实用翻译教程（第三版）

Translation
A Practical Course

刘季春◎编著

中山大学出版社
·广州·

版权所有 翻印必究

图书在版编目（CIP）数据

实用翻译教程/刘季春编著 . —3 版 . —广州：中山大学出版社，2016.8
ISBN 978 - 7 - 306 - 05774 - 7

Ⅰ. ①实… Ⅱ. ①刘… Ⅲ. ①英语—翻译—教材 Ⅳ. ①H315.9

中国版本图书馆 CIP 数据核字（2016）第 181900 号

出 版 人：徐　劲
策划编辑：刘学谦
责任编辑：刘学谦
封面设计：林绵华
责任校对：林彩云
责任技编：何雅涛
出版发行：中山大学出版社
电　　话：编辑部 020 - 84111996，84113349
　　　　　发行部 020 - 84111998，84111981，84111160
地　　址：广州市新港西路 135 号
邮　　编：510275　传　真：020 - 84036565
网　　址：http://www.zsup.com.cn　E-mail：zdcbs@mail.sysu.edu.cn
印 刷 者：广州家联印刷有限公司
规　　格：787mm×1092mm　1/16　22.5 印张　430 千字
版次印次：1996 年 8 月第 1 版　2007 年 8 月修订
　　　　　2016 年 8 月第 3 版　2021 年 12 月第 17 次印刷
印　　数：55001～57500 册
定　　价：39.80 元

如发现本书因印装质量问题影响阅读，请与出版社发行部联系调换

第三版前言

本教程的第一版在1996年，修订版在2007年，现在是2016年，整整20年。此时的我，真是百感交集。没想到我年轻时的一项工作，竟延续了20年。

自上次修订，教程的整体框架已经固定，包括内容和体例。因此，这次修订总的原则就是精益求精。具体的工作主要在以下三个方面：

一是完善内容。本次修订最大的变化是第十章。除两个附录，我重写了这章，去芜存菁，条理更为清楚。这一章讲的是对外传播，是上次修订时新增的内容。重读这一章，我发现其内容和观点都很好，只是材料的取舍和组织有欠周到。再者，我这些年读了别的学者的一些文章，在教学和实践中又有了新体会，所以决定重写这一章。其他章节也都做了不同程度的修订，包括增加了部分变化了的内容，替换了一些不够典型的例子，以期讨论的问题更翔实，更可信。

二是精编练习。练习的编写很考验教材编者。记得上次修订，我将初版时的练习推倒重来，一大特色就是有过半的练习为开放性设计，没有提供参考答案。原本是想给任课教师发挥的空间，或减轻他们另外出题的负担。但我在网上众多的评论中注意到，有不少读者希望我提供练习答案，以便于他们自学。可见这是个两难的问题。为此我趁这次修订的机会，视练习的性质和难度，对练习又做了较大的调整，力求取得一个平衡。此外，我的另一个指导思想，就是尽可能采用第一手资料和尽可能采用自己的翻译。因此，若对比两个版本，读者会发现我已经替换了大量的句子。我精挑细选，但苦于找不到更多心仪的材料，只好减少了练习的数量。

三是锤炼文字。我很羡慕一些作者，他们的语言似有魔力。因此，我为这次修订设定的另一个重要目标就是锤炼文字。我一遍又一遍朗读书稿，能改的尽量改，哪怕只改动一两个字。我很希望我的这本教程，不但言之有据，还能朗朗上口、让人爱读。

最后，值本教程20周年、三版付梓之际，我要感谢我教过的历届学生，正是你们的参与，给了我教学的灵感和喜悦；我要感谢那些不曾谋面的广大读者，正是你们的喜爱，给了我做完美教材的愿望和动力。

这是本教程的第三版，本想在各方面做到尽善尽美，以后就不再修订了。但等到现在交稿的时候，我的心情已经完全不一样了，因为我自知仍有可以改进的地方，就说练习的设计吧，戚戚然心有不甘。是为记。

作者
2016 年 7 月 11 日
于广州白云山麓

修订版前言

自本教程初版,至今不觉已11载,其间重印5次,每次印数不多,三两千册,细水长流,共计发行了22000册。作为自选课题,没有刻意宣传,在自生自灭的状况下,能有这个成绩应该是很欣慰的了。我在内心感激我的上帝:本书亲爱的读者。

"书又脱销了",这是近年来出版社和作者面临的一个共同问题:是按旧版继续重印呢,还是推出全新的修订版?显然,一再重印是不合适的,因为教程的某些内容已显得陈旧,并且也需要及时反映这些年翻译研究的最新成果。经再三思考并和出版社协商,作者最终着手了本教程的修订工作。

今天看来,在编写体例上,教程初版所确立的原则是正确的:一是重描写性、轻规定性;二是翻译标准多元化(见"初版前言")。正所谓初生牛犊不畏虎,当时自己未曾涉猎多少理论,也没有出过国门,只是凭直觉,认为翻译教材应该这样编写。后来去英国做访问学者才发现,描写性、多元化正是国际上许多人文学科所倡导的。可喜的是,翻译标准采用多家之说的做法,现在已经为国内同行广泛采用。

本次修订,仍坚持重描写、多元化这一原则,具体情况说明如下:

1. 将初版第三章"翻译的标准"改为"翻译的理念"。这不是字词上的简单变化,而是作者翻译观的又一次深化。标准是一种尺度,目的在于统一和规范,而理念则是一种观点或一种态度。尺度多了,形同虚设;而观点或态度,则自然可以是多种多样的。这一章有增有删,增添了国外两大学术流派,删减的是国内的翻译观点。对每一理念,除阐述其基本精神外,还详细介绍了该理念产生的背景。

2. 重点改进叙述方式和各章练习设计。目前书市上各类翻译教材唾手可得,但多数任课教师却宁愿自编讲义。为什么呢?作者近年来发现一个重大"秘密",就是不少翻译教材,作者说得过多,没有给任课教师发挥的余地,所以,只宜作读本,不宜作教材。有鉴于此,本书穿插了一些重要的例子,却有意不给答案,不作分析,或延迟评价。这次修订,各章的练习,几乎是推倒重来,除提供多项选择外,一大特色就是,有一半以上的练习题都是开放式的,可以选作课外的材料,也可以用来课堂讨论。

3. 精选例子,整合内容。本次修订增添了许多文学的例子。虽然教程的重心是实用文体的翻译,但从翻译原理的角度,缺了文学的例子,似乎谈不深,谈不透。在内容上也进行了较大的调整:将第四章"涉外文书的翻译原则"和第十章"涉外合同的特点与翻译"合并为第八章,增写现在的第十章。另外,初版的附录2"合资经营合同实例"和附录4"涉外文书常用词语英汉对照表",因已经有相关的法规和词典可以替代,故全部删除。初版的附录1改放在第7章后,附录3重写为附录1,增补附录2。总的来说,初版共23万字,修订版直接删除了约6万字,增写的(不含改写部分)在12万字以上。

4. 详注出处。本次修订,对于重要的译例、材料、观点,除在书后的参考文献中列出之外,仍尽可能在当页作脚注。由于初版时间较早,某些材料自己也忘了是从哪里来的。这次为了某个出处,作者曾在图书馆和阅览室整架、整架书地去翻查(仍有个别未查实)。我认为,遵守著作权法,尊重和保护好别的作者,也是对自己的最好保护。

修订历时整整15个月,这是开始时没有预料到的,除了日常工作,几乎是全身心地投入。很荣幸,修订版被列为教育部普通高等教育"十一五"国家级规划教材,我想,在主观上,一定要对得起这个称号。

在本教程修订过程中,作者得到过许多人的帮助。著名书画家陈永祥先生欣然应允使用他画集中的文字材料;本单位的谢栋元、罗可群两位中文教授,是经常求助的对象;英国朋友Ms Claire V. Gore不时帮助解决一些英语的疑难,并提供难得的资料。还有我的前后两届研究生、双学位本科生,帮我将初版书稿和新增的材料陆续输入电脑。这次修订之所以能顺利完成,还与本书责任编辑刘学谦老师的督促分不开,谨在此一并致谢。

作者
2007年6月6日
于广州白云山麓

初版前言

有关文学翻译和科技翻译的教程，早已有之，但有关实用文体翻译的教材却还未见到，教学时也苦于找不到这类材料。为了填补这一空白，笔者不避浅陋，在教学实践的基础上进行了这方面的尝试。

研究以往的翻译教材，笔者发现，在编写体例上，大多按部就班，重规定性（Prescriptive），轻描写性（Descriptive），倘若举例不当，难免误导一般的读者。笔者以为，译无定规，因此，"授人以鱼，不如授人以渔"是编著《实用翻译教程》的指导思想。"翻译的标准"一章采用的是多家之说，以期读者有所判断，知所抉择。其他各章除介绍有关翻译的一般知识和技巧外，笔者也斗胆穿插了不少个人的学习心得和评论。但愿读者在不完全同意笔者意见之时，也能够受到点滴启发，从而对翻译有个较为全面的认识。

目前，关于实用文体翻译的研究，国内还刚刚起步，笔者也只是广泛地涉猎，许多东西还来不及消化，而且实践的时间也不长。因此，书中的许多提法也只是探讨，难免有偏颇和谬误之处，欢迎读者的反馈，更欢迎读者的批评指正。

在本书编写过程中，笔者参阅过大量中外书刊（详见"主要参考书目"），没有这些书籍和论文作者的辛勤劳动，本书的完成是不可能的。书中引证的重要例句佳译（除少数出处不明，如某些广告标题、口号的译文外），一般均注明出处，不敢掠美；还有相当译例则是笔者为说明某个翻译要点而从原文直接翻译或在别的译文基础上改译的。书中所有译例和练习答案仅供参考，并非范译。

广东外语外贸大学的何自然教授、罗可群教授对本书的编写给予了热情的鼓励和关怀，中山大学出版社的副总编辑杨权同志对本书的出版给予了大力支持，责任编辑夏华同志从全书的格局到文字的技术处理都提出过宝贵的意见，现趁本书出版之际，谨向上述诸位致以衷心的谢忱。

编著者
1996 年 4 月于广州

目 录

原 理 编

第一章 绪论 ········· 2
第一节 什么是翻译 ········· 2
第二节 翻译工作者的修养 ········· 3
一、良好的英语基础 ········· 3
二、扎实的汉语功底 ········· 3
三、懂点翻译理论 ········· 4
四、一丝不苟、精益求精的精神 ········· 4
第三节 如何学习翻译 ········· 7

第二章 翻译的过程 ········· 11
第一节 理解阶段 ········· 11
一、双语能力的局限 ········· 11
二、专业知识的局限 ········· 12
三、思维与文化差异 ········· 15
第二节 表达阶段 ········· 17
一、重视上下文,避免孤立处理词句 ········· 17
二、从情景出发,摆脱表层结构的束缚 ········· 21
第三节 校对阶段 ········· 24
一、校对的步骤 ········· 25
二、校对的方法 ········· 25
三、商务文本的校对 ········· 26
附录:本章第一节 4 个句子的分析 ········· 28
【练习题】 ········· 34

第三章 翻译的理念 ········· 38
第一节 严复:信、达、雅 ········· 38

第二节　傅雷：重神似不重形似 ·· 40
　　第三节　许渊冲：美化之艺术，创优似竞赛 ································· 43
　　第四节　亚历山大·弗雷泽·泰特勒：翻译三原则 ······················ 51
　　第五节　尤金·奈达：动态对等 ·· 53
　　第六节　操纵学派 ·· 56
　　第七节　德国功能翻译学派 ·· 58
　　第八节　小结 ·· 61
　　【进修书目】 ··· 62

技　巧　编

第四章　翻译的重要环节之一：措辞精当 ··· 64
　　第一节　注意词的多义性 ·· 66
　　第二节　注意词的语体色彩 ·· 71
　　第三节　注意培养语感，提高鉴赏力 ·· 74
　　【练习题】 ··· 78

第五章　翻译的重要环节之二：活用技巧 ··· 81
　　第一节　词量的增减 ·· 86
　　　一、增词法 ·· 86
　　　二、减词法 ·· 91
　　第二节　词类的转换 ·· 93
　　第三节　反面着笔 ·· 95
　　　一、表达习惯的需要 ·· 95
　　　二、立场、语气的需要 ·· 97
　　【练习题】 ··· 100

第六章　翻译的重要环节之三：方法相宜 ······································· 102
　　第一节　直译法 ··· 103
　　第二节　意译法 ··· 103
　　第三节　直译与意译的关系 ·· 104
　　第四节　直译与意译的条件 ·· 110
　　【练习题】 ··· 115

实 用 编

第七章　外贸信函的特点与翻译 ······ 118
第一节　格式问题 ······ 120
第二节　称呼与结尾礼辞问题 ······ 124
第三节　措辞问题 ······ 127
　一、汉语"请"字的英译 ······ 127
　二、敬辞与谦辞 ······ 129
　三、其他婉转词语的使用 ······ 132
第四节　摘译问题 ······ 133
　附录：外贸信函常用缩略语 ······ 137
【练习题】 ······ 139

第八章　契约语言的特点与翻译 ······ 142
第一节　程式化 ······ 142
第二节　准确性 ······ 149
第三节　严谨性 ······ 150
　一、注意时间的表示法 ······ 151
　二、注意金额、数字的表示法 ······ 152
　三、注意增加限制性词语 ······ 154
第四节　一致性 ······ 157
第五节　庄重性 ······ 162
第六节　简明化 ······ 168
第七节　小结 ······ 175
【练习题】 ······ 176

第九章　涉外广告的特点与翻译 ······ 185
第一节　广告标题、口号的句法与修辞特点 ······ 185
　一、巧设问句 ······ 186
　二、使用省略句，诱发联想 ······ 187
　三、使用祈使句，发出召唤 ······ 188
　四、突出利益 ······ 188

五、利用反论 ………………………………………………… 189
　　六、活用成语、名句或谚语 ………………………………… 190
　　七、巧用修辞 ………………………………………………… 191
　第二节　广告标题、口号的翻译 ………………………………… 193
　　一、直译法 …………………………………………………… 193
　　二、意译法 …………………………………………………… 196
　　三、四字结构法 ……………………………………………… 197
　　四、套译法 …………………………………………………… 199
　第三节　广告标题、口号翻译应注意的问题 …………………… 203
　　一、广告标题或口号的翻译贵在创新，切忌步人后尘 …… 203
　　二、广告标题或口号的翻译应注意中英广告语的不同特点 … 203
　　三、广告标题或口号的翻译可采用更为灵活的方法 ……… 204
　第四节　商标的特点与翻译 ……………………………………… 205
　　一、商标的特点 ……………………………………………… 205
　　二、商标的翻译 ……………………………………………… 207
　　三、商标翻译应注意的事项 ………………………………… 212
　第五节　广告正文的特点与翻译 ………………………………… 213
　第六节　广告正文汉译英存在的问题 …………………………… 219
　【练习题】 ………………………………………………………… 221

第十章　对外传播的问题与对策 ………………………………… 225
　第一节　问题产生的原因 ………………………………………… 225
　　一、人们对翻译的普遍误解 ………………………………… 225
　　二、人们对原文的过度迷信 ………………………………… 228
　第二节　解决问题的对策 ………………………………………… 236
　　一、普及翻译教育 …………………………………………… 236
　　二、培养多元翻译观 ………………………………………… 236
　　三、增强跨文化意识 ………………………………………… 237
　第三节　小结 ……………………………………………………… 246
　　附录1：翻译项目实例　"千年古楼遗址"与"千年古道遗址" …… 247
　　附录2：应用翻译示例　《北京老街》前言 ………………… 260
　【练习题】 ………………………………………………………… 265

第十一章 涉外文书常用词语的翻译 ········ 271
- 第一节 be interested in ········ 271
- 第二节 (be) subject to ········ 272
- 第三节 responsible for / responsibility 与 liable for / liability ········ 274
- 第四节 abide by / comply with; according to / in line with / in accordance with ········ 276
- 第五节 against ········ 277
- 第六节 offer, quote / quotation, bid ········ 279
- 第七节 if, in case 及其他 ········ 281
- 第八节 shall 及其他 ········ 282
- 【练习题】 ········ 286

第十二章 企业名称的翻译 ········ 288
- 第一节 英语企业名称的汉译 ········ 288
- 第二节 汉语企业名称的英译 ········ 289
  - 一、"公司"的译法 ········ 290
  - 二、"总公司"的译法 ········ 292
  - 三、"分公司"的译法 ········ 294
  - 四、其他各类"公司"和"厂"的译法 ········ 296
- 第三节 小结 ········ 297

主要参考文献 ········ 298

附录一 常用英语公示语例解 ········ 303

附录二 补充练习材料 ········ 320

附录三 各章练习参考答案 ········ 334

Principles 原理编

第一章
绪　论

第一节　什么是翻译

什么是翻译？实际做翻译的人一般不会问这个问题，因为在他们的心目中，那不是不言自明的事吗？写教材的人或做理论研究的人，往往都试图给出一个完美的定义，然而至今似乎还没有谁真正做到了。我不比别的作者聪明，所以不想再多给一个多余的定义。不过，我还是觉得，了解一下美国语言学家罗曼·雅各布森（Roman Jakobson，1896—1982）在《论翻译的语言学问题》[①]中对翻译的分类还是会有些好处，他将翻译分成三大类：

（1）语内翻译，或称"重新措辞"（Intralingual translation or rewording），即用同一种语言中的某些符号来解释另一些符号。

（2）语际翻译，或称"狭义翻译"（Interlingual translation or translation proper），即用某种语言符号来解释另一种语言符号。

（3）符际翻译，或称"跨类翻译"（Intersemiotic translation or transmutation），即用非语言符号系统的符号来解释语言符号。

根据这个分类法，翻译研究的范围就十分宽泛了：解释或转述都可称作翻译，将古代语言转换成现代语言，或将少数族群的语言转换成通用语言，更是翻译；设计交通信号也是一种翻译。推而广之，绘画、雕塑、器乐、舞蹈、京剧的脸谱甚至交通信号等等，都牵涉翻译。

然而，这种对翻译的认识，还不是最宽泛的。美国学者乔治·斯坦纳（George Steiner，1929—）在其力著《通天塔之后》（*After Babel*）中指出"理解即翻译"（understanding as translation）。我很钦佩作者的洞察力。说穿了，理解的过程就是翻译的过程。在他的启发下，我认识到"说话也是一种翻译"：说

[①] 引自 Jakobson, Roman (1959). On Linguistic Aspects of Translation, in Lawrence Venuti (ed.) *The Translation Studies Reader*. London and New York: Routledge, 2000, 作者译文。

话——不就是将无声的思维转换成有声的言语吗？我们平时常说的"言不尽意"，不就是没有"翻译"好吗？这样理解翻译，翻译便无处不在、无时不在，人只要一息尚存，他就在翻译了。可见翻译之普遍以及研究翻译的意义。

不过，我觉得对于学习翻译的人，最励志的定义（而不是完美的定义），还是英国学者莫娜·贝克（Mona Baker）选来用作翻译教材名字的表达：*In Other Words*。北京的外语教学与研究出版社引进该书时，将其翻译成《换言之》，口语化一点，就是"换句话说"。这是对翻译的大彻大悟。我后来了解到，这并不是贝克的首创，用作书名也不是第一次，并且古今中外还有不少智者说过类似的话。总之，翻译是种选择的艺术，好的翻译，总是在众多备选项中精挑细选的结果。因此，"换句话说"，可以变成"换两句话说""换三句话说"，套句时髦的语言就是：翻译没有最好，只有更好。

第二节 翻译工作者的修养

一、良好的英语基础

学习英语的人很多，但学得好的人却极少。有的人考 TOEFL 和 GRE 能考高分，但英语的实际运用能力却很低。能记许多生僻古怪的词语，而一些简单基本的词汇却不会灵活运用，这不等于学好了英语。良好的英语修养，除能听说外，还包括能读、能写、能译；能读各种体裁的文章，有较高的鉴赏能力；能写出内心的各种感受，用词达意；能译出原文的意蕴，行文地道。有人认为，只要学了几年英语，借助于几本词典，就可胜任翻译工作，这是大错特错。一旦动笔翻译，立觉笔下有鬼，连自己也怀疑自己了。

二、扎实的汉语功底

我们在汉语的环境中长大，学了几十年的汉语，按理说，汉语的水平该不错了。事实上，学习母语也不例外，要讲方法，要有意识地训练，才能卓有成效。不但要破"万卷"书，还要善于思考，勤于练笔。不然，许多人天天看报，看了一辈子，为什么连一封书信都写不好呢？给学生上英汉翻译课时，常听到学生说，这不仅考我们的英语，也考我们的汉语，这话一点不假。如果是英译汉，汉语水平较好，而英语略差，译出来的东西还能像个样子；而如果汉语太差，不管英语如何"精通"，译出来的东西，一定拿不出去。如果不能很好地用中文遣词造句，就不必奢谈翻译。因此，我在课堂上常常告诫以外语为专业的学生，千万不能只抱着几本英语教科书，而不继续加强汉语的修养。要知道：母语学好了，外语才有学好的可能。

三、懂点翻译理论

这里说"懂点"，并不是说懂得多些不好，而是说不要专谈理论不实践。要实践 —— 理论 —— 再实践 —— 再上升到理论，从而逐步完善。有人会反对说，我从来都没有学过什么理论，不是照样译得很好吗？我们不否认有这样的天才，但大多数"凡人"，还得学点基本功。翻译理论是前人的经验总结，学点翻译理论，可以少走弯路，事半功倍。倘若是位天才，再学点理论，那更是如虎添翼，何乐而不为呢？我们认为翻译教学更不能忽视这一点。课堂的翻译练习和课外作业，数量毕竟有限，不能奢望每周几学时的学习，翻译水平就能一下子有很大的提高。因此，翻译教学的关键，在于传授学生原理与方法。"授人以鱼，不如授人以渔"正是本书用较大篇幅介绍翻译原理的目的所在。

四、一丝不苟、精益求精的精神

具有良好的英语基础和扎实的汉语功底，并且熟悉翻译的基本理论，这些固然重要，但翻译工作者最重要的一个素质，就是一丝不苟、精益求精的精神。因此，初学翻译的人，首先必须培养一种态度。

（一）培养勤查词典的习惯，避免望文生义

在当今中国，大学的英语教学及各种类型的英语考试，毫无例外都有惊人分量的阅读理解，好像分量不大得惊人，就不足以考核学生的理解水平。要求学生一目十行，然后做一些似是而非的选择题。课堂的阅读教学也步调一致，鼓励学生猜测词义。这种教学方法，对提高学生的阅读速度和理解能力显然会有好处。但是，不管它有何成效，不可否认的是，它也容易产生负面效应，比如养成学生囫囵吞枣、不求甚解的懒惰作风，这就给翻译教学带来很大的困难。

翻译的大忌就是望文生义。哪怕是有一丁点疑问，也得查词典。同一个词，有时还得查好几本工具书，进行交叉比较和考证，否则就可能出错，甚至闹笑话。如若不信，不妨猜猜下列词语的意义，写在纸上，然后查查词典，再对照书后的答案，自己就可得出结论。

a) dry goods
b) wet goods
c) dry state

d) wet state

e) dry law

f) white goods

g) white wine

h) dry white wine

i) toilet water

j) to close the switch

（二）培养修改译文的习惯，避免满足于"差不多"

初学翻译的人，最大的毛病就是不愿修改译文。笔译与口译不同，口译要求敏捷、达意，时间要求很严；而笔译时间相对宽松，因此要求准确、简明。若是文学翻译，还要求传神、有文采。要提高口译能力，必须敢于开口；要提高笔译能力，则必须勤于练笔。笔译课常有这种情形，老师问："你的译文呢？"学生回答说："我想好了。"这种只想不写的学生，很难提高笔译能力。殊不知"想"与"写"有很大的距离。"想"的东西飘忽不定，只有"写"下来的东西，白纸黑字，才是具体的东西；也只有写下来，才方便修改。

笔译课和英语基础课（如《大学英语》）也不同。英语基础课包括听、说、读、写、译五项基本技能，其中"译"排在最后（教学原则一般是听说领先、读写跟上、适当翻译）。因此，按基础课的要求，翻译只要正确、达意，就可得满分。笔译课是对笔译的专项技能训练，如果仅仅是正确、达意，理论上说，充其量只能得60%的分。

有许多人，大学修了4年英语，毕业后又从事多年翻译，但译文质量却总是不尽人意。其根本原因，就在于平时要求不严，容易满足于"可以""差不多"。因此，懂英语的人很多，但合格的笔译人员却很少。翻译能力达到一定水平，若要再上一个台阶，一定要养成字斟句酌、精益求精的习惯。一个句子译下来，即使功底很好的人，也常得修改。要是功底弱些，改进的余地则更大。试看下面的例子：

1. He will come again in autumn to discuss business for next year.
   他秋天将再来讨论明年的生意。

2. The firm was closed owing to large losses.
   这个公司由于损失很大而倒闭。

3. This is a special offer and is not subject to our usual discounts.

这是特殊报盘，不以我方通常折扣为条件。

4. Please reply whether we are to insure the above shipment.

   请回答我方要不要对上述货物保险。

5. Please let us know as soon as you have made choice so we can make necessary arrangements for shipment without delay.

   一旦做出选择，请马上让我们知道，以便我们为及时装运做必要的安排。

6. You are kindly requested to let us have your best quotation for the canned fish.

   请你们报给我们鱼罐头的最优惠的价格。

以上6个英语句子的汉译，若按照大学英语的要求，已经是符合要求了。但若按笔译课的标准，则大有改进的余地。试分别改译如下：

1. 他秋天将再来洽谈明年的业务。
2. 这家公司由于巨大亏损而倒闭。
3. 这是特惠报盘，我方通常折扣不适应于此盘。
4. 请答复我方是否对上述货物保险。
5. 一旦做出选择，请马上通知我们，以便为及时装运做必要的安排。
6. 请报鱼罐头最优惠的价格。

这6句译文，你是否感觉比初译好了许多呢？但只要你肯花时间，再推敲一番，仍有改进的余地，比如可再改译如下：

1. 他秋季将再来洽谈明年的业务。
2. 该公司因巨额亏损而倒闭。
3. 此系特惠报盘，不另加我方通常折扣。
4. 请告我方是否投保上述货物。
5. 选妥请即通知，我方好及时安排装运。
6. 请报鱼罐头最惠价。

其中最后一句，笔者曾在课堂试验过多次。让学生翻译时，不作任何要求，译完之后，再叫学生数数自己的译文中有多少个汉字。结果，多数学生的译文在16个字左右，最多的将近20个字。接着我要求学生将译文压缩到8个字，几分钟后，居然多数学生将译文压缩到了这个字数，并与我提供的参考译文非常接近。**可见，能否写出好的译文，往往取决于你是否有修改译文的意愿和习惯。**最后，学生译文的主要区别在于对原文中 the canned fish 的措辞，有的译"鱼罐头"，有的则译"罐头鱼"。哪种说法对？哪种说法错？还是两种说法都对？若要认真的话，它们倒真的有分别：这是两个偏正结构的短语，在"鱼罐头"中，"罐头"是中心词，"鱼"是修饰语；但在"罐头鱼"中，"鱼"是中心词，而"罐头"成了修饰语。在外贸业务中，作为商品，严格说来，应称"鱼罐头"。比如说，人家问你："你是做什么的啊？"你回答说："我是做生意的。"人家又问你："做什么生意的？"你回答说："做罐头生意的。"人家要是再问你："做什么罐头的啊？"你就会说："做鱼罐头的。"但如果在餐桌上作为一道菜，那就要改称"罐头鱼"了。

第三节　如何学习翻译

翻译是可以自学的，许多杰出的前辈翻译工作者都不是学校培养出来的，有的根本就没有上过翻译课。但翻译做得好的人，一定研读过前人的翻译和汲取了前人的经验。现在自学的条件比以前不知好多少，各种翻译教材、书籍和工具书，可说是唾手可得。当然，如果没有老师的指点，要在琳琅满目、令人眼花缭乱的书海里找到合适的书也不是件容易的事。这里我想给初涉翻译的读者推荐几本好书和好的词典。

自学翻译的最好方法，在我看来，就是对照阅读，即选择名著名译来对照阅读。什么增词、减词啊，什么词类转换、正反、反正表达等翻译技巧，都可在对照阅读中慢慢学到。由于语境的关系，读者更能体会译者匠心独运、曲尽其妙的心路历程，远胜阅读技巧类书籍。对照阅读的时间长了，鉴赏力也会逐步提高。名著名译有很多，但学习翻译的学生，不能不知夏济安编译的两册英汉对照（《名家散文选读》，香港今日世界社，1976 年第 1 版）。夏先生的翻译不着痕迹，恰如他的中文写作，文字之美，叹为观止！另一个不可多得的英汉对照的好本子，是外语教学与研究出版社编的《吕叔湘译文三种》（1992 年第 1 版），其中有个中篇叫《伊坦·弗洛美》（*Ethan Frome*），我还是十多年前第一次读到，后来又细读过几次，每次都为原作的悲剧情节暗自惊心，更为译者再现原作的语言功力深深折服。吕先生是我国成绩卓著的语言学家，但若因此错过了学习他的翻译艺术，那就是莫大的损失和遗憾了。长篇小说的汉译有口皆碑的首推杨必译的《名利场》（人民文学出版社，1957 年第 1 版），许多翻译教材都选过她的译文，尤其是开篇的那段话，简直翻译得出神入化！另外，现在有很多世界文学名著的重译本，因此，只要有心，找同源译文来对照阅读不是太难。常言道：不怕不识货，就怕货比货。多数情况下，不要老师的指点，译文的好坏，读者在比读中自己就能判断。汉译英可用作范本的书比较难找，原因是有的好本子难度太大。这里我乐于推荐陈文伯编的《教你如何掌握汉译英技巧》（世界知识出版社，1999年第1版）。该书分4个部分，其中的亮点是第一部分的"对照阅读"，共11个短篇，每篇提供了两个译文，为读者多提供了一个参照。第三部分的"文章练习"，共50个短篇，也是很好的练习材料，在做完练习后，可对照阅读第四部分提供的参考译文。该书最大的好处，就是所选文章短小精悍，又各有胜处，方便练习，也不易令人厌烦。最后，我要特别强调对照阅读的方法，若要事半功倍，一定要自己先试译一遍再对照名家的翻译。对于中、长篇小说，这样做可能需要极大的毅力，或可选择其中的段落来练习，但对于短篇，就不能偷懒了。

论述翻译的书籍也不能不看。我认为美国专家Joan Pinkham（琼·平卡姆）编写的 *The Translator's Guide to Chinglish*（《中式英语之鉴》，外语教学与研究出版社，2000年第1版），或许是近20年来在国内出版的汉英翻译最有用的书。该书作者曾先后在北京的外文出版社和中央编译局工作过8年，是专门为中国翻译工作者的英译文改稿的专家。8年中她收集了大量的典型中式英语实例，然后分门别类指出它们的病症。在国内学习英语的人，无论英语学得有多好，都能从中得到教益。该书也可作为英语写作课的辅助读本。翻译技巧方面的书，钱歌川编的《翻译的技巧》（商务印书馆，1981年第1版）是不能被遗忘的。该书在20世纪80年代深受大学生的喜爱，但时隔30多年，同类的书可能仍无出其右。全书分为3编，第一编为"汉译英与英语句型"，第二编为"英语惯用法及其翻译"（重点在英译汉），第三编为"疑难句法及文章译例"（包括汉译英和英译汉）。该书与现在一般教材讨论的翻译技巧不同，最大的特色就是系统例解了英语的各种句型。从英语句型入手，据我个人的经验，是学习汉译英的一个有效途径。介绍讨论翻译的通俗读物时，我要向读者极力推荐金圣华的《齐向译道行》（商务印书馆，2011年第1版）。该书收录了80篇翻译随笔，其中绝大多数是刊登在《英语世界》里的专栏文章。这些文章都是作者翻译教学或翻译实践的经验之谈，娓娓道来，有的放矢。它不同于高头讲章的枯燥论文，而是文字极美的翻译散文，读来赏心悦目，轻松愉快，特别适合青年学生。

学习翻译与做翻译，都离不开词典，一个好的翻译工作者，往往也是使用各种工具书的专家。我们鼓励学生扩大知识面，但翻译涉及的领域可以说是无所不包，在知识爆炸的今天，即使是在某一特定领域，一个人也不可能样样精通。因此，做翻译，懂的东西多，固然重要；然而，也许更为重要的是，遇到难题，他

第一章 绪 论

应该知道在哪里可以找到答案。懂得正确使用工具书，就等于有许许多多的专家不分昼夜、随时听候你的差遣。

词典，对于翻译工作者来说，是多多益善。词典的种类五花八门：有外语词典，有汉语词典；有单语词典，有双语词典；有一般语言词典（释义为主），有各种专科词典（如化工、医药、法律、经济）；有综合性百科词典，还有专门用途词典（如发音词典，引语词典，缩略语词典，人名、地名词典，同义词、反义词词典，搭配词典，倒序词典，成语、俚语、寓言、典故词典，分类词典，文化词典，图解词典，应有尽有）。作为个人，不可能，也没有必要全部备齐，应根据自己的需要慢慢添置。

开始学习翻译，至少要备三本一般语言词典，即一本英汉词典、一本汉英词典、一本英英词典。学生毕业参加工作后，可根据工作的性质再备两本专科词典。比如，从事外贸的，就再备一本《英汉经贸词典》和一本《汉英经贸词典》。有人反对使用英汉词典，实际上，对于查找一些物件的名称和各学科的术语，英汉词典更直截了当，省时省力，有不可替代的优势。对于其他词类，如动词、副词、形容词，其主要作用则在于诱发联想，由此及彼。英英词典的主要作用则在"辨义"。

最常用的英汉词典，要数上海译文出版社出版的《新英汉词典》（2000年第1版），对于一般学习英语的人已经基本够用。另一本值得推荐的英汉词典，尤其是对于做翻译，是上海三联书店出版的郑易里、曹成修编的《英华大词典》（1956年第1版），后来出了几次修订版。汉英词典，要数吴光华等主编、上海交通大学出版社出版的《汉英大词典》（1993年第1版），该词典的长处是兼顾文学、科技和商贸，是目前同类词典中的佼佼者。英英词典可分美国系列和英国系列，美国系列最有影响的当是Webster's（一般译作"韦氏"词典），另一本口碑很好的词典是 *The American Heritage Dictionary of the English Language*，该词典图文并茂，一大特色是，对某些疑难词条还专列"Usage"一栏。英国系列的词典最出名的是Oxford和Collins。上面所列，无论是美国系列，还是英国系列的词典，都一版再版，质量可靠，享誉世界。对于一般的读者，只要有其中一本（中大型的）就基本够用。

除了3本必备的词典之外，笔者还想特别推荐两本词典，一本是 *Collins Cobuild English Language Dictionary*（1987年第1版）。Cobuild 是 the Collins Birmingham University International Language Database 的缩写形式。该词典可以称作用法词典，与传统词典不同，它依据的是语用学原则，其词条的释义反映了该词或短语特定的使用环境，释义以真实的句子表述，从中可以看出其基本词类和使用方法。例如，"door"这个词条可能是这样表述的："A door is ...",看到位于该词前面的不定冠词，读者就知道那是一个可数名词。"conceal"这个词条又可能会这样表述："If you **conceal** something, you…"。这表明该词是一个及物动词，要求主语为"人"，而宾语所涉及的范围很广，必须是无生命的物体或抽象的概念。如果一个释义是这样开始的："to **sink** a ship means to …"，则暗示该词对主语的要求不严，包括有生命的人和无生命的物，但是该义项要求的宾语只限于船只或船只类的物体。该词典的不足在于收词有限，但也是它的长处所在，如果能查得着的词语，解释就几乎是详尽无遗，往往让你感觉到量身定造的尊贵。

另一本要特别推荐的词典是梅家驹等编、上海辞书出版社出版的《同义词词林》(1983年第1版)，该词典可用12个字来概括：雅俗共赏，兴趣盎然，开卷有益。"词林"（英语中的对应词语是"thesaurus"）与一般的同义词（"synonym"）词典不同，它的功能不在于"辨义"，而在于"提供选择"（个别特殊用法，编者则在括号里以常用搭配的形式加以解释，点到即止，一目了然）。因此，做英汉翻译时，尤其是做文学翻译时，每当苦于想不起某个妥帖的表达（心里明白得很，却一时想不起来），只要查一个近义词，该词典就会如数家珍，一一给你道来（很多时候还提供反义词），你苦思冥想的那个词可能就在其中。笔者多年使用这本词典，还经常把它当作读本，有时读着读着，不禁开怀大笑。编词典能编到这个水准，真让人羡慕！

做翻译离不开词典，对于专业翻译工作者，同一类词典还可能备上几本，以便交叉参考。但也要防止过度依赖词典。俗话说，尽信书不如没书，词典也是如此。做翻译，除严谨之外，还需要悟性和想象。

第二章
翻译的过程

翻译的过程,大致可分为理解、表达和校对三个阶段。

在翻译实践中,理解是表达的前提,表达是理解的具体化、深刻化。理解和表达并非截然分开的两个阶段,译者在理解的同时,也在考虑如何遣词造句,如何再现原文的风貌。

理解和表达同等重要。有人说理解比表达更重要,也有人说表达比理解更重要,甚至有人说,在翻译过程中,理解占百分之多少,表达占百分之多少,这些看法都是片面的。具体地说,理解、表达的难易,各占百分比的多少,都会因材料的不同而不同,也会因译者的不同而不同。容易的材料,表达占主导地位;较难的材料,理解占主导地位。母语水平高的,理解是主要矛盾;外语水平高的,表达是主要矛盾。总之,所有这一切,都不能一概而论。

第一节 理解阶段

要正确、透彻地理解原文,往往并非易事,其原因是多方面的:

一、双语能力的局限

译者的双语能力有限:在外语方面,可能有不认识的词语,不明确的语法关系,或不了解的知识、背景和文化;在母语方面,可能缺乏写作的经验,缺乏必要的想象或不具备融会贯通的能力。且外语能力与母语能力又会相互影响。例如:

1. Evolution is a conservative process, wasting little of value.
2. When the history of the Nixon Administration is finally written, the chances are that his Chinese policy will stand out <u>as a model of common sense and</u>

good diplomacy. ①

3. I soon perceived that she possessed in combination the qualities which in all other persons whom I had known I had been only too happy to find singly. ②

4. Time goes fast for one who has a sense of beauty, when there are pretty children in a pool and a young Diana on the edge, to receive with wonder anything you can catch! ③

  以上4个句子，在理解上可以说都有相当的难度。例1的句型和用字都十分平常，但可能要求译者有相关的知识储备及推理与联想的能力；例2的难点在对画线短语的理解，可能需要相关的背景知识；例3的关键在结构，分不清各部分间的关系就无从下手；例4的困惑在于缺乏上下文，因此就更需要凭借分析句法关系，当然对字词的理解也不能掉以轻心。此处暂不给参考译文，请读者先分析和试译一遍，再与本章后"附录"中的译文和讲解对照，这样会更有收获，因为看了人家的译文，就难免被牵着鼻子走了。

二、专业知识的局限

  翻译工作所涉及的知识，有一般性知识，还有各行各业的专门知识。俗话说隔行如隔山！因此，早有学者指出，翻译要做得好，译者必须是个"杂家"。但要做个"杂家"，却是说来容易做来难。一个人的时间和精力毕竟有限，即使学到老，也不可能行行都懂，门门都通。因此，做个"杂家"只能当作是有志者的追求或理想，更好的途径，还是应鼓励译者成为某个方面的专家。记得20世纪90年代，我在西安听过叶笃庄先生的一次讲演，大意是说，30年之内，很难有人能够超过他所译的达尔文著《物种起源》。叶先生是我国知名的农学家，也是《物种起源》译本的总校和译者之一。他这番话的依据就是，英语好过他的人，未必能应对该书中无以计数的动植物名称及相关的知识；专业知识过硬的人，其英语水平又未必能胜过他。近年来，我有一个发现，商务印书馆从20世纪50年代开始，直到现在一直在引进的《汉译世界学术名著丛书》（大约有400多种）的译者中，有相当比例的人不是外语专业出身的。这些都值得我们思考。

---

  ① 引自张培基等：《英汉翻译教程》，上海外语教育出版社1981年版，第146页。下划线为编者所加。
  ② 引自钱歌川：《翻译的技巧》，商务印书馆1981年版，第218页习题。
  ③ 出处同①，第152页。

这里举一个保险行业方面的例子。《中国翻译》杂志 1986 年第 6 期有一篇题为《如何翻译工程合同中 subject to 引出的短语和类似从句》的文章。其中有这样一个例句:

5. Subject to the Contractor's responsibilities and liabilities under the contract, the Contractor shall bear the amount of <u>the retained liabilities (excess)</u> stated in Appendix 12 in cases where the Contractor is responsible for the loss, damage or injury.

原译文是:

5-1. 承包方必须根据本合同规定的承包方责任和赔偿责任范围,在承包方对灭失、损坏或人身伤害负有责任时,承担附件 12 中所述的**保留责任部分金额** (免赔额)。

一年后,《中国翻译》杂志 1987 年第 6 期,刊有另一篇文章,题为《谈谈工程合同翻译的严肃性和缜密性》,对上述译文提出了质疑,指出:"既然免赔,那承包方还有什么负担呢?"并将原文改译如下:

5-2. 在承包方应对设备的丢失、损坏或损伤负责的情况下,承包方应根据本合同规定的承包方应负的责任和赔偿义务负担附件 12 中所说的**残余赔款额** (即超额部分)。

我本人对保险行业的术语也是一知半解,只是出于翻译职业的好奇,对此做过一番调查。可以看出,上述两个译者的主要分歧在于对"excess"的理解。因此,我查阅了多种工具书。如:J. H. Adam 1982 年编的 *Longman Dictionary of Business English*;香港万源财经资讯公司 1985 年出版的《商用英汉辞典》;薛立亚、张慧敏主编,中国对外翻译出版公司 1986 年出版的《英汉经济综合词典》;黎孝先主编,台湾五南图书出版公司 1988 年出版的《国际贸易英汉大辞典》;牛津大学出版社 1990 年出版的 *A Concise Dictionary of Business*。这些辞典的解释基本是一致的,其中以《商用英汉辞典》的解释最为详尽:

Excess (扣除免赔额):在海上货物保险中,规定保险人对于承保货物的单独海损超过约定限度(比率)时,仅就超过部分予以赔偿者,称为 excess 或 excess franchise。例如，一批货物保险金额为US$10 000，而约定适用 3% 的 excess 时，假定损害金额未超过US$300（3%），保险人不予赔偿；假如损害金额为 US$480，保险人仅对超过 US$300 的部分损害即 US$180 予以赔偿，并不是对 US$480 全部损害予以赔偿。因为这种赔偿条件系将免赔额（franchise）予以扣除后赔偿，所以在美国又称为 deductible franchise 或称 deductible。例如：Average payable in excess of 3%.（海损超过 3% 始予赔偿。）

Franchise（免赔额、免赔限度、免赔百分比）：在海上货物保险中，规定保险人对于损失之逾越约定限度中，始就全部损害予以赔偿（换言之，损害之未达约定限度者，保险人不予赔偿）。其界限称为 franchise 或 non-deductible franchise。再者，货物损害虽逾越约定限度，但保险人仅就逾越的部分损害予以赔偿者，即称 deductible franchise 或称 excess，或以 excess（deductible）表示。假定一批货物投保金额为美金 10 000 元，而约定适应 franchise 3% 时，如损害金额为美金 350 元，保险人即按全部损害金额照赔。设使适用 excess 3% 时，保险人仅赔偿美金 50 元，此将两者差异比较如下：

损害额	Franchise 3%	Excess 3%
US$200（2%）	不赔	不赔
US$300（3%）	赔偿 US$300	不赔
US$350（3.5%）	赔偿 US$350	赔偿 US$50
US$500（5%）	赔偿 US$500	赔偿 US$200

根据以上的解释，我们似可得出结论，译文 5－1 的确有误，它错把 excess（扣除免赔额）当 franchise（免赔额）了。但后者的批评也不准确，"免赔额"在特定的情况下还是要"赔"的。综合两个译文的长处，试再改译如下：

5－3. 根据本合同规定的承包方责任和赔偿义务，承包方在对设备的灭失、毁坏或破损负有责任时，必须承担附件 12 中所述的**剩余赔款额**（即**扣除免赔额**）。

如此烦琐的讨论，对于一般的读者，可能头脑都要发胀。总之，翻译难，批评人家也难。翻译多了，就少不了要出错。从事翻译的时间愈长，胆子可能会愈

第二章 翻译的过程

小。因为专业知识的欠缺,我们有太多的东西无能为力。

三、思维与文化差异

我们从小到大,受同一文化的熏陶,对周围发生的一切,不拘大小,都司空见惯、习以为常,久而久之,便形成某种思维定式。但译者面临的是另一国文化,所接触的事物和人们的行为方式与自己的大不相同。因此,在两种语言的转换过程中,每当语言甲与语言乙表达方式不一致的时候,就可能造成译者理解的困难,甚至导致错误。还往往出现这样的情况,对原语文化的人来说,可能是 ABC 常识性的东西,但对译者来说,却有可能莫测高深。例如:

6. 我们希望产品的图案和色彩能照顾到欧洲人的**心理**。
7. 本协议及附件用中英文书就,两种**文字**具有同等法律效力。
6 – 1: We hope that the design and color of the products would suit European <u>psychology</u>.
7 – 1: This Agreement and Appendix are rendered in Chinese and English. Both <u>languages</u> shall possess the same legal validity.

上述两句汉语,是再简单不过的了,但学生在做翻译时却出现了错误。在例 6 – 1 中,译者将"心理"理解为"psychology"。如稍加推敲就会知道,这是简单比附、误用词典所致。在例 7 – 1 中,译者将"两种文字"译为"both languages"。表面上看旗鼓相当,却犯了逻辑不通的毛病。试想:我们能说哪种"文字"享有更高或更低的法律效力吗?试比较下面的译文:

6 – 2. We hope that the design and color of the products would suit the European <u>taste</u>.①
7 – 2. This Agreement and Appendix are rendered in Chinese and English. Both <u>texts</u> shall possess the same legal validity.

如果将这两个词回译成汉语,"taste"原来指的是人的"偏爱"和"情趣",而"texts"则指的是"用两种文字写成的文本"。字面不相当,骨子里却正好是一回事。有人认为,汉译英的主要矛盾是表达,但要是麻痹大意,就会成为祸害。

---

① 引自北京语言学院/北京对外贸易学院编:*Business Chinese* 500,外文出版社 1982 年版。

汉英翻译中因比附犯的错误最多。在中国进出口商品交易会会刊《中国商品》中，曾有不少企业都为自己拥有"国家二级企业"的称号而自豪，但看看广告的英译却大感意外，而且凡是有"国家二级企业"这个桂冠的，一律都给译成了"State Second-class Enterprise"。其实这里所说的"二级企业"，如果要用英语来解释的话，应该是"the second best enterprise"，这里强调的是"好"。可是，如果查查英文词典，second-class 却意为"below a standard；inferior（低于标准；次等的）"，强调的则是"差"。人们常说的"二等公民"，就是"second-class citizens"。如果将"Second-class Enterprise"回译成中文的话，就会是"二流企业"。殊不知，"二级企业"和"二流企业"仅一字之差，意思却大相径庭！这种广告岂不倒了招牌？"国家二级企业"及类似的短语如何英译，值得探讨，比如，能否将"国家二级企业"改译为"State-level II Enterprise"？

看看英译汉的情况又是怎样的呢？在第一章里所列举的几个词中，"white wine"，有的人很可能信手就会把它译为"白酒"，而事实上却是"白葡萄酒"。在英语中，"wine"传统上是指以水果汁为原料酿造的酒，如 apple wine，cherry wine。如果在"wine"之前没有冠上某种水果的名称，则是专指葡萄酒。"dry white wine"，也许有人一眼之下又把它译成了"白干"。"白干"者，白酒也。因无色、含水分少而得名。但英语中的"dry"，若用来指"酒"，并非"含水分少"的意思，否则，下面国外某酒厂的广告标题①就要让人莫名其妙了：

> What is it that makes Sainsbury's
> Manzanilla
> Such a dry sherry?
>
> Water, of course.

既然是"干"（dry），怎么能因为有"水"（water）呢？原来"dry"是与"sweet"相对，用英语解释就是"lack of sugar"。"dry white wine"，即"不含糖分的葡萄酒"。这样，上面那则广告标题就有解了：

---

① 引自 Sally King, *Pocket Guide to Advertising*. Basil Blackwell（UK）and the Economist Publications, 1989, p. 153。

第二章 翻译的过程

> 是什么使得 Sainsbury 酒厂的
> Manzanilla 葡萄酒的
> **口味那么纯正自然呢？**
>
> 那当然是**水**了！①

我们知道酒厂广告的一个共同特点就是强调"水"好。"酒"好，即因"水"好，故好酒者买酒时必要看准酒的产地。"dry white wine"的汉语名叫"干白葡萄酒"。说实话，这是个"将错就错"的意译名，致使许多中国人都不明白它的真正含义。但我们发现商务印书馆 1989 年出版的《现代汉语词典》补编已将"干酒"（即"干白葡萄酒"的简称）列为一个词条，释义为"一种不含糖分的酒，多用葡萄酿成"，这显然是从英语翻译过来的。像"white wine"，"dry white wine"，"dry state"这类"简单"的词组，之所以给理解带来困难，关键就在于译者不熟悉原语文化。

第二节 表达阶段

表达错误，肯定是理解错了，或似懂非懂（这种情况占很大比例）。但理解正确，却也未必能充分表达出来。这说明，表达要讲究一定的方法。本节重点谈两个方面。

一、重视上下文，避免孤立处理词句

初做翻译的人，往往容易看一个句子译一个句子，遇有生词，也只是在句子的语境下考虑词义。译到后面，才发现前面的翻译有问题，得重来，既浪费了时间，自信心也受到打击。也有人逢山开路，遇水搭桥，筚路蓝缕地翻译下来，结果却前言不搭后语也浑然不知。正确的方法，应考虑词与词、词与句、句与段、段与段、段与篇章的关系。因此，开译之前，通读全文是最紧要的，

---

① 当然，这样的翻译只是个大意，还没有传达出原广告的幽默，作者正是利用了英语中"dry"这个词的一词多义。但在中文里找不到相当的词语来表达。

往往通读一遍还不够。只有这样，才能从大处着眼，小处着手，前后贯通。在译完之后，还应从词、句、段中跳出来，通读几遍译文。比如，看看选词用字是否有失分寸？词句表达是否合乎习惯？叙事状物是否有违情理？起承转合是否圆通自然？有时，从单个的词或句子看，译文似乎不错，但从整体上看却显得貌合神离，或"不够味儿"。正所谓"只见树木，不见森林"。因此，在精打细敲之后，进行全盘的加工润色是十分必要的。好比画家作幅巨画，画上几笔，总要抬起头来，或是退后几步，审视整个画面，然后再在什么地方添加几笔。如果一味低头描绘，画中的一草一木可能惟妙惟肖，但最后的作品很可能并不动人，因为画面缺乏总的氛围。试看下面一个片段：

On a cold gray morning of last week I duly turned up at Euston Station, to see off an old friend who was starting for America.

Overnight, we had given him a farewell dinner, in which sadness was well mingled with festivity. Years probably would elapse before his return. Some of us might never see him again. Not ignoring the shadow of the future, we gaily celebrated the past. We were as thankful to have known our guest as we were grieved to lose him; and both these emotions were made evident. It was a perfect farewell.

And now, here we were, stiff and self-conscious on the platform; and, framed in the window of the railway-carriage was the face of our friend; but it was like the face of a stranger, — a stranger anxious to please, an appealing stranger, an awkward stranger, … (Max Beerbohm：*Yet Again*, Chapter 2 Seeing People Off)①

这篇节选的英语曾出现在多年前自学考试的翻译试卷里。表面上看，前两段没有什么理解方面的问题，只是最后一段有点费解，但有过类似的经历，或发挥一点想象，也不是不可以对付的。作者曾把它翻译成汉语，并在课堂给学生讲评过，当时暗自得意，将"It was a perfect farewell."译成"那真是一个令人难忘的送别"，而没有将其中的"perfect"照字面译成"完美的"。这次写入书稿，找出了整篇原文，原来是 Max Beerbohm 的小说 *Yet Again* 里描写"送别"的情景。但待我读完它之前的几个段落，我就怎么也得意不起来了。请看：

---

① http：//www. worldwideschool. org/about. html.

I am not good at it. To do it well seems to me one of the most difficult things in the world, and probably seems so to you, too.

To see a friend off from Waterloo to Vauxhall were easy enough. But we are never called on to perform that small feat. It is only when a friend is going on a longish journey, and will be absent for a longish time, that we turn up at the railway station. The dearer the friend, and the longer the journey, and the longer the likely absence, the earlier do we turn up, and the more lamentably do we fail. Our failure is in exact ratio to the seriousness of the occasion, and to the depth of our feeling.

In a room, or even on a door-step, we can make the farewell quite worthily. We can express in our faces the genuine sorrow we feel. Nor do words fail us. There is no awkwardness, no restraint, on either side. The thread of our intimacy has not been snapped. The leave-taking is an ideal one. Why not, then, leave the leave-taking at that? Always, departing friends implore us not to bother to come to the railway station next morning. Always, we are deaf to these entreaties, knowing them to be not quite sincere. The departing friends would think it very odd of us if we took them at their word. Besides, they really do want to see us again. And that wish is heartily reciprocated. We duly turn up. And then, oh then, what a gulf yawns! We stretch our arms vainly across it. We have utterly lost touch. We have nothing at all to say. We gaze at each other as dumb animals gaze at human beings. We "make conversation" —and such conversation! We know that these are the friends from whom we parted overnight. They know that we have not altered. Yet, on the surface, everything is different; and the tension is such that we only long for the guard to blow his whistle and put an end to the farce.

至此，相信读者也在改变看法，而且对原文最后一段的措辞也会更有信心，比如怎样翻译"self-conscious"，然而，如果要对故事中"I"的心理世界有个全面的把握，至少应该将这一小节读完，原文是这样接下去的：

"Have you got everything?" asked one of us, breaking a silence. "Yes, everything," said our friend, with a pleasant nod. "Everything," he repeated, with the emphasis of an empty brain. "You'll be able to lunch on the train," said I, though this prophecy had already been made more than once. "Oh yes," he said with conviction. He added that the train went straight through to Liverpool. This fact seemed to strike us as rather odd. We exchanged glances. "Doesn't it stop at Crewe?" asked one of us. "No," said our friend, briefly. He seemed almost disagreeable. There was a long pause. One of us, with a nod and a forced smile at the traveller, said "Well!" The nod, the smile, and the unmeaning monosyllable, were returned conscientiously. Another pause was broken by one of us with a fit of coughing. It was an obviously assumed fit, but it served to pass the time. The bustle of the platform was unabated. There was no sign of the train's departure. Release—ours, and our friend's—was not yet.

忽视上下文的联系，教训有时是惨重的。看过本书第一版的读者也许会发现，在第六章"词类的转换"那一节的开头，笔者曾津津乐道的一整段，现在全部给删除了。原来那段讲解的是如何通过词类的转换来翻译罗素（Bertrand Russell，1872—1970）写的一篇文章的标题"How to Grow Old"。文章的主要内容是劝诫老年人不要怕死，主张生活应达观开朗。笔者当时反对将该标题直译为《如何变老》（也反对其他现成的译法，如《老年人须知》《怎样安度晚年》），而主张翻译成《老年人生活艺术》，并指出："从词类上进行分析，原文标题是'副词 + to 动词不定式 + 系动词 + 形容词'，而译文则是'名词 + 名词 + 名词'；从词序上分析，译文与原文正好互为颠倒。由此，译文与原文在形式上可谓大相径庭。但从意义上来说，懂得'如何'在最恰当的时候做最恰当的事，这不正是一种'艺术'吗！仔细分析起来，译文虽经重大转换和调整，但却仍紧扣原文标题字面（'老年人'译'old'，'生活'译'grow'，'艺术'译'how'），同时又忠实于正文内容。"但后来我真是叫苦不迭，因为是偷懒而酿成的大错。虽然没有哪个当面说我"自以为是"，但这件事一直像麦芒般扎着我，唯有在此坦白才能得以解脱。原来，笔者是针对 L. G. Alexander 主编的 *New Concept English* 第四册上那段文字来讨论的，但不幸的是，那只是个节选。更不幸的是，事实上，还是笔者念大学时在吴景荣等编选的《当代英文散文选读》里就学过那篇完整的文章，后来淡忘了。偶然的原因找出来一看，让我大惊失色。文章是这样开头的："In spite of the title, this article will really be on how not to grow old, which, at my time of life, is a much more important subject." 如果将标题译成《老年人生活艺术》，后面怎样能接下去呢？恰恰相反，《如何变老》才是得体的翻译，因此译文就可这样顺其自然："尽管标题这样写，实际上，本篇要讨论的是'如何不变老'。这个话题，对于像我这个年纪的人来说，尤为重要。"这件事给我的另一个启示就是：不能为技巧而技巧，技巧的运用必须服从于文章的内容。

二、从情景出发，摆脱表层结构的束缚

做翻译的另一常见毛病，就是习惯于"对号入座"。这种习惯一方面来源于词典释义（如果是双语词典，上面已经标注了"对等"的词语，拿来便用；如果是单语外文词典，读者也会下意识地在大脑里将其转换成母语中某个"相当"的词语）。比如，我们见到"good"，就将它与"好的"画等号；见到"better"，就将它与"较好的"或"更好的"画等号；见到"best"，就将它与"最好的"画等号。**实际上，词典释义与行文翻译往往相去甚远。**例如，将"Any experience is good."这句英语译作"任何经历都是好的"自然不能算错，但显然不如译作"凡是经历都很珍贵"[①]。又如，将"Honesty is the best policy."译作"诚实是最好的策略"，也能看懂（很多翻译就是这个模样），但纯净的中文则应该是"诚实为上"。再看看"我们破例给2%的佣金，不能再高了"，这句汉语中间没有任何"好"字，却可能译作："We will give a 2% commission as an exception. This is the best we can do."

"对号入座"的另一来源是受某些外语教师或语法、用法类书籍的影响。比如，我们从一开始就被告知："so... that..."相当于"太……以至于……"，"too...to..."相当于"太……以至于不能……"，"as... as..."相当于"像……一样"，"more than"相当于"比……更"。这样的典型结构还有很多很多，多年下来，等外语学到一定程度，这些"对等"的结构在大脑里安营扎寨，直至根深蒂固，因此，翻译时到处都充满诱惑。翁显良就举过这样一个例子："He was so angry that he couldn't speak."最不伤脑筋的译法就是逐词转换：He = 他，was = 是，so = 那样，angry = 愤怒，that = 以致，he = 他，couldn't = 不会，speak = 说话。连在一起就是："他是那样愤怒，以致他不会说话。"而纯正的汉语则应该是："他气得连话都说不出来。"

要克服"对号入座"，摆脱原文表层结构的束缚，除了可以通过学习翻译技巧外（如学会"转换词类"和"反面着笔"等，参见第五章），还可借助改变思维定式的一些训练。这里介绍两种训练方法，一是"**回避法**"[②]，二是"**情景法**"。

先说"回避法"。"回避法"主要针对的是单个词语的处理。具体地说，就

[①] 引自苏福忠：《译事余墨》，生活·读书·新知三联书店2006年版，第1页。

[②] 这一点是受到乔海清的启发，见《翻译新论》，北京语言大学出版社1993年版。该作者主张，翻译应从实际出发，表达应多样化。

是每当看到一个词语,最早出现在脑子里的译文,尽可能避免使用,而是尝试从不同的角度切入(如语体有雅俗之分,语气有强弱之别,色彩有褒贬的差异,句式有陈述、反诘、感叹、主动与被动、正说与反说等等的不同)。例如:

1. In fact, ...(尝试不使用"事实上")
    a)原来……
    b)说白了……
    c)归根到底……
    d)不瞒你说……
    e)你有所不知……

2. Fortunately, ...(尝试不使用"很幸运"或"幸而")
    a)还好……
    b)好在……
    c)巧得很……
    d)真走运……
    e)谢天谢地……

3. the best opportunity(尝试不使用"最好的机会")
    a)大好时机
    b)形势再好不过了
    c)天时、地利、人和
    d)机不可失,时不再来
    e)过了这个村,就没那个店

4. You must help.(尝试不使用"你必须帮忙")
    a)全靠你了。
    b)请多关照。
    c)帮帮忙,好不好?
    d)你不帮忙可不行。
    e)这忙你帮也得帮,不帮也得帮!

可见,思维定式打破了,表达的潜力是很大的。以上同一词语或句子的不同译法,在潜在的语境中都是可能的表达,即使在同一语境中,也未必是(或更准确地说,往往不是)最早想到的译法是最巧的译法。

再说"情景法"。该方法主要针对的是表层结构。心里明白,却表达不出来,一般都是原文的表层结构在作怪。余光中提供了一个很有趣的例子①:"Don't cough more than you can help."这句话该怎么译成汉语呢?是"不要比你能忍的咳得更多"呢?还是"不要咳得多于你能不咳的"呢?看来两者都不像地道的汉语,因为怎样念也感到别扭。仔细想想,不就是"能不咳,就不咳"嘛!难道这样简单的话我们都不会说吗?但翻译就是这样奇怪,话虽简单,有时就是怎么也绕不过来。遇到这种情形,行之有效的方法,就是在吃透原文的意思之后,要设法将原文的词、句结构暂时抛之脑后,再想象一下,在同样的情景下,我们平常是怎么说的,然后用自己的话写下来。下面是从书籍中摘录的几个实例:

1. If you know the answer, raise your hand.
   如果你知道答案,请举手。
2. Smith fell down when he ran fast to meet them.
   当史密斯跑得很快去会见他们时,他摔倒了。
3. I was admittedly shy.
   我是以腼腆胆怯著称的。
4. If we can help you further, please don't hesitate to get in touch with us.
   愿意为你们进一步服务,如有需要,请与我们联系,请勿犹豫。
5. The murderer ran away as fast as he could, so that he might not be caught red-handed.
   凶手尽快地跑开,以免被人当场抓住。
6. Your friend is familiar with the culture-specific non-verbal or verbal markers giving away the policeman's ignorance. (Christiane Nord: *Translating as a Purposeful Activity*, p. 2)
   你的朋友熟悉印尼文化,因此他从警察的言语或非言语标志中看出,该警察对那条街一无所知。②

显然,以上6个句子的翻译,都不同程度地受了原文表层结构的影响。读者不妨根据这里推荐的方法试译一遍,相信结果会大不一样。一些翻译大师,他们

---

① 引自余光中:《余光中选集》第四卷(语文及翻译论集),安徽教育出版社1999年版,第145页。

② 上下文是假设读者"你"身处雅加达闹市,又不会印尼语,在当地朋友的帮助下向警察问路的情形。

之所以能翻译得那么妥帖自然，原因就在于他们都擅于化解原文的表层结构，在译文中重新组装信息。请欣赏下面几个漂亮的译文：

1. Nothing except a battle lost can be half so melancholy as a battle won. — The Duke of Wellington

   都道战败苦，谁知战胜惨！（许渊冲 译）①

2. These alterations of mood were the despair and joy of Ethan Frome. (Edith Wharaton：*Ethan Frome*)

   她这种**一会儿一个**情调，叫伊坦**时而**灰心**时而**高兴。（吕叔湘 译）②

3. I did not want a ring, but Mother presented this one to me with such affection that I saw no way to get out of accepting it. She put it on my finger and kissed me. (Clarence Day：*Life with Father*)

   我是不要戴戒指的，可是母亲的**盛意**真是叫人难以拒绝。她把戒指给我套在指头上，又亲了我一下。（吕叔湘 译）③

4. "Eating between meals," Mrs. Baines said, "What would your mother say, Master Philip?" (Graham Greene：*The Basement Room*)

   "**三顿不够，这会儿还要吃，**"贝恩思太太开腔了："你妈知道了会怎么说呢，菲力少爷？"（翁显良 译）④

第三节　校对阶段

校对阶段是理解与表达的进一步深化。换言之，校对的过程，就是对原文内容进一步理解、表达、核实的过程，表达是逐步完善的。我们在翻译时尽管十分细心，但译文错漏或文句欠妥都在所难免。因此，校对是保证译文质量不可缺少的阶段。本节重点谈三个问题。

---

① 引自许渊冲：《文学翻译谈》，（台北）书林出版有限公司1998年版，第353页。这句深富哲理的名言，是出自击败拿破仑的英国名将威灵顿公爵之口。
② 引自吕叔湘：《吕叔湘译文三种》，外语教学与研究出版社1992年版，第55页。
③ 引自吕叔湘：《吕叔湘译文三种》，外语教学与研究出版社1992年版，第407页
④ 引自翁显良：《意态由来画不成？》，中国对外翻译出版公司1983年版，第83页。

一、校对的步骤

一般说来，校对可以分四个步骤。

第一步，当然是检查是否有错漏。较长的文本，有经验的译者会在原文的段首标上序号，然后在译文的段首也标上序号，这样就不容易遗漏段落（遗漏整段文字的情况时有发生），没有特殊原因，译文不要轻易改变原来的段落，如要改变，也最好在初校后进行。

第二步，检查是否有逻辑问题。比如，文中是否有不相干的句子，前后是否矛盾，或是否有不合常理或看不明白的地方。逻辑问题几乎总是理解的问题，个别情况属于原文本身的毛病。若是后者，可考虑根据文本的性质或翻译的目的作适当处理。

第三步，设法消除英译汉中的欧化结构。这是一个艰巨的工作，对译者的要求很高，但也不是不可作为。除上一节重点讨论的外，还有一些行之有效的方法。首先，要了解英文与中文的基本不同在哪里。比如：①英文重形合（即句子各部分的关系主要依靠有形的连接，如英文中有大量的 that，which，where，when，if，and，of，in），中文重意合（主要依靠词序和意念的连贯，散而不乱）；②英文句子一般不能缺少主语，中文句子称为"流水句"，其显著特点就是多个分句可共享一个主语；③英文句子称"绵长句"，习以为常的是环环相扣的后置修饰语，中文句子则基本为前置修饰语，结构简洁；④英文的大半名词前要用冠词，非 the 即 a，而中文里完全没有冠词的概念；⑤英文里的名词有单复数的形态之分，中文里的单复数多数情况只靠意会，不必明示；⑥英文里大量使用被动语态，中文虽有被动语态，但远不如英文用得那么广泛，且表达方式更为多样化。了解了这些基本特点，在校对时才能对症下药：设法删减连接词语（比如少用"如果"，少用"和"字，少用"当……时候"及类似结构）；设法删减主语；设法删减"的"字结构，学会化整为零；设法删减"一个""一种""那个"（这是上了冠词的当）；设法删减"们"字；设法删减或替换"被"字。能满足上述要件，译文便能朗朗上口了。

第四步，加工润色，文学翻译尤其重要。常听人说，好的文章是改出来的，翻译也不例外。认真的译者，文稿在排版阶段还在修改，有了这种精神，才能不断超越自己。

校对的四个步骤只是大致的说法，或为叙述的方便，不是截然分开的。

二、校对的方法

校对可分初校和复校（复校又可分二校、三校等，视文本性质而定）。初校的目标是消除错漏，复校则致力于行文流畅，文学翻译更追求色彩的斑斓，但两者并不是截然分开。以下是两点建议：

一是抛开原文校对。这是初校和终校不可缺少的环节。背后的理念是：**译文必须独立成篇**。换言之，它必须是不依赖于原文而独立存在，因为一般的译文读者是看不懂原文或无须对照原文。因此，原文是篇好文章，译文也必须是篇好文章。极端而言，原文是首好诗，译文首先必须是首诗，然后再看是否是首好诗。主体准确和传神，比细节真实更为重要，要知道：并非所有的细节都同等重要。实际上，翻译中的多数毛病在不看原文时就能发现。抛开原文校对的理想方法，就是朗读。所谓朗读，就是要读出声音来。在朗读的过程中，哪里拗口，哪里声音不对，哪里语气不合，都能逐一发现和纠正。如果时间允许，初校之后，先放上一段时间，再进行校对，这样更容易发现问题。往往译者原来觉得不错的句子，重读后，又觉得不满意了，再次加工，译文质量可大大改观。

二是请别人校对。自己写的东西，最终是给别人看的。自己觉得明白易懂，没有问题，并不完全等于别人的感觉也是如此，角度不同，知识储备和背景不同，见解有时会很不一样。因此，请别人校对，最能发现问题。哪怕不同意别人提出的看法，总不会有坏处，只会使自己考虑得更周全，因而使译文更严密和完美。如果是英译汉，可请有中文写作经验的人帮助校对（英文不熟的更好）。如果是汉译英，在定稿前，最好能请母语是英语的人看看，译文是否地道，他们最有发言权。

三、商务文本的校对

商务文本，重在记实，在校对内容方面另有侧重，除要求简明、严谨、准确外，还要特别注意事实细节，包括日期、金额、数量、代号等。

（一）日期

经贸业务方面，凡涉及有关日期的文字，都应严格认真，丝毫不能马虎。特别是对外签订合同，有关年、月、日都得大写。例如：

本合同于一九九九年二月十八日在广州签订。
The Contract is signed in Guangzhou this eighteenth day of February, one thousand nine hundred and ninety nine.

关于日期，还应注意一些（复合）介词的特定含义，如"on and about"，"on and after"，"on and before"，"until"等。如果使用"from…to…"结构，还

应注意是否包括起止日期。

（二）金额

表示金额，一是要注意货币单位。如果是美元，应写成 US$ 或 USD；是港币，应写成 HK$；是人民币，应写成 RMB￥，即 Renminbi yuan 的缩写；是日元，就应写成 JP￥，即 Japanese yen 的缩写。二是要注意在小写之后，是否有必要再大写。金额的小写，应注意货币符号与金额数之间不留空格，例如：HK$ 152 348.00，不应写成 HK$　152 348.00。

（三）重量

表示重量，要注意其单位，如不要把 kg（公斤）错译为"斤"，也不要把 kg（公斤）错译为"公吨"（ton）。此外，还应注意是净重还是毛重等事项。

（四）缩略语和代号

经贸英语中，有许多缩写、代号。这些缩写和代号都有特定含义，如表示价格，有 CIF（cost, insurance and freight）价格（即到岸价格/船上交货价）。支付条款中，有 D/P（documents against payment），即"付款交单"；有 D/A（documents against acceptance），即"承兑交单"；等等。翻译时应特别小心，一个字母之差，就可能带来重大经济损失。

（五）倍数词

如果是英译汉，要注意"增加了……倍"与"增加到……倍"或"是原来的……倍"的区别。表示减少，要注意汉语的表达习惯，一般不译成"减少……倍"，而是化成分数或百分数。（参见第八章第三节）

（六）数字

使用数字，比如 152 348.00，翻译时千万不能遗漏小数点，否则酿成大错。书写数字，有时使用分节号，如上面这个数字还可以写成 152,348，不要误把分节号当作小数点，译成 152.348，结果相差 1000 倍。如果是英文数字，特别注意"billion"的用法。在美国和法国，billion 等于"10 亿"，即 1 000 000 000。在英国和德国则等于"兆"（万亿），即 1 000 000 000 000。另外，使用数字也应注意数字前后的"近""多""约""左右"等表示分寸的字样。

（七）注意一些易混结构

如"out of question"（毫无问题）与"out of the question"（绝不可能）；"25% of invoice value"（发票金额的25%）与"25% off invoice value"（发票金额减去25%）；等等。

附　录：本章第一节4个句子的分析

1. Evolution is a conservative process, wasting little of value.

    参考译文：物质的进化是个极其缓慢的过程，**物质在短时间内不会起质的变化**。

这个句子摘自一本外国人编写的写作教材，谈的是如何巧用分词短语化解定语从句，以达到简洁句子的目的。没有任何上下文，也不需要任何上下文。笔者只是出于职业的敏感，觉得这个句子很有趣，可用来说明翻译的道理。

该句子的结构无须分析，用词也很简单，对每个三四年级的大学生来说都不会有生词，但要了解这些单词组合在一起又形成了一个什么样的概念，却很不简单。不简单在哪里呢？就在于它背后隐藏的知识。比如，你至少要了解进化论是怎么一回事，否则翻译就无从下手。从译文中可以看到，我增加了一些词。你的译文又是怎样的呢？

2. When the history of the Nixon Administration is finally written, the chances are that his Chinese policy will stand out <u>as a model of common sense and good diplomacy</u>.

    原译文：当最后撰写尼克松政府的历史时，他的对华政策可能成为**懂得常识**和处理外交的楷模。（转引自张培基等《英汉翻译教程》第146页）

原译文不太好懂，什么是"懂得常识和处理外交的楷模"呢？后来在《翻译通讯》1985年第4期李端严先生对原译文提出了批评，认为所谓"common sense"，无非是说他的对华政策符合一般人的正常看法，因此引申为"通情达理"较好，他的改译如下：

第二章 翻译的过程

译文二：当最后撰写尼克松政府的历史时，他的对华政策可能成为**通情达理**和善于处理外交事务的楷模。（李端严 译）

我基本同意他的看法，只是觉得修改后的译文仍不好懂。要翻译好这个句子，如果对那段历史有所了解当然会有帮助。简单地说，1972年，时任美国总统的尼克松应周恩来总理的邀请访华，断绝了20多年的中美交往的大门重新打开，他的访问堪称"破冰之旅"。尼克松访华期间，中美双方于1972年2月28日在上海发表了《中美联合公报》（即《上海公报》），正式宣布谋求两国关系正常化。从此，世界上最大的发展中国家和世界上最发达的国家结束了敌对状态。尼克松的对华政策符合美国的根本利益，又何尝不符合中国的根本利益呢？（当时中苏关系降到了冰点，台湾问题纠缠不清）按今天时髦的语言来说，这是"双赢"的大好事，连普通百姓也知道的，因此这是"common sense"（常识）。如果要把这句话说得通顺好懂些，不妨将原来的并列结构"a model of common sense and good diplomacy"（常识和好外交的楷模）做点调整①，试再改译如下：

译文三：当人们最后撰写尼克松政府的历史时，他的对华政策可能**尤为引人注目，成为灵活运用常识来处理外交事务的楷模**。

3.

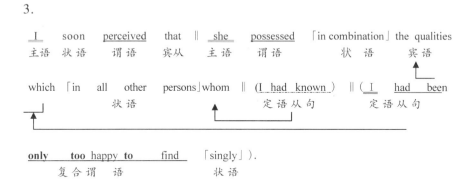

这是一个用词不多、结构却十分复杂的句子。因此，要准确翻译，第一步，

---

① 未查到英语原文出自哪本书，但我读书时发现，在齐沛合译卡尔布兄弟（Marvin Kalb & Bernard Kalb）著《基辛格》（上册）第432页（北京三联书店，1975年版）里，该书作者引用了这句话的后半句。齐沛合的译文是："他（尼克松）的对华政策树立了一个遵从常识的典范，一个正确外交的典范。"可见，齐沛合译本保留了原文的并列结构，意思也很清楚。这里多提供一个译文，可帮助读者加深对这句话的理解。

必须厘清各部分的关系。如上图所示,这个复合句是个"主 — 谓 — 宾"结构,宾语为一个从句,宾语从句也是个"主 — 谓 — 宾"结构,其中宾语引出一个定语从句和一个状语,而状语再携带一个定语从句。在词语方面,要特别注意粗体字部分的"only too ... to"结构,因为阅读课教师常常将"too ... to"结构中的不定式诠释为含否定意义,但如果在"too"的前面有"only""all""but"等字修饰,后面的动词不定式就不具有否定意义,不了解这一点,就会把意思弄反了。另外,句中的"singly"和"in combination"为对应的表述,处理好这对词语,对翻译好整个句子也很关键。试译如下:

参考译文:在我所熟悉的人身上,我很高兴能发现**这样或那样的**(singly)优良品德。然而我很快就惊喜地注意到,许多人的优良品德,**她却一人兼而有之**。(in combination)

4. Time goes fast for one who has a sense of beauty, when there are pretty children in a pool and a young Diana on the edge, to receive with wonder anything you can catch!

这个句子在笔者的脑子里有十多年了。当时被委派教翻译课,没想到订购的教材竟是自己念大学时学过的国家统编《英汉翻译教程》。当时老师是怎么教我们的,也没有多少印象,为了不受原来翻译的影响,对准备讲解的例子,都盖起书来自己先译一遍,没想到却发现不少问题,而这个句子给我的印象最为深刻,因为我的翻译与书上所给的译文几乎讲的不是一回事。请比较:

教材译文:当你跟可爱的孩子们站在池子里,又有个年轻的狄安娜在池边好奇地**接受你捉上来的任何东西的时候**,如果你懂得什么叫美的话,时间是过得很快的。

笔者译文:当可爱的孩子们在池子里戏水玩耍,池边又有个年轻貌美的姑娘**尽收眼底**的时候,对于一个有美感的人来说,他一定会**赞叹不已**,时间不知不觉就过去了。

注意两个译文的粗体字部分。回过头来仔细分析,我们的重要区别有两点,一是语法分析的不同,原译者认为 to receive 的逻辑主语是 Diana,而笔者认为是 one,理由是中间的分句只能当作插入成分,因为它的前后都有一个逗号隔开;一是对 receive 和 catch 的理解,原译者认为它们对应的是具体的"接受"和

"捉",而笔者认为两者都可以理解成更为抽象的"看见"(to see 或 to perceive)。因教材没有标明出处,没有上下文,很难判断谁对谁错,但毕竟原译者是有上下文的。尽管如此,笔者仍相信自己的语法分析更有道理。这次修订教材,又想起了这个句子,因此下定决心要找出它的源头。请看:

When he followed Halliday into the sitting-room for lunch, three faces, very fair and blue-eyed, were turned suddenly at the words: "This is Frank Ashurst — my young sisters."

Two were indeed young, about eleven and ten. The third was perhaps seventeen, tall and fair-haired too, with pink-and-white cheeks just touched by the sun, and eyebrows, rather darker than the hair, running a little upwards from her nose to their outer points. The voices of all three were like Halliday's, high and cheerful; they stood up straight, shook hands with a quick movement, looked at Ashurst critically, away again at once, and began to talk of what they were going to do in the afternoon. <u>A regular Diana and attendant nymphs</u>! After the farm this crisp, slangy, eager talk, this cool, clean, off-hand refinement, was queer at first, and then so natural that what he had come from became suddenly remote. The names of the two little ones seemed to be Sabina and Freda; of the eldest, Stella.

Presently the one called Sabina turned to him and said:

"I say, <u>will you come shrimping with us</u>? — it's awful fun!"

Surprised by this unexpected friendliness, Ashurst murmured:

"I'm afraid I've got to get back this afternoon."

"Oh!"

"Can't you put it off?"

Ashurst turned to the new speaker, Stella, shook his head, and smiled. She was very pretty! Sabina said regretfully: "You might!" Then the talk switched off to caves and swimming.

"Can you swim far?"

"About two miles."

"Oh!"

"I say!"

"How jolly!"

The three pairs of blue eyes, fixed on him, made him conscious of his new importance — The sensation was agreeable. Halliday said:

"I say, you simply must stop and have a bathe. You'd better stay the night."

"Yes, do!"

But again Ashurst smiled and shook his head. Then suddenly he found himself being catechised about his physical achievements. He had rowed — it seemed — in his college boat, played in his college football team, won his college mile; and he rose from table a sort of hero. The two little girls insisted that he must see "their" cave, and they set forth chattering like magpies, Ashurst between them, Stella and her brother a little behind. In the cave, damp and darkish like any other cave, <u>the great feature was a pool with possibility of creatures which might be caught and put into bottles</u>. Sabina and Freda, who wore no stockings on their shapely brown legs, exhorted Ashurst to join them <u>in the middle of it</u>, and help **sieve** the water. He too was soon bootless and sockless. <u>Time goes fast for one who has a sense of beauty, when there are pretty children in a pool and a young Diana on the edge, to receive with wonder anything you can catch</u>! Ashurst never had much sense of time. It was a shock when, pulling out his watch, he saw it was well past three. <u>No cashing his cheque today, the bank would be closed before he could get there</u>. Watching his expression, the little girls cried out at once:

"Hurrah! Now you'll have to stay!"

原来这是出自 1932 年诺贝尔文学奖获得者、英国作家约翰·高尔斯华绥 (John Galsworthy, 1867—1933) 的中篇小说《苹果树》(*The Apple Tree*)。①请注意画有底线的句子，显然，原译者有三个根据，一是前面有一句"你跟我们去摸虾好吗"，中间有一处说"池子里可能有些小生物，抓到后可以装到小瓶子里玩"，后面还有一处说"帮助筛水"（也可以理解为用"网"或"筛"淘虾）。看完整

---

① 故事是这样的：男主人公 Ashurst 还是个大学生的时候曾在一个农庄借宿，偶然结识了乡村姑娘 Megan。双方一见钟情，在美丽的苹果树下海誓山盟，Ashurst 决意带姑娘去伦敦一起生活。但是当他去附近的城镇银行取钱购置行装的时候，意外遇见了老朋友 Halliday 和他的 3 个妹妹，而很快被其中年长的妙龄少女 Stella 的美貌俘虏了。结果 Ashurst 失诺于 Megan，与 Stella 结婚。在多年后的银婚纪念日，他故地重游，发现了 Megan 因精神错乱而死去后的坟墓。一切照旧，然而没有了生活中最美好的东西——"那苹果树，那歌声和那金子"。

个上下文，笔者认为这三个根据仍不足为凭，理由如下：

其一，从句法上分析，如果"to receive"的逻辑主语是 Diana 的话，那么"children"也应是并列的逻辑主语，但"children"是在池子的中央（也是直接参与"摸虾"的人），而 Diana 是在池子的边上，这不合常情。另外，从写作的角度，如果是循着这个思路，动词不定式后面的句子这样写会更生动："to receive any creatures you <u>hand over</u>"。

其二，"帮助筛水"，并没有明确表示是"淘虾"。另外，就两个动词"to receive"和"to catch"来说，选用具体意义的"接受"和"捉"，远不如选用抽象意义的"接收"和"捕捉"所唤起的意境那么优美。

其三，最为重要的是，我们发现这句话是作者随景插入的一个评论，换言之，这是"虚境"与"真境"的结合，你中有我，我中有你。所谓"虚境"，就是说，所涉及的事件是一个真理，可以泛泛而论，所以作者没有说池子里有"两个"小女孩，也没有用女主人公的真名 Stella，而换用了一个美女化身的月亮女神 Diana；所谓"真境"，是说此情此景，可正相比附。句首的"时间过得快"（"虚境"），也是与后面的"错过了去银行兑支票的时间"（"真境"）相对照。

这里我们还收集到另外两个译文，再作一番比较，也许对这个句子的理解会更深刻些：

译文一：对于有美感的人来说，时间是过得很快的，尤其是池子里有两个孩子，池边上站着一位年轻的狄安娜，你无论逮到什么，她们都欢叫。①（董衡巽 译。原注：Diana：罗马神话里的月亮女神）

译文二：一个富于审美感的人，遇到水塘里这些可爱的孩子们，水塘边又有一位年轻美丽的狄安娜，她们从你手里接过任何你能捉到的东西时就发出一阵欢叫，这时，对你来说，时间当然过得飞快！②（屠枫 译。原注：Diana：罗马神话里的月亮和狩猎女神）

从上面两个译文看，两个译者都加了脚注，说明都知道这是虚境，但第一个译者根据上下文将"children"译成"两个孩子"，前后不统一，就有点弄巧成拙了，另外，漏译了"to receive"，同时又增添了想象的"欢叫"。第二个译者则将"children"和"Diana"看成是"to receive"的共同逻辑主语。根据以上的分

---

① 董衡巽译：《苹果树》，中国和平出版社 2005 年版，第 64 页。
② 屠枫译：《苹果树》，人民文学出版社 2006 年版，第 129 页。

析，笔者将这句英语再改译如下：

修改译文：对于一个有美感的人来说，当置身于一个**胜景迭起、满目惊喜**的世界，时间会过得飞快，就如眼下天真烂漫的孩子们在水潭里戏水玩耍，岸边又有一位月神般的少女。（阿瑟斯特从来没有多少时间概念，等他掏出表来一看，早已过了3点，不免大吃一惊。他的支票今天无法兑现了，不要等他赶到，银行早就关门了。）

拿这个译文与笔者最早的那个译文比较，重要的区别在于后者突出了主要信息，回过头来看看原文，也是先叙述时间过得快，再补叙水潭周围的活动，因此，这样的安排应该说是合适的。笔者将Diana的意思引申出来，有两个好处，一是省去作脚注的麻烦，一是避免读者将它误读为女主人公的名字。按笔者对后半句两个主要动词的理解，要翻译成相当的汉语，也感到力不从心。现在给的译文只能说是暂时的。读者看完之后也许同意笔者的观点，也许不同意笔者的观点，这都不重要，重要的是，通过这样的分析，我们对翻译的过程便有了更深刻的了解。

【练习题】

Ⅰ. 下列精选的这组句子包含某些特别的字词或结构，可能会给翻译带来理解或表达上的困难。请尝试将它们译成汉语，力求表达自然，避免翻译腔。请在认真修改自己的译文之后，再对照书后提供的参考译文。

1. Wait here until I come.
2. Don't open the door till the bus stops.
3. The stereo radio is now a standard feature.
4. The earth rotates as it travels through space.
5. We had barely dropped off to sleep when the doorbell began to ring.
6. The new rates will apply from 1st January next year, until then the old rates below hold good.
7. Jobs felt that design simplicity should be linked to making products easy to use. (Walter Isaacson: *Steve Jobs*, p. 127)
8. I think most creative people want to express appreciation for being able to take advantage of the work that's been done by others before us. (Walter Isaacson: *Steve Jobs*, p. 570)
9. I think Henry Ford once said, "If I'd asked customers what they wanted, they

would have told me,'A faster horse!'" People don't know what they want until you show it to them. That's why I never rely on market research. Our task is to read things that are not yet on the page. (Walter Isaacson: *Steve Jobs*, p. 567)

10. Interest in historical methods had arisen less through external challenge to the validity of history as an intellectual discipline and more from internal quarrels among historians themselves.

11. Usage is the only test. I would prefer a phrase that was easy and unaffected to a phrase that was grammatical. (W. Somerset Maugham: *Lucidity*, *Simplicity*, *Euphony*)

12. I have written few pages that I feel I could not improve and far too many that I have left with dissatisfaction, because, try as I would, I could do no better. (W. Somerset Maugham: *Lucidity*, *Simplicity*, *Euphony*)

13. It is a valuable work. I do not think anyone writes so well that he can not learn much from it. (W. Somerset Maugham: *Lucidity*, *Simplicity*, *Euphony*)

14. Some writers who do not think clearly are inclined to suppose that their thoughts have a significance greater than at first sight appears. (W. Somerset Maugham: *Lucidity*, *Simplicity*, *Euphony*)

15. Don't forget that Jerusalem is also a modern, thriving city, and there are plenty of excellent shops and restaurants to temp you away from sightseeing for a while.

Ⅱ. 请根据原文，校改下列译文。

1. All the items enquired for in your letter are not handled by this Corporation.
   译文：来函所询商品不是这家公司经营的。

2. These documents are detailed with names, dates, places and full descriptions of the incidents investigated.
   译文：这些文件详细载明了姓名、日期、地点和所调查事件的全部经过。

3. We are enclosing herewith the captioned contract in two originals, of which please return one copy to us duly countersigned for our records.
   译文：今寄上标题合同正本两份，请会签后寄回一份，以便存档。

4. … require the Contractor to promptly re-perform the project services in which the error was discovered at no additional cost to the Purchaser, provided that the working and living conditions as specified in Appendix 8 shall be provided by the Purchaser.
   译文：……要求承包方对发现有错误的工程服务迅速返工而不增加购买方的费用。但是，购买方要按附件八规定向返工人员提供工作和生活条件。

5. Any event or circumstance beyond the control of the Parties shall be deemed an event of Force Majeure and shall include, but not be restricted to, fire, storm, flood, earthquake, explosion, war, rebellion, insurrection, epidemic and quarantine restrictions.

译文：任何双方无法控制的事件或情况，均应视为不可抗力事件，应该包括，但不限于火灾、水灾、地震、爆炸、战争、叛乱、暴动、传染病及检疫。

Ⅲ. 下面是同一原文的3个版本的译文①，试采用初校不看原文的办法，看看能发现什么问题，做好记号，再对照原文复校。原文放在书后的练习答案部分。

宝 岛
〔英〕R. L. 史蒂文森 著 欣 若 译

第十五章 岛上的人

山丘的一边，在这一带显得陡峭而坚硬。从那上面，有一堆沙砾扑扑簌簌地掉下来，在树丛间滚动。我本能地把眼睛朝那个方向转去，看见一个影子在一棵松树的树干后面急速地跳跃着。它究竟是什么，是熊，是人，还是猴子，我完全说不上来。它看上去是黑黝黝、毛蓬蓬的，再多的我就搞不清楚了。但是，由这个新的幻影引起的惊恐使我停了下来。

金银岛
〔英〕R. L. 史蒂文生 著 荣如德 译

第十五章 岛中人

从小山这一侧陡峭而多石的山坡上，许多沙砾喀啦啦跳动着穿过树木纷纷落下。我的眼睛本能地转向那边，看见一个身影以极其迅捷的动作跳到一棵松树背后。那究竟是熊、是人，还是猿猴，我怎么也说不上来。反正是黑乎乎、毛茸茸的，此外我什么也没看清楚。但这个新出现的幽灵却把我吓得不敢向前。

---

① 转引自许国烈编：《中英文学名著译文比录》，陕西人民出版社1985年版，第246－247页。

荒岛探宝记

〔英〕R. L. 史蒂文生 著 张友松 译

第十五章 岛上的奇人

这儿有一处山腰是陡峭的石崖,那上面有一个砂石的尖嘴松开了,轰隆轰隆地从树木当中急滚下来。我的眼睛本能地朝那边望去,便看见一个人形的动物在一棵松树后面飞快地跳动。那究竟是什么,是熊、是人,或是猴子,我根本就看不清。这东西是黑乎乎的,满身长着粗毛。别的我就什么也不知道了。可是,这个怪物引起的恐惧却使我站住了。

第三章
翻译的理念

翻译的理念是人们对翻译本质的认识和信仰。人们认识事物总是有差异，因此信仰自然也有所不同。信仰不同，行为方式就不尽一样。在翻译实践中，我们有必要了解在中外翻译史上产生过重大影响的翻译理念，这样，我们就能在宏观上把握方向，在微观上取舍有据。

翻译的理念是一个动态的概念。时代不同，实践的内容不同，人们对事物的理念就会发生变化。翻译也不例外，理念会不断超越。

第一节 严复：信、达、雅

严复（1854—1921），近代启蒙思想家、翻译家。字又陵，又字几道，福建侯官（今福州）人。福州船政学堂第一届毕业，光绪三年（1877年）受清廷派遣留学英国格林尼治海军学院，归任北洋水师学堂总教习，升总办（校长）。1895年"甲午"惨败后，发表《论世变之亟》《救亡决论》等文，狠批顽固保守，宣传维新思想。严复留学英国期间无意研修航海和军事技术，却醉心西方文物制度，一生的巨大贡献体现在翻译方面。他的译著主要收集在《严译名著丛刊》《侯官严氏丛刊》里，计有：

《天演论》（T. Henry Huxley：*Evolution and Ethics and Other Essays*）

《群己权界论》（John Stuart Mill：*On Liberty*）

《穆勒名学》（John Stuart Mill：*System of Logic*）

《群学肄言》（H. Spencer：*Study of Sociology*）

《原富》（A. Smith：*Inquiry into the Nature and Cause of the Wealth of Nations*）

《法意》（C. D. S. Montesquien：*Spirit of Law*）

《社会通诠》（E. Jenks：*History of Politics*）

《名学浅说》（W. S. Jevons：*Logic*）

以上均是西方学者社会科学的学术名著，它们的引进在中国思想界起了振聋发聩的启蒙作用。

第三章 翻译的理念

严复的巨大贡献还体现于他在我国译学思想史上建立了一座丰碑。我国约有2000年的翻译史，但影响最广的翻译理念出自严复1898年发表的《天演论·译例言》。在这里，严复把对翻译的感悟浓缩为经典的"信、达、雅"3个字。这三字理念在半个多世纪里几乎成了我国翻译界普遍接受的"翻译标准"。以下是《天演论·译例言》里的精彩片段：

> 译事三难：信、达、雅。求其信，已大难矣！顾信矣不达，虽译犹不译也，则达尚焉。……译文取明深义，故词句之间时有所颠倒附益，不斤斤于字比句次，而意义则不倍本文。

> 故西文句法，少者二三字，多者数十百言。假令仿此为译，则恐必不可通，而删削取径，又恐意义有漏。此在译者将全文神理融会于心，则下笔抒词自善互备。至原文词理本深，难于共喻，则当前后引衬以显其意。凡此经营，皆以为达；为达即所以为信也。

> 《易》曰："修辞立诚。"子曰："辞达而已。"又曰："言之无文，行之不远"。三者乃文章正轨，亦即为译事楷模。故信、达而外，求其尔雅。

> 新理踵出，名目繁多，索之中文，渺不可得，即有牵合，终嫌参差。译者遇此，独有自具衡量，即义定名。……一名之立，旬月踟蹰，我罪我知，是存明哲。

由上可见，严复提出的"信、达、雅"三字也是"前后引衬，自善互备"。然而并不是所有人都全盘接受这一理念。随着翻译实践的深入和对翻译的思考，人们开始注意到这三字有相互矛盾的地方，而其中"雅"字引发的批评最多。有人指出：如果原文不"达"、不"雅"，而译文却既"达"又"雅"，这岂不过犹不及，仍然不"信"吗？另一方面，也有人尝试重新注解这三字的内涵：所谓忠实、通顺、美；达意、传神、文采；正确、通顺、易懂；求实为信，流畅为达，可读为雅，不一而足。尤其是对"雅"字，似乎人人能解，但解各不相同。近年来，由于西方"操纵论""目的论"在国内的传播，严氏理念的地位才从根本上受到撼动，然而，仍有不少人在经过一番比较之后不无感慨地说："还是'信、达、雅'好！"

严复的精神遗产还体现在他对待翻译的态度上。他做翻译的目的很明确，即传播西方先进思想,以实现其"教育救国"的理想。他译《天演论》是为了传播"物竞天择"的进化论原理,向国民敲响"国家危亡"的警钟。他翻译的每一本书都是事先经过严肃的挑选,为当时中国政治、经济所急需。他的译作常附有例言、案语或详尽的注释,他厘定专名尤为审慎:"一名之立,旬月踟蹰"这句名言将永远垂范后世译者。

第二节　傅雷:重神似不重形似

傅雷(1908—1966),我国著名文学翻译家。原名怒安(又作怒庵),上海南汇县(今浦东新区)人。19岁自费留学法国,在巴黎大学文科学习艺术理论,同时去卢浮美术史学院和梭邦艺术讲座听讲。留法期间,曾流连于卢浮艺术博物馆以及巴黎和日内瓦、布鲁塞尔、罗马等地众多博物馆、艺术馆,观摩和研究美术大师的不朽之作。1931年回国,抵沪之日,适逢"九一八"事变。回国后曾短暂从事过美术考古工作及在上海美专任职,因与流俗的氛围格格不入,无法与人共事,最终选择了闭门译述的事业,以稿费为经济来源。自20世纪30年代始,即致力于法国文学的翻译,毕生翻译作品30余部,约计500万言,代表译作有罗曼·罗兰长篇巨著《约翰·克利斯朵夫》,传记《贝多芬传》《托尔斯泰传》《米盖朗琪罗传》,巴尔扎克系列小说《高老头》《欧也妮·葛朗台》《贝姨》《邦斯舅舅》《夏倍上校》《搅水女人》《都尔的本堂神甫》《幻灭》,服尔德的《老实人》《天真汉》《查第格》,梅里美的《嘉尔曼》《高龙巴》,丹纳的《艺术哲学》,等等,奠定了他在当代中国翻译界法国文学,尤其是巴尔扎克作品权威翻译家的地位。此外,还写有《傅雷家书》《世界美术名作二十讲》《与傅聪谈音乐》等。

傅雷译作等身,译笔生花。遗憾的是他鲜谈翻译理论。用他自己的话说,是因为有顾虑:一方面怕犯了自高自大的嫌疑,另一方面怕引起争论,于事无补。更重要的是,他认为"翻译重在实践",自己一向"以眼高手低为苦"。因此,生前正式发表的译论只有两篇,一是《高老头》重译本序(1951年9月),一是应《文艺报》(1957年第10期)之约的《翻译经验点滴》。后来刊印的还有两封书信,一封是《致林以亮论翻译书》(1951年4月5日),另一封是《致罗新璋论文学翻译书》(1963年1月6日)。然而,这仅有的4篇文字,或音调铿锵,或语重心长,充满真知灼见。此摘录片段如下:

以效果而论,翻译应当像临画一样,所求的不在形似而在神似。以实际工作而论，翻译比临画更难。临画与原画，素材相同（颜色、画布，或纸或绢），法则相同（色彩学、解剖学、透视学）。译本与原作，文字既不侔，规则又大异。各种文字各有特色，各有无可模仿的优点，各有无法补救的缺陷，同时又各有不能侵犯的戒律。像英法、英德那样接近的语言，尚且有许多难以互译的地方；中西文字的扞格远过于此，要求传神达意，铢两悉称，自非死抓字典，按照原文句法拼凑堆砌所能济事。（《高老头》重译本序）

愚对译事看法实甚简单：重神似不重形似；译文必须为纯粹之中文，无生硬拗口之病，又须能朗朗上口，求音节和谐；至节奏与 tempo，当然以原作为依归。尊札所称"傅译"，似可成为一宗一派，愧不敢当。以行文流畅，用字丰富，色彩变化而论，自问与预定目标相距尚远。（《致罗新璋论文学翻译书》）

鄙人对自己译文从未满意，苦闷之处亦复与先生同感。传神云云，谈何容易！年岁经验愈增，对原作体会愈深，而传神愈感不足。领悟为一事，用中文表达为又一事。况东方人与西方人之思想方式有基本分歧，我人重综合，重归纳，重暗示，重含蓄；西方人则重分析，细微曲折，挖掘唯恐不尽，描写唯恐不周；此两种 mentalité，殊难彼此融洽交流。（《致罗新璋论文学翻译书》）

两国文字词类的不同，句法构造的不同，文法与习惯的不同，修辞格律的不同，俗语的不同，即反映民族思想方式的不同，感觉深浅的不同，观点角度的不同，风格传统信仰的不同，社会背景的不同，表现方法的不同，以甲国文字传达乙国文字所包含的那些特点，必须像伯乐相马，要"得其精而忘其粗，在其内而忘其外"。（《高老头》重译本序）

我有个缺点：把什么事看得千难万难，保守思想很重，不必说出版社指定的书，我不敢担承，便是自己喜爱的作品也要踌躇再三。……我这样的踌躇当然有思想根源。第一，由于我热爱文艺，视文艺工作为崇高神圣的事业，不但把损害艺术品看作像歪曲真理一样严重，并且介绍一件艺术品不能还它一件艺术品，就觉得不能容忍。（《翻译经验点滴》）

任何作品，不精读四五遍决不动笔，是为译事基本法门。第一要求将原作（连同思想、感情、气氛、情调等等）化为我有，方能谈到迻译。……总之译事虽近舌人，要以艺术修养为根本：无敏感之心灵，无热烈之同情，无适当之鉴赏能力，无相当之社会经验，无充分之常识（即所谓杂学），势难彻底理解原作，即或理解，亦未必能深切领悟。（《致罗新璋论文学翻译书》）

  选择原作好比交朋友：有的人始终与我格格不入，那就不必勉强；有的人与我一见如故，甚至相见恨晚。但即使对一见如故的朋友，也非一朝一夕所能真切了解。想译一部喜欢的作品要读到四遍五遍，才能把情节、故事记得烂熟，分析彻底，人物历历如在目前，隐藏在字里行间的微言大义也能慢慢咂摸出来。但做了这些工夫是不是翻译的条件就具备了呢？不。因为翻译作品不仅仅在于了解与体会，还需要进一步把我所了解的、体会的，又忠实又动人地表达出来。（《翻译经验点滴》）

  因此，我深深地感到：（一）从文学的类别来说，译书要认清自己的所短所长，不善于说理的人不必勉强译理论书，不会作诗的人千万不要译诗，弄得不仅诗意全无，连散文都不像，用哈哈镜介绍作品，无异自甘作文艺的罪人。（二）从文学的派别来说，我们得弄清楚自己最适宜于哪一派：浪漫派还是古典派？写实派还是现代派？每一派中又是哪几个作家？同一作家又是哪几部作品？我们的界限与适应力（幅度）只能在实践中见分晓。勉强不来的，即使试译了几万字，也得"报废"，毫不可惜；能适应的还须格外加工。（《翻译经验点滴》）

  文学的对象既然以人为主，人生经验不丰富，就不能充分体会一部作品的妙处，而人情世故是没有具体知识可学的。所以我们除了专业修养、广泛涉猎以外，还得训练我们观察、感受、想象的能力；平时要深入生活，了解人，关心人，关心一切，才能亦步亦趋地跟在伟大的作家后面，把他的心曲诉说给读者听。因为文学家是解剖社会的医生，挖掘灵魂的探险家，悲天悯人的宗教家，热心如沸的革命家；所以要做他的代言人，也得像宗教家一般的虔诚，像科学家一般的精密，像革命志士一般的刻苦顽强。（《翻译经验点滴》）

  读完以上论述，我们可以窥见一位译界先贤的伟岸形象。实际上，传神、神韵、神似说原是我国古典文论的寻常话题，将其引入翻译加以讨论的也并不始自傅雷。但开篇标举"重神似不重形似"并以大量优秀译作实践自己翻译理念的,只有傅雷,因此,他的理念为更多的人所熟知。"神似"说是傅雷对严复以来我国50年的翻译经验的总结,对初涉翻译的人有很大的指导意义。值得特别指出的是,《傅雷家书》凝聚了傅雷对人生、对艺术的深刻见解,可作为青年学生和翻译学徒不可多得的修养读物。

我们今天所要传承的,不仅是傅雷的翻译思想,更有他作为知识分子的人格风范。傅雷是一个完美主义者,他秉性孤傲倔强,几乎不近人情,但他的赤子之心,又使人芥蒂全释,肃然起敬。傅雷一身傲骨,是一个宁可站着死、不愿跪着生的人。抗日战争期间,他东不至黄浦江,北不至白渡桥,为的是避免向日本宪兵行礼。1958年反右运动开始即受到批判,有位好心的领导暗示他把检查的调子定得高一点以便过关,但傅雷坚持:"没有廉价的检讨,人格比任何东西都可贵!"结果被错划为右派。从此他更是深居简出,专心译事。但直到1962年,人民文学出版社的约稿没有出版一本,原因是傅雷不同意另用笔名,以至于靠"预支稿费"维系生活。1966年"文化大革命"伊始,傅雷夫妇再次遭受厄运,因不堪凌辱,于批斗折磨之后,9月3日凌晨夫妇俩共赴危难,双双自尽。傅雷享年58岁,成为中国翻译史上悲壮的一页!

第三节 许渊冲:美化之艺术,创优似竞赛

许渊冲(1921—),江西南昌人。先后毕业于西南联大、巴黎大学。退休前为北京大学教授。许渊冲是我国杰出的文学翻译家和翻译理论家,尤其是在古典诗词的翻译和理论建构方面成绩卓著。中文代表作有《翻译的艺术》《文学与翻译》《追忆逝水年华》等;英文著作有《中诗英韵探胜》(*On Chinese Verse in English Rhyme*)("北大名家名著文丛")和 *Vanished Springs*(分别在北京和纽约出版);汉译英作品有 *Songs of the Immortals*(《不朽之歌》,英国 Penguin Books)、《诗经》《论语》《楚辞》《西厢记》《老子道德经》《唐诗三百首》《宋词三百首》《元曲三百首》《毛泽东诗词选》等;汉译法作品有《毛泽东诗词四十二首》《中国古诗词三百首》等;外译汉有德莱顿的《一切为了爱情》、罗曼·罗兰的《约翰·克里斯托夫》等英、法文豪的名著10种。各种版本的著译共计100多本(种)。为表彰其杰出贡献,2010年12月2日,中国翻译工作者协会授予许渊冲"翻译文化终身成就奖",2014年8月2日,在柏林举行的第20届世界翻译大会上,国际翻译家联盟授予许渊冲"北极光"杰出文学翻译奖。该奖项是国际翻译界文学翻译最高奖项之一,许渊冲是该奖项自1999年设立以来首位获奖的亚

洲翻译家,也是中国迄今为止获得国际翻译界最高奖项的第一人。

许渊冲的翻译理论独树一帜,自成体系。他将他的理论概括为"美化之艺术,创优似竞赛"10个字,代表文学翻译的八论,下面分别介绍。

一论"美":即"三美论",包括"意美、音美、形美",是根据鲁迅在《汉文学史纲要》第一篇中提出的文章"三美"("意美以感心,一也;音美以感耳,二也;形美以感目,三也")。意美是第一位的,音美第二,形美第三,应努力做到"三美"齐备。例如毛泽东《冬云》里的两行诗:

高天滚滚寒流急,
大地微微暖气吹。
In the steep sky cold waves are swiftly sweeping by;
On the vast earth warm winds gradually growing high.

原诗对仗工整,译诗也毫厘不差:主语对主语,谓语对谓语,状语对状语;原诗重复了"滚滚"和"微微",译文用重复头韵 sw 和 gr 的方法来传达。"滚滚"和"微微"是叠词,译文用了双声来译,可以说基本上传达了原诗的"三美"。

二论"化":即"三化论",包括"等化、浅化、深化",是根据钱钟书的"化境说"。"三化"指的是翻译的方法,运用之妙,可出神入化。"等化"包括静态和动态的对等,把"无风不起浪"译成"there is no smoke without fire"可算是"等化"的译法,"等化"还包括词性转换、同词异译、异词同译、正反反正、错位补偿等翻译技巧。"浅化"就是化繁为简,以浅显的译文形式表达深奥的原文内容,如把"黄粱美梦"只译成"a golden dream"。而"深化"与"浅化"正好相反,就是透过原文的表层形式,进入原文的深层内容,使译文比原文变得更深刻。比较杜甫"文章千古事,得失寸心知"诗句中"得失"的三种译法:

A poem may long, long remain,
Who knows the poet's loss and gain (joy and pain)?

A work may last a thousand years,
Who knows the author's smiles and tears?

三论"之":即"三之论",包括"知之、好之、乐之",是根据孔子在《论语》中提出的"知之者不如好之者,好之者不如乐之者"和王国维在《人间词话》中提出的"境界说"。所谓"知之",就是知道原文说了什么;所谓"好

之",就是喜欢译文;所谓"乐之",就是读了译文产生共鸣,甚至拍案叫绝。例如《诗经·采薇》中的千古丽句和英译:

昔我往矣,	When I left here,
杨柳依依。	Willows shed tear.
今我来思,	I come back now,
雨雪霏霏。	Snow bends the bough.
行道迟迟,	Long, long the way,
载饥载渴。	Hard, hard the day,
我心伤悲,	My grief o'erflows.
莫知我哀!	Who knows? Who knows?

这一段描写的是战后士兵回家途中的痛苦,情景交融,天人合一。译者把"杨柳依依"译成"依依不舍,甚至流下了眼泪"(英文的"垂柳"正巧就是 weeping willow, 即垂泪的杨柳),把"雨雪霏霏"译成"大雪压弯了柳枝",象征压弯了士兵的腰肢,一二行与三四行形成强烈对照,巧妙传神。译者将"载饥载渴"浅化为"日子难熬",是为了形似而多少牺牲了意美,如果不愿牺牲意美,也可以增加两行"Hunger and thirst, Press me the worst",那就是为了意美而损害了形美。原诗每行4字,英译每行4个音节;原诗有韵,英译两行一韵。整首译诗虽然没有完全与原诗音似、意似和形似,但整体的意美有增无减。译诗形象逼真,咏之音调哀婉,韵味不尽。

四论"艺术":即"翻译是艺术,不是科学",来源于朱光潜在《诗论》中说的"'从心所欲,不逾矩'是一切艺术的成熟境界"。"不逾矩"是低标准,是必然王国的问题;"从心所欲"是高标准,是自由王国的问题。科学和艺术的矛盾,表现在文学翻译上,就是真(似)与美的矛盾。科学研究的是"真",艺术研究的是"美"。科学研究的是"有之必然,无之必不然"之理;艺术研究的是"有之不必然,无之不必不然"之艺。如以译诗而论,求真是低标准,求美是高标准;译诗不能不似,但似而不美也不行。如果真与美能统一,自然是再好没有;如果真与美有矛盾,那不是为了真而牺牲美,就是为了美而失真。如译得似的诗远不如原诗美,那牺牲美就是得不偿失;如果译得"失真"却可以与原诗比美,那倒可以说是以得补失;如果所得大于所失,那就是译诗胜过了原诗。为了求美,甚至不妨失真。如果原文有不同的解释,很难说哪种解释更"意似",就不必拘泥正误问题,不妨看看哪种译文更美。例如,李白《送友人》中的第一、二句"青山横北郭,白水绕东城"的英语译文:

Green mountains bar the northern sky;
White water girds the eastern town.

有人提出疑问，南阳东边离城三里有清水环流，为一城之胜，俗称白水，今名白河，所以"绕东城"是绕于城之东，并非如许译的"东城"。但许渊冲说，根据艺术的原则，就不必拘泥于"绕东城"是不是"绕于城之东"，而更应表达出"青山"对"白水"，"北郭"对"东城"的对仗美（1996：161）。又如贺知章的《回乡偶书》：

少小离家老大回，
乡音无改鬓毛衰。
儿童相见不相识，
笑问客从何处来？
Old, I come back to my homeland I left while young;
Thinner has grown my hair though I speak the same tongue.
My children whom I meet do not know who am I.
"Where are you from, dear sir?" they ask with beaming eye.

许渊冲说，这首诗是贺知章离家50多年之后，86岁回乡时写的。本来只是一己小我的感伤，但到了1200多年后的今天，台湾同胞回祖国大陆探亲，还能引起心灵的共鸣，这就是"个相"转为"共相"（叶嘉莹语），浅显的内容也深化了。第三句的"儿童"，究竟是指自家的儿女，还是指村中的儿童？一般说来，诗人已经80多岁，儿女已不会再是儿童。这样就事论事的解释，只能说是"个相"的。但如解释为自己家的儿童都"相见不相识"，那就更富戏剧性（也就是更美，编者注），引起的共鸣更广，即"个相"深化为"共相"了。

五论"创"：即"文学翻译等于创作"，来源于郭沫若的"创作论"。再创的译法就是原作者用译语的创作，或者说译者设身处地，假如自己是原作者会怎么用译语来写，自己就怎么译。例如李延年的《北方有佳人》：

北方有佳人，	There is a beauty in the northern lands;
绝世而独立。	Unequaled, high above the world she stands.
一顾倾人城，	At her first glance, soldiers would lose their town;
再顾倾人国。	At her second, a monarch would his crown.
宁不知倾城与倾国？	How could the soldiers and monarch neglect their duty?

| 佳人难再得! | For town and crown are overshadowed by her beauty. |

"倾城倾国"并不是倾覆国家和城池的意思,短诗内容和形式有矛盾,所以译者用再创作的"失城、失国、失职、失色"来翻译。

六论"优":即"翻译要发挥译文语言优势"。许渊冲指出:"忠实于原文内容,通顺的译文形式,发挥译文的优势,可以当作文学翻译的标准。……翻译可以不发扬译文语言的优势,但发扬了译文语言优势的却是更好的翻译。是否符合**必要条件**是个对错问题,是否符合**充分条件**却是个好坏问题。"(粗体为编者所加)例如:

1. —"How much did you suffer?"
   —"Plenty," the old man said. (*The Old Man and the Sea*)
   —"你吃了多少苦呵?"
   —"一言难尽,"老头说。

2. —"Hyde Park you said, didn't you? I'll be there to cheer you."
   —"It's a promise," he said. (*Betrayed Spring*)
   —"你说海德公园,是不是?我准来给你打气。"
   —"那就一言为定啦。"他说。

两例中,原文的"Plenty"和"It's a promise"平淡无奇,但在译者的笔下,译文却情景交融。"发挥译文语言优势"是改变定向思维、突破表层结构的一种立竿见影的方法。例如:

1. as rich as a king
2. commit the same error
3. fellow sufferers
4. make a superficial change
5. miss a good chance
6. underestimate one's own capabilities

以上6个短语,如果只求正确,可分别译成:

1. 像国王那样富有
2. 犯同样的错误
3. 一道受苦的人

4. 只作表面的改变
5. 失去一个好机会
6. 低估自己的能力

但是，如果发挥译文语言的优势，它们则可分别改译如下：

1. 富可敌国
2. 重蹈覆辙
3. 难兄难弟
4. 换汤不换药
5. 失之交臂
6. 妄自菲薄

如果能在段落、篇章的层面发挥译文的语言优势，就能大大提高译文的质量。例如：

The jousts and tournaments, the entertainments and revels, which each petty court displayed, invited to France every wandering adventurer; and it was seldom that, when arrived there, he failed to employ his rash courage, and headlong spirit of enterprise, in actions for which his happier native country afforded no free stage. (Scott: *Quentin Durward*)

初稿：各个小朝廷都夸耀的比枪演武、饮酒作乐，把每个胆大妄为的流浪汉都吸引到法兰西来了；很少有个流浪汉来后不能显示他鲁莽的勇气和轻率的冒险精神的，而他更幸运的故乡，却没有为这些活动提供自由的舞台。

定稿：各个小朝廷都引以为荣的比枪演武、饮酒作乐，使四海为家的玩命英雄闻风而来；难得有个好汉到了法兰西不能一显身手，表现他的匹夫之勇和冒险精神的，而他幸运的故国却没有提供这些英雄的用武之地。（司各特：《昆廷·杜沃德》，许渊冲 译）

定稿中的"引以为荣""四海为家""玩命英雄""闻风而来""好汉""一显身手""匹夫之勇""英雄用武之地"，都是比初稿中相应的措辞更好的表达方式，可以说是发挥了译文语言的优势。

七论"似":即"三似论",包括"形似、意似、神似",是根据傅雷的"神似说"。"形似"是"三似"的最低层次,如果内容和形式一致,那"形似"就等于"意似";如果内容和形式有矛盾,那"形似"就成了"貌合神离";"意似"是"三似"的中间层次,要在原文与译文内容和形式上都一致的条件下才能做到。如果内容和形式有矛盾,那就要得"意"忘"形",得其精而忘其粗,那就成了"神似",也就是"三似"中的最高层次。如杜甫《登高》中的名句:

无边落木萧萧下,
不尽长江滚滚来。
The boundless forest sheds its leaves shower by shower,
The endless river rolls its waves hour after hour.

原诗"落木萧萧"3个草字头,译诗也有3个词是"sh"的头韵;原诗"长江滚滚"3个三点水,译诗也有两个词是"r"的头韵;原诗"萧萧"和"滚滚"是叠字,译诗也有两个叠词 shower by shower 和 hour after hour,且 shower 与"萧萧"还音似;原诗"无边"和"不尽"对仗工整,译诗 boundless 和 endless 也遥相呼应。原诗字形和视觉上的冲击几乎都移注到了译诗里。这两句英文诗如要还原,大约就是:无边无际的树林一阵一阵地洒下了树叶,无穷无尽的长江时时刻刻波涛滚滚而来。这个英译基本上可以说是包含了形似、意似和音似的神似。

八论"竞赛":即"翻译是两种语言的竞赛,文学翻译更是两种文化的竞赛"。例如毛泽东《为女民兵题照》中的两句:

中华儿女多奇志,
不爱红装爱武装。
Most Chinese daughters have desire so strong,
To be battle-dressed and not rosy-gowned. (tr. Xu, 1981)
To face the powder and not to powder the face. (tr. Xu, 1992)

两次翻译,译者一方面是在与自己竞赛,另一方面又在与表达同一内容的原语及原语文化竞赛。从形式上讲,原诗重复了"爱"和"装"字,从内涵上讲,"红装"与"武装"同列并不指代服饰本身。因此,初译无论在形式上还是在文化内涵上都处于竞赛的劣势。而后译重复了"face"和"powder"两个词,首先在形式上取得均势。第二次世界大战时报纸上常说"to face the powder",意指"面对战场的硝烟",说明在内涵上也旗鼓相当。原诗两个"爱"字都是动词,两个"装"字都是名词;译文"face"一个是动词,当"面对"讲,一个是名词,当"脸"讲;"powder"同样一个是名词,当"硝烟"讲,一个是动词,当"抹粉"讲,这就发挥了英语动名互类的优势,取得了竞赛的胜利。

总括起来,"三美"是许渊冲翻译哲学的本体论;"三化"是方法论;"三之""神似"是目的论;"艺术""创作"和"竞赛"是认识论;"发挥优势"既是认识论,又是方法论,统帅全局。许渊冲还模仿老子《道德经》第一章,通俗地写了一篇《译经》:

译可译,非常译。	Translation is possible; it's not transliteration.
忘其形,得其意。	Forget the original form; get the original idea!
得意,理解之始;	Getting the idea, you understand the original;
忘形,表达之母。	Forgetting the form, you express the idea.
故应得意,以求其同;	Be true to the idea common to two languages;
故可忘形,以存其异。	Be free from the form peculiar to the original!
两者同出,异名同理。	Idea and form are two sides of one thing.
得意忘形,求同存异:	Get the common idea, forget the peculiar form:
翻译之道。	That's the way of literary translation.

许渊冲的翻译理论曾引起不小的争论,持怀疑或否定意见的人中也包括一些知名学者和翻译家,批评主要集中在三个方面:

一是以诗体译诗会不会"因声损义"?

二是怎能说"求真是低标准""为了求美,不妨失真"呢?

三是什么是发挥译文语言优势?各国语言和文化何来优劣,何来竞赛?会不会导致滥用四字成语,使一部外国文学作品成了中文陈词滥调的堆砌?

针对第一个问题,许渊冲是这样回答的:译诗要得其精而忘其粗。所谓"精"就是"意美""音美"和"形美"。唐诗的"音美"首先在押韵,如果丢掉了音韵,翻译出来的东西能够算是诗词吗?因此,用韵固然可能因声损义,不用韵则一定因声损义。

针对第二个问题,许渊冲指出:在译诗的问题上,诗是本体,是第一位的;译是方法,是第二位的。诗求美,译求真。如果把美的诗译得不美,那不可能算是存真;只有在不失真的条件下,尽可能传达原诗的美,才是译诗应该采用的原则。"求真"论者认为译文只要意似,越近似越好,音和形都是次要的,不能因声损义,更不能以形害义;"求美"论者认为译诗的结果应该是一首诗,如果原诗具有"三美"而译诗只是意似,那无论多么近似,也不能算是好的译文。

针对第三个问题,许渊冲认为,这里存在一个认识问题。创作和翻译都可以比作绘画,创作以现实为模特,所以翻译就不能只以原作为模特,而要以原作所写的现实为模特。两种不同的文字要表达同一内容,总有一种文字表达得好一点、一种差一点,或者两种文字不相上下的三种可能。无论哪种可能,在他看来都是竞赛。表达得好一点的叫"优势",差一点的叫"劣势",不相上下的叫"均势"。西方文字之间差距较小,做到均势比较容易,中西文字之间差距较大,要做到均势就不容易,有时甚至是不可能。因此,将一种语言翻译成另一种语言,就应该扭转劣势,争取均势,最好能发挥优势。发挥译文语言优势,就是要用目的语最好的表达方式。中西语言各有优势,四字成语是汉语的优势之一,就像关系从句是英语的优势之一。但发挥汉语优势并不限于用四字成语,也不等于用四字成语。一个词是不是陈词滥调,要看它用在什么场合。至于为什么翻译还是两种文化的竞赛呢?那是因为语言文字往往还包含文化信息。

许渊冲指出:"如果地图不符合实际的地形,那么,应该修改的不是地形,而是地图。"

许渊冲不仅译著等身,更难能可贵的是,他积 60 多年的译事经验,构建了一整套简洁、易用的翻译理论。许渊冲的翻译理论充溢着东方的智慧,具有超前意识,虽然质疑之声曾此起彼伏,但现在越来越多的人感觉到许渊冲翻译理论的魅力,并开始认同其价值。我们认为,严复以来,如果说傅雷的"重神似不重形似"是我国传统翻译理论研究的第一次飞跃的话,许渊冲以"发挥译文语言优势"为核心的理论便是第二次飞跃。

第四节 亚历山大·弗雷泽·泰特勒:翻译三原则

泰特勒(Alexander Fraser Tytler,1747—1814):在西方,最早且影响最广而深远的翻译理念可以说是近代英国的亚历山大·弗雷泽·泰特勒提出的翻译三原则。

泰特勒于 1790 年出版了他里程碑式的著作《论翻译的原理》(*Essay on the Principles of Translation*)。在这本书里,他指出:"好的译文是将原作的长处完完全全地移注到另一种语言里,使得译文语言所属国的人能明白地领悟,强烈地感受,正像原作语言所属国的人所领悟、所感受的一样。"由此,他推演出翻译的三条原则:

(1)译文应完整再现出原作的思想。(The translation should give a complete transcript of the ideas of the original work.)

（2）译文的风格和笔调应与原作的性质相同。（The style and manner of writing should be of the same character with that of the original.）

（3）译文应与原创作品那样行文自然。（The translation should have all the ease of original composition.）

以上三条原则的前后顺序，根据泰特勒的说明，是依其重要性的大小排列的。如果不能同时兼顾这三条原则，为了保证满足第一条原则，可以牺牲第三条原则，必要的话，再牺牲第二条原则。对翻译的其他相关问题，泰特勒还有精辟的论述：

> 如果译者应该完整再现原作的思想，那么就产生一个问题：是否在任何情况下，比如原作缺乏力度，或语焉不详，或行文拖沓，译者都无权增减原作的思想呢？若要给这个问题一个总的回答，我会说，译者不是不可以有这个自由，但必须十二分地小心。必须进一步注意的是，那个外加的思想要与原作的思想血肉相连，并确实增强了原作思想的力量。另一方面，译者每次删减某个思想，这个被删除的思想在该从句或主句中只能是个附属品，而决不是中心内容。同理，它还必须确定无疑是个冗余信息。这样，删减的结果就不至于损害或削弱原作总的思想。（编者译，原书第22页）

> 如果所有的语言其特征和性质是一样的话，把一种语言译成另一种语言就不会是件艰巨的任务了……但是，众所周知，各种语言的特征和差异甚大，因此，人们普遍认为，译者的职责只在于顾全原作的思想和精神（sense and spirit），使自己对作者的思想了然于胸，然后用他认为最合适的言语把这些思想准确无误地传达出来。另一方面，为了使译文尽善尽美，译文不仅要传达原文作者的思想和情感，还要同样传达原文作者的风格和行文方式（his style and manner of writing）。（编者译，原书第8页）

> 即使是一流的画家，要在一幅临摹的画里完全保存原作风格的挥洒自如和意境的逼真传神，也是不容易的；然而，画家所使用的毕竟是完全相同的原料，他唯一的任务，只不过是把摆在他面前的那幅画的笔调和神态临摹下来。如果原作是挥洒自如、优雅脱俗，那么所临摹的画，也具有同样的特征，因为其比例与原作丝毫不差。然而，译者的任务却很不一样，他使用与原作不同的颜料，但却要求给他的画创造出同样的力量和效果。

他不许模仿原作的手法,可是必须用他自己的手法画出完全相同的作品。他愈加注意仔细地临摹,他的作品就愈不能表现出原作的挥洒自如了。那么,译者如何才能克服困难,做到既挥洒自如,又忠实于原作呢?用个大胆的比喻:他必须借用原作者本人的灵魂,而使用他自己的发音器官来说话。(编者译,原书第114页)

泰特勒的翻译理论在西方产生过重大影响,至今还在广为引用。我国早在20世纪20年代初就有介绍。泰特勒提出的三条原则,与严复的"信、达、雅"相比,长则虽长,但不可否认,泰特勒行文严谨,措辞精确,叙述科学,三原则相辅相成,自成体系。

第五节 尤金·奈达:动态对等

尤金·奈达(Eugene A. Nida,1914 — 2011),美国著名语言学家、翻译理论家。1968年当选过一届美国语言学会(The Linguistic Society of America)会长,是联合圣经学会(The United Bible Societies)1949年创刊的《圣经翻译家》(*The Bible Translator*)的主要编辑和撰稿人之一。

奈达自幼笃信基督,立志做一名传教士。求学期间,对语言科目表现出特别的兴趣,中学开始学习拉丁语,大学专修外语,主攻希腊语,兼修拉丁语、德语和法语。1939年在南加州大学获希腊语《圣经·新约》研究的硕士学位。1941年入密执安大学,主修描写语言学和文化人类学,在弗赖斯(Charles C. Fries)等知名教授的指导下,于1943年以学位论文《英语句法要略》(*A Synopsis of English Syntax*)获语言学博士学位。同年加入美国圣经学会(The American Bible Society)。因其在语言学方面的背景和造诣,不久就被推荐为该组织及联合圣经学会的语言顾问(1943 —1981),负责调研和改善世界各地《圣经》译本的语言问题和接受情况。1937 — 1952年间在美国圣经学会的姊妹机构暑期语言学院长期任教。奈达本人并未翻译过《圣经》,但自1946年担任圣经翻译部的执行秘书起,承担过大量《圣经》翻译的组织工作,包括制订工作计划、培训译员、审校译稿、编写翻译指导书、与世界各地《圣经》译者探讨和解决实际问题。由于工作关系,在长达60年的时间里,奈达有机会游历了90多个国家和地区,实地考察过200多种语言,尤其是非洲、拉丁美洲、太平洋岛屿上的一些小语种。这些经历成为他学术生涯的坚实基础,也给他的著述打上了宗教的烙印。

奈达的学术成就斐然,单独或合作出版了40多部书,发表论文250余篇。

早期代表作有《形态学》(Morphology, 1946)、《圣经翻译》(Bible Translating, 1946)、《信息与传教》(Message and Mission, 1960)。中期，在西方翻译界，而不仅仅是圣经翻译界，奠定其泰斗地位的著作有《翻译科学探索》(Toward a Science of Translating, 1964) 和与查理·泰伯 (Charles R. Taber) 合写的《翻译的理论与实践》(The Theory and Practice of Translation, 1969)。晚期，影响较大的著作有《从一种语言到另一种语言》(From One Language to Another) (与Jan de. Waard 合写，1986)、《跨文化交际社会语言学》(The Sociolinguistics of Intercultural Communication, 1996)。最近的著作有《翻译与语境》(Translation in Context, 2002)、《语言的魅力》(Fascinated by Languages, 2003)。奈达被誉为世界译坛的一位长青学者。

奈达在翻译理论方面最重要的贡献就是提出了"动态对等" (dynamic equivalence) 的原则，运用交际理论和信息论的原理，将焦点从传统的译文与原文两个文本的比较转移到两个过程的比较，使人们注意到影响信息接收的各种语言和文化因素。"动态对等"具体是怎样一个原则呢？下面摘译的部分论述可以反映其概貌：

> 过去，人们往往主张以教育的手段来提高读者的阅读能力，然而现在，在翻译所有大众文学的时候，常规的做法是，把同一原文译成不同层次的译文，这样，不同阅历水平的人就可以根据自身的条件，选择相应译本。比如，美国圣经学会正在着手以三种译文形式把《圣经》译成西班牙语：一种是传统型的，对象是目前新教教徒；另一种在性质上更为现代化，难度也更大，对象是受过良好教育的非教会成员；第三种，使用非常简朴的西班牙语，对象尤其是那些初识文化、平时又和新教教会少有接触的人。(《翻译科学探索》，编者译，原书第144页)

> 翻译求动态对等，而不求形式对等，是建立在"等效原则"的基础之上。这样的翻译，与其说关心的是接受语与原语两种语言间信息的匹配，不如说更关心它们间的动态关系，即译文接受者和译文信息之间的关系，应该与原文接受者和原文信息之间的关系大致相同。(《翻译科学探索》，编者译，原书第159页)

> 动态对等翻译的目标在于表达自然，丝毫不留痕迹，力求把原语文化背景下的行为模式转换成译入语文化背景下相关的行为模式，……在用现代英语翻译的作品中，也许比任何其他作品都更能体现追求等效

的,算是 J. B. 菲力普所译的《新约全书》了,在其《罗马书》第16章第16节中,他理直气壮地把"Greet one another with a holy kiss"(请你们以圣吻互相致意)译成"give one another a hearty handshake all around"(请你们一一诚挚地握手)。(《翻译科学探索》,编者译,原书第159-160页)

过去,翻译的焦点是如何保存信息的形式,译者往往以能够复制原文特有风格(如节奏、韵律、双关、交错配列、平行结构、怪异语法)而自鸣得意。然而,如今的焦点已经从信息的形式转移到信息接收者的反应。因此,译者必须抉择的,是接收者对翻译信息的反应。这个反应又必须与推想的原文接收者在原语背景下的反应加以比较。甚至那个古老的问题:"这个翻译正确吗?"也必须换另一个问题来回答:对谁而言呢?(《翻译的理论与实践》,编者译,原书第1页)

谈到翻译,对于普通人来说,是否能用一种语言里潜在的等值物来代替另一种语言里实际的等值物,这也许是争论最激烈的一点了。他难以想象,那些从未见过"雪"的人能读懂《圣经》里关于雪的描写。如果那个民族不知"雪"为何物,他们怎能会有一个词来指代"雪"呢?并且,如果他们没有一个词来指代"雪",那么,《圣经》又怎能翻译呢?……许多语言里都有等值的成语,比如"白如鹭羽"或"白如蘑菇";或者它们还可以用非比喻的短语,诸如"非常非常白"来表达"白如雪"这个概念。其要点是,是否用"雪"这东西来表达,并不影响该句话的意思。(《翻译的理论与实践》,编者译,原书第4页)

要保持信息的内容,语言的形式就必须改变:如果所有的语言在形式上都是不同的(不然它们怎能叫作不同的语言呢!),那么,为了保持信息的内容,改变语言的形式就再自然不过的了。(《翻译的理论与实践》,编者译,原书第5页)

翻译的实质,就是用最贴近自然的译文语言再现原文信息,首先在意义方面,其次在风格方面。(《翻译的理论与实践》,编者译,原书第12页)

显然,奈达是主张意译的。他的极端的归化的做法曾引起不少批评。在后来的《从一种语言到另一种语言》里,奈达对他的翻译思想做了一定的修正。比如，将"动态对等"的提法改成"功能对等"（functional equivalence），并特别提出了改变语言形式的五个条件（原书第 38—39 页）：

(1) 直译会传递完全错误的意义时；
(2) 引入外来语会形成语义"空缺"，因此人们有可能填入错误的意义时；
(3) 形式对应会引起严重的意义晦涩时；
(4) 形式对应会导致明显的非原文作者之意图的歧义时；
(5) 形式对应会导致不合译文语言语法或文体规范时。

奈达的翻译理论在 20 世纪 80 年代初被介绍进入我国，也是我国实行改革开放政策后最早引进的当代西方翻译理论。他的理论像一股春风席卷了中国整个翻译界，引发了广大翻译工作者对西方翻译理论的浓厚兴趣与密切关注，从此打破了"信、达、雅"的一统天下。奈达本人也曾十多次来到中国，在广州、北京、南京、上海、重庆、西安等地的高校讲学。奈达是一个学术视野宽广、不囿成见、谦虚谨慎的学者，与中国翻译界有广泛的交往和良好的人缘。

第六节　操　纵　学　派

操纵学派（Manipulation School）这个近乎半玩笑式的学名，指的是一个在研究方法方面具有广泛共识的学术群体。该学术群体内部则更喜欢自称为"翻译研究学派"（Translation Studies），或"低地国家学派"（Low Countries Group）（"低地国家"指西欧的比利时、卢森堡和荷兰），尽管后者可能引起误会，因为该群体的学者实际上并不局限于该地区。该群体也以"描写学派"和"系统学派"而著称。该学派的代表人物有荷兰的詹姆斯·霍尔姆斯（James S. Holmes）、雷蒙·梵·登·勃鲁克（Raymond van den Broeck），以色列的伊特玛尔·埃文·佐哈尔（Itamar Even-Zohar）、吉迪恩·图里（Gideon Toury），比利时的若泽·朗贝尔（José Lambert），英国的苏珊·巴斯奈特（Susan Bassnett-McGuire）、西奥·赫尔曼斯（Theo Hermans），美国的安德烈·勒菲弗尔（André Lefevere）等。

大致从 20 世纪 70 年代中期开始，这批学者曾多次在一起召开研讨会，其成果结集出版或散见于各类期刊和非正式出版物（如博士论文），多数论文是在比利时、荷兰和以色列出版，且用荷兰语、法语或希伯来语写成。1985 年，西奥·赫尔曼斯以约稿和收集旧作的方式，以英语为写作语言（或翻译成英语），将论文结集成册，取名《对文学的操纵——文学翻译研究》（*The Manipulation of Literature: Studies in Literary Translation*），试图反映该学派的整体面貌，并使英语世界的广大读者得以了解他们的观点。赫尔曼斯为该论文集撰写了一篇影响深远的纲领性序言:"翻译研究:一个全新的范式"(*Translation Studies and a New Paradigm*)。他认为,翻译研究学者最大的敌人往往就是他们自己:他们天真地认为文学家是具有艺术禀赋的创造天才,理所当然地承认原著至高无上的地位。因此,翻译研究的目的无非是通过凸显各种译本的错误和缺陷来说明原著的优越。现在这个新的学术群体正致力于打破传统文学翻译研究的瓶颈,目标就是要在一个普遍理论和个案研究的基础上建立一个新的范式。下面两段话能基本反映该学派的观点:

> 他们所认同的,简单地说,就是把文学看成是个复杂的动态系统;他们相信理论模型与实际个案研究为互动的关系;他们遵循的是描写的、以目的语为取向的、功能主义的和系统的文学翻译方法;他们感兴趣的是,是什么制约着译本的产生与接受,翻译过程与其他类型的文本处理有何联系,翻译在某一特定文学中以及翻译在文学系统间相互作用的过程中处于怎样的地位和扮演怎样的角色。(Hermans,1985,编者译,原书第10-11页)

> 多元系统理论认为,系统内的各层级和分支系统都在不断争夺主导地位,而文学翻译则是其中之一。在某个特定的文学里,文学翻译在某个特定的阶段,有可能构成一个具有自身特点和模式的、相对独立的分支系统。在目的语文学系统中,翻译可能成为主流文学的一部分,也可能成为一种处于边缘状态的文学现象。它们可能被用作向目的语文学的主导诗学发起挑战的有力武器,也可能被用来支持和加强目的语中的文学传统。从目的语文学的角度看,所有的翻译都是译者为某个特定的目的而对原语文本进行某种程度的操纵。(Hermans,1985,编者译,原书第11页)

操纵学派实际上不是通常意义上的一个学派,他们之间的"共识"也只是大家能够共同讨论问题的基础,而不是共奉一个教条。它汇聚了一批地域分布很广、各有专攻的学者,且学者之间的研究还在不断分化。该学派的代表作还有霍尔姆斯的《翻译研究的名与实》(*The Name and Nature of Translation Studies*,1972),埃文·佐哈尔的《多元系统研究》(*Polysystem Studies*,1990),图里的《翻译理论探索》(*In Search of a Theory of Translation*,1980),《描述翻译学及其他》(*Descriptive Translation Studies and Beyond*,1995),勒菲弗尔的《翻译、重写和对文学声名的操纵》(*Translation, Rewriting and the Manipulation of Literary*

Fame，1992）等。他们的成果很多，我们也许可以从他们研究的一些关键词中更能把握到该学派的走向，比如操纵（manipulation）、重写（rewriting）、描写研究（descriptive studies）、多元系统（polysystem）、赞助人（patronage）、诗学观念（poetics）、意识形态（ideology）。

操纵学派的理论无疑是划时代的，它的贡献在于：①以目的语为取向，突破了"对等"和"忠实"的概念，肯定了译者的主体意识，从而提高了译者和翻译文学的地位；②跳出了"文本结构"的框框，让人们认识到翻译的背后始终隐藏着种种制约关系，从而融通了翻译研究与文化研究（有人称之为"翻译研究的文化转向"，反过来，又有人称之为"文化研究的翻译转向"，因为操纵学派的学者中有不少人是从事文化研究的）、意识形态、政治学等社会科学，大大拓宽了翻译研究的领域，促进了跨学科研究的发展。

第七节 德国功能翻译学派

功能翻译的理念并不是在 20 世纪发明的，翻译史上早有文学和/或《圣经》的译者注意到不同的情景要求不同的处理（Nord，1997：4）。德国功能翻译学派（German School of Functionalist Approaches to Translation）则始于 20 世纪 70 年代。第一代代表人物有卡塔琳娜·莱丝（Katharina Reiss）、汉斯·J. 弗美尔（Hans J. Vermeer）和尤斯塔·霍尔茨－门泰里（Justa Holz－Mänttäri），第二代代表人物有玛格利特·阿曼（Margret Ammann）、汉斯·霍里希（Hans Hönig）、保罗·库斯茅尔（Paul Kussmaul）、西格里特·库普斯－罗瑟莱特（Sigrid Kupsch-Losereit）、克里斯蒂安·诺德（Christiane Nord）、海顿·维特（Heidrun Witte）等。后面还有许多倡导者，且也不局限于德国。其中弗美尔和诺德都是莱丝的学生，几代学人不断推动、丰富、完善了该派理论。

莱丝在她 1971 年出版的《翻译批评的可能与限制》（*Möglichkeiten und Grenzen derübersetzungskritik*）里，一方面仍坚持以原作为中心的等值理念，另一方面又建立了一个以原作和译作的功能对等为标准的翻译批评模式，因为她注意到，在实际翻译中，等值并不总是能够做到的，有时甚至还未必是所希望的。莱丝的理论存在明显的矛盾，但开启了德国翻译研究的新方向。

德国功能翻译学派的核心理论是"目的论"（Skopos theory，德语：Skopostheorie，Skopos 一词来源于希腊语，相当于"目的""目标"或"意图"），是弗美尔在 1978 年出版的《普遍翻译理论架构》（*Ein Rahmen für eine allgemeine Translationstheorie*）里第一次提出来的。"目的论"的理论基础是"行为理论"

(action theory)。行为理论认为,任何行为都有其目的,或更为精确地说,"目的"是人类行为的属性。因此,翻译作为一种行为,其方法和策略也取决于其目的。"目的论"还糅合了"交际理论"(theory of communication)、文化理论(theory of culture)等理论,认为任何行为都是在特定时间、特定地点和特定文化背景下发生的。也就是说,原文是作者在原语背景下(时间、地点、文化、情景)为某个特定目的和特定接收者制作的一个文本,译文则是译者在目的语背景下(时间、地点、文化、情景)为另一个特定目的和特定接收者制作的一个文本。在这个理论框架下,所谓翻译的"目的",自然是指译文的目的。

后来,在《翻译行为的目的性与委托性》(Vermeer, 1989, 转译自 Andrew Chesterman 的英语译文)一文中,弗美尔对"目的论"进行了更充分的阐释。他认为翻译除"目的性"之外,另一个重要特性就是"委托性",即一个人从事翻译,要么出于自己的意愿,要么出于别人的意愿,无论哪种情形,他的行为都是为了完成一项"委托"(如果是前者,就等于自己委托自己)。这样,翻译就牵涉到交际的各方:原文作者—原文—委托人(包括发起者/客户)—译者—译文—译文接收者,委托者对翻译的运作起重要作用,确定翻译的目的主要考虑的是翻译的接收者。为使翻译达到预期的功能,委托者须给译者提供"翻译指令"(translation brief),它包括:①目标,即对所委托任务目的的描述(如译文接收者,译文使用的时间、地点、场合,译文的传播方式,译文的功能,等等);②实现目标的条件(如交稿期限和费用等实际问题)。"翻译指令"应在委托人与译者之间协商决定。译者是翻译行为"最具权威"的专家,他有权决定怎样实现某项翻译。当委托人不了解,甚至误解目标文化时,译者就有责任给委托人提供专业意见。比如,说服委托人允许译者调整或修改原文,在个别情况下,还可建议委托人放弃某项翻译,因为提供翻译咨询也视为翻译行为。总而言之,翻译的最高原则就是"目的原则","只要达到目的,可以不择手段。"(the end justifies the means)(Reiss and Vermeer, 1984: 101, 转引自 Nord, 1997: 29)。

"目的论"还有三条次生原则,一条是"篇内连贯"(intra-textual coherence),或"连贯原则"(coherence rule),指的是译文与译文接收者之间的关系,即译文必须能够被目的语文化背景下的译文接收者所理解和接纳;另一条是"篇际连贯"(inter-textual coherence),或称"忠实原则"(fidelity rule),指的是译文与原文之间的关系,即翻译不是无本之木。这里的"忠实"近似我国的传统译论,所不同的是其在翻译中的地位。最后一条是"充分原则"(adequacy),指的是译文与"翻译指令"(translation brief)之间的关系,即如果译文的目的不同于原文的目的,译文必须满足"翻译指令"的要求。在这个系统中,"篇际连贯"从属于"篇内连贯","篇内连贯"从属于"充分原则",三者又从属于总的"目的原则"。

霍尔茨-门泰里则在行为理论的基础上比弗美尔更进了一步,提出了"翻译行为"(translational action, Holz-Mänttäri, 1984)的概念。她甚至回避使用"翻译"(translation)这个词,取而代之使用了"信息传递物"(translation transmitters)这样一个怪僻的术语(可指配有图片、声音和肢体动作的文字资料)。在她的理论里,"翻译行为"涵盖所有形式的跨文化转换形式,也包括不牵涉原语或目的语文本的转换。霍尔茨-门泰里特别重视翻译过程中各种角色的作用,尤其是译者的地位。她把译者推崇为"跨文化交际的专家"。

为防止极端功能主义倾向,诺德提出了她自己的"功能翻译理论"模式,即"功能+忠诚"(function plus loyalty)。不同于传统的"忠实原则"(译文与原文的关系),"忠诚原则"指的是翻译过程中的人际关系,即译者必须考虑三方的合法权益:发起人、译文接收者和原文作者。这样,"忠诚原则"一方面限制了某一原文之译文功能的随意扩张,另一方面又增加了译者与有关各方对翻译任务的必要协商。由此,她认为"功能"和"忠诚"是该理论的两大支柱。德国功能翻译学派的成果几乎都是用德语发表的,影响力受到极大的限制,诺德意识到写作语言的重要意义,直接用英语撰写了 *Translating as a Purposeful Activity*: *Functionalist Approaches Explained* 一书,使该理论在英语世界甚至世界范围内得以迅速推广。

德国功能翻译理论是翻译理论研究的又一次革命。第一,它扩大了翻译研究的外延,改写了"翻译"的定义。第二,它与长期主导的语言学等值理论分道扬镳。等值理论视原文为衡量译文的唯一标准,而功能理论则视原文为"参考的信息"(an offer of information),使原文在翻译过程中的地位大大降低,从而突出了译者的责任与主体意识,因此也提高了译文与译者的地位。第三,它视翻译为跨文化的人际互动行为(intercultural and interpersonal interaction),而不仅仅是文本处理和语码转换(text-processing and code-switching),更为真实地反映了翻译的复杂过程,拉近了翻译理论与实践的距离。第四,目的的多样性暗示了一个原文不可能只有一个"正确的"译文,从而为各种变译提供了理论依据,改变了翻译批评和译文评价的单一模式。

德国功能翻译理论的传播并不是一帆风顺的,也遭遇过各种批评和质疑,例如,有学者指出:

(1)并非所有行为都有目的;

(2)并非所有翻译都有目的,如文学,真正的文学是艺术,而艺术是不具目的的;

(3)功能主义不尊重原文。

针对上述三个问题,他们是这样回答的:根据"行为"的定义,如果一个行为不具任何目的,那它就不成其为行为了。某个具体的行为,无论是赞成还是反对,一定是在两个或多个行为模式里自由抉择的结果,即使不做任何选择也是选择的一种表现。因此,即使是"为艺术而艺术"的运动也必然暗示了某种意图,即创造出仅仅为艺术而存在的艺术的意图。在"目的论"里,"原文"被"从王位的宝座上拉了下来",但这并不排除以原文为"衡量一切的标准"的可能,因为对原文最大限度的忠实可以是众多翻译目的中的一个。为使目的语文化的学者了解原文的句法,译者在翻译时可以严格模仿原文的句法。为什么不呢?问题的关键在于,译者必须知道他在做什么,清楚他的行为将带来怎样的结果。(Vermeer, 1989; Nord, 1997)。

第八节　小　结

翻译不能没有理念,就如人不能没有信仰一样。对待不同的翻译理念,我们应该持怎样一个态度呢?我们想,首先要有一个海纳百川的胸怀。显然,人们对翻译的认识比以往更深刻了,视野更宽广了,不再抱着"不信"或"不忠实"就"不是翻译"的老观念了。

综观上述中西不同时期的翻译理念,我们可以看出,在这令人眼花缭乱的理念背后,实质上反映的是两大类研究,即翻译的本体研究和翻译的外部研究。所谓本体研究,主要涉及的是语言本身的转换问题,而外部研究则主要涉及影响语言转换的其他关系。仔细比较同类研究中的不同理念,我们会发现,只要认真从事过翻译实践和理论思考的人,其理念又是何等相似!有学者指出,严复的理论来自泰特勒,也有的学者指出,严复的"信、达、雅"三字可追溯到我国古代佛经翻译家支谦的《法句经序》。实际上,英雄所见略同,或在两者的交互启发下提出自己的主张都是有可能的。

即使在不同大类的研究中,若再往深处看,总的来说,都是在研究翻译中如何对待"原文"的问题。这里面又可分为对等的理念、再生的理念和实效的理念(参考周兆祥,1996)。对等理念的背后有一个假设,即翻译就是复制原文,所以,翻译应尽可能存"真";再生理念的背后也有一个假设,即译文是原文的"借尸还魂",翻译就是要让作者及其意念在另一个时空里得到新的生命,就如钢琴演奏家凭借乐谱为当场的听众再度演绎一首作品。实效理念的背后则又有一个完全不同的假设,即翻译是一项服务,原文只是提供的不定形的"面团"。翻译的成败取决于消费者(委托人、雇主等)的满意程度,换言之,取决于是否达到某个具体的目的(如推销商品、传递资讯、提供乐趣等)。这样,忠实于原文的译文未必是合乎要求的译文，不忠实于原文的译文又未必是不合乎要求的译文。原来每一种翻译理念都有其自身的翻译哲学。我们过去看重的只是第一种理念，怀疑的是第二种理念，而几乎完全忽视的是第三种理念。

由此可见，任何一种翻译理念都是片面的，反映的只是局部"真理"。因此，我们一方面既要防止对某种理念的盲目崇拜，另一方面又要避免对某种理念的苛求。奈达的翻译理论在我国的遭遇值得认真反省：起初是"言必称奈达"，后来变成了"言必称奈达理论之缺陷"（参考杨晓荣，1996）。现在的"操纵论"和"目的论"又似乎是如日中天，不少人开口闭口就是"目的论"。但我们要清醒地认识到，"操纵论"和"目的论"关注的毕竟是翻译的外部研究，主要起宏观的指导作用。作为学习翻译的学生，仍不能忽视以"忠实"为取向的翻译训练。

中国传统译论注重经验，讲究悟性，见效于指导微观实践；西方当代译论推崇实证，善用推演，成就在构建宏观理论，很难说孰优孰劣，只能说各具功能。重要的是：知其所长，为我所用。若能融会中西，继往开来，定能使翻译研究更上层楼！

【进修书目】

1. Nida, Eugene. *Toward a Science of Translating* / 奈达：《翻译科学探索》，上海：上海外语教育出版社，2004.

2. Nida, Eugene & Taber, Charles. *The Theory and Practice of Translation* / 奈达等：《翻译理论与实践》，上海：上海外语教育出版社，2004.

3. Newmark, Peter. *A Textbook of Translation* / 纽马克：《翻译教程》，上海：上海外语教育出版社，2001.

4. Nord, Christiane. *Translating as a Purposeful Activity—Functionalist Approaches Explained* /诺德：《目的性行为——析功能翻译理论》，上海：上海外语教育出版社，2001.

5. 罗新璋，陈应年：《翻译论集》（修订本），北京：商务印书馆，2009.

6. 思果：《翻译研究》，北京：中国对外翻译出版公司，2001.

7. 翁显良：《意态由来画不成?》，北京：中国对外翻译出版公司，1983.

8. 许渊冲：《翻译的艺术》，北京：中国对外翻译出版公司，1984.

9. 许渊冲：《文学翻译谈》，台北：书林出版有限公司，1998.

10. 周兆祥：《翻译与人生》，北京：中国对外翻译出版公司，1998.

Techniques 技巧编

第四章
翻译的重要环节之一：措辞精当

我国古代文学理论家刘勰指出："因字而生句，积句而成章，积章而成篇。篇之彪炳，章无瑕也；章之明靡，句无玷也；句之清英，字不妄也。"（《文心雕龙》章句第三十四）刘勰论述的是写文章时字、句、章（段）、篇的关系；文章要写得好，一方面要从全篇的宏旨着眼，另一方面又要从具体的单字着手。翻译也是如此，一篇译文的好坏，除了句段之间的衔接，最终还取决于字词的选择是否精当。英国语言学家弗斯（J. R. Firth）说："每个词用在不同的上下文中就是一个新词。"（Each word when used in a new context is a new word.）从翻译的角度说，每个具体上下文中的词，理论上讲，只有一种译法，可见翻译之困难。鲁迅曾感叹："我向来总以为翻译比创作容易，因为至少是无须构想。但到真的一译，就会遇着难关，譬如一个名词或动词，写不出，创作时候可以回避，翻译上却不成，也还得想，一直弄到头昏眼花，好像在脑子里面摸一个急于要开箱子的钥匙，却没有。"（《且介亭杂文二集》）这种在脑子里寻觅那一个最为精当的字词的痛苦是每一个认真做过翻译的人都经历过的。

翻译时怎样才称得上措辞精当呢？我们可以先看一些例子：

1. By some happy fortune I was not seasick.
   说来有几分走运，我竟没有晕船[①]。
2. From peak to peak leaps the live thunder.
   雷声隆隆，翻山越岭而来[②]。
3. Now and then he turned his eyes from the girl's face to that of the partner, which, in the exhilaration of the dance, had <u>taken on a look of impudent ownership</u>. (Edith Wharaton: *Ethan Frome*)
   他时而转移他的目光从女子的脸上到他的舞伴的脸上，那张脸在跳

[①] 转引自苏福忠：《译事余墨》，生活·读书·新知三联书店2006年版，第130页。
[②] 引自黄自来：《英汉语法对比》，（台北）文鹤出版有限公司1987年版，第156页。

第四章 翻译的重要环节之一：措词精当

舞的狂热之中俨然有"佳人属我"的精神。(吕叔湘 译)①

4. Nixon had been flashing signals to Peking since the spring but there had been no positive response; <u>significantly</u>, there had not been any of the usual denunciations either. (Marvin Kalb & Bernard Kalb: *Kissinger*, p. 227)

尼克松自那年春天以来一直向北京发出信号，可是没有得到积极的反应；但**意味深长的是**，也没有挨到那种老一套的痛斥。(齐沛合 译)②

<u>查查词典</u>，再仔细品味，我们不得不佩服译者的高明。翻译时要做到措辞精当之所以那么困难，是因为这不仅涉及字词在特定上下文中的基本意思，还涉及字词的搭配与色彩，思维与表达的不同习惯，还有文学语言独特的意态与神韵，等等，只要哪里稍微差了一点，就会言不尽意。笔者也经常饱尝这种寻觅一个字词的痛苦，当然也有过无以言表的喜悦。兹举数例，与读者一起分享：

5. "Writing is a tough trade. <u>Don't get mixed up in it if you can help it.</u>" (Ernest Hemingway)③

写作是个辛苦的行当，**除非万不得已，切莫以身相许**。(或：……，切勿入错了行。)

6. A good style should show no <u>sign of effort</u>. What is written should seem <u>a happy accident</u>. (W. Somerset Maugham: *Lucidity*, *Simplicity*, *Euphony*)

好的风格不应露出**刻意的**痕迹，写下来的东西应像是**信手拈来的**。

或：好的风格不应露出**斧凿的**痕迹，写下来的东西应像是**信手拈来的**。

7. This modern and spacious hotel is designed to <u>make the most of its advantageous position</u>, in the hills above Sorrento overlooking the enchanting Bay of Naples.

这家现代、宽敞的酒店位于山腰之上，近可俯瞰苏莲托小城，远可眺望令人陶醉的那不勒斯海湾，其设计**占尽地势之利**。

8. Elliot was <u>too clever not to see</u> that many of the persons who accepted his invitations did so only to get a free meal and that of these some were stupid

---

① 引自吕叔湘:《吕叔湘译文三种》，外语教学与研究出版社 1992 年版，第 37 页。

② 引自马文·卡尔布等:《基辛格》，齐沛合译，生活·读书·新知三联书店 1975 年版，第 350 页。

③ 引自 Gregory H. Hemingway. *To Make Papa Proud*. 作者为 Ernest Hemingway 的儿子。

and some worthless. (W. S. Maugham: *The Razor's Edge*)①

艾略特**何等聪明，怎会看不出**，许多接受他邀请的人，只是为了免费饱餐一顿。他很清楚，他们中有些人是愚蠢无知，另一些则是无足轻重。

显然，翻译时要做到措辞精当，非一朝一夕所能成就。本章根据学习者的特点，重点谈三个方面。

第一节　注意词的多义性

同一个词，由于语境的不同，其词义可千差万别。比如汉语的"打"字，我们就有"打鱼""打柴""打篮球""打喷嚏""打酱油"……如果要把它们译成英语，同是一个"打"字，十之八九须译成不同的词，才能体现"打"字的不同含义，或示其细微差别。同样，英语里的"make"一词也能构成许许多多的词组，如"make paper""make cloth""make a fire""make a promise""make tea""make trouble""make money"。同是一个"make"，如果译成汉语，绝大多数也须译成不同的汉字。试看下面两个例子：

1. Poets as we know have always made a great use of alliteration. They are persuaded that the repetition of a sound gives an effect of beauty. I do not think it does so in prose. It seems to me that in prose alliteration should be used only for a special reason; when used **by accident** it falls on the ear very disagreeably. (W. Somerset Maugham: *Lucidity, Simplicity, Euphony*)

   正如我们所知，诗人总是大量地使用头韵，因为他们从不怀疑重复使用某个声音可以增添美感。但我不相信写散文时也能产生同样的效果。在我看来，除非有特殊的理由，在散文里一般是不使用头韵的，如果**毫无缘由地**使用头韵，耳朵则必然受罪。

---

① 英语原文转引自钱歌川：《翻译的技巧》，商务印书馆 1981 年版，第 439 页。原来有译文，前半部分是："艾略特是一个聪明的人，必然看得出来，……"笔者总觉得韵味差了那么一点。

第四章 翻译的重要环节之一：措词精当

这个例子与上一节的第6例是选自同一篇文章，两处都使用了accident这个词语，其基本意思都是"偶然"，但我们却在一处翻译成"信手拈来"，一处翻译成"毫无缘由"，如果单从汉语来看，几乎很难想象它们原来是译自同一个词语。

2. Each **change** of season, every **change** of weather, indeed, every hour of the day, produces some **change** in the magical hues and shapes of these mountains, and they are regarded by all the good wives, far and near, as perfect barometers. (Washington Irving: *Rip Van Winkle*)
季节**更替**，寒暑**变迁**，甚至**须臾之间**，群山都呈现出**不同的奇姿异彩**。远近贤德的主妇会把它们看作精确的晴雨表。(笔者译文)①

原文有4个"change"（包括一个暗含的），意思都是一个，但根据汉语的搭配习惯，这里却运用了4个不同的表述方式。

在应用文体中，我们还要注意区分日常生活用语和专业用语，且同一个专业用语在不同的语境下又有不同的意义。请看下面的例子：

1. He got all the credit for the discovery.
2. The ledger shows 300 pounds on the debit side and 50 pounds on the credit side.
3. The availability of cheap long-term credit would help small businesses.
4. They sold grain on credit during time of famine.
5. How much do I have to my credit?
6. They cannot obtain credit at all in the trade.
7. They have opened the covering credit with the Bank of China, London.

以上7个句子都包含有"credit"这个词，但每个句子中的"credit"，其词义都有所区别：

---

① 万紫、雨宁的译文是："四季的每一转换，气候的每一变化，乃至一天中每一小时，都能使这些山峦的奇幻的色彩和形态变换，远近的好主妇会把它们看作精确的晴雨表。"（见王佐良编选《美国短篇小说选》，中国青年出版社1980版）。有学者批评说，在旧英语中，"good wife"当作一个词语，作"主妇"解，不应错译成"好主妇"。笔者就此查阅了几部权威的英语词典，发现作"主妇"解时，该词语应是连写，即"goodwife"，而不是分开书写的"good wife"。根据上下文，本书将"good"一词译成"贤德的"，似无不妥。

1. 他由于这项发现而获得各种**荣誉**。
2. 从分类账上可以看出，发生金额借方 300 英镑，**贷方** 50 英镑。
3. 低息长期**贷款**可以扶持小型企业。
4. 饥荒季节，他们则**赊销**粮食。
5. 我的**银行户头**上还有多少存款？
6. 他们的生意**信誉**已荡然无存。
7. 他们已从伦敦中国银行开立了有关的**信用证**。

只要翻开一本词典，我们就可知道，一词多义是语言的普遍现象。因此，同词异译是翻译的常态。再看几个汉译英的例子：

1. **价廉**物美。
2. 我们不销售**廉价**质次的货物。
3. 我们已按**很低**的价格向你们报盘。
4. 你们将会看出我们这批货物的价格是很**便宜**的。
5. 请报体温表**最低价**。
6. 对我们的业务建议如有兴趣，请寄样品，并告**最惠条款**。
7. 我们的报价已是**最低价**，折扣不能再多给了。

以上 7 个句子都涉及"价格低"这个概念，但若要译得贴切，却可能须用不同的词语来表达。试译如下：

1. fine and <u>inexpensive</u>
2. We do not sell <u>cheap</u> quality goods.
3. We have made you an offer at a very <u>competitive</u> price.
4. You will find our prices for these goods very <u>popular</u>.
5. Please make us your <u>lowest</u> quotation for Clinical Thermometers.
6. If you are interested in our business proposal, please send us the samples together with your <u>best</u> terms and conditions.
7. As we have quoted you our <u>rock-bottom</u> price, we can't give you any more discounts.

查阅一般的汉英词典，比如查"便宜"这个词条，往往不可能给出所有的释义。即使倒过来去查英汉词典，也并非每个词都能找到确切的对应汉语词语，

第四章 翻译的重要环节之一：措词精当

如"best"一词，只是在特定的搭配中，才具有"优惠的""便宜的"等类含义。许多学生，一谈到"便宜"，可能马上就联想到"cheap"一词，但这个词多数情况含有贬义，这点不能不知。

字词除了其基本意义外，在漫长的岁月中，词义会不断演变，形成种种引申意义，这也给译者带来困难，不仅在表达上，而且在理解上。如果不能确切把握其上下文的具体含义，则表达必然生搬硬套，轻者不知所云，重者导致错误。试比较：

1. The overriding **lesson** of the **history** of civilizations, however, is that many things are probable but nothing is inevitable. (*The Clash of Civilizations and the Remaking of World Order* by Samuel P. Huntington, New York: Simon & Schuster, 1996: 307)

    译文一：然而，文明**史**中压倒一切的**教训**是，很多事情都是可能的，但任何事情都不是不可避免的。（某译本）

    译文二：然而，文明的**兴衰更替**给我们上的最重要的**一课**就是，很多事情都是可能的，但任何事情都不是不可避免的。

将"history"译为"史"似乎不能算错，但不引申出来，意思就不清楚。"lesson"是个多义词，就看你选哪个意思了。选词不当也会造成意思的混乱。

2. Discipline means choices. Every time you say yes to a goal or objective, you say no to many more. Every prize has its price. The prize is the yes; the price is the no. ("Rules Every Achiever Knows" by Sybil Stanton— *Reader's Digest*, Nov, 1987)

    译文一：纪律意味着选择。每当你对一个目标或对象说"是"，你实际上是对许多别的目标或对象说了"不"。任何奖赏都有它的代价，奖赏就是你说的"是"，代价就是你说的"不"。

    译文二：**自律**意味着选择，每当你**肯定**一个目标或对象，你同时也**否定**了更多的目标或对象。每个奖赏都有它的代价，**肯定**的是奖赏，**否定**的就是代价。

    译文三：自律意味着**有取有舍**，每当你**肯定**一个目标或对象，你同时也**否定**了更多的目标或对象。每个奖赏都有它的代价，**得到奖赏是因为你说了"是"，付出代价是因为你说了"不"**。

    译文四：**成人不自在，自在不成人。每当你想有所作为，你就得决心更多不为**。要想获大奖就得付出相应的代价。**若要有所**

· 69 ·

"得",就得有所"失"。

这里的4个译文是有意为之的。译文一尽可能复制原文,但意思若隐若现,让人感觉不快;译文二、三、四体现了不同程度的引申,引申到怎样的程度才为合适,则取决于具体的语言环境和译者的翻译思想。

应用文体中也不乏词义引申的情况,翻译时也要仔细分辨。请看下面的例子:

1. We have an interest for your athletic goods.
2. We enclose a list showing our present availabilities.
3. The arrivals do not conform to the sample. You must have shipped the wrong parcel.
4. It is one of the most useful of the household conveniences.
5. Oil prices came tumbling down, brightening the outlook for inflation and helping to touch off a rally on Wall Street.
6. To cover our shipment, we would request you to establish a commercial letter of credit in our favor for the contracted amount through an American Bank.

以上6个句子中的"interest""availabilities""arrivals""conveniences"和"Wall Street""shipment",如查词典,它们的基本含义可分别是"兴趣""可得到的东西""到达(的东西)""便利(设施)""华尔街"和"装运"。如果将这些词义直接放入译文,就很难充分表达原文的含义,故须进一步引申:

1. 我们有一个**买主**愿购你们的体育用品。
2. 兹附上我方**现货**货单一份。
3. **到货**与样品不符,你们谅必装错了货。
4. 这是最为便利的**家用设备**之一。
5. 石油价格猛跌,使通货膨胀问题出现曙光,促使**华尔街股票市场**恢复活力。
6. 请通过一家美国银行按合同金额开立以我公司为受益人的商业信用证,用以支付**货款**。

传统上,词义引申分成具体化引申和抽象化引申两种。由于具体语言环境千差万别,常常很难绝对划分何者为具体化引申,何者为抽象化引申,因此本书没有分开叙述。

必须强调的是，词义引申的一个重要前提就是，必须从原词固有的基本含义出发，注意掌握分寸，不可离开上下文和内在的逻辑关系任意发挥，否则就失去了引申的依据。

第二节　注意词的语体色彩

译什么，像什么，这是措辞精当与否的一个重要标志。文学作品偏爱意境的再现，着力于事件的铺陈或人物的描写，用词趋向口语化，色彩斑斓。请看下面的例子：

> It was Miss Murdstone who was arrived, and a gloomy-looking lady she was; dark, like her brother, whom she greatly resembled in face and voice; and with very heavy eyebrows, nearly meeting over her large nose, as if, being disabled by the wrongs of her sex from wearing whiskers, she had carried them to that account. She brought with her two uncompromising hard black boxes, with her initials on the lids in hard brass nails. When she paid the coachman she took her money out of a hard steel purse, and she kept the purse in a very jail of a bag which hung upon her arm by heavy chains, and shut up like a bite. I had never, at that time, seen such a metallic lady altogether as Miss Murdstone was. (Charles Dickens: *David Copperfield*)

> 来的不是别人，正是枚得孙小姐。只见这个妇人，满脸肃杀，发肤深色，和她兄弟一样，面目嗓音，也都和他兄弟非常地像。两道眉毛非常地浓，在大鼻子上面几乎都连到一块了，好像因为她是女性，受了冤屈，天生地不能长胡子，所以才把胡子这笔账，转到眉毛的账上了。她带来了两个棱角崚嶒、非常坚硬的大黑箱子，用非常坚硬的铜钉，把她那姓名的字头，在箱子的盖儿上钉出来。她开发车钱的时候，她的钱是从一个非常坚硬的钢制钱包儿里拿出来的，而她这个钱包儿，又是装在一个和监狱似的手提包里，用一条粗链子挂在胳膊上，关上的时候像狠狠地咬了一口一样。我长到那个时候，还从来没见过别的妇人，有像枚

得孙小姐那样完全如钢似铁的。（张谷若 译，第60页）①

张谷若译英国小说家狄更斯代表作《大卫·考坡菲》，被称作小说翻译的一个典范（袁锦翔，1990：295）。这一段描写的是枚得孙的姐姐兼管家初到考坡菲家时的情状。枚得孙小姐是个铁石心肠的女人，作者竭尽嘲讽之能事，不仅把她描写得相貌骇人，连她随身携带的物件也人格化了，呈现出狰狞的面目，试看那极度夸张和沉重色彩的词语：greatly, very, hard, hard, hard, gloomy-looking, dark, uncompromising, heavy eyebrows, large nose, heavy chains, black boxes, brass nails, steel purse, in a very jail of, a metallic lady, altogether。

译者的手法也是出神入化，第一句采用的是拆句（一分为二），逆序和增词（增加了"不是别人"）的方法，把一个强调句型处理得妥妥帖帖，以"只见"开启下一句，旋即进入正题，前后衔接得天衣无缝（看不出还有什么更好的译法！）。为了复制原文的风格，译者也毫不吝啬，前后使用了5个"非常"，外加一个"完全"，突出两个"坚硬"，衬以一"铜"一"钢"和一条"粗链子"，再加上关上时"像狠狠咬了一口"的"监狱似的"手提包，使得狄更斯笔下的那个浓眉大鼻、发肤暗淡、如钢似铁、满脸肃杀的枚得孙小姐活脱脱地站在了译文读者的面前。

与文学作品不同，公文类文书则注重信息的准确，讲究行文的严密，用词趋向书面化，稳健庄重。（参见第八章）翻译时应充分体现这些特点。试举例说明：

1. It causes a loss of time and thus a loss of money.
   不仅损失了时间，也因此损失了金钱。
2. This offer is subject to the goods being unsold on receipt of your reply.
   这个报盘以收到你们的答复时货还没有卖掉为有效。
3. The responsibilities of the carrier shall commence from the time when the goods are loaded on board the ship and shall cease when they are discharged from the ship.
   承运人的责任期限应该从货物装上船舶的时候起到货物卸离船舶的时候止。
4. Party A shall have the responsibilities and duties to assist the company in the handling of the following matters concerned.

---

① 引自（英）狄更斯著：《大卫·考坡菲》，张谷若译，上海译文出版社2003年版，第60页。

第四章 翻译的重要环节之一：措词精当

甲方有责任和义务帮助公司办理下面的有关事情。

对照以上 4 个中英文句子，从内容和意义上看，应该说译文是忠实于原文的。但不足之处是，读起来不像经贸方面的文字材料，原因就是译文所使用的都是口语体词语。事实上，只要在措辞方面稍作修改（包括适当使用某些汉语虚词），译文就可大大改观：

1. 这不仅浪费了时间，也因此损失了**资金**。
2. **此盘**以收到你方答复货**未**售出为有效。
3. 承运人责任期限应从货物装上船舶**时始**至货物卸离船舶**时止**。
4. 甲方有责任和义务**协助**公司办理以下有关**事宜**。

再看一组例子：

1. We want two originals and six copies.
   我们需要 2 本原件和 6 本复印件。
2. What do your insurance clauses cover?
   你们的保险条款包括哪些内容？
3. We wish to insure the following consignment against all risks for the sum of US$3 600.
   我们希望为下面的货物保综合险，总金额为 3600 美元。
4. Do you allow any quantity difference when the goods are loaded on board the ship?
   装船时，货物数量是否允许有差额？

以上 4 个句子的译文，意思也正确，也能让人看懂，但却不算是好的译文，因为全部都使用了"大白话"。如果用上一些术语和行话，译文效果就会好得多。试分别改译如下：

1. 我方需要**正本** 2 份，**副本** 6 份。
2. 你们的保险条款中有哪些**险别**？
3. 我们要为下列货物按 3600 美元保额**投保**综合险。
4. 装船数量是否允许有**增减幅度**？

经贸类文书有许多专业术语，而其中大多数都已有通用译名。除此之外，还有一些较为固定的短语或表示法。作为涉外工作者，平时应注意积累，在翻译时才可能以"行话"译"行话"。下面再举一些例子，注意画线部分：

1. Owing to <u>force majeure</u>, we cannot execute these orders.
   由于**不可抗力**，我们无法执行这些订单。

2. We are pleased to advise you that <u>the captioned goods</u> were shipped yesterday per S. S. "Da Qing".
   兹通知，**标题货物**已于昨天由"大庆"轮装出。

3. Your proposal for payment by <u>time draft</u> for Order No. 1156 is acceptable to us, and we shall draw on you at 60 days' sight after the goods have been shipped. Please honor our draft when it falls due.
   我们同意贵方以**远期汇票**支付 1156 号订单，我们将于货物装出后开出 60 天期的汇票，请到时即付。

4. In reply to your cable of 3rd June, which asked us to make an offer for our Blanket No. 33, we wish to confirm our cable dispatched on 6th June offering you <u>without engagement</u> the following.
   6 月 3 日来电嘱报第 33 号毛毯盘，现确认我方 6 月 6 日电报**不受约束盘**如下。

5. Please quote both <u>F. O. B.</u> China port and <u>C. I. F.</u> Mombasa prices.
   请同时报中国口岸**离岸价**和蒙巴萨**到岸价**。

6. In order to enable you to apply for the necessary import licence, we are sending you Proforma Invoice No. 234 <u>in triplicate</u>. Please note that if there is any change in price or delivery, we shall keep you informed.
   为您方申请必备的进口许可证，兹寄形式发票第 234 号**一式三份**，其中价格或交货期若有变更，我方将另行通知。
   （注：类似的短语，如一式二份、一式四份、一式五份可分别译成"in duplicate""in quadruplicate"和"in quintuplicate"。）

第三节 注意培养语感，提高鉴赏力

我们常可听说"眼高手低"的情形，但却不会有"眼低手高"的可能。措辞能否精当与鉴赏水平密切相关。作为学习者，可以从培养语感入手，比如学会

发现句子中的"异常"现象。下面举例说明:

1. Such a chance was denied me.
   我没有得到这样一个机会。
2. I'm blest if I know.
   我一点儿也不知道。
3. These were the meetings that engineered Khrushchev's "resignation" on ground of "advancing age and deteriorating health."
   这些会议促使赫鲁晓夫"辞职",其理由是他的"年纪越来越大,而且健康状况恶化"。

这3个句子①,没有上下文,给理解带来一定的困难,但细心和语感较好的读者仍能觉察到一些"蛛丝马迹"。比如,例1是个被动句,例2包含了一个我们不大常用的词(blest),例3有个词是被引号框起来了,且"engineer"这个词很少用作动词。只要这么简单的分析,你就不会满足于原来的译文了:首先,例1中的译文显然没有表达出被动结构的意义,而例2中的译文,如果将它回译成英文,似乎也用不着使用"blest"这么"生僻"的一个词,例3中的译文虽然也使用了引号,但却看不出有什么特别的意思,原因可能是它没有很好地与动词搭配使用。

要准确翻译上面的句子,有必要查实两个单词,*Collins Co-build English Language Dictionary*(1987年版)是这样解释的:

blessed: as a mild swear word or exclamation. EG. I'm blessed if I know! (p. 139)

engineer: If you **engineer** an event or situation, you arrange or cause it in a clever or indirect way, especially in order to obtain some advantage for yourself (p. 467)

Co-build 好像是专门为这两个句子设计的,问题全解决了。试改译如下:

1. 这样的好机会哪有我的份!

---

① 引自张培基等:《英汉翻译教程》,上海外语教育出版社1980年版,第105页,第117页,第138页。

2. 知道的是小狗！（或：我怎会知道呢！）
3. 这些**精心策划**的会议**迫使**赫鲁晓夫"辞职"，其理由是他"年事日高，健康恶化"。

好的原文，本来就是原作者刻意追求和周密安排的，尤其会体现在一些关键词语上，如诗歌中有"诗眼"，散文中有"文眼"。因此，翻译要做到措辞精当，首先要能揣摩到原作者选词用字的心思，得作者之志。例如：

1. A few of the committee had <u>urged</u> hanging him as a <u>possible</u> example.①
2. He (Fowler) had a sound feeling that idiom was the backbone of a language and he was <u>all for the racy phrase</u>. He was no slavish admirer of logic and was willing enough to give usage right of way through the exact demesnes of grammar. (W. Somerset Maugham: *Lucidity, Simplicity, Euphony*)
3. <u>To begin my life with the beginning of my life</u>, I record that I was born (as I have been informed and believe) on a Friday, at twelve o'clock at night. It was remarked that <u>the clock began to strike</u>, and <u>I began to cry</u>, simultaneously. (Charles Dickens: *David Copperfield*, p. 1)

例1是个很简单的句子，但用字却十分讲究，一个"urge"和一个"possible"前后呼应，使句子赫然生威。例2是个长句，但最感棘手的恐怕还是一个短语，即"all for **the** racy phrase"，翻译时还不能忽略了其中那个特别的定冠词。例3的开头以改变词性的手法使一个动词短语和一个名词短语产生回环，句子的结尾又特意安排了两个中韵（strike 和 cry），使整个句子读起来余音缭绕，文采斐然。这是狄更斯的大手笔。试看下面的译文：

1. 有些委员**强烈要求**将他处以绞刑，**以儆效尤**（或：**以期杀一儆百**）。（笔者译文）
2. 福勒的观点是正确的：约定俗成是语言之本。因此，写作时他**最讲究词趣，若言不尽意，决不罢休**。他注重逻辑，但又时有变通，坚持要语法正确，但又不排斥惯用法。（笔者译文）

---

① 英文句子转引自刘宓庆：《英汉翻译技能训练手册》，上海外语教育出版社1987年版，第105页。

3. **为的是从我一生的开始,**来开始我一生的记叙,我就下笔写道:我生在一个星期五夜里十二点。别人这样告诉我,我自己也这样相信。据说那一会儿,**当当的钟声,**和呱呱的啼声,恰好同时并作。(张谷若 译,第3页)①

鉴赏力的提高,一个有效的途径,就是向名家学习,尤其是通过名著名译的对照阅读,如果能自己先做一遍,再对照阅读,就能事半功倍。名著之所以成为名著,要么意义深刻,要么语言过人,要么情节曲折,凡此等等;而名译之所以成为名译,就在于译者能还其本来面目,手段之高明让你叹服!英译汉如本教程引用过的《吕叔湘译文三种》,杨必译的《名利场》,张谷若译的《大卫·考坡菲》,都是不可多得的好模本。下面再选几个漂亮的译文,供欣赏:

1. For twins they are very dissimilar. Colin is tall and active and Johnny is short and middle-aged.

   孪生兄弟本应相似,然而不然。科林高而活跃,约翰矮而老成。(翁显良 译,第19 – 20页)

2. The builder [Hale] refused genially, as he did everything else. (Edith Wharaton: *Ethan Frome*)

   郝尔的拒绝是很婉转的,这人**无往而不婉转**。(吕叔湘 译,第83页)

3. The room was a pleasant one, at the top of the house, overlooking the sea, on which the moon was shining brilliantly. (Charles Dickens: *David Copperfield*)

   我那个屋子很叫人可心,它坐落在这所房子最高的一层,俯临大海,那时月光正**澄澈晶明**地照在海面上。(张谷若 译,第233页)

4. The Flower Girl: Will you pay me for them? ②

   The Daughter: Do nothing of the sort, mother. The idea! (Bernard Shaw: *Pygmalion*)

   译文一:卖花女:你肯给钱吗?
   　　　　女儿:一点不要给她,母亲。**她想得倒好**!③
   译文二:卖花女:你替他给钱吧?

---

① (英) 狄更斯著:《大卫·考坡菲》,张谷若译,上海译文出版社2003年版,第3页。
② 英文此处为土语方言,原文是:Will ye – oo py me fthem?
③ 引自许渊冲:《翻译的艺术》,中国对外翻译出版公司1984年版,第12页。

女儿：妈，别给她。**听她的！**（杨宪益 译，第11页）

5. It was a day as fresh as grass growing up and clouds going over and butterflies coming down can make it. It was a day compounded from silences of bee and flower and ocean and sea.

芳草萋萋，白云悠悠，彩蝶翩翩，天朗气晴，蜜蜂无言，春花不语，海不扬波，大地寂寥，四周是如此安静。①

例1的第一分句，虽然只有6个单词，不看人家的译文，不知道翻译竟有云泥之别！试想将它译成："作为双胞胎，他们非常不像"，不也是"忠实"于原文的意思么？然而翁显良对"for"与"dissimilar"之间的关系了然于胸，再用锤炼的汉语译出，音韵典雅，难出其右。例2的后半句是个平常不过的表达，但吕叔湘却能化腐朽为神奇，使被描写的人的神态历历如在目前。翻译常常是这样，越是看似简单的地方，越见译者的功力。例3中的"brilliantly"，是个意思"缥缈"的副词，很难把握住，即使"把握"住了，往往也难于准确地言表。张谷若用"澄澈晶明"译之，宛如一幅精彩绝伦的木刻，不愧为翻译大家的手笔！例4有两个译文，原文的"The idea!"，对于一般人恐怕不知如何是好，现在一个译文是"她想得倒好！"，一个译文是"听她的！"，译得真是活脱，亏他们想得出来！例5的出处不详，但可以看出，译者充分发挥了汉语之长，以8个四字结构的短语，再加一个小句压尾，把两个"剪不断，理还乱"的句子翻译得韵意圆转，叫人不得不佩服。

上面只谈了要做到措辞精当应注意的三个方面，实际上，影响措辞的远不止这些。翻译，体现在技巧上，如八仙过海，各显神通；但它更应体现在译者的态度上：言不尽意，决不罢休！总之，措辞精当，是一种不懈的追求，翻译应当像经典创作那样，在文字上千锤百炼。

【练习题】

Ⅰ. 请将下列外贸业务中的常用句子译成英语，注意选词和使用行话。

1. 银行拒绝给该公司提供新的贷款。
2. 一有新货，我们即与贵方联系。
3. 随函附上装船单据副本，请查收。
4. 我们相信，你方定会见票即付。

---

① 转引自张梅岗：《实用翻译教程》（上），湖北科技出版社1993年版。译文显然借用了崔颢的《黄鹤楼》中的诗句。

5. 请将信用证修改为"在广州议付"。
6. 如果一方未能执行合同,另一方有权中止本合同。
7. 很遗憾,我们不能接受你方报盘,你方价格太高,不敢问津。
8. 为促成交易,我们认为你们至少得让5%才行。
9. 我们的支付条款是保兑的、不可撤销的信用证,凭即期汇票支付。
10. 随函寄上第4567号购物确认书一式两份,请尽快签退一份,以备我方存查。

Ⅱ. 下列句子选自本人翻译的一位美国传教士的日记,原著为 *An Eventful Year in the Orient*,描写的是20世纪20年代该传教士从美国出发,途经日本来到中国,以及在中国(因战乱辗转南京、如皋、上海等地)逗留期间(1926—1927年)的所见所闻。所选句子可能会在理解和表达上遇到困难,请尝试将这些句子翻译成中文。(注意:请在反复修改译文,达到自己认为的最佳状态后,再对照书后提供的参考答案,这样更有助于增加对翻译的认识。)

1. During this time one of the panes in a window kept up a continuous rattle. There was practically no wind blowing. This lower Yangtze Valley would be about the last place in the world to expect an earthquake, but I shall be interested in seeing the next newspaper to note if there has been any evidence of it elsewhere. (注:作者当时在南京)

2. Rev. and Mrs. George Synder of the German Reformed Church are a bit farther inland. They were sent a telegram telling them to get out, …but in view of the fact that there was no disturbance at their station they wired back that they were going to stay. A second telegram, more urgent than the first, was sent, but no reply was received to this. We are personally interested in the Synders because they were fellow-passengers on the "President Wilson" last summer and we thoroughly enjoyed each other's companionship. (注:作者当时在南京,他们一家也是乘"President Wilson"轮船来中国的)

3. On our way to the boat dock we began to appreciate some of the tenseness of the situation—the crowds of rude soldiers, hard coolies, general anticipation of trouble.

4. Shortly after we could hear automobiles with reinforcements rushing up the street, and we wondered whether we would have to dash to the warships for safety. (注:作者当时在上海)

5. One of these grammars, a large, bulky thing with fine print, was written by a Mr. Poutsma of Groningen, and I was wondering if the gentleman was some distant cousin. (注:作者也姓Poutsma,美籍荷兰裔;Groningen为荷兰地名。语境:

作者一行在日本东京逛书店）

6. The first morning we were here we were awakened by the sound of firing of rifles and machine guns. I knew they were fighting a couple of hundred miles up the river, and wondered if a force had quietly gotten this far down the river and were attacking Nanking. However, I learned later that it was merely rifle practice. （注：作者当时在南京）

7. I have been told that legally gambling is forbidden in Nanking, although I have seen plenty of evidence that this rule is not enforced, but during the days of New Year celebration the "lid is off" legally and gambling may be done without any restraint. These sights made us think of the Lord Jesus in the temple at Jerusalem, driving the business men out with a whip, and we wondered why the heathen priests did not do the same to these people who were desecrating the courtyard of their gods. （注：作者一行游南京夫子庙）

8. We noticed several groups of hogs. Usually there was a sow with three to seven pigs feeding on the sparse grass. A boy keeps watch over these animals. They are not exactly razor back hogs, but surely rather thin around the middle, and I just wondered how these black-skinned animals would appreciate about a month in the fields of our Iowa farmers. （注：作者一行在南京郊外远足）

9. At many places (along the top of the Wall of Nanking) we observed slabs of stone, six inches thick, a foot wide, and about four feet high. They were erected parallel to each other. Each slab had two holes four inches in diameter cut into them. The slabs were set very firmly into the top of the wall. We wondered what they were used for in the good old days. Perhaps blocks of wood were inserted into the holes to accommodate ropes for pulling up men and materials onto the wall.

10. We are all wondering, wondering, wondering what the next month or two holds in store for us. To me it looks as though there are very stormy days ahead.

第五章
翻译的重要环节之二：活用技巧

有人误以为，所谓合乎标准的翻译，就是在把一种语言转换为另一种语言的时候，做到"不增""不减""不改"。翻译实践告诉我们，由于两种语言表达方式的差异，翻译的过程往往是"既增、又减、还改"的过程。这种根据各自语言的特点，在具体的上下文中适当地"增、减、改"，就是我们要讨论的翻译技巧。

这种翻译时适当的"增、减、改"，传统上称为词量的增减、词类的转换、词句的拆合、反面着笔等。灵活运用这些技巧，可以帮助我们在实际翻译时妥善解决内容与形式之间的矛盾，使译文做到内容忠实、文字通顺、行文简洁、明确易懂，否则，译文就可能生硬、别扭、拖沓、晦涩，或导致错误。因此，译文质量的高低与译者能否灵活运用翻译技巧有着十分密切的联系。

如何运用这些翻译技巧呢？为了给学习者一个整体印象，我们先以语段为单位综合剖析两个例子。

原文：

BEFORE THE CURTAIN

As the Manager of the Performance sits before the curtain on the boards, and looks into the Fair, a feeling of profound melancholy comes over him in his survey of the bustling place. There is **a great quantity of** eating and drinking, making love and jilting, laughing and the contrary, smoking, cheating, fighting, dancing, and fiddling: there are bullies pushing about, bucks ogling the women, knaves picking pockets, policemen on the looking out, quacks (*other* quacks, plague take them!) bawling in front of their booths, and yokels looking up at the tinseled dancers and poor old rugged tumblers, **while** the light-fingered folk are operating upon their pockets behind. Yes, this is VANITY FAIR: not a moral place certainly; nor a merry one, though very noisy. Look at the faces of the actors and buffoons when they come off from their business; and Tom Fool washing the paint off his cheeks **before** he sits down to dinner with his wife and the little Jack Puddings behind the canvas. The curtain will be up presently, and he will be turning over his head and heels, and crying, "How are you?" (William Makepeace Thackeray: *Vanity Fair*，粗体格式为本书作者所加)

译文：

开幕以前的几句话

领班的坐在戏台上幔子前面，对着**底下**闹哄哄的市场，瞧了半晌，心里不觉悲惨起来。市场上的人有的在吃喝，有的在调情，有的得了新宠就丢了旧爱；有在笑的，也有在哭的，还有在抽烟的，打架的，跳舞的，拉提琴的，诓骗哄人的。有些是到处横行的强梁汉子，有些是对女人飞眼儿的花花公子，也有扒儿手和到处巡逻的警察，还有走江湖吃十方的，在自己摊子前面扯起嗓子嚷嚷（这些人偏和我同行，真该死！）。跳舞的穿着浑身发亮的衣服，可怜的翻斤斗老头儿涂着**两腮帮子**胭脂，**引得**那些乡下佬睁着眼瞧，**不提防**后面就有三只手的家伙在掏他们的口袋。是了，这就是**我们的**名利场。这里虽然是个热闹去处，**却**是道德沦亡，说不上有什么快活。

你瞧瞧戏子们丑角们下场以后的脸色——譬如那**逗人发笑**的傻小子汤姆回到后台洗净了脸上的油彩，**准备**和老婆儿子（一群小傻小子）坐下吃饭时候的**形景**，你就明白了。不久开场做戏，汤姆又会出来连连翻斤斗，嘴里叫唤着说："您好哇？"（杨必译《名利场》，人民文学出版社1994年版。粗体格式为本书作者所加）

杨必女士译萨克雷的《名利场》在中国翻译界备受称赞，如果有谁能静下心来拿她的译文与原文对照着看一遍，想来比读任何翻译技巧的书都强，如果能自己先认真翻译一遍，再与之比较，就能学到更多的东西，即使功力上好的译者，恐怕也不得不佩服她。这里所选取的只是小说开篇的一小段，供分析之用。

对一般读者来说，可能还有不少生词。为了将注意力集中在翻译技巧上，我们先将可能的生词标注出来（以出现先后为序）。

jilt：*v.* 抛弃（情人）

bully：*n.* 恃强凌弱者

buck：*n.* 花花公子

ogle：*v.* 向……抛媚眼

knave：*n.* 恶棍、无赖

quack：*n.* 冒牌医生；江湖骗子

bawl：*v.* 高声叫喊

yokel：*n.* 乡巴佬

tinsel：*v.* 用金属箔装饰

rouge：*v.* （在……上）涂胭脂

tumbler：*n.* 翻斤斗者

buffoon：*n.* 滑稽戏演员；小丑

canvas：*n.* 马戏团帐篷

仔细对照阅读，可以归纳出以下几个方面：

（1）**选词用字**。译者特别擅长使用口语和方言词汇，比如，"领班的""幔子""瞧了半晌""有的得了新宠就丢了旧爱""强梁汉子""飞眼儿""扒儿手""走江湖吃十方的""扯起嗓子嚷嚷""两腮帮子""有三只手的家伙在掏他们的口袋""戏子们"。另外，"领班的""幔子"和"戏子们"等的措辞非常得体，试想，假如将它们分别翻译成"戏团的经理""幕布"和"演员们"，又会是怎样的效果呢？

（2）**合译与拆译**。如用"领班的"译"the Manager of the Performance"，用"下场以后"译"when they come off from their business"，可属"合译"；而用"有的得了新宠就丢了旧爱"译"jilting"，用"走江湖吃十方的"译"quacks"，则属"拆译"。可以看出，无论是合译还是拆译，都显示了译者对生活的深刻领悟和信手拈来般驾驭母语的本领。

（3）**增译与略译**。比如（见译文段落中粗体部分），"底下""两腮帮子"（原文只是用作形容词的过去分词"rouged"），"引得""不提防"（原文只是表示时间的"while"，按字面至多译成"与此同时"），"我们的""却""脸色"（原文只是"face"），"逗人发笑的""准备""傻"和"形景"都是根据行文、情景或逻辑关系而添加的。另一方面，译者又将原文第二句的"a great quantity of"略去了，这样处理显然很高明，因为随后一连串的"吃喝""哭笑""打架""跳舞"等对此已经有了交代。此外，一些连词（如"while"和"before"，见原文中粗体部分）也给巧妙地给隐去了。

（4）**调整次序**。有两处用心独到的次序调整。第一处调整在第一句的后半句，原文的次序是：① and looks into the Fair, ② a feeling of profound melancholy comes over him ③ in his survey of the bustling place，译文的次序是：③对着底下闹哄哄的市场，①瞧了半晌，②心里不觉悲惨起来。第二处调整在第三分句的后半句，原文的次序是：and ①yokels looking up at ②the tinseled dancers and poor old rugged tumblers, ③ while the light-fingered folk are operating upon their pockets behind，译文的次序是：②跳舞的穿着浑身发亮的衣服，可怜的翻斤斗老头儿涂着两颊帮子胭脂，①引得那些乡下佬睁着眼瞧，③不提防后面就有三只手的家伙在掏他们的口袋。这一调整使得原文暗藏的三层语义关系（跳舞的和翻斤斗的 —— 引得……睁着眼瞧 —— 不提防……）更为清楚，由此可见译者的手段。

（5）**改译和创造性译法**。原文第二句中的"and the contrary"，译者没有照字面翻译，而改为"也有在哭的"，与前面的"也有在笑的"配成对，本段最后一句的前半句"The curtain will be up presently"，译者也没有照字面翻译，而改译为"不久**开场做戏**"，这两处更改都更合乎汉语的行文习惯。第三句括号里的"*other* quacks, plague take them!"，其中"*other*"为斜体，译者没有借用改变字体的方式，而是将隐含的意义用文字传达出来（这些人**偏**和我同行，真该死!），可以说是创造性译法。要译得如此传神，非创造不能（不同的译者，结果可能大不相同，因为原文提供了创造的空间）。第四句中的"noisy"，在英语里本是一个贬义词，但因为有"though"表让步，译者改为褒义词"**热闹**去处"，才能与后面的（原文是"前面的"，这里也做了次序的调整） "not a moral place certainly, **nor a merry** one"承接上去。这种翻译时**合理化**①的做法在许多大译家的作品里常能看到，值得我们学习。将第五句"and Tom Fool"中的"and"改译成"譬如"，采用的也是这种方法。

（6）**其他译法**。原文有三处介词短语："in his survey of the bustling place"，"on the looking out"和"behind the canvas"，译者都将它们译成了动词性短语："**对着**底下闹哄哄的市场"，"**到处巡逻**的警察"，"**回到**后台"，这些都属于"词类的转换"；译者将"not a moral place certainly"译成"却是道德沦亡"，则属于"反面着笔"。另外，最后一句"and he will be turning over his head and heels"，译者用叠词"连连"（"汤姆又会出来**连连**翻斤斗"）翻译原文的进行时态，则很难归类，也可称之为创造性译法。

要译好这一段，真不容易，简直让人眼花缭乱！以上是文学翻译的情形，应

---

① 我们之所以称这种方法为"合理化"，是因为在实际翻译时译者常常会碰到原文不合理的情形，换言之，有时原文本身有瑕疵，比如在逻辑上不够严密。

用文体的翻译又会是怎样呢?请看第二个例子①。

原文:

Article 38

a. Credits should stipulate the type of insurance required and if any, the additional risks which are to be covered. Imprecise terms such as "usual risks" or "customary risks" should not be used; if they are used, banks will accept insurance documents as presented, without responsibility for any risks not being covered.

b. Failing specific stipulations in the credit, banks will accept insurance documents as presented, without responsibility for any risks not being covered.

译文:

第 38 条

a. 信用证应规定所需要保险的类型以及应投保的附加险别。不应使用诸如"通常险别"或"惯常险别"一类含义不明确的条款。如使用了这类条款,银行将接受提交的保险单据,而不**负**任何险别漏保之责。

b. 信用证如无明确规定,银行将接受提交的保险单据,而不负任何险别漏保之责。

这是国际商会第 400 号出版物《跟单信用证统一惯例》(1983 年修订本)第 38 条,属于法律性文献,行文和措辞都极为严谨。翻译这类文献时,不可任意发挥。所附译文已很好地反映了原文的语体风格和措辞特点。但如果仔细对照原文和译文,我们就会发现,译者在"亦步亦趋"的同时,同样也进行了一系列的选择、调整或变通。

(1) 词义的选择。将"risks"和"cover"分别译为专业术语"险别"和"投保"。

(2) 语态的转换。将两个被动语态的句子译成了主动语态。

(3) 词量的增减。译文第一段第二句增加了表示概括的词"一类",译文第

---

① 引自王萍:《外贸应用文大全》,现代出版社 1991 年版,第 629 页。

二段第一句增加了表示条件的"如",译文第一段第一句减去了原文表示可能性的"if any"(如果是汉译英的话,就是"增词"了。这是英语措辞严谨的一个表现)。在两段译文中,还省去了原文中的许多冠词、介词或连词。

(4)词类的转换。如原文两处都使用了介词"without",但译文都改成了汉语的动词"**不负任何险别漏保之责**"。

(5)反面着笔。原文第一段末的"not being covered"这一否定形式,在译文中是以"漏保"这一肯定形式来表达的;原文第二段第一句的"Failing"这一肯定形式,在译文中却是以否定词"无"来表达的。

到此为止,读者自己便可得出结论了。本章拟重点介绍四种翻译技巧。在翻译实践中,人们往往综合运用各种技巧,下面分别论述,仅是为了行文的方便。

第一节 词量的增减

在翻译实践中,词量的增减是一个事物的两个方面,要表达同一个意思,如果英译汉时需要增词,反过来,汉译英时就往往需要减词。词量的增减,指的是根据原文上下文的意思、逻辑关系以及译文语言的句法特点和表达习惯,在翻译时有时增加原文字面没有出现但实际内容已经包含的词,或者减去原文虽有但译文语言表达用不着的词。必须指出的是,词量的增减必须防止两个倾向:一是添枝加叶,任意发挥;二是避难就易,肆意删节。

一、增词法

增词,从理论上说可以增加任何词。根据具体的上下文,可增加动词、形容词、名词或别的词类,但在什么时候增加什么样的词才能恰到好处,而不超出一定的界限,则需要悉心体会。下面试分析几个译例:

1. A book, tight shut, is but a block of paper.
   译文一:一本书,紧紧合上,只是一叠纸。
   译文二:一本书,如果紧紧合上不读,只是一叠纸。
   译文三:一本书,如果紧紧合上不读,只是一叠废纸。
   译文四:闲置之书只是一叠废纸。[①]

[①] 英语原文及译文四转引自张达聪:《翻译之原理与技巧》,(台北)国家书店有限公司1983年版,第259页。此处译文略作修改。

第五章　翻译的重要环节之二：活用技巧

上面同一个句子的 4 个译文，可以体现翻译的不同层次。译文一与原文似乎丝丝入扣，但却显得支离破碎、关系不清、语意不足；译文二增加了"如果……不读"，意思明白无误，只是觉得"言犹未尽"；译文三又增加了一个"废"字，这可是点睛之举。能否译出这个"废"字，是翻译这个句子的关键，也是判断这个译文优劣的一个重要标准。不读的书，不仅是一叠纸，而且是叠废纸。因为如果是叠白纸，还可画出最新最美的图画，只是废纸才是无价值的东西。一个"废"字，说话者的语意才得以充分表达。译文三的不足之处，就是行文拖沓累赘；而译文四则简明扼要，笔酣墨浓了。

2. Success is often just an idea away.
　　译文一：成功往往只是一个念头的距离。
　　译文二：成功往往只是一念之差。
　　译文三：成功**与否**，往往只是一念之差。①

译文一让人看后莫名其妙；译文二改变说法，但仍让人似懂非懂；而译文三只是简简单单增加了一个"与否"，却使人豁然开朗！原句的意思表达得淋漓尽致。

3. Nothing happened in the night.
　　译文一：夜间什么事也没发生。
　　译文二：夜间**倒是风平浪静**，什么事也没发生。②

上面这个句子，如果要译得传神，需要凭借一定的想象力。译文一给人的感觉是"孤孤零零"，似乎与周围的环境毫无关系。试想，若是平常，人们见面时会对你说上这么一句话吗？显然，说这话的时候是处于一个"非常时期"，换言之，说话者和听话者本来预料是要发生什么"异乎寻常"的事情的。译文二增加了一个"倒是"和"风平浪静"，一下就使译文氛围毕现，让人领略到话语的弦外之音。

4. Away flies the arrow!

---

① 英语原文及译文三转引自张达聪：《翻译之原理与技巧》，（台北）国家书店有限公司 1983 年版，第 259 页。
② 转引自《中国翻译》1989 年第 4 期，译文略作修改。

译文一：箭飞走了！

译文二：箭嗖的一声飞走了！（或：嗖——，箭飞走了！）

这是摘自一本翻译专著里的英语句子，原译文是"箭飞走了！"。但试想一下，假如将"箭飞走了！"这个汉语句子回译成英语，不就是"The arrow flies away!"吗？但你再深入想想，作家在这里为什么不使用陈述句而选用倒装句呢？高明的作家，往往造句运字都十分讲究，这样安排想必是有原因的。我们试用增词法，将原句改译。译文二中增加一个象声词，再衬以句末的感叹号，让人感到突如其来，如闻其声，如临其境。这样的译文也许更贴近作者的原意。

5. 有个搭船过江的人，一不小心，将所带的一柄剑，从船边落到江里去了。那人马上在剑落下去的地方，画了个记号。

A man was ferrying across a river. When, by accident, his sword dropped into the water, he immediately carved a notch on the side of the boat to mark the place where his weapon was lost.

这是《刻舟求剑》故事的一部分，表面上看，译文是忠实于原文的，但显然故事的关键没有表达出来，问题在哪儿呢？请仔细对比下面修改后的译文：

A man was ferrying across a river. When, by accident, his sword dropped into the water, he immediately carved a notch on the side of the moving boat to mark the place where his weapon was lost.[①]

原来只是一字之别，但从中却可窥见译者对原文理解的深度和英文表达的非凡功力。

6. Kissinger left the palace encouraged by Thieu's reaction. He failed to understand that the Vietnamese, like other Asians, prefer to avoid direct personal confrontation. Rather than say no, they will often respond with an

---

[①] 引自司徒谈编：*Best Chinese Idioms*，赵书汉、汤博文译，（香港）海峰出版社1986年版，第115页。

ambiguous nod. (Marvin Kalb & Bernard Kalb: *Kissinger*, pp. 364 – 365)①

阮文韶的这种反应,使基辛格离开总统府时感到大有希望。**殊不知**,越南人同其他亚洲人一样,也是极力避免当面与人顶撞的。他们往往只是模棱两可地点点头,而不**轻易**说个"不"字。(齐沛合 译)②

搞英汉对比的人都知道,英语是典型的形合型语言,而汉语是典型的意合型语言。自然也有例外。英语原文中前两个句子之间并没有连接词,但它们之间的关系还可意会。不过在中文译文中,假如不增加这个"殊不知",恐怕你就不知道作者在说什么了。这是非常高明的翻译。后面那个"轻易"也增加得很漂亮。

以上所举例子,均选自文学类书籍,很能说明增词的原理。从这些译例可以看出,任何"增词"都得有一定的理据。下面我们再来看看经贸文献的翻译情况。

如同文学翻译一样,经贸文献翻译的增词现象也是千变万化。有的教材试图将形形色色的增词加以概括和归类,但结果却都有牵强之嫌,因为许多例子都很难说属于某一具体范畴,很可能几种情况兼而有之。但从整体上来说,增词要么为使译文意思明确,要么为使译文结构完整,要么为使译文符合目的语的行文习惯,要么为使译文具有某种修辞或语体色彩,等等。下面的实例可以帮助学习者进一步了解增词的原理。

1. All cash bonus shall be subject to income tax.
   所有现金红利,均需**缴纳**所得税。(根据汉语行文习惯,增加动词)
2. It's more expensive than it was last time but not as good.
   价钱比上次的高,但**质量**却比上次的差。(增补原文省略部分,原句后半句的完整形式应该是: ... but it's not as good as it was last time.)
3. The application of plastics in automobile industry has brought about great increase of the consumption.
   塑料在汽车工业上的使用大大增加了**塑料**的消费量。(增补原文省略部分,以使意思更加清楚)

---

① 阮文韶(Thieu)时任南越总统。基辛格为美国尼克松总统助理兼特使,当时正极力斡旋谋求南北越停战,抽身越南战争。
② 引自马文·卡尔布等:《基辛格》,齐沛合译,生活·读书·新知三联书店1975年版,第558—559页。

4. Commission depends on the quantity of goods ordered.

   佣金的**多少**取决于订货量的**大小**。(增词以使译文语意完整，更合汉语表达习惯)

5. All the multilateral arrangements need to be examined for clauses that restrict the free trade.

   所有多边安排都必须加以审查，以研讨**其中有无**限制自由贸易的条款。(范存恒译，此处译文略作修改。这是一个增词佳例，不增词则难以传达原文的含义)

6. As agreed, the terms of payment for the above orders are letter (s) of credit of 60 days' sight or D/P sight draft.

   双方同意，上述订货货款以60天期信用证或即期付款交单方式支付。(增加概括性词语，以使译文更为具体明确)

7. We have paid the freight and marked the cases "Urgent. For Immediate Delivery".

   我方已付运费，并在箱面标刷了"急件、速运"**字样**。(增词以使句子语气完整)

8. This is to inform you that by mutual consent, the agency contract with Messrs. A. Green & Co. London will cease to exist at the end of this June. We welcome your direct inquiries to our office.

   与伦敦格林公司所签代理合约，经双方同意，将于6月底失效。**因此，从7月初起**，欢迎向我公司直接询购，特此通知。(增译承上启下的词语，以使译文连贯)

9. According to our record, your corporation bought substantial quantity of chemicals from us. Unfortunately the business between us has been interrupted in the last few years.

   根据我们的记录，贵公司**过去**购买我们的化工产品的数量相当可观，可惜近年来业务一度中断了。(增加表示原文时态的词，并与后面的时间形成对照)

10. The fan, with its modern, elegant, bright, and harmoniously coloured design, is an excellent electrical household appliance for cooling purposes on hot summer days.

    本电扇**款式**新颖，**造型**大方，**色彩**鲜艳，**色泽**调和，是炎炎夏日消暑纳凉之家电精品。(修辞性增词，以使译文音节对称，朗朗上口)

11. The shipper shall be liable for all damage caused by such goods to the

ship and/or cargo on board.
如果上述货物对船舶和（或）船上**其他**货物造成任何损害，托运人应负全责。（增词以使译文意思明确，条理清楚）

12. 买卖双方同意按下述条款购买、出售下列商品并签订本合同。
This Contract is made by **and between** the Buyer and the Seller, whereby the Buyer agrees to buy and the Seller agrees to sell the under-mentioned commodity subject to the terms and conditions stipulated below. （增词以使译文严谨。这是英语合同语言的一个特色）

13. 如果每件或每一计算单位的货物的实际价值超过上述协议中所载的申报价值，承运人所负的责任不应超过该申报价值。
Should the actual value of the goods per package or freight unit exceed the declared value stated in the aforesaid agreement, the carrier's liability, **if any**, shall not exceed the declared value. （增词以使译文语气委婉）

14. 此保证金有效期为120天，从19＿＿年＿＿月＿＿日始至19＿＿年＿＿月＿＿日止，过期失效。
This Bond shall be valid for 120 (**ONE HUNDRED AND TWENTY**) days, i. e. from ＿＿, 19 ＿＿, until ＿＿, 19 ＿＿, after which this Bond shall become null and void. （增加括号中的大写数字以使译文严谨，增加"i. e."以使译文连贯）

二、减词法

由于两种语言表达习惯的不同，翻译时如果一字不漏地照搬，往往会显得累赘、拖沓、冗杂或不合行文习惯，甚至产生歧义。采取减词译法可以使译文言简意赅。涉外文书的翻译常有以下几种减词情况：

第一，减去代词，这种情况尤见于外贸信件的翻译。例如：

1. Please let <u>us</u> know the detailed information on your market.
   请告贵方市场详情。
2. We assure <u>you</u> of <u>our</u> prompt attention to this matter.
   我们保证立即处理此事。

第二，减去陈腐或不必要的套话。例如：

1. We <u>take this opportunity</u> to inform you that we are now in a position to

make prompt shipment of the merchandise.

兹奉告，该商品可即期装运。（译文比原文大为简明，除减去了"take this opportunity"这一陈腐的表达外，还省略了3个代词，并用一个"可"字代替了原文中"in a position"这样繁复的表达方式）

2. Enclosed is the technical information on the air compressors. Please <u>do not hesitate</u> to contact us if you require any further information.

兹附上气体压缩机技术资料，若还需其他资料，敬请告知。

第三，减去不言而喻或冗杂的词语。例如：

1. Any expenses accruing from this credit inquiry will be <u>gladly</u> paid upon receipt of your bill.

对此信用咨询所需任何费用，在接到账单后即付。（以"即付"译"will be gladly paid"，言简意赅，恰到好处）

2. <u>On condition</u> that you sign this receipt. I will pay the money.

你在收据上签字，我就付款。（原文是通过连接词来表示"条件"的，而汉语则是通过从句和主句的前后顺序来表达这一关系的）

3. The price of the products should be set according to the price in the international market. It should be fixed by the two parties <u>at a level</u> that will bring profit to both.

产品价格应该根据国际市场的价格，由双方共同商定，须照顾到双方的利益。（译文看似没译"at a level"，但字里行间却含有其意）

4. Part-time waitress applicants who had worked at a job would receive preference <u>over those who had not</u>.

应聘业余女服务员者，有工作经验的优先录用。（如果不作省略，译成"应聘业余女服务员者，有工作经验的比没有工作经验的优先录用"，其中"比没有工作经验的"就纯属多余了）

5. 男女老少咸宜

   suitable for men, women and children

6. 互通有无

   the exchange of needed goods（试比较：the exchange of what one has for what one needs）

从以上译例可以看出，减词译法也是炼词炼句的一种最重要的手段，可以充分显示译文语言的优势。减词译法的情况同样也十分复杂，往往一个句子中多种情况的省略兼而有之，因此很难加以归类，以上编排仅是为了叙述方便。除所列几种情况外，我们可以看出，许多冠词、介词、连词都没有在译文中出现，它们往往都是翻译时的减词对象。

第二节 词类的转换

词类转换是翻译时最为常用的一种变通手段，是突破原文词、句格局，化阻滞通行文的重要方法。许多生硬、别扭、拖沓的欧化中文（英译汉）或中式英文（汉译英）往往都是没有进行词类转换的结果，而若能善于运用词类转换，尤其是英译汉（因为汉译英对译者的外语水平要求很高），常常能起到化腐朽为神奇的效果。

美国总统林肯在葛斯底堡著名的演说词末尾有句话是"…and that government of the people, by the people, for the people…"有人把它译为"**民有、民治、民享的政府**"，原文中有3个介词"of""by""for"分别译成了3个动词"有""治""享"，铿锵有力，言简意赅，是词类转换的绝佳例子。

许多翻译教科书在阐述"词类转换"一节时，将词类转换分成若干类型，如名词转换成动词、副词转换成形容词等。这种做法容易束缚初学者的思想。事实上，从理论上来说，翻译时词类的转换是没有限制的。一个名词在不同的上下文中，或在不同的译者笔下，既可能译成动词，也可能译成副词，或可能译成别的词类，其他词类的转换也无不如此。当然，词类转换有一定的原则，既不违背原文的意思，又有助于译文的流畅。下面试举一些译例，学习者可以从中领悟该技巧的奥妙。

1. We have decided to place <u>a trial order</u> for the following on the terms stated in your letter.
   根据来函条款，我公司决定**试订**下列货物。（名词 → 动词）

2. Your <u>information</u> as to discounts for a large order would be appreciated.
   请**告**大批订货的折扣。（名词 → 动词）

3. Please let us know if our terms are <u>acceptable</u>.
   请告是否**接受**我方条款。（形容词 → 动词）

4. Kindly give our claims your <u>prompt attention</u> and let us have your <u>remittance</u> in due course.

请**立即处理**我方索赔并及时**汇来**赔款。(形容词 → 副词；名词 → 动词；名词 → 动词)

5. Please send us the following <u>by</u> the first steamer sailing for Singapore next month, and draw on us for the invoice amount.

   下列货物请**装**下月第一艘驶往新加坡的班轮，并按发票金额开具汇票向我方收款。(介词 → 动词)

6. The new contract would be <u>good</u> for 5 years.

   该新合同的**有效期**为5年。(形容词 → 名词)

7. We learn that you have been <u>dealers</u> of Chinese products for many years.

   据我们了解，贵公司**经营**中国产品已有多年历史。(名词 → 动词)

8. Weapons are more <u>lethal</u> and more <u>manoeuvrable</u> by many orders of magnitude than they were in the past.

   现代武器的**杀伤力**和**机动性**不知要比旧式武器强多少倍。(范存恒译)(形容词 → 名词)

9. No critic has praised Dryden's prose more aptly. He (Dr. Johnson) said of him that he appeared to have no art other than that of <u>expressing with clearness what he thought with vigor</u>. (W. Somerset Maugham: *Lucidity, Simplicity, Euphony*)

   没有谁比他评论德莱顿的散文更中肯的了。他说，德莱顿的写作艺术看来无非是能**用明晰的语言表达活跃的思想**。(笔者译文)(名词 → 形容词)

词类转换虽无限制，但由于英汉两种语言某些固有的表达特点，在大量实践中，我们也可发现一些规律性的东西。比如在英语中，NP（名词性短语）+ of + NP 这种偏正结构十分常见。而这种偏正结构又往往可以译成汉语的动宾结构。

1. We are <u>exporters of</u> the above goods, having <u>a background of</u> some 30 years.

   我们**出口**上述商品，已经**经营**了三十来年。

2. We hereby register a claim with you for the shortage of 1 000kg in the <u>shipment of</u> chemical fertilizer ex S. S. "Olympia".

   由"奥林匹亚"轮装来的化肥短重1000公斤，我们特此向你们提出索赔。

3. It is certainly a pleasure to have this order from you and we wish you the best of success in your sales promotion of the goods.

   承你方订货，实感荣幸，祝你们**推销**货物圆满成功。

4. The cat, who had been a puzzled observer of these unusual movements, jumped up into Zeena's chair. (Edith Wharton: *Etham Frome*)

   那个猫儿一直**莫名其妙**地在旁边看着这些和平常不同的行动，这个时候一跳跳上细娜的椅子.（吕叔湘 译）

此外，我们也可看出，英汉互译时，名词与动词之间的转换是最为普遍的。英语多用名词，汉语多用动词，了解并充分利用这些特点，无疑有助于提高译文的质量。

第三节　反面着笔

人们在表达同一事物或同一概念时，往往既可以从正面叙述，也可以从反面叙述。英语如此，汉语也是如此。比如说某事做起来"很困难（quite difficult）"，也可改说"很不容易（far from easy）"；说做某事"竭尽全力（do one's utmost）"，也可改说"不遗余力（spare no effort）"；说某个学生成绩"还好（good）"，也可改说"不错（not bad）"；等等。翻译时，这种反译正说或正译反说，我们称之为"反面着笔"。也有人称这种译法为"同义反译"或"正反、反正译法"，反面着笔不仅仅指肯定句与否定句之间的相互转换，还包括使用反义词和从不同角度叙述同一意义等方法。

翻译时为什么要反面着笔呢？归纳起来，其原因主要有下列两种：

一、表达习惯的需要

叙述同一件事或同一概念，有时两种语言的表达方式相差很大，形成相对固定的表达模式，不这般表达，就感觉不顺，不自然。因此，翻译时就必须"客从主"，进行适当的转换。例如：

1. Wet Paint!

   油漆未干！

这是一则公示语，英汉两个句子的意思完全相同，但表达各异。英译"油漆未干"，只能是"Wet Paint"，而不能是"Paint Not Dry"；而汉译只能是"油漆未干",而不能是"湿的油漆"。没有别的理由,习惯而已。

2. Admission by Invitation Only
   非请莫入。(公示语)
3. Keep Upright!
   切勿倒置!(货物装箱标志用语)
4. But that's the beginning of the problem.
   然而,问题还远不止这些。
5. Agreeable Sweetness
   甜而不腻(这是一则食品广告语,若从正面着笔,实难表达,现在反面着笔,意思豁然贯通)
6. <u>If any matter should be added</u> after this contract comes into force, then such a matter shall be agreed upon by both sides through friendly consultations and confirmed by means of exchanging official documents, which shall form <u>an integral part</u> of this contract.

   译文一:本合同生效后,**如还要增加某些事情**,须经双方友好协商同意后,以交换正式文件确认,该文件同样作为合同的一个**有机组成部分**。

   译文二:本合同生效后,**如有未尽事宜**,须经双方友好协商同意后,以交换正式文件确认,该文件应视为本合同**不可分割的一部分**。

比较两个译文,主要区别在于,一个从正面着笔,一个从反面着笔。显然,译文二更合汉语公文语体。

7. We shall be pleased to <u>receive</u> a check from you for the settlement of your account to the end of last month.

   如蒙**寄来**支票结清截至上月底的你方账目,我方将不胜感激。(原文从收函人的角度使用"receive",译文则从发函人的角度使用"寄来")
8. 在收据**尚未签字**前,不得付款。
   Before the receipt <u>has been signed</u>, the money must not be paid.

按照汉语的习惯可以说"在……没有……以前",但是这种说法在英语中不合乎习惯,上面这句如果照字面直译:Before the receipt has <u>not</u> been signed , the money must not be paid. 那就令人费解了。

二、立场、语气的需要

"还好（good）"与"不错（not bad）"等类似成对的表达法，实际上是有区别的。一个句子是从正面着笔，还是从反面着笔，往往传递了说话者微妙的情感和立场，而反面着笔对表达强弱轻重的语气很起作用。因此，在翻译时（尤其是文学翻译），该技巧被广泛运用。例如：

9. ...and I had not known you a month before I felt that you were the last man in the world whom I could ever be prevailed on to marry. (Jane Austen: *Pride and Prejudice*)

   认识你还没有一个月，我就觉得像你这样一个人，哪怕天下的男人死光了，我也不愿嫁给你。（王科一 译，此处译文略作修改）

这是一个反面着笔的佳译，女主人公说话时的情状跃然纸上。

10. If I had not lost my watch!

    我把手表给丢了，真倒霉！①

这又是一个大胆使用反面着笔的佳译。原句是个虚拟句，许多人对这个句型都相当熟悉，一看到上面这个句子，很可能就译成"要是我没有把手表丢了该有多好啊！"。若是如此，又是句经典的欧化中文。我们平时在这种场合是这样说话的吗？该用手表的时候，手表却丢了，试想说话者当时是多么懊恼！译文用"真倒霉"而不用"该有多好啊"，更能体现说话者的心情和语气。

11. Though they extol the virtues of the peaceful life, only one of them has ever gone to live in the country and he was back in town within six months. (L. G. Alexander: *New Concept English*)

    虽然他们对那宁静的生活赞不绝口，事实上，他们中仅有一人真正在农村生活过，然而此人**不到半年**就返回了城市。

---

① 转引自张梅岗等：《实用翻译教程》（上册），湖北教育出版社1993年版，第243页，译文略作修改。

原文中的"within six months"如果正面着笔，就会译成"在6个月之内"。"6个月"时间，可以说是段"较长的时间"，也可以说是段"很短的时间"，这要看对什么事情而言。原文作者显然是反对那种"乡村生活优于城市生活"的观点。为了体现作者这一立场，故采用反面着笔，并将"6个月"改成"半年"，两者意思虽然一样，但语感却大不相同。

12. We are not completely satisfied with your manner of doing business.
    译文一：我们**不十分满意**贵方做生意的态度。
    译文二：贵方做生意的态度**有待改进**。

原文如果将"completely"拿走，就是一句令人十分尴尬的生硬说法，可见该词在缓和语气上的作用。译文一从正面着笔，似乎太直；译文二从反面着笔，因此更能体现说话者的用心和口吻。

13. While trade is good, money is very tight at present.
    译文一：尽管生意**很好**，但目前资金仍十分短缺。
    译文二：尽管生意**不错**，但目前资金仍十分短缺。

这里说话者所强调的并不是生意"好"，而是资金严重"不足"，故译文二更符合说话者的立场。

14. The Autumn Report also touched upon the serious economic problems that would crop up.
    译文一：秋季报告**也顺便提到了**可能出现的严重经济问题。
    译文二：秋季报告**也没有回避**可能出现的严重经济问题。

两个译文不同的措辞反映了截然不同的态度，哪个更为合适，则要看具体情况了。这个例子也告诉我们，译者的情感也有可能影响翻译的结果。

当然，也有这样的情况，有的句子既可正面着笔，也可反面着笔，两者很难说有多少差别，有时只是个人的偏爱，或在具体的上下文中某种译法好些。但懂得多种表达方法也是种长处，到用时就有了选择的余地。例如：

15. If you find our terms and conditions agreeable, please cable us your order for our confirmation.

译文一：**若同意**我方条款，请即来电订货，以便我方确认。

译文二：对我方条款**如无异议**，请即来电订货，以便我方确认。

16. The highest discount we can allow on this article is 10%.

    译文一：对这件商品，我们最多只能给10%**的折扣**。

    译文二：对这件商品，我们最多只能**打九折**。

17. 供不应求

    译文一：Supply falls short of demand.

    译文二：The supply is inadequate to meet the demand.

    译文三：Demand exceeds supply.

    （以上3个译文都属正确，但采用反面着笔的译文三最为简洁）

18. Now <u>I am a grandfather</u>, Mr. Brownlow. But I remember these dinners in the old days. (R. U. Joyce：*A Question of Ethics*)

    现在，**我已经抱了孙子了**，白朗劳先生，可是我忘不了早年的那些个小宴。（吕叔湘 译，见《吕叔湘译文三种》，这样处理很新鲜，当然，也可以正面着笔，译成："我已经是做爷爷的人了。"）

另外，值得一提的是，英语中有许多**隐性否定词**（即形式肯定但意义否定的词），在译成汉语时，往往可采用反面着笔，转换成否定句。最常见的隐性否定词有：fail/failure, in the absence of, the last, beyond, be prevented from, too…to, instead of, rather than 等。下面试举几例：

19. This is <u>the last place</u> where I expected to meet you.

    我**怎么也没有**想到会在这里见到你。

20. We are sorry about <u>the delay in sending</u> you the revised specifications.

    迟迟未告你方修正规格，甚歉。

21. We regret to learn that you have <u>failed</u> in obtaining the licence.

    得知你方**未能**获得许可证，深表遗憾。

22. We believe the quality of this material will <u>not fail</u> in answering your purpose.

    我们相信此货的质量**一定**符合你方要求。（此句为否定句，故可转换成肯定句）

23. Owing to <u>the absence of</u> any news from you, we have sold the goods elsewhere.

    由于**没有得到**你方任何消息，我们已将该货另售别处。

24. The seeds are to be free from admixture.

 油籽**不得**含有杂质。

25. In the event of force majeure or any other contingencies beyond our control, we shall not be held responsible for the late delivery or non-delivery of the goods.

 如果发生不可抗力事件，或我们**无法**控制的任何其他意外事故，我方对迟交或不交货概不负责。

翻译技巧是前人经验的总结，学习翻译技巧，可以帮助我们认识翻译的本质。本章的举例只在说明原理，远非完备。实际操作时，情况千差万别，所附译文，也仅供参考，并非一定得如此这般地增减或转换。搞翻译，可说是八仙过海，各显神通。总的来说，要提高翻译水平，首先要提高运用语言的能力，并在正确思想的指导下进行大量的翻译实践，唯如此，才能融会贯通各种翻译技巧。

【练习题】
请综合运用各种翻译技巧将下列句子译成汉语。请在认真修改自己的译文之后，再对照书后提供的参考译文。

1. If once virtue is lost, all is lost.
2. If water is cold enough, it changes to ice.
3. There is no clue to the identity of the murderer.
4. Ice is not so dense as water and therefore it floats.
5. The wrong power-line connection will damage the motor.
6. Those waitresses recruited shall undergo a three-to-six-month probationary period.
7. The man was wearing a black suit, a pair of black shoes, a black beard, and a troubled look.
8. Evidently he had the first quality of an angler, which is not to measure the pleasure by the catch.
9. That substances expand when heated and contract when cooled is a common physical phenomenon.
10. Energy losses range from 10% to 20% when fuels are used directly to 65% to 70% for electrical generation and transmission.
11. In the absence of a settlement through negotiation, the case under dispute can be submitted to arbitration.

12. We regret our inability to accept your claim because the cases, when being loaded, left nothing to be desired.
13. We have come to depend on the availability of three principal kinds of transportation: land, sea, and air.
14. From him I learned that a good politician is marked to a great extent by his sense of timing. He says the right thing at the right moment.　（Marvin Kalb & Bernard Kalb: *Kissinger*）
15. Nor do I teach because I think I know answers, or because I have knowledge I feel compelled to share. Sometimes I am amazed that my students actually take notes on what I say in class! (Peter G. Beidler: *Why I Teach*)

第六章
翻译的重要环节之三：方法相宜

在翻译方法上，向来有直译与意译之分。人们对于这两种翻译方法，毁誉俱有，褒贬不一，一直存在着争议。译界为什么对直译与意译如此兴趣不衰呢？这至少可说明两点：第一，直译与意译是翻译的两大根本方法，方法是否相宜，将直接影响译文的质量；第二，关于直译与意译，还有许多理论问题尚待解决。纵观许多学者有关直译与意译的论述，这种争议的主要原因，似乎是人们对于直译与意译的界说不尽相同。往往出现这样的情况，主张意译者把某些生搬硬套、佶屈聱牙的死译贬之为直译，因而否定直译；而主张直译者则将某些添枝加叶、肆意增删的胡译斥之为意译，因而否定意译。结果，直译和意译的本来面目都给扭曲了。事实上，直译与死译，意译与胡译，应严格区分开来，决不可混为一谈。在直译与意译的论战中，总的说来，直译受到了更多的质疑，所以，严复以来的翻译理论大多"重神似而不重形似"。究其根本原因，那就是，什么是"直译"？其答案比之于什么是"意译"更多种多样和游移不定。即使在直译派之间，人们对于直译的理解也可能大相径庭。比如说，多数人认为，既忠实于原文的内容，又保留原文形式的译文是直译。但何谓"形式"？人们又难于达成一致的意见，比如说，改变原文的词序，算不算改变了原文的形式？

然而，如果从句子结构上来讨论（即以句子结构改变的大小为标准），任何翻译都只是一个"度"的问题，即它必定处于直译与意译这个连续体的某个位置上，要么偏向直译，要么偏向意译，也可能重叠，这种关系可图示如下：

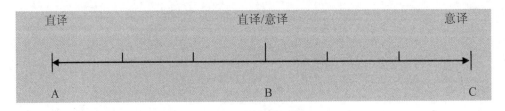

图 6-1　直译与意译的关系

因此，关于直译与意译的定义，为避免不必要的繁杂和分歧，可以只从习语

（成语）层面来讨论，不牵涉句法层面。

第一节 直译法

那么，从习语层面来讨论，什么是直译呢？本书采用一种说法，即在符合译文语言规范的前提下（自然在许多时候是不得不改变词序和词性的），既保持原文的内容，同时又不改变其修辞或措辞特点（如形象、比喻、民族或地方特色等）的译文为直译。下面的例子可视为典型的直译。

black market	黑市
go into the red	出现赤字
dollar diplomacy	金元外交
pillar industry	支柱产业
two-way trade	双向贸易（即进出口贸易）
the open-door policy	门户开放政策
stony-hearted	铁石心肠的
to use both the stick and the carrot	胡萝卜加大棒
Among the blind the one-eyed man is king.	盲人国里，独眼为王。
铁饭碗	iron rice-bowl
三角债	triangle debts
拳头产品	fist products（此译尚有争议）
米袋子菜篮子工程	the project of rice bags and vegetable baskets
一寸光阴一寸金	An inch of time is an inch of gold.
（深圳）世界之窗	Window of the World（注：其中的介词"of"，正确的写法应该是"on"。）

第二节 意译法

什么又是意译呢？简单地说，保持原文的内容，但不能同时兼顾其修辞特点，不得不改变说法的译文为意译。由于地理、风俗、历史等差异，对同一事物，各民族的语言都有其独特的表达方式。直译有时佶屈聱牙，有时晦涩难懂，有时拖沓累赘，有时引起歧义，有时则不能充分传达原文的神韵，凡此种种情况，我们就采取意译。意译并不等于随心所欲地偏离原文。意译只是用不同的译文形式，表达与原文相同的内容。例如：

technical know-how	专有技术
talk shop all the time	三句话不离本行
a land of honey and milk	鱼米之乡
a Napoleon of finance	金融巨头
to get the upper hand	占上风
to use both the stick and the carrot	软硬兼施
penny wise, pound foolish	小事聪明，大事糊涂
五湖四海	all corners of the country
拳头产品	competitive products / quality products
十全大补酒	far-reaching tonic wine
吃不了兜着走	to be in serious trouble

第三节　直译与意译的关系

从理论上说，无论是直译，还是意译，在根本上都没有问题。原想直译，结果变成了死译；原想意译，结果变成了胡译。对于初学者来说，分寸拿不准，这也是常有的事，但这不是直译或意译本身的毛病，而是译者经验不足和驾驭语言的能力问题。

翻译常识告诉我们，直译和意译是翻译的两大根本方法。任何从事实际翻译的人，都不可能自始至终在任何场合只使用直译，或只使用意译一种方法。因此，我们主张，直译和意译为互补的关系，即不宜直译的地方，我们就采取意译，不宜意译的地方，我们就采取直译。**强调直译和意译为互补的两种翻译方法**(complementary methods)**，就是说，两种方法不分彼此，同等重要**。在实际操作时，可能要经过尝试直译——意译——直译的反复比较，最后选定较为贴切的译法。有的学者指出，直译法是主要的或基本的翻译方法（the primary or basic method），意译法是次要的或补充的翻译方法（the secondary or supplementary method）。我们认为这样措辞来区分并不妥当。因为，这又势必要循环到直译与意译谁是谁非的问题。直译与意译的互补关系可图示如下：

第六章 翻译的重要环节之三：方法相宜

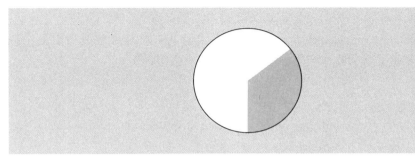

图 6-2 直译与意译的互补关系

为了说明直译与意译的关系，下面请看行文翻译中的一些实例：

1. Exporting to a certain number of countries is made difficult by the quantity of <u>red tape</u>.
   意译：政府部门的**繁文缛节**使得向某些国家的出口贸易困难重重。

这句中的"red tape"，如果直译成"红带子"，势必令读者莫名其妙。原来，英国的律师和政府官员习惯用红带子捆扎文件，后来，"red tape"就引申为"公事手续"上的形式主义。这里将"the quantity of red tape"意译为政府部门的"繁文缛节"，颇为允当。

2. Earnings per share have <u>mushroomed</u> at a 34% annual compounded rate.
   意译：若以复利计算，则每股的利益每年**激增**了34%。

"mushroom"一词作动词用，比喻像蘑菇般地迅速增长。如果直译，一定费解。汉语里的"雨后春笋"近似此意，但使用场合不同，故也不便套用。

3. We are very sorry to disappoint you, but hope you will understand that <u>stock offers are a touch-and-go kind of things</u>.
   意译：使你们失望，十分抱歉，但望你们能够理解，销售现货**成交快，一有买主，就会立即脱手**。[①]

[①] 引自诸葛霖：《外贸实用英语手册》，商务印书馆1981年版，第267页。

· 105 ·

"touch-and-go",一眼看去,就是汉语的"一触即发",但原意却是"risky; uncertain whether it will happen or succeed(冒风险的;对结果或成功缺乏把握的)"。译者根据上下文略作变通,很好地传达了原文的含义。

4. Business is a two-way street and to keep it open in both directions there must be a sense that both partners are doing their utmost to ensure a steady growth in each other's markets.

直译:生意好比**双行道**,伙伴双方都必须明白,只有竭尽全力确保对方向自己市场的出口稳步增长,道路的两个方向才得以畅通。

意译+直译:做生意得**有来有往**,伙伴双方都必须明白,只有竭尽全力确保对方向自己市场的出口稳步增长,**道路的两个方向**才得以畅通。

"two-way street"是城市交通方面人们十分熟悉的一个词语,将它直译为"双行道",其喻义十分清楚,然而将它一拆为二,意译为"有来有往",也令人耳目一新。两种译法各有长处,可根据上下文选用。

5. Among so many well-dressed and cultured people, the country girl felt like a fish out of water.

意译:同这么多穿着体面而又有教养的人在一起,这位乡下姑娘感到**很不自在**。①

直译:同这么多穿着体面、举止文雅的人在一起,这位乡下姑娘感到自己**就像是离水之鱼**。

直译+意译:这位乡下姑娘待在这一大帮穿着体面、举止文雅的人中间**感到难受极了**,**就像鱼待在岸上**。

意译失去了原文的韵味,不如直译。直译的理由是:鱼离不开水,是一种自然现象,中西方皆然。至于鱼离水之后的滋味如何,可让读者自己去体会。第三种译法是作者的一位老师建议的,色彩斑斓,从反面着笔,也很新鲜。

6. 现在合同已签了,真是**木已成舟**, **生米煮成了熟饭**,只好如此了。

---

① 引自张培基、喻云根等:《英汉翻译教程》,上海外语教育出版社1980年版,第169-170页。

意译：As the contract has been signed, what's done is done and can't be undone.①

这句话如果照字面直译，译文想必冗长，而且外国人也不可能看明白。这里采取意译，既精炼，又达意。

7. We feel that if as you say you have no problem selling these gloves elsewhere, you have our blessing to do so.
   意译：我们感到，如照你方所说，你方能在别处售出这批手套，那我们真是**求之不得**。

原来"blessing"是"赐福"的意思，若照字面翻译文理不通，现改用反面着笔，意思和语气都出来了。

8. 男男女女都**七嘴八舌**地说出他们的惦记和盼念。
   直译：With seven mouths and eight tongues, all were talking together. They tried to tell Hsiao how they had missed him.②
9. 方案一公布，大家就**七嘴八舌**地议论开了。
   意译：Publication of the draft plan touched off a lively discussion with everybody eager to put in a word.

在汉语里，许多成语中包含有数字，如一举两得、三心二意，其中有些是实指，有些是虚指，翻译时应严格区分开来。显然，例8中"七嘴八舌"的"七"与"八"是虚指，不宜直译。

10. 正如一些传媒指出的，对中央决定了的事，有的人借口情况特殊不尽力去办；有的人用取巧的办法搞所谓"变通"；有的人虚应敷衍，只说不做；有的人搞"上有政策，下有对策"。很明显，这样的步调不一致，国家再好的政策也行不通。因此，近一时期高层人士一再强调要树立全国一盘棋的思想，反对分散主义和地方主义。
    Some media have given this observation: With respect to central

---

① 引自陈浩然：《外贸英语翻译》，中国对外经济贸易出版社1987年版，第244页。
② 转引自张培基：《习语汉译英研究》（修订本），商务印书馆1979年版，第51页。

government decisions, some people **give only half-hearted effort** for their execution under the pretext of their special local conditions; some get around the issue in the name of "flexibility"; some **pay lip service but make no move**; still others resort to the practice that the higher authorities have their policies while the localities have their "counter-measures". Evidently, such discordance in action will only spell failure for State policies however well-formulated they may be. That is why highly-placed officials have been crying for **treating local work as part of coordinated move in "a game on the national chessboard"** and opposing decentralism and regionalism. (*China Economic News*)

这个译文忠实、流畅，以直译为主，但巧妙地穿插了意译，并多处发挥了译文语言的优势（如half-hearted effort，pay lip service）。其中"全国一盘棋"的处理方法叫人叹服，看来在这个上下文中，采取纯粹的意译或直译是很难达到这种效果的。

从上述译例可以看出，直译与意译是翻译习语的主要方法。习语包括成语、俗语、谚语、歇后语、格言等。在翻译史上，习语的翻译大致经历了三个阶段：纯意译——意直结合偏重意译——直译为主，意译为辅。这种越来越偏重直译的趋势是有一定根据的，因为习语反映了一个民族的风土人情，更是该语言修辞手段的集中体现，而直译则能加强各民族的文化交流，还能将原文中别具一格的词汇及新鲜生动的表现形式介绍到另一种语言中去，从而增强译文语言的表现力。

由英语（或通过第三种语言转译）直译成汉语的典型例子如：

cold war	冷战
iron curtain	铁幕
golden age	黄金时代
chain reactions	连锁反应
to show one's cards	摊牌
to be armed to the teeth	武装到牙齿

由汉语直译成英语的典型例子如：

纸老虎	paper tiger
赤脚医生	barefoot doctor

第六章　翻译的重要环节之三：方法相宜

丢脸	to lose face
保面子	to save face
打破饭碗	to break one's rice bowl
走后门	to get in by the back door（此说尚有争议）

各种语言里都存在大量的外来语，越是大的语种越是如此。时间长了，许多外来语都被译文语言同化了，以至于人们感觉不到它们是"外来"的，甚至要弄清楚某个词语的来历还需专门的考据工夫。我们强调直译与意译为互补的两种翻译方法，不分彼此，同等重要，但从积极的意义上说，在翻译习语的时候，应该解放思想，大胆创新，先试直译，不相宜，再改换意译。《毛泽东选集》英译本中有许多成功的直译，为我们树立了榜样。例如：

竭泽而渔	draining the pond to get all the fish
削足适履	cutting the feet to fit the shoes
君子动口不动手	A gentlemen uses his tongue, not his fists.
吃一堑长一智	a fall into the pit, a gain in your wit
树欲静而风不止	The tree may prefer calm, but the wind will not subside.

按理说，这些汉语习语，在英语中有的是不难找到近似的习语采用归化的译法的（如用"to kill the goose that lays the golden eggs"来译"竭泽而渔"）。但译者没有轻易放弃直译，这种探索的精神值得赞赏。

除直译与意译两种主要的翻译方法外，还可综合使用各种翻译方法。例如：

1. 下海　　　plunging into the sea of business
2. 盲人瞎马　a blind man on a blind horse——rushing headlong to disaster
3. 瞎子点灯白费蜡

    (a) like lighting a candle for a blind man ——a sheer waste

    (b) as useless as a blind man lighting a candle

4. IBM was all set to go into full production for the orders that were destined for the USSR, then the Government embargo hit them <u>like a bolt out of the blue</u>.

    IBM 公司已经做好全面生产苏联订单的准备，可是，政府突然下令禁止输出，这消息对 IBM 公司**无异是个晴天霹雳**。（张信雄译，p.54）

5. My brother is a lawyer and my sister is a doctor. They say I am <u>the black</u>

sheep of the family because I decided to be an actor.

我哥哥是律师，我姐姐是医生，而我却决定当演员，因此，他们说我是**家里的黑羊，没出息**。①

例 1 中，plunging into the sea 为直译，of business 为意译。例 2、例 3（a）和例 5 为"歇后语"式（或称"解释"性）翻译，前面部分为直译，后面部分为意译。例 3（b）很巧妙，把喻义镶嵌在短语中间，这相当于直译的一个注脚。在例 4 中，英语的"like a bolt out of the blue"和汉语成语"晴天霹雳"，在设喻和用法上都十分吻合，这是采用"借用习语"的方法。

第四节 直译与意译的条件②

翻译界多数人认同这么一个说法，即"能直译时就直译，不能直译时就意译"。这种说法对翻译习语尤其适应。这样有保留地说，是因为如果牵涉到句法层面，也有人会说"能意译时就意译，不能意译时就直译"，两种说法都可能说得通，看你怎样理解了。当然，"能"与"不能"直译，会因人而异的，你认为"不能"，若换一个高手，却可能柳暗花明。比如上文提到的"君子动口不动手"的英语译文"A gentlemen uses his tongue, not his fists."，相信多数人都会认为译得很妙，但如果这句话给替换两个词语，给译成"A gentlemen uses his mouth, not his hands."，效果就大大打折扣了。

主张先尝试直译，是从丰富本族语和促进文化交流的角度来说的。但毕竟外

---

① black sheep 源自谚语 There is a black sheep in every flock. 是说在白的羊群中常会有因基因变异产出黑羊的情形，牧羊人往往不喜欢黑羊，一是因为黑羊不那么值钱，一是因为迷信黑羊是不吉利的征兆。后引申为在每一个团体中至少会有一个名声不好的成员。现在有不少英汉词典将这个词条注译为"害群之马"或"败家子"，应该说是不准确的。根据 *Brewer's Dictionary of Phrase and Fable*, the black sheep of the family 指的是给家里人带来耻辱的成员。这里采用直译加解释，只是权宜和过渡的做法，能否被接受有待时间的检验，但汉语中已经有类似的例子，比如我们已经接受了将"dark horse"翻译成"黑马"，当然也许是因为后者出现的频率更高的缘故。

② 本节归纳了五条参考原则，其中第二、三、四条是在陈文伯的启发下（见参考文献）写成的，第五条原则"优选法"是本书作者的一家之言。五条原则均是编者 1991 年硕士论文中的部分成果，一直没有正式发表，但近十多年来这方面的研究并没有多少进展，现趁本书修订的机会增加一节，就正于同行。

第六章　翻译的重要环节之三：方法相宜

来语中新的表现法有些难免与本族语格格不入。因此，研究直译与意译的条件就显得十分有意义。下面归纳了几条"原则"（使用"原则"一词，只是为了行文的方便），可用来判断是否采用直译，供参考。

原则一，判断是否易懂。应该承认，这种判断有时是很主观的。但各种语言中都包含一些人类普适的道理（universals），从一种语言直接转换成另一种语言，不会造成多少理解上的困难，如上文提到的 "like a fish out of water"，英语中还有 "throw the baby out with the bathwater" "A bird in the hand is worth two in the bush."，等等。又比如汉语中的"水中捞月""缘木求鱼""画饼充饥""鸡蛋碰石头"等等，像这样的成语可以大胆地尝试直译。

原则二，判断典故的"隐"与"显"。许多成语都有出典，有些典故与日常生活关系密切，往往还能在大脑里唤起生动的图像，我们称这样的典故为显性典故，如英语中的 "Judas kiss" "Achilles heel"，汉语中的"东施效颦""守株待兔"；相反，有些成语的典故在逐渐隐退（甚至看不出有什么出典），日常使用多取其抽象意义，我们称这样的典故为隐性典故，如英语中的 "blow hot and cold" 和汉语中的"朝三暮四""南柯一梦"。通常情况下，处理隐性典故时更适宜采用意译，而处理显性典故时则更适宜采用直译。但典故的"隐"与"显"在不同的上下文中是不尽相同的，也就是说它们有可能相互转换。例如，汉语中的"自相矛盾"，多数情况可以把它当作隐性典故处理，比如简单地意译为 "to be self-contradictory"，但假如是"以子之矛，陷子之盾，何如？"，就是一个十足的显性典故了，这时只有直译其中的"矛"和"盾"了，比如译成 "But what if you should use one of your spears to pierce one of your shields?"。

原则三，判断比喻的"死"与"活"。语言随时代而发展，人们的审美情趣也会因事过境迁和生活环境的改变而变化，原来新鲜活泼的比喻到了今天也许就变得了无生气，甚至莫名其妙了，因此比喻有"死"和"活"之分别。死的比喻如英语中的 "to rain cats and dogs" 和 "as cool as a cucumber"，汉语中的"粗枝大叶""大刀阔斧"。翻译这样死的比喻只能意译；如果是活的比喻，比如英语中的 "a dark horse" 和汉语中的"老鼠过街，人人喊打"，一般应尽可能地直译。成语中的比喻与该语言的文化密不可分。因此，就某个特定成语的翻译，究竟应直译还是意译，学者间常存在分歧。比如 "as timid as a rabbit" 的汉译（该译成"胆小如鼠"呢，还是译成"胆小如兔"呢？）就曾经引起过争论。

原则四，判断成语中成分的"虚"与"实"。成语中常常包含一些数字，而这些数字有的是虚指，有的是实指，应仔细分辨。"实"数多数情况自然更适合"实"译（或称直译），而"虚"数只能译其大意（或称意译）。在汉语中这类成语尤其多。例如"七嘴八舌"（上文已经分析到）"三番五次""五颜六色""三心二意""一穷二白"。这些成语中的数字均为虚数。如果将"虚"数译"实"了，就可能闹笑话。比如汉语中的"女大十八变"，如果译"实"了，不就成了妖怪了吗（就像孙悟空有七十二变）？又如"一举两得""一着不慎，满盘皆输""十之八九"，这些成语中的数字都是"实"数（或可视为"实"数）。但判断成语中数字的"虚"与"实"并不总是那么容易，比如"三头六臂"中的数字是"虚"还是"实"呢？同是"女大十八变"，在特定的上下文中也可能"实"译（比如在引语中），还有的成语中的数字既可当作实数，也可当作虚数。请看下列对"十五个吊桶打水，七上八下"的不同处理：

1. 他这一阵心头如十五个吊桶打水，七上八下，老是宁静不下来。（周而复《上海的早晨》第一部第五十二章，北京外文出版社，1962）①
   His mind was in a turmoil these days and he was quite unable to think straight. （A. C. Barnes 译）
2. 那胡正卿心头"十五个吊桶打水，七上八下"。（施耐庵、罗贯中《水浒》第二十六回）② Hu Cheng-qing was very much upset by this, and his heart was beating like fifteen buckets being hurriedly lowered into a well for water — eight going down while seven were coming up. （Jackson 译）

原则五，判断表达方式的"优"与"劣"。这种方法或称"**优选法**"。首先需要说明的是，这里所说的"优"与"劣"，并不是说语言有优劣之分，而是说在表现某一具体情景时不同语言在遣词造句上的高下。在英汉两种语言中有许多表达同一意义的成语，但它们在设喻或表达方式上大不相同，在翻译时，有人采用直译（或称"异化"的方法），有人则采用意译（或称"归化"的方法），没有明确的标准。"**优选法**"可以提供这方面的帮助。下面举例说明：

1. 十赊不如一现。
   A bird in the hand is worth two in the bush.

在这一组里，汉语的表达就远不如英语。因此，汉译英时，只需简单地借用英语这个现成的说法，但英译汉时，一般情况下显然不会借用汉语这个过时的表

---

① 转引自张培基：《习语汉译英研究》（修订本），商务印书馆1979年版，第118页。
② 转引自陈文伯：《英语成语与汉语成语》，外语教学与研究出版社1982年版，第338页。

达法，而会采用直译，比如现在多数英汉词典的译文就是直译："双鸟在林，不如一鸟在手"。

2. spend money like water
   挥金如土

在这一组里，英语的表现手法更贴近当代生活，尤其是我们很容易联想到自来水的使用，因此直译成"花钱如（哗哗的）流水"显得很自然。但如果倒过来把"挥金如土"直译成英语，就会很费解。

3. look for a needle in haystack
   大海捞针

在这一组里，汉语的表达优于英语的表达，因为汉语的表达更为夸张，如果直译成英语，英美人自然能够领会，甚至欣然接纳，从而丰富英语的表达方式。

4. the crocodile's tears
   猫哭耗子
5. to kill two birds with one stone
   一箭双雕
6. There is no smoke without fire.
   无风不起浪。

以上 3 组又是另一番情形，英语和汉语都使用了形象，但使用的是不同的形象，很难说孰"优"孰"劣"，只能说英语的表达，其起源更贴近英美人的生活，汉语的表达，其起源更贴近中国人的生活。如果相互直译，并不是不可接受，但每种语言都具有相当的"排异"功能，因此多数人更乐于接受本土的说法。这也可以部分地解释为什么在英译汉的小说中（或讨论中西文化的书籍中）我们可以见到"鳄鱼的眼泪""一石二鸟""无火不生烟"的说法，但在中国人自己写文章时却几乎总是使用"猫哭耗子""一箭双雕"和"无风不起浪"。

7. to be beaten black and blue
   被打得青一块紫一块

有意思的是，在这一组里，英语和汉语都使用了颜色词，但为什么英语选择了"黑"与"蓝"，而汉语却选择了"青"与"紫"，恐怕都是偶然使成，因此也无法分辨出其间的高下。如果相互直译势必严重违反译入语的用词习惯，这个时候采用"入乡随俗"的办法也许是唯一的选择。

8. one in a thousand
   百里挑一

在这一组里，英语和汉语的意思完全一致，虽然夸张的程度不同。根据"约定俗成"的原则，我们仍用"百里挑一"，当然，根据本书提出的"优选法"原则，译成"千里挑一"也未尝不可。但值得注意的是，如果是汉译英，最好译成"one in a thousand"，而不宜译成"one in a hundred"，这不仅仅因为后者违背了上述两条原则，还因为它可能产生言外之意。英语和汉语中类似的语对还有很多。例如，on second thoughts（三思）。如果把"三思而后行"翻译成英语，我们可以写成"think twice before you act"，当然也可以写成"think thrice before you act"。

中西习语的互译研究是一个十分有趣和复杂的课题，远非几条原则所能概括。人们在翻译习语时，遇到译入语中有近似的习语的情况，往往有归化的倾向，即喜欢借用现成的说法，但有几点值得注意：

（1）当心似是而非的习语。英汉两种语言中有许多习语在表面上看十分对等，而实际上却相去甚远，或根本不对等。例如，"eat one's words"与"食言"，"dog-eat-dog"与"狗咬狗"，"love me, love my dog"与"爱屋及乌"。

（2）避免借用民族或地方色彩过浓的习语。例如，不宜将"Many heads are better than one."译成"三个臭皮匠，胜过诸葛亮。"；也不宜将"Everybody's business is nobody's business."译成"三个和尚没水吃。"。换句话说，可以将民族色彩浓郁的习语译成中性的习语，而不是相反的方向。

（3）注意习语的一词多义和使用场合。例如，上文提到英语里的"a bolt out of the blue"可褒可贬，但汉语里的"晴天霹雳"只用来形容不好的事情。再如，"at sixes and sevens"与"乱七八糟"，"a black sheep"与"害群之马"，"Strike while the iron is still hot."与"趁热打铁"，"to fan the flame"与"煽风点火"都不完全对等。

总之，在英汉两种语言里，意义和使用场合都相等的习语（equivalents）不是没有，如"to burn one's boats"与"破釜沉舟"，但这种情况毕竟太少了。较多的是两者相当（corresponding），而绝大部分是既不相等，又不相当。因此，借用习语应十分小心。在行文翻译时，实际的情形是，英语习语往往不一定能译成汉语习语，而非习语的英语词语倒有可能译成汉语习语，反之亦然。

从以上直译与意译的讨论中，基本可以得出结论：直译与意译没有好坏之分，只是职能不同，运用的场合不同。直译与意译，好比译者的两条腿，缺一不可，只要运用得当，可以左右逢源，相得益彰。

【练习题】

I. 试选用适当的翻译方法，将下列汉语习语译成英语，并讨论其得失。

1. 赴汤蹈火
2. 画饼充饥
3. 三从四德
4. 三头六臂
5. 水中捞月
6. 先礼后兵
7. 易如反掌
8. 缘木求鱼
9. 走马观花
10. 像只落汤鸡
11. 急得像热锅上的蚂蚁
12. 老鼠过街，人人喊打
13. 谋事在人，成事在天
14. 跑了和尚，跑不了庙
15. 三天打鱼，两天晒网
16. 一着不慎，满盘皆输

II. 试选用适当的翻译方法，将下列英语习语译成汉语，并讨论其得失。

1. a bull in a china shop
2. a skeleton in the closet
3. a walking skeleton
4. Achilles' heel
5. as cool as a cucumber
6. as poor as a church mouse
7. at a stone's throw

8. Care killed the cat.

9. child's play

10. like a cat on hot bricks

11. Pandora's box

12. Spare the rod and spoil the child.

13. A wise fox will never rob his neighbor's hen-roost.

14. Every lover sees a thousand graces in the beloved object.

15. One boy is a boy, two boys half a boy, three boys no boy.

III. 下面是"一个和尚挑水吃，两个和尚抬水吃，三个和尚没水吃"的三种译文，试分析它们的得失及其原因。

One monk, two buckets; two monks, one bucket; three monks, no bucket, no water—more hands, less work done. （引自邓炎昌、刘润清：《语言与文化》，外语教学与研究出版社1989年版，第52页）

"Didn't you ever hear the saying? A lone monk brings his bucket of water to drink, two monks carry their bucket of water jointly, but when three monks are together, there is no water at all." （艾芜：《百炼成钢》英译本 *Steeled and Tempered*，北京外文出版社，1961）

One monk got to carry two buckets of water with one pole as the temple needs water; but two monks carry only one bucket with the same pole; if there are three monks, nobody is willing to go and bring the needed water. (T. K. Ann: *Cracking the Chinese Puzzles*, Vol. 1, p. 142)

Special Topics 实用编

第七章
外贸信函的特点与翻译

　　国际贸易涉及大量的外贸信函,这些外贸信函是公司、企业间商务往来最重要的沟通手段。一封外贸信函写得好不好,往往可以决定一桩生意的成败。请先看下面的信函①:

Dear Ms. Obermann,

Although thousands of orders come in at this time of the year, the ones that get the warmest greetings are those from loyal customers, like you. You've given us your Christmas order for many years. Every transaction we've had with you has been exceptionally pleasant.

Undoubtedly, at this time of the year you are snowed under with catalogs from many mail order houses. It would be nice to think that our catalog was the only one that claimed your attention, but of course that isn't so, nor would it be good business on your part. Evidently, you read at least one other catalog this year. The Desk Clocks you specified are not carried by us.

I've done some checking for you. The clock you ordered is offered by Joe Stow & Co., 212, 98th Street in Keokok, Iowa. If you feel that the Stow clocks will serve your purpose best, that's where you are.

But, Ms. Obermann, I hope you will take another look at the Desk Clock on page 131 of our catalog. You'll be particularly interested in Model 41. Model 41 is almost identical to the clock you selected, with two exceptions. Our

---

① 引自 Ferd Nauheim, *Letter Perfect*, U.S.A: Van Nostrand Reinhold, 1982, p. 206。

clock has a radium dial and swivel base, giving your customers added convenience. The prices of the two clocks are almost the same. The additional values in Model 41 add only $1.50 a unit to your cost. In case your copy of the catalog has been discarded, I'm enclosing another one for you.

Desk Clocks seem to be unusually popular this year and Model 41 has been selling immensely well. To be certain that your needs will be covered. I'm putting aside the 100 you want. I'll hold them until I hear from you.

After you've read this letter, please phone me collect to tell me whether you want the folks on your Christmas list to have Model 41. Your clocks are sitting on the shipping room "hold" counter, all prettied up in their sparkling Christmas wrappings. They're ready to go to you the moment you say "Okay." I'll be grateful if you'll give me your decision by Friday of this week.

Sincerely,

笔者参考译文：
奥伯曼女士：

您好！

每年此时，尽管成千上万的订单蜂拥而至，但像您这样忠实的客户的订单是最受欢迎的。多年来承蒙发来圣诞订单，与您的每次生意都尤为称心如意。想必此时您又忙于应付雪片般飞至的函购商品目录，真希望我们的目录是唯一引起您注意的一份。然而那当然不可能。若果真如此，从您的角度来说，缺乏比较，也未必是件好事。显然，您今年至少翻阅了一份其他公司的商品目录，因为您所订的座钟并不在我们的目录之列。

经我们查核，您所订的座钟是由依阿华州凯克市第98街212号的乔·斯托公司经营。假如斯托公司的座钟正合您意，当然就没有必要选择别的了。

但是，奥伯曼女士，我们仍希望您不妨再翻阅一下我们目录中131页上所介绍的座钟。相信您会对其中的41型尤为青睐。41型座钟与您选定的座钟相比，款式不但几乎完全相同，还另具两大特色：一是夜光指示，二是可旋底座。这给您的顾客带来额外便利。两种座钟的价格也相差无几。41型座钟额外的功能仅使其单价略增1.50美元。以防您手头没有留存我公司目录，现随函奉上另一份。

今年的座钟生意似乎特别看好，而我们的41型更是十分畅销，为了确保您的需求，我会特意为您留下100只，专候回复！

阅信后请打受话方付款电话，告知您是否选定41型座钟作为馈赠亲友的圣诞礼品。给您的这批座钟都饰以闪亮的圣诞包装，正存列在发货仓的"特留"专柜，只要您说声"行"，我们立刻就给您发货。如蒙在本周五前得悉您的决定，我们将不胜感激！

　　此致
敬礼！

这是一封十分诚恳而又格外讲究技巧的外贸信函（要翻译得语气相当，也不是一件容易的事），恐怕没有谁收到这样的信能不为之感动。一位涉外文秘人员若有如此才干一定是该公司的福气。有关外贸信函写作的书籍很多，本章拟从翻译的角度对其格式、称呼、措辞、摘译等方面加以阐述。

第一节　格　式　问　题

在格式上，中、英外贸信函存在很大的差异。中文外贸信函与日常生活信函没有多大区别；而英文外贸信函，与日常生活信函相比，却增加了许多特殊部分。英语是世界贸易的主要语言，因此，英语外贸信函历史悠久、内容完整、自成系统。为了与国际贸易惯例协调，以及分类归档诸多便利，外贸信函汉译英时，应依照英文外贸信函正式程式；外贸信函英译汉时，可保留英文信函正式程式，也可套用我国传统格式，具体做法，可依据每个公司的习惯决定。

英文外贸信函的格式，在长期形成的过程中，主要有三种：

(1) **绝对平头式**（Block Form）。分段时（包括日期和签名）都从左边开始，每行对齐，成一垂直线。打字时不必考虑左边的留空，段与段之间要用双行距。（见图7-1）

(2) **缩行式**（Indented Form）。地址及其他需分行的地方，下行比上行缩进2~3个英文字母，日期位于信笺的右上端，签名位于中间偏右下方。每段开始一般缩进3~4个英文字母。

(3) **折中式**（Semi-block Form）。大致与缩行式相似，所不同的是，姓名、地址不用逐行缩进成斜向排列。混合采用上述两种格式，故称折中式。

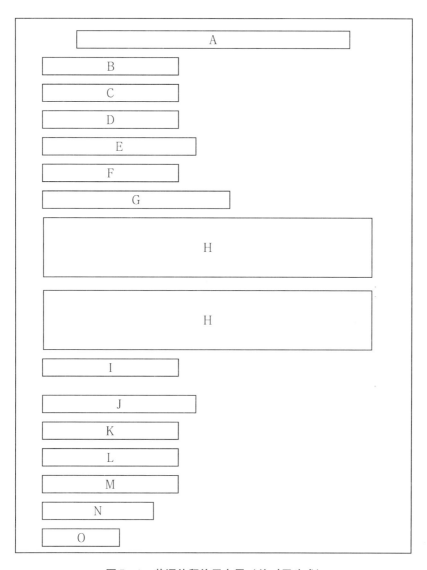

图 7-1 英语外贸信函布局（绝对平头式）

布局说明：

A = Letterhead 信头（通常印在信笺上，包括公司名称、地址，也有的包括电话号码、电传或电报挂号、简短广告语等，位置可居中、居左或居右）

B = Date 日期

C = Reference No.（Our Ref. /Your Ref.）查询号（包括我方查询号或贵方查询号）

D = Inside Address 封内地址（包括收信人姓名及地址）

E = Attention 经办

F = Salutation 称呼

G = Subject 事由（或"Caption:"，或信笺上已打好的"Re:"符号）
H = Body of Letter 正文
I = Complimentary Close 结尾礼辞
J = The Name of the Company Represented by the Writer 写信人所代表之公司名称
K = Signature 签名（签名下方为打字署名及职务）
L = Initials 口述人/打字员姓名首字母，如 RGM/mwe 或 RGM：mwe
M = Enclosure（Encl. 或 Enc.）附件
N = C. C.（Carbon Copy）抄送
O = P. S.（Postscript）附言

以上 A—O 共 15 个部分，是英文外贸信函中可能的组成部分。实际的外贸信函，因具体情况不同，往往不是那么完整。应注意的是，汉译英时，中文原件可能没有"查询号""经办"或"事由"部分。公司的涉外文秘人员，在可能的情况下，有责任和义务在翻译时补上，这样有利于加快信函的传递，为公司赢得时间。

采用哪种格式，取决于个人偏好，但作为公司或企业，所有对外贸易信函的格式最好能保持一致。本节为节省篇幅，仅图解绝对平头式。以下是两封英文外贸信函的实例，可作汉译英时格式之参考。

英语外贸信函实例 1[①]

Diadem Office Supplies Ltd.

Star Chamber

119 – 125 Cambridge Road

Reading

19 November 2003

Ref. ORD / 056

Gripsure Office Machinery Co., Ltd.

244 High Street West

East Ealing

LONDON W14

[①] 本节例 1 和例 2 均选自 Bryan Allen，*The Business Letter*. London：Evans Brothers Limited，1978。此处略作调整。

第七章 外贸信函的特点与翻译

(Attention of Mr. R. G. Miles)
Dear Mr. Miles:

Delays in Delivery

Following my telephone call today, I am sorry to inform you that the 15 "Gripsure" Miniature Electric Typewriters we ordered on 25 September have not yet been received.

As they are urgently needed for export we should be glad if you could arrange for their dispatch without delay.

Six of these typewriters have been promised to an important overseas customer and are due to leave London Airport on Saturday 27 November.

Will you please let us know by return when we can expect the delivery?

Yours Sincerely,

Diadem Office Supplies Ltd.

Brian O'Behan
BRIAN O'BEHAN
Sales Manager

英语外贸信函实例 2

Gripsure Office Machinery Co. Ltd.
Founded 1887
244 High Street West
East Ealing
London W14

20 November 2003

Your Ref. ORD / 056
Our Ref: CONT / 203

Mr. Brian O'Behan
Sales Manager
Diadem Office Supplies Ltd
119 – 125 Cambridge Road
READING

Dear Mr. O'Behan:

Thank you for your letter ORD / 056 of 19 November. We very much regret that we have been unable to complete your order.

The delay was due to a strike of delivery drivers but we are happy to inform you that this has been settled.

We are working through the backlog of orders and will deliver six of our "Gripsure" Miniature Electric Typewriters on Friday 26 November. The balance will follow in seven days.

We apologize for the inconvenience caused to you by this delay.

Yours sincerely,

R. G. Miles

R. G. MILES
Production Manager
RGM/ mwe

第二节　称呼与结尾礼辞问题

英语外贸信函最常见的称呼有:
Dear Sirs:
Dear Madam:
My dear Sir:

Dear Mr. Brown:

My dear Mrs. Hartley:

Gentlemen:

有几点应注意：

（1）对女性的称呼，无论是已婚还是未婚，都统称 Dear Madam，切忌使用 Dear Miss。

（2）英国人偏爱使用 Dear Sirs，而美国人偏爱使用 Gentlemen。

（3）Gentlemen 仅用复数形式，不用单数形式 Gentleman，也不用 Dear Gentlemen。

（4）My dear Mrs. Hartley 并不意味着比 Dear Mrs. Hartley 更亲密，相反，前者是种更为正式的称呼。

英文外贸信函里的称呼往往是和结尾礼辞紧密相关的。英语外贸信函中最常见的结尾礼辞有：

Yours truly,

Yours sincerely,

Yours faithfully,

如何将这些看似简单的称呼和结尾礼辞翻译成贴切的汉语，仍不可掉以轻心。最糟糕的莫过于按英汉词典里的单词翻译将"Dear Madam"译成"亲爱的夫人"，而将"Yours sincerely"译成"您的忠诚的"。这样的称呼和结尾与公函格格不入。

我们认为，英文外贸信函中的"Dear"，是一种对收信人的**尊称**，只不过是种礼节、俗套而已；而在汉语的书信称呼中，"亲爱的"却是一种**昵称**，仅用于家人或情侣之间。因此，"Dear"和"亲爱的"在外贸信函里的称呼并不等值。英语外贸信函的结尾礼辞"Yours sincerely"等，也只是程式上的要求，同样不能按字面直译。

那么该如何翻译英语外贸信函中的称呼和结尾礼辞呢？从许许多多英汉对照的有关外贸信函的书籍看来，其做法不尽相同。如果称呼是泛称"Gentlemen"或"Dear Sirs"，或"My dear Sirs"，有的作者干脆回避不译，画条底线"＿＿＿＿＿"了之；有的则简单地译作"先生"，略过"Dear"或"My dear"；还有很大部分将称呼中的"Dear"译成了"亲爱的"；还有的则沿用我国旧式书信中的启事语，如"敬启者""谨启者"；也有采用我国旧式书信中的敬称，如"执事先生""台鉴"；如果是确称具体的人，如"Dear Mr. Yang"，则译为"杨先生台鉴"。除"台鉴"外，类似的敬辞还有"惠鉴""玉鉴""钧鉴""大鉴""尊鉴""勋鉴"等。必须指出的是，这些汉语旧式书信中敬辞的使用，还得根据对象（是长辈还是平辈，是政界还是商界等）加以选择。

这种翻译时套用汉语旧式书信称呼的做法尤其多见于港台出版的书籍，是否可取，值得商榷。但有一点可以肯定，那就是至少比译成"亲爱的某某先生""亲爱的某某女士"之类的更符合汉语的表达习惯。另一方面，我们也必须指出，这种旧式书信的称呼，主要是在上了年纪、受过良好教育的人之间使用。作为公司的文秘人员，如果你要翻译的信函是给这类人看的话，那么这种译法就比较得体。否则，现在的年轻人并不喜欢这样的称呼，这种措辞显然已不合时宜，倒不如按现代书信的格式，简单地译成："某某先生（某某女士／某某同志）：您好！"

汉译英的情况也值得注意。在汉语的书信称呼里，如果是寄给个人的，人们往往习惯于在收信人的姓氏后加上头衔或职业名称，如"李教授""王老师""张局长""肖经理"等。但在英语信函中，只有少数几个显要的头衔才可用于称呼，如"Professor（教授）""Doctor（博士）""President（总统）""Mayor（市长）"。因此，"布朗教授"，在称呼里就可英译为"Dear Professor Brown"，但"布朗老师""布朗局长""布朗经理"等，只好按照英语的表达习惯，统称为"Dear Mr. Brown"。如果收信人是已婚女性，则译为"Dear Mrs. Brown"。

至于英文外贸信函的结尾礼辞，事实上只不过是写信人对收信人的一种谦称，不必照字面直译为"您的忠诚的"或"您的忠实的"，这不合语体，也不合汉语的习惯。我国公函中有相当的礼辞，如"谨启""谨上""敬上"，可不妨套用。如果是较为正式的公函，也可分写两行，译为"此致／敬礼！"。

如果是回信，也可译成"×××谨复"。在信函本身有比较得体的结束语的情况下，这种结尾礼辞甚至可以忽略不译。另外，某些单证（如信用证）里也常见到"Yours faithfully"，这种套语，在这种场合译成"谨此"也很得体。

如果是汉译英，解决的办法就更为简单，什么"谨启""谨上""敬上"之类，则可根据信头的称呼，统统还原为"Yours sincerely"或"Yours truly"等。但有一点值得注意，即汉语信尾的那些礼辞是可有可无的，但英文信函的结尾礼辞则是不可缺少的组成部分。因此，汉语原文信尾即使没有使用像"谨启""谨上""敬上"之类，也必须相应地增译"Yours sincerely"或"Yours truly"等。此外，英语外贸信函的结尾常常使用一些套语。例如：

1. Your favourable information will be appreciated.
2. Your early reply will be highly appreciated.
3. Awaiting your immediate reply.

有的学生可能将上面3句分别译成：

1. 我们期望得到你们的好消息。

2. 我们将会十分感激你们的早日答复。
3. 等候你们的早日回信。

这些译文虽说没有曲解原文的意思,但却行文啰嗦,有失汉语信函的语言风格。实际上,汉语也有类似的客套话,言简意赅,译者可充分发挥译文语言的优势。比如将上面3句分别译成:

1. 恭候佳音!
2. 如蒙早复,不胜感激!
3. 候复!(或:请即复!)

第三节 措 辞 问 题

外贸信函源远流长,风格独具。其最大的特点就是行文庄重、措辞婉约、套语迭出、自成系统。因此,无论是英译汉,还是汉译英,外贸信函的翻译,质量的好坏,很大程度上取决于译者能否做到遣词运字的得体,语气句调的相仿。下面就几个典型的问题进行探讨。

一、汉语"请"字的英译

在中文外贸信函里,凡是向对方提出某种要求,出于礼貌往往都得用上个"请"字,因此,"请"字也许可以说是中文外贸信函使用频率最高的词语。

说到汉语里的"请"字,凡是懂点英语的人,都会联想到"please"。随手翻开汉英或英汉词典,"请"与"please"也似乎是绝对相等之词。但翻译并不如此简单,若不知变通,或图省力,每次"对号入座",定出差错。高明的译者,必是依据具体的情景,采用不同的词汇和句法手段。请看下面各种不同情况下"请"字的译法:

1. 使用"please":
  请告我方交货日期与付款要求。
  <u>Please</u> let us know your delivery date and conditions of payment.
2. 使用"kindly":
  请将两份提单由不同的邮班寄来,同时开来30天汇票以便承兑。
  <u>Kindly</u> send us 2 Bills of Lading by separate posts, together with your draft

at 30 days for acceptance.

3. 使用"be appreciated"：

   请从速办理本订单为荷。

   Your prompt attention to this order would <u>be highly appreciated</u>.

4. 使用"It would be appreciated if you would..."结构：

   请寄贵公司产品图解目录一份为荷。

   <u>It would be appreciated if you would</u> send us an illustrated catalog of your manufactures.

5. 使用"We shall appreciate it if you will..."结构：

   请报50吨花生实盘。

   <u>We shall appreciate it if you will</u> make us a firm offer for 50 tons of peanuts.

6. 使用"We shall (should) be grateful (或 obliged) if you would (或 can/will/ could)"结构：

   请告你方市场详情。

   <u>We shall be grateful / obliged if you can</u> provide us with all possible information on your market.

7. 使用疑问句：

   这是我们的包装设计，请转给厂方，供他们参考。

   This is our design for the packing. Could you possibly give it to the manufacturers for their reference?

8. 使用主动语态：

   根据双方协议条款，我们已开具了该批船货的即期汇票，通过此处中国银行转去，请见票即付。

   According to the terms agreed upon, we have drawn on you at sight against shipment through Bank of China here. We would ask you to protect the draft upon presentation.

9. 使用被动语态：

   恳请你方尽力早日解决这一悬而未决的问题。

   You're kindly requested to exert your best effort to wind up the long-standing issue at an early date.

10. 根据上下文省译：

    请即复（信尾套语）。

    Awaiting your immediate reply.

11. 使用"wish":

敬请注意，我方客户急需合同货物。

We <u>wish</u> to draw your attention to the fact that our clients are in urgent need of the contracted goods.

以上"请"字的许多译例可以说明几个问题：一是"请"字在不同的上下文中，其意思有细微区别，比如要求程度的强弱、表达方式的直接与间接、措辞或句式的正式与否，翻译前须悉心领会；二是"请"字的适应范围很大，英译汉时，许多客套话不必照字面直译，可考虑能否译成汉语的"请"字；三是"请"字的英译，不必千篇一律。

二、敬辞与谦辞

除了"请 / please"之外，中英文外贸信函还大量使用其他套语。涉及对方时，常用敬辞，提到自己时，则常用谦辞。汉语里常用的敬辞有"台鉴""您""惠函""惠顾""赐复""奉告""恭候""承蒙""敬悉""贵方""贵公司""阁下"等，常见的谦辞有"过奖""不敢当""愚见""拙作""寒舍""敝人""敝公司"等。英语里也有敬、谦词语，敬辞如"Dear Mr. Brown"中的"Dear"，以及"favour""kindly"等；谦辞如"be appreciated""be obliged""be grateful"以及信尾落款的"Sincerely yours"等。

中英两种语言在措辞上虽然都有敬、谦之分，但它们在大多数场合下都不对应，或表达习惯不尽相同，因此给英汉互译带来许多问题。比如，在汉语里，提到对方，第二人称有"你"和"您"之分；但在英语里，有时也需要用比较尊敬的语气，却不论对方年龄多大，级别或地位多高，"you"就是"you"，无须改用什么特殊的词语，也不应加什么词缀。又如，在汉语里，提到对方公司，可说"你公司"，也可说"贵公司"，提到自己的公司，可说"我公司"，也可说"敝公司"；但在英语里只能是"your company"和"our company"。翻译时如何处理这些问题呢？通过大量译例的分析，可归纳出三种主要方法：

一是"套译"。所谓"套译"，就是用一种语言里的礼貌词语或套语来翻译另一种语言里相当的礼貌词语或套语，而不必按原文句式逐词直译，如前面谈到的信头称呼与信尾礼辞的翻译就属这种情况。请再看几个例子：

1. We should <u>appreciate</u> a prompt reply.

   如蒙即复，不胜感激。

2. We <u>shall be very much obliged</u> if you will quote us the price for this model.

如蒙开报这种型号的价格，**不胜感激**。

3. Your immediate attention <u>would be appreciated</u>.

   请即办理**为荷**。

4. 从十月二十一日来函**欣悉**，贵公司决定按我公司十月十一日报价大量订购多种产品。

   We are <u>glad to learn</u> from your letter of 21 October that you have decided to place a large order for a number of the items included in our quotation of 11 October. （中英两种表达方式不谋而合）

二是"略译"。相对来说，汉语里的敬辞与谦辞比英语里的敬辞和谦辞多得多。因此，汉译英时，遇到敬辞或谦辞很难找到合适的对应词时，只好略去不译，勉强直译，反而觉得不自然。请看下面几个译例：

1. 根据贵方来函要求，现寄上**敝**公司产品目录一份。

   According to the request in your letter, we are sending you a catalog of our products.

2. **承蒙惠函**祝贺本人当选本公司董事长一事，特表谢忱。

   Thank you very much for your letter congratulating me on my election as president of this Corporation.

3. 再次感谢你方订货，今后如需零件，请再**惠顾**。

   Thank you again for your order. Please keep us in mind whenever you need more parts.

英译汉有时也可略去某些毫无意义的套语：

1. We are looking forward <u>to the pleasure of</u> hearing from you.

   请即复！

2. If you are not interested in <u>taking advantage of</u> the offerings on the list, please <u>be good enough</u> to forward it to some of the firms with which you have established business relationships.

   如果你们无意购买我方产品，烦请将货单转寄与贵公司有业务往来的其他商行。

三是译"语气"。在中英文两种语言敬谦词语不对应的情况下，翻译时最好的办法也许是复制原文语气。比如，汉语的"请你在这签字"，可以英译为"Please sign here."。但如果说得客气些："**请您**在这签字"，就可译为"Would you please sign here?"。汉语中的"您"在译文里虽然没有体现在词汇上，仍然是用"you"，但却体现在整个句子的语气上。许多学生不懂这种**错位补偿**的方法，所以许多译文显得生硬。比如，有的学生可能把这个英文句子："In reply to your inquiry of 25th March, we are pleased to offer you the following."翻译成："现答复你们 3 月 25 日来信询问，我们很高兴地向你们报盘如下。"这个翻译紧扣原文字面，说通也通，但却不能算是个好的译文。原文里的"are pleased"并非"高兴不高兴"的问题，只不过是客套而已，因此没有必要字字对译。如果仿制原文语气，我们就可译成"兹复贵方 3 月 25 日询价，并报盘如下"。译文省去了"are pleased"，但却把"your inquiry"译成了"**贵方询价**"。整个译文，不仅意思正确，并且语气吻合。再分析下面一些译例：

1. We <u>are pleased to inform</u> you that goods have been dispatched today.
   货物今日业已启运，特此奉告。（使用中文敬辞，将"be pleased to inform"译成"奉告"）
2. <u>Please</u> accept my <u>heart-felt</u> appreciation for your patronage and cooperation.
   承蒙贵公司惠顾与合作，本人谨表谢忱。（译文虽未直译"Please"和"heart-felt"，但字里行间却充分体现了原文恭敬虔诚的语气）
3. We hope to <u>have the pleasure of</u> serving you in the near future.
   我们希望在不久的将来，能为贵方效劳。（使用敬谦词语"贵方"与"效劳"来补译"have the pleasure of"之语气）

敬谦词语的处理，除上面谈到的外，还应注意以下两点：

（1）语言是活的、发展的，应尽量避免使用一些陈腐的词语，如英语里的"favor（=letter/order）""your esteemed letter"；汉语里的"阁下""昨悉大函""笑纳""顿首"等。

（2）使用谦辞时应注意分寸，既要彬彬有礼，又要不卑不亢。应坚决摒弃使用像"beg"这样有损人格、有损国格的词语。对外业务中提到自己时，过去在汉语里常用"敝人""敝公司"等。现在汉译英时，可忽略其谦辞成分，若英译汉则可采取折中的办法。例如：

1. 对**敝公司** 15 周年纪念典礼，承蒙拨出宝贵时间出席，再次向您致谢。
   This is to thank you again for taking the time and trouble to join us in

celebrating our 15th anniversary.

2. We handle various kinds of hardware products.

    本公司经营各种五金产品。

3. We hereby engage that payment will be duly made against documents presented in conformity with terms of this credit.

    本行兹保证若所交单证符合本信用证条款，本行即予付款。

三、其他婉转词语的使用

俗话说"和气生财"。这是生意人的金科玉律。因此，无论是英文外贸信函还是中文外贸信函，措辞都十分讲究分寸、得体，避免刺激对方，即使是向对方抱怨，甚至索赔，也须彬彬有礼。请看下面的例子，注意画线部分：

1. 兹通知，有关信用证业已开出。

    We wish to advise you that the relative L/C has been established.

2. 十分抱歉，我们暂时不能接受贵方报盘。

    We regret that we are not in a position to accept your offer.

3. 你方必须按合同规定的期限将货装上"东风轮"，否则，**万一出现空舱**，空舱费将由你方负责。

    You must deliver the goods on board the S. S. "East Wind" within the time limit as stipulated in our contract, otherwise dead freight, if any, should be borne by you.

4. I'm afraid we can't accept your counter-bid.

    很抱歉，我们无法接受你方还盘。

5. I'm afraid we can't come to terms if you won't give us 3% discount.

    如果不给3%的折扣，我们恐怕很难成交。

6. We presume that there must be some reason for your having trouble with this article.

    我方产品给你们带来麻烦，谅必事出有因。

像以上句子中画底线的词语，在外贸信函中随处可见，从意义的角度说，都不是必不可少的，但有了它们，就像机器上了润滑油，可以将贸易摩擦减少到最低限度。因此，在起草或英汉互译外贸信函时，在语气方面适当增减变通，是非常有必要的。

此外，要翻译好外贸信函，自然还需具备一定的经贸知识和熟悉相关的习惯表达，这不是本章的任务。再者，外贸信函属于公文，措辞应尽可能庄重，避免过多地使用口语词语，有关要点，请参阅第八章第五节。

第四节　摘译问题

在实际工作中，多数情况，文秘人员不需要从头到尾将外语信函翻译成汉语，而只需摘译，这对翻译人员和信函使用者来说，都节省大量时间。摘译信函应注意以下几个方面：

（1）译者必须通读信函全文，对有疑问处必须查阅有关此事的往返信函，或请教承办过此事的人员。摘译须内容完整，交代清楚信函的来龙去脉，做到一目了然。

（2）摘译应包括所有主要事实细节，如时间、地址、支付条件、产品规格等。应特别注意的是，信函的重要内容除包括在信函正文外，还常常出现在信函正文后的"附言"里。

（3）摘译的长短取决于信函的内容和使用者的要求，短的可用一两句话概括，长的需用一两段加以归纳。

（4）摘译信函不必拘泥原文的词句，但务必与事实相符，语气吻合。

试比较下列英文信函的两个译文：

ROBIN REDGRAVE[①]

Lincoln Meadows, Apt. 4

320 Sterling Street

Lyndon City, TX 75212

November 15, 2001

Mr. Thomas Ireland

Vice President for Public Relations

Global Vision, Inc.

---

① 引自 Jacqueline Trace. *Style and Strategy of the Business Letter*. New Jersey：Prentice-Hall, Inc., 1985, p. 36, 此处略作调整。

3200 Jefferson Blvd.
Reagansville, CA 92040

Dear Mr. Ireland:

Will you please send me some information about Global Vision's semi-rigid, gas-permeable lenses?

In a recent *Fortune* article (October 10, 2001) on new contact lens technology, I read that your company has developed and marketed this new lens. I have been wearing hard contacts for ten years but want to switch to a softer, more comfortable lens. Because I have astigmatism, however, the traditional soft lens doesn't fit my needs. Your new lens, according to the *Fortune* article, can be shaped to correct for astigmatism.

I will be thankful for any information you can send. In addition, I would like answers to the following questions:

Can they be worn during the night, i.e., are they designed for extended wear?
What has been the success rate for wearers so far?
What is the price to the consumer?
Has a bifocal been designed for this type of lens?
Where are the lenses being distributed? Is there a distributor in my area?

Since my optometrist is uninformed about your new lens, I will greatly appreciate your help.

Sincerely yours,

Robin Redgrave

(M's) Robin Redgrave

全译：

罗宾·雷德格雷夫

得克萨斯州（75212）林敦市
史特林大街 320 号 林肯草坪 4 号公寓

爱尔兰先生：

  您好！

  我很想了解一些有关环球眼镜公司半硬式、可透气隐形眼镜的情况。

  在最近一期《财富》杂志上（2001 年 10 月 10 日版），我读到一篇介绍新型隐形眼镜的文章，得知贵公司研制并在市场上推出了这种新型眼镜。我戴硬式眼镜已有 10 年之久，现在想换一种更为柔软、舒适的镜片。但因我患有散光，而传统的软式隐形眼镜又不适合于我。根据《财富》杂志上的那篇文章，贵公司的新式眼镜可以矫正散光。

  如蒙提供任何信息，我将十分感激。此外，我还想了解如下几个具体问题：

1. 该眼镜能否夜间也不取下，即是否为"长戴型"设计？
2. 目前为止，散光治愈率有多高？
3. 零售价多少？
4. 是否为双焦设计？
5. 该眼镜哪里有售？我居住区有无经销商？

因为我的配镜师对你们的新型眼镜不甚了解，如蒙帮助，我将十分感激。

  此致
敬礼！

罗宾·雷德格雷夫（女士）
2001 年 11 月 15 日

摘译：

罗宾·雷德格雷夫
得克萨斯州（75212）林敦市
史特林大街320号 林肯草坪4号公寓

爱尔兰先生：
　　您好！
　　我很想了解一些有关环球眼镜公司半硬式、可透气隐形眼镜的情况。
　　该眼镜能否夜间也不取下，即是否为"长戴型"设计？
　　目前为止，散光治愈率有多高？
　　零售价多少？
　　是否为双焦设计？
　　该眼镜哪里有售？我居住区有无经销商？
　　如蒙帮助，我将十分感激。

　　此致
敬礼！

罗宾·雷德格雷夫（女士）
2001年11月15日

　　无论是全译还是摘译，一般来说，信头都应全译，这有助于信函使用者了解信的全过程，当然，自己的地址不必翻译。摘译常用第一人称，语气更为真切。如果是老客户，双方都相当熟悉，信头也可免译。
　　摘译也可用第三人称，以摘要形式译出。现以本章第一节所附两封英文外贸信函为例分别摘译如下：

信函一摘译

来函时间：2003年11月19日
收件时间：_____
贵方查询号：ORD/056

王冠办公设备供应公司催交15台"格别优"小型电动打字机，其中6台须于11月27日前交货，并要求即刻回函，明确交货时间。

信函二摘译

来函时间：2003年11月20日
收件时间：_____
我方查询号：ORD/056
贵方查询号：CONT/203

"格别优"办公设备有限公司回函，告因装运司机罢工致交货误期，并保证6台"格别优"小型电动打字机将于11月26日交货，其余数将于7天后补足。

附录：外贸信函常用缩略语

一、地址常用缩略语

Apt.	Apartment	Rd.	Road
Ave.	Avenue	Sq.	Square
Bldg.	Building	St.	Street
Blvd.	Boulevard	Ter.	Territory
Dr.	Drive		

二、美国州名缩略语（与邮政编码连用）[①]

1. AL	Alabama		27. MT	Montana
2. AK	Alaska		28. NE	Nebraska
3. AZ	Arizona		29. NV	Nevada
4. AR	Arkansas		30. NH	New Hampshire
5. CA	California		31. NJ	New Jersey
6. CO	Colorado		32. NM	New Mexico
7. CT	Connecticut		33. NY	New York
8. DE	Delaware		34. NC	North Carolina
9. DC	District of Columbia		35. ND	North Dakota
10. FL	Florida		36. OH	Ohio
11. GA	Georgia		37. OK	Oklahoma
12. HI	Hawaii		38. OR	Oregon
13. ID	Idaho		39. PA	Pennsylvania
14. IL	Illinois		40. RI	Rhode Island
15. IN	Indiana		41. SC	South Carolina
16. IA	Iowa		42. SD	South Dakota
17. KS	Kansas		43. TN	Tennessee
18. KY	Kentucky		44. TX	Texas
19. LA	Louisiana		45. UT	Utah
20. ME	Maine		46. VT	Vermont
21. MD	Maryland		47. VA	Virginia
22. MA	Massachusetts		48. WA	Washington
23. MI	Michigan		49. WV	West Virginia
24. MN	Minnesota		50. WI	Wisconsin
25. MS	Mississippi		51. WY	Wyoming
26. MO	Missouri			

[①] 选自 Bryan Allen, *The Business Letter*, London: Evans Brothers Limited, 1978.

第七章 外贸信函的特点与翻译

【练习题】

Ⅰ. 注意外贸信函措辞庄重、婉约的特点，将下列句子翻译成英语。

1. 请告贵公司贸易条款。
2. 承蒙大力推销我方拖鞋，不胜感激！
3. 请将下列货品尽快寄至上述地址，谢谢。
4. 兹通知，标题货物已于昨日由"和平"轮装出。
5. 现随寄我方销售合同第 HN38 号一式两份，请查收。
6. 请托运人特别注意本提单内与该货保险效力有关的免责事项和条款。
7. 现另邮我方最新产品目录及价目单。希望价格和质量均适合你方需要。
8. 承蒙建议做我方代理，但因我们之间尚不十分熟悉，不如待日后做开交易，再谈此事为宜。
9. 贵公司 2005 年 8 月 31 日的传真函敬悉。感谢你们合作的诚意，我厂将以积极的态度早日促成合作的到来。
10. 兹附上我方第 5368 号形式发票一式两份；计 500 辆 "永久牌" 自行车，1993 年 10 月交货。务请注意，该形式发票有效期至 1993 年 9 月 1 日止。

Ⅱ. 注意外贸信函措辞庄重、婉约的特点，将下列句子翻译成汉语。

1. While we appreciate what you stated in your letter of Dec. 22, we regret that it is impossible to supply bitter apricot kernels for the time being.
2. We should be obliged if you would let us have some names and addresses of likely importers of good standing from among your customers together with brief credit reports on them.
3. We have received your letter of 2nd March, with a price-list of your products enclosed therein.
4. We are pleased to inform you that we have booked shipping space for our Order No. 4265 of chemical fertilizer on S. S "Peace" with ETA the 15th May.
5. The smallest order we can fill for the goods is 1 000 yards. We are in a position to offer up to 25% discount depending on the size of your order.
6. Enclosed are our latest catalogs and price-list. Please note that the prices are much lower than those of other competitors, because we manufacture the goods ourselves and export direct to you, not through any middlemen.
7. Herewith we have pleasure in handing you an order for immediate shipment of 100 bales of Merino Wool.
8. Claims, if any, must be made within 30 days after the arrival of the goods at the

destination, after which no claims will be entertained.

9. Thank you very much for your letter of June 5 with samples and price-list. We have made our choice and take pleasure in enclosing our Order No. 368.

10. We would appreciate your sending us a catalogue of your Rubber Boots together with terms of payment and the largest discount you can allow.

Ⅲ. 请摘译本章开头所列信函，注意发挥汉语优势，做到言简意赅、措辞婉约和不漏要点。

Ⅳ. 下面是一封典型的外贸信函①，麻雀虽小，五脏俱全。请全译信函（包括封内地址），重点考查对外贸信函格式的熟悉程度，要求电脑打印稿。

---

① 引自 Jacqueline Trace. *Style and Strategy of the Business Letter.* New Jersey: Prentice-Hall, Inc., 1985, p. 46。

第七章　外贸信函的特点与翻译

The American Heritage Bookstore
250 Central Avenue
Lyndon City, TX 75236

ROBIN REDGARVE. Manager   (814) 973-1000

December 15, 198 __

M's BarbaraWardzinski
Sales Manager
Horizon Publishing Company
82 Salinas Street
Little Apple, WI 53405

Re: Imperfect Condition of *TEN EASY STEPS TO DECORATING YOUR HOME*, Invoice
　　No. 98600
―――

Dear M's Wardzinski:

Our order of 100 copies of *Ten Easy Steps to Decorating Your Home* by Lenore Goodman, order no. RC 28, which arrived yesterday from your warehouse, is not suitable for sale.

We were eagerly awaiting the arrival of this publication after its favorable review in *Publishers Weekly*. In fact, several of our regular customers have already requested the book. You can imagine our disappointment, therefore, when we opened the shipment to find a large faded spot across the upper left-hand corner of each of the covers.

Since the book should prove to be a popular gift item, you can understand why we cannot accept this shipment. We are therefore returning the cartons to your warehouse today and asking that you send a duplicate order right away.

Since we need these books for our Christmas sales, we are confident you'll get the duplicate order to us quickly.

Sincerely,

Robin Redgrave
(M's) Robin Redgrave
Manager
RR/jc

第八章
契约语言的特点与翻译

契约语言涉及面相当广，包括个人间的字据，资格认定的各种证书，行业内部的各种规章，企事业单位经贸往来的各种合同、协议，银行、信托、保险业务的各种单证，司法程序的各种诉状、判决，政府机构的各类公文，国家的各种法律法规，以及国家间的各种协定，等等。

契约语言与通常的书面语言不同，与技术语言也不同，与文学语言的距离则更远，这给一般的译者无论是在理解还是在表达方面都带来困难。契约语言具体有哪些特点呢？翻译时又应注意哪些方面呢？这是本章要探讨的问题。

第一节 程式化

多数契约文本都有沿用已久的格式，同业见之，照此办理，省时高效。与文学翻译不同，契约语言的翻译讲究的不是标新立异，而是合乎惯例。因此，熟悉各种契约文本的格式是译者入行的基本要求。例如，英语贸易合同的开头都是大同小异：

This contract is made and entered into this _____ day of _____, one thousand nine hundred _____ by and between _____ Co., at _____ (hereinafter referred to as Party A) and _____ Co., at _____ (hereinafter referred to as Party B).

本合同于 _____ 年 _____ 月 _____ 日由 _____ 公司，地址：_____（以下简称甲方）与 _____ 公司，地址：_____（以下简称乙方）签订。

例1：

购销合同

本合同于2003年8月8日在北京签订。一方为中国公司——ABC贸易有限公司，注册地址为中华人民共和国北京（以下简称"卖方"）。一方为纽约公司——国际贸易有限公司，注册地址为美利坚合众国纽约州纽约市（以下简称"买方"）。

Sales Agreement

The agreement, (is) made in Beijing this eighth day of August 2003 by and between ABC Trading Co., Ltd., a Chinese Corporation having its registered office at Beijing, the People's Republic of China (hereinafter called "Seller") and International Trading Co., Ltd., a New York Corporation having its registered office at New York, N.Y., U.S.A. (hereinafter called "Buyer").

例2：

出口合同

本合同由ABC贸易有限公司（以下简称"卖方"）和XYZ贸易有限公司（以下简称"买方"）于2005年8月5日签订。买卖双方同意按以下条款购买、出售下述商品。

Export Contract

This Contract is entered into this 5th day of August 2005 between ABC Trading Co., Ltd. (hereinafter called "Seller") who agrees to sell, and XYZ Trading Co., Ltd. (hereinafter called "Buyer") who agrees to buy the following goods on the following terms and conditions.

例3：
合作经营企业合同

_____有限公司，遵照_____法律注册的_____公司（简称_____），地址：_____ 为甲方与_____有限公司，遵照_____法律注册的_____公司（简称_____），地址：_____为乙方。

甲方和乙方（简称双方）同意根据《中华人民共和国中外合资经营企业法》和《中华人民共和国中外合资经营企业法实施条例》及其他有关法律的规定，共同成立一家合作经营企业（简称"合营企业"）。

Contract for Joint-Operation Enterprise

_____ COMPANY LTD., a company duly organized under Law of _____ and having its registered office at _____ (hereinafter called "Party A")

AND

_____ COMPANY LTD., a company duly organized under Law of _____ and having its registered office at _____ (hereinafter called "Party B")

Party A and Party B (hereinafter referred to as the "Parties") agree to jointly form an Equity Joint Ventures (hereinafter referred to as the "JV") in accordance with *The Law of the People's Republic of China on Chinese Foreign Equity Joint Ventures* and *Regulations for the Implementation of the Laws of the People's Republic of China on Chinese Foreign Equity Joint Ventures* and other applicable laws and regulations.

有时，为了便于涉外经济活动，提高办事效率，公司、企业间还经常使用**格式合同**。

例4：

MODEL CONTRACT

Contract No. _____   Date: _____
Seller: _____   Signed at: _____
Address: _____   Cable Address: _____
Buyer: _____
Address: _____   Cable Address: _____

The Seller and the Buyer have agreed to conclude the following transactions according to the terms and conditions stipulated below:

1. Name of Commodity: _____
2. Specifications: _____
3. Quantity: _____
4. Unit Price: _____
5. Total Price: U. S. $: _____
6. Packing: _____
7. Time of Shipment: _____ days after receipt of L/C.
8. Loading Port & Destination Port: From _____ via _____ to _____.
9. Insurance: _____
10. Terms of Payment: _____

   (1) The Buyer shall send a confirmed, irrevocable, transferable, and divisible Letter of Credit to be drawn by sight draft to the Seller before _____, _____. The L/C remains valid until _____ days after the above-mentioned delivery and will expire on _____.

   (2) A deposit of _____% shall be paid by the Buyer immediately after signing the contract.

11. Shipping Mark & Clearance: Shipping mark to be at the Seller's option.
12. N. B. Please mention contract number when opening L/C.
13. Remarks: _____

The Seller: _____   The Buyer: _____

格式合同

合同编号：_____　　　　日　　期：_____

卖方：_____　　签约地点：_____

地址：_____　　电报挂号：_____

买方：_____

地址：_____　　电报挂号：_____

兹经买卖双方同意成交下列商品订立条款如下：

1. 商品：_____
2. 规格：_____
3. 数量：_____
4. 单价：_____
5. 总值：_____ U. S. D. （_____）
6. 包装：_____
7. 装运期：_____ 收到信用证后_____ 天。
8. 装运口岸和目的地：从_____ 经_____ 至_____。
9. 保险：_____
10. 付款条件：_____

　　（1）买方须于_____ 年_____ 月_____ 日前将保兑的、不可撤销的、可转让、可分割的即期信用证开到卖方。信用证议付有效期延至上列装运期后_____ 天在_____ 到期。

　　（2）买方须于签约后即付定金_____ %。

11. 装船标记及交货条件：货运标记由卖方指定。
12. 注意：开立信用证时请注明合同编号号码。
13. 备注：_____

卖方：_____　　买方：_____

格式合同，或称标准合同（Standard Contract），是国际贸易中由一个国际组织或外贸商业组织或律师事务所根据买卖合同应该具有的基本内容而拟定的固定条文，印成固定格式的空白标准合同。格式合同须经双方当事人签字后方为有效合同。

契约文本，种类繁杂，格式各有面貌，需要长期积累。比如，要英译一份看似十分简单的文凭证书，如果从来没有见过目的语中同类文本的格式，译者也会感到无从下手。

例5（学位证书）：

THE UNIVERSITY OF LANCASTER

It is hereby certified that

KASEY CARVER

has been duly admitted to the

Degree of Bachelor of Arts

in

American Studies

Vice-Chancellor   Acting Secretary of the University

Date   July 2000

例6（毕业证书）：

THE UNIVERSITY OF HULL

THIS IS TO CERTIFY THAT

KASEY CARVER

Having pursued the prescribed courses

of study and satisfied the Examiners

was today awarded the

Postgraduate Certificate in Education

Main Curriculum Subject: English

With Distinction in Theory & Practice

9 July, 2003

Registrar   Vice-Chancellor

第二节　准确性

在契约文本中，用词准确是第一要旨，因此，在涉及重要概念的翻译时，负责任的译者都会再三斟酌。下面是《中华人民共和国中外合资经营企业法》中几个条款的三种英译文（上海中华印刷所，1987；中国对外经济贸易出版社，1992；法律出版社，2002。它们分别冠以A、B、C以示区别），在翻译过程中都曾反复征询过各方专家的意见，但显然意见难以统一。试分析哪个译文的措辞更为准确，或提出改进的办法。

1. 此法中多处提到"外国合营者"和"中国合营者"。译文如下：
   （A）foreign participants; Chinese participants
   （B）foreign parties; Chinese parties
   （C）foreign joint ventures; Chinese joint ventures

2. 此法第四条规定："合营者的注册资本如果转让须经合营各方同意。"译文如下：
   （A）The transfer of one party's share in the registered capital shall be effected only with the consent of the other parties to the venture.
   （B）The transfer of one party's share in the registered capital shall be effected only with the consent of the other parties to the venture.（与A相同）
   （C）If any of the joint ventures wishes to assign its registered capital, it must obtain the consent of the other parties to the venture.

3. 此法第十条规定："鼓励外国合营者将可汇出的外币存入中国银行。"译文如下：
   （A）A foreign participant shall receive encouragements for depositing in the Bank of China any part of the foreign exchange which he is entitled to remit abroad.
   （B）A foreign party is encouraged to deposit in the Bank of China any part of foreign exchange which he is entitled to remit abroad.
   （C）A foreign joint venture shall be encouraged to deposit in the Bank of China the foreign exchange which it is entitled to remit abroad.（该版本为第十一条）

我国目前主要的涉外法规基本上都已经有了英文版本。法规翻译的量很大，措辞不够准确的地方在所难免，但要提高法规翻译的质量，精益求精的精神是不可少的。也正因为有了这种精神，同一法规，陆续出了不同的英文版本，目的就是要不断地完善现有的译文。可以想见，这项工作今后一定还会继续下去。

要做到措辞准确，还必须严格界定近义词的含义。下面以中国加入世界贸易组织谈判过程中《乌拉圭回合多边贸易谈判结果：法律文本》(*The Results of the Uruguay Round of Multilateral Trade Negotiations*：*the Legal Texts*)（法律出版社，2000。以下简称《乌拉圭回合协议》）的翻译为例加以说明：①

在《乌拉圭回合协议》中，表示"实施""执行"意思的词有"application""enforcement""implementation"和"operation"，但既然是用不同的词来表述就应该具有不同的含义，因此，中译文就必须有所区别。根据法律词典的释义，在定稿中专家们将"application"翻译为"适用"，以强调实施的对象，即实施是否恰当的问题；将"enforcement"翻译为"执行"，以强调实施的力度，即实施是否符合规定的问题；将"implementation"翻译为"实施"，以强调实施的方式，即实施是否按照计划或程序进行的问题；将"operation"翻译为"运用"，以强调实施的状态，即实施是否产生预期的效果。

又如，在《乌拉圭回合协议》中，出现了几个有关"损害"的词，即"harm""injury""prejudice""nullify"和"impair"。根据法律词典的释义和具体的语言环境，专家们将"harm"译为"损害"，将"material injury"译为"实质损害"，将"serious injury"译为"严重损害"，将"serious prejudice"译为"严重侵害"，将"nullify"译为"丧失"，而将"impair"译为"减损"。

契约文书中还存在大量这类近义词，一条基本的原则就是为含义相近的不同词语分别确定特定的译法，尽量避免出现多个词语同一译法（或避免同一词语多种译法，参见第四节"一致性原则"）的情况，以确保特定译法具有单一解释的要求。

第三节　严谨性

契约语言，顾名思义，是一种谨慎的语言，言出必践。比如协议，明确规定了当事人双方（或各方）的权利与义务，行文措辞都必须滴水不漏。如有差错，

---

① 参见索必成："谈《中国加入世界贸易组织法律文件》的中文翻译"，见陆文慧：《法律翻译——从实践出发》，法律出版社2003年版，第287—327页。

小则带来不便,重则造成不良政治影响,或导致经济纠纷。因此,在翻译之前,要仔细分析原文的词句结构和逻辑关系,表达时力求清晰,避免歧义。如何使译文严谨,可以从以下几个方面入手:

一、注意时间的表示法

合同、银行单证等对时间的要求十分严格,丝毫不能含糊。为了使时间不致歧义,英语中常常同时使用两个介词,或采用其他增词手段加以限制。例如:

1. 装运:2005年12月31日前 (**含31日**) 装运,但需以卖方2005年10月底前收到可接受信用证为条件,允许分批装运和转运。
   Shipment: To be shipped <u>on or before</u> December 31, 2005, subject to acceptable L/C reaching Seller before the end of October, 2005 and partial shipments allowed, transshipment allowed.

2. 装运日期**不得晚于**2003年3月31日,并须由"和平"轮装运。
   Shipment is to be made <u>on or before</u> March 31, 2003, per S. S. "Peace".

3. 约翰·史密斯先生1986年以来任我公司驻纽约代表,能力卓著,现已决定退休。**自**2002**年**3**月**31**日**起,他已无权接受任何订单或收账。
   Mr. John Smith, who has been showing an excellent ability as our New York representative since 1986, has now decided to retire from the service. Accordingly he will be unauthorized to accept any orders or to collect any account <u>on and after</u> March 31, 2002.

4. 本报盘有效期至2006年5月22日 (**含22日**)。
   The offer remains in force till May 22, 2006 (<u>inclusive</u>).
   或:The offer remains in force <u>till and including</u> May 22, 2006.
   (如果不包括22日,则说 till and not including)

5. 装船须在1月1日至1月15日之间完成 (**含15日**)。
   Shipment must be made from January 1 to January 15, <u>both days included</u>.

6. 新的价格表将**自(在)**6月1日始生效。
   The new pricelist will become effective <u>from (on)</u> June 1.

若指某一特定日期,则用介词 on。例如:

1. Party A shall deliver the goods to Party B **on** July 30.

甲方将于 7 月 30 日将该货交给乙方。

2. This credit expires on 16th October, 2003 for negotiation in China.
   本信用证在中国议付，有效期至 2003 年 10 月 16 日。

若以终止时间为对象，表示"在某月某日之前"，则用 by 或 before。例如：

Party A shall deliver the goods to Party B **by** July 30, 2003.
或：Party A shall deliver the goods to Party B **before** July 31, 2003.
甲方须在 7 月 30 日前将该货交给乙方。

注意：用 by 时，包括所写日期，用 before 时指所写日期的前一天，故须写作 July 31。此外，对于一些重要的涉外合同，日期应坚持大写，如 6 月 1 日：the first of June。在可能的情况下，还应避免使用一些不确定的时间副词或介词，如 "promptly" "immediately" "as soon as possible" "about August 20"。

二、注意金额、数字的表示法

为了堵塞漏洞，便于核对，避免差错，凡涉及金额及其他数字时，都应坚持大小写并用，即在小写之后，再在括号内用大写重复一次。在大写金额前后习惯上要分别加上"SAY"和"ONLY"，即分别相当于汉语的"大写"和"整"。例如：

1. You are hereby authorized to draw on Golden Dragon Hardware Co. Singapore not exceeding RMB ￥2375.00 CIF (<u>SAY</u>：RMB ￥TWO THOUSAND THREE HUNDRED AND SEVENTY FIVE <u>ONLY</u>) available by your drafts, drawn in duplicate, on them at 60 days' sight.
   现授权你方开立汇票向新加坡五金公司索取到岸价不超过人民币 2375.00 元 (**大写**：人民币贰仟叁佰柒拾伍元**整**) 凭你方出具以上公司为付款人 60 天后见票即付的汇票一式二份。

2. The registered capital of the Joint Venture Company shall be _____ (SAY：_____ U. S. Dollars) of which Party A and Party B shall each invent <u>fifty percent (50%)</u>, that is _____ (<u>Say</u>：_____ U. S. Dollars). The Parties shall share the profits, losses and risks in proportion to their investment contributed.
   合资公司的注册资本为_____ (**大写**：_____美元)，甲方和乙方各出资**百分之五十** (50%)，计_____ (**大写**：_____美元)，双方将按上述投资比例分享利润,分担亏损和风险。
(注:例中的"百分之五十"和括号中的阿拉伯数字"50%",可有双重作用,一是出于慎重,二是为了醒目。)

3. The increase of investment was one and a half times or from one million U. S. D. to one and a half million U. S. D.
投资金额增加了 0.5 倍,**即从原来的 100 万美元增加到现在的 150 万美元。**

关于倍数的翻译,两种语言的思维和表达习惯不一致,在英语中说"增加了多少倍"是连基数包括在内的,表示增加后的结果;而在汉语中却不算基数,只表示纯粹增加的倍数,两种语言正好相差一倍。例如:

1. The turnover of the company has grown six-fold over the past ten years.
公司的销售额 10 年来增加了 5 倍。
2. Traffic accidents now are five times less than before.
现在的交通事故比以前减少了 80% (或:……减少了五分之四)。

英语中可以说"减少了多少倍",但汉语中没有这种说法,故应转换成百分数或分数。另外,英语中表示"倍数"的结构很多,并不是凡有"times"或"-fold"等字样都遵循"相差一倍"的规律,并且许多书上的说法也不尽统一。因此,翻译涉外合同或其他重要文献时,如果涉及倍数词,严谨的做法就是写出或重复具体的数字。

金额的表示,还应特别注意区分不同的货币名称和符号:

"$" 可作"美元"的符号,但也可作其他货币的符号。为严谨起见,都须在"$"前加上有关国家的货币缩写字母。常见的表示法有:

U. S. $ = United States Dollar
HK$ = Hong Kong Dollar
A$ = Australian Dollar
NZ$ = New Zealand Dollar
S$ = Singapore Dollar
Can$ = Canadian Dollar

"£" 是英镑符号,代替"pound",冠在数字之前,但在"£"符号之后如还有大写缩写字母,则指相关国家的货币。如:

£ C   = Cyprus pound (塞浦路斯镑)

£ Ir　＝ Irish pound（爱尔兰镑）

£ M　＝ Maltese pound（马耳他镑）

£ S　＝ Sudanese pound（苏丹镑）

￥既可以是人民币符号，代表 yuan/元，（有时在"￥"前还有 RMB，则是 Renminbi 的缩写），又可以是日本货币单位，代替 Japanese yen（日元）。实际使用中须加以区别，人民币元写成 RMB￥，日元写成 JP￥。例如：

The unit price of this machine is 34 652 Japanese yen（SAY JP￥ THIRTY FOUR THOUSAND SIX HUNDRED AND FIFTY TWO ONLY）.

这种型号的机器每台单价为 34652 日元（大写：叁万肆仟陆佰伍拾贰日元整）。

三、注意增加限制性词语

1. Advance freight and/or freight payable at destination shall be paid to the carrier in full, irrespective of whatever damage or loss may happen to ship and cargo or either of them.
   预付运费和到付运费，**或其中之一**，无论船舶及所载货物，**或其中之一**遭受任何损坏或灭失，都应毫不例外地全额付给承运人。
2. The carrier is entitled, at port of shipment and/or port of destination, to verify the quantity, weight, measurement and contents of the goods as declared by the shipper.
   对托运人申报的货物数量、重量、尺码与内容，承运人有权在启运港或目的港**选择核查**，也有权在上述两个港口**重复核查**。

为使行文严谨、准确，合同文字常常使用 and/or 这一结构。and/or 是一种连接并列结构的省略形式，其完整的结构是"A and B + A or B"。英译汉的问题主要是措辞单调。比如，很多人不管在什么场合都把它译成"和（或）"，省事倒是省事，但很难让人形成准确的概念。实际上，多动脑筋，也可以做到富于变化、层次分明。

3. **第五条** 合营企业各方可以现金、实物、工业产权等进行投资。（《中华人民共和国中外合资经营企业法》）
   （a）**Article 5** The parties to an equity joint venture may make their

investment in cash, in kind <u>or</u> in industrial property rights, etc. (北京：法律出版社，2002)
(b) Article 5 Each party to an equity joint venture may contribute cash, capital goods, industrial property rights, etc, as its investment in the venture. (上海：中华印刷所，1987)

"现金、实物、工业产权"三者之间的关系，A译理解为"选择"关系，B译则理解为"并列"关系，但按照立法意图应兼及上述两种关系，即"X, Y and/or Z"。因此，上述译文可改译如下：

(c) Article 5 Each party to a joint venture may contribute cash, capital goods <u>and/or</u> industrial property as its investment.

4. 买卖双方同意，按下列条款由买方购进，由卖方出售下述商品，并签订本合同。
The Contract is <u>made by and between</u> the Buyer and the Seller, whereby the Buyer agrees to buy and the Seller agrees to sell the under-mentioned commodity according to <u>the terms and conditions</u> stipulated below.

这是"售购合同"里非常程式化的句子。首先，合同的订立，英语里同时使用了"by"和"between"两个介词，目的是要强调"合同"是由双方订立，并在双方之间执行，不涉及任何第三方。其次，"条款"的表述，译文也使用了两个单词"terms"和"conditions"，因为某个合同条款的达成经常包括若干条件。以合同中的"支付条款（terms of payment）"为例，在合同签订前，买卖双方首先要商讨采用什么方式支付：是采用信用证支付，还是采用银行托收。如果双方商定采用信用证支付方式，也就是把"terms"定下来了。此后双方须进一步商讨与此有关的"conditions"，比如买方何时开立信用证，如果买方不按时开证怎么办等，这些有关支付的"terms"和"conditions"合在一起，才构成合同中的"支付条款"。

5. The Tenant shall make every effort at all times <u>including but not limited to</u> the hours between 11:00 PM and 7:00 AM not to play nor operate any musical instruments, radio, television or other like devices in the leased premises as not to create a disturbance to anyone outside the premises leased by the Tenant.

承租人须保证任何时候不在租住的房舍内弹奏乐器、收听广播、观看电视，或拨弄其他类似装置，**特别**是在晚上 11 点至次日早晨 7 点，**但不限于**以上时间，以免干扰房舍周边的居民。

6. Claims Procedure: Upon occurrence of an accident covered by this Policy, the Applicant, the Insured, or the designated beneficiary should notice the company at least 5 days later from the date he knows <u>or should reasonably know</u> of the accident. Notification delay attributable to Force Majeure is excluded.

   索赔手续： 投保人、被保险人或指定受益人应于知道**或理应知道**保险事故发生之日起至迟 5 日内通知保险公司，因不可抗力导致的延误除外。

7. INTERNATIONAL— NOTICE OF BAGGAGE LIABILITY LIMITATIONS: For most international travel (<u>including domestic portions of international journeys</u>) liability for loss, delay, or damage to baggage is limited to approximately $20.00 per kilo for checked baggage and $400 per passenger for unchecked baggage unless a higher value is declared in advance and additional charges are paid.

   国际航班 —— 行李有限责任通告： 大多数国际旅行（**包括国际行程的国内部分**）对于行李的灭失、延误或损坏，除非乘客事先声明携带贵重行李及缴纳追加的费用，通常情况最高赔额每公斤交运的行李约为 20 美元，随身携带的行李每位乘客约为 400 美元。

8. Parents or guardians may avoid liability for their children's crimes if they can satisfy the court that they have done everything they can to prevent it.

   孩子的父母或监护人，只要能向法庭证明，他们已采取一切必要措施防止其孩子**或被监护人**犯罪，可免除承担其孩子**或被监护人**犯罪的法律责任。

9. 12 岁以下儿童可免费与父母同住。（宾馆）
   No extra charge for **one** child under 12 years of age sharing same room with parents.

从上述 5 (5-9) 个例子可以看出撰稿人或译者的心思要多么缜密，这也是契约语言最为典型的特点。

第四节　一致性

在契约语言中，为了避免造成概念混乱，使读者疑为另有所指，原则上要求某一文本中的关键词语（主要是名词和动词）的译法前后保持一致，防止同义异译。在重要的合同里，关键词常有明确的书面定义。例如：

Article 1 Party A shall deliver to Party B as soon as possible after this Agreement becomes effective, but in any event within 60 days thereafter, at Party B's address set forth above, all the Technical and Sales Information relating to Licensed Products.

第一条 甲方应尽快在协议生效后，或最迟在本协议生效后六十天内，按上开乙方地址交给乙方有关**特许产品**的全部**技术与销售情报**。

Definitions：

Article 1 The term Technical and Sales Information as used herein shall mean all data and information which Party A owns on the date hereof or may develop or acquire during the term of this agreement, and which relates to the manufacture and/ or sale of Licensed Products and includes detailed assembly drawings, parts lists, material specifications and manufacturing methods and procedures relating to the Licensed Products as well as sales and publicity materials such as catalogs, explanation materials, pamphlets, photographs, layout books, and sales materials.

定义：

第一条 本协议所用"**技术与销售情报**"的含义，是指甲方在本协议签订之日或存续期间发展或获得的，同生产和（或）销售"**特许产品**"有关的所有数据和情报，包括与"**特许产品**"相关的详尽组装图纸、配件表、原料规格、生产方法、生产程序以及诸如产品目录、使用说明书、小册子、照片、图样书册、销售等宣传资料。

如果一开始将"information"译为"情报"，就不要中途改译"信息"。类似一词多译的情况经常会遇到。例如，"technical know-how"可能译成"专有技术"，也可能译成"技术秘密"或"专门技术"；在一份保险单中，可能多次出现"the insured"一词，可将其译成"投保人"，也可以将其译成"被保险人"，问题的关键是在特定文本的翻译中只选择其一,不可前后交替使用。本章第二节里谈到,在《乌拉圭回合协议》中,"application""enforcement""implementation"和"operation" 4 个词反复出现,译者首先要确定它们各自的译法("适用""执行""实施""运用"),不可错位,同时还得保证每个词前后只有一个译法。

前后一致的要求(也适用于技术文本),译者应时刻注意:

第九条 外资企业应当在审查批准机关核准的期限内在中国境内投资;逾期不投资的,工商行政管理机关有权**吊销**营业执照。

Article 9 An enterprise with foreign capital shall make investments in China within the period approved by the authorities in charge of examination and approval. If it fails to do so, the administrative departments for industry and commerce shall have the power to <u>cancel</u> its business licence.

第十四条 外资企业拒绝在中国境内设置会计账簿的,财政税务机关可以处以罚款,工商行政管理机关可以责令停止营业或者**吊销**营业执照。

If an enterprise with foreign capital refuses to maintain account books in China, the financial and tax authorities may impose a fine on it, and the administrative department for industry and commerce may order it to suspend operation or may <u>revoke</u> its business licence.

以上是摘自汉英对照《中华人民共和国外资企业法》(法律出版社,2002)中的第九条和第十四条。在英译两处"吊销营业执照"时使用两个不同动词的做法是不合适的。在我国某些正式出版的中英对照的法规文本中,还有不少措辞不一致的情况。比如,在同样表示条件的平行条款中,有的用一连串的 if 引导,但突然间又用一个 where 引导,在内容上看不出有任何区别。

一致性原则的另一层含义就是要求译者了解契约语言翻译的历史沿革。例如,在合同类文本中,凡作过定义的词语或涉及的主要人和物,按惯例均以大写字母开头。有不少词已有定译,约定俗成,译者无须、也不宜另起炉灶,相反,译者应维护其延续性(除少数的确有改进必要的以外)。例如,中国改革开放后出现的"三资"企业(外资企业、中外合资经营企业和中外合作经营企业)相应的英译名分别为 foreign capital enterprises, Chinese foreign equity joint ventures 和 Chinese foreign contractual joint ventures。类似的常见词语还有很多,需要长期积累和勤查词典。如果自己翻译,一方面很费事,也未必译得准确,另一方面还容易引起混乱。我国各种法规的名称,通常有比较固定的英译:

法 规 名 称	英 译
法	Law
条例	Regulations
规定	Provisions for
办法	Measures; Procedures
说明	Explanations (on)
决定	Decision
草案	Draft
修正案	Amendment (to)
实施细则	Implementing Rules; Rules for Implementation of
暂行规定	Interim Provisions; Provisional Regulations
试行办法	Trial Measures
管理规定	Provisions for the Administration of
补充规定／附则	Supplementary Provisions

契约文本中条款名称和序号标记也有一套可供参照的处理方法：

中文条款名称及标记形式	英文条款名称及标记形式
第一章／第一部分	Chapter I / Part I
第一节	Section 1
第一条	Article 1
第一款	Paragraph 1
(a) 项	Subparagraph (a)
(i) 目	Item (i)

以上是一套完整的条款名称及其标记形式，在实际引用某一条款时，通常有两种形式，一种如"Paragraph 2 of Article 1"，中文译为"第一条第二款"，一种如"Article 2.3"，中文译为"第 2.3 款"，而不是"第 2.3 条"。

然而，多数契约文本（如一般的合同）采用的是更为简明的条、款、项结构。如"条"以"Article"加阿拉伯数字表示，其余款项在"条"之下直接使用阿拉伯数字和字母表示：

第一条／Article 1
（款）：1.1　　　　1.2　　　　1.3　……
（项）：a.　　　　 b.　　　　 c.　……

第二条／Article 2
（款）：2.1　　　　　2.2　　　　　2.3 ……
（项）：a.　　　　　b.　　　　　c. ……
……

可以看出，标记形式可有所不同，但无论采用哪种标记形式，原则就是，在特定的文本中只能选用一套符号系统。条款标记的划一，不仅能起到提纲挈领、层次清楚的作用，更为重要的是，并列的条目还表明同等的法律地位。

在涉外合同里，还有一套反复出现的词语，译法已约定俗成，熟悉和掌握这套词语，无疑有助于提高合同翻译的效率。例如：

甲方/乙方	Party A / Party B
甲方/乙方	Side A / Side B
甲方/乙方	the First Party / the Second Party
甲方/乙方	the Party of the first Part / the Party of the second Part
丙方/第三方	the Third Party
当事人	the Party
当事人一方	one Party
双方	both Parties
另一方当事人	the other Party
双方当事人/各方	the Parties
有关方	Parties concerned
买方	the Buyer / the Vendee / the Purchaser
卖方	the Seller / the Vendor / the Supplier
派出方/接受方	the Sending Party / the Receiving Party
委托人/代理人	the Principal / the Agent
转让方/受让方	the Transferor / the Transferee
出让方/受让方	the Licensor / the Licensee
承包方/建造方	the Contractor / the Builder
承租人/出租人	the Tenant / the Lessor
以下简称（甲方）	hereinafter referred to as (Party A) / hereinafter called (Party A) / hereinafter termed (Party A) /

	hereinafter（Party A）/
	called（Party A）
	（注：第一和第二种说法最为正式。该短语一般都放于括号内，如属于连续行文，其前后应有逗号隔开。）
（表示金额）大写	SAY
（表示金额）整	ONLY
鉴于	whereas
上述	said
为了	for the purpose of
前款	the proceeding paragraph
有效	remain valid; remain in force; remain good
生效	come into force; take effect; become effective
无效	null and void
	（e.g. ... shall become automatically null and void）
期满、失效	expire/expiration
具有同等法律效力	possess the same legal validity;
	be equally authentic
对……具有约束力	be binding upon
遵守	comply with; abide by; conform to
依据、按照	in accordance with; in compliance with; according to
属于下列情形之一的	under any of the following circumstances;
	falling into any of the following categories
另有规定的除外	except as otherwise provided for by/in;
	except where otherwise provided for by/in;
	unless otherwise specified by;
	unless otherwise specified herein
除另有协议的以外	unless otherwise agreed upon
特别许可的除外	except as specifically authorized by

第五节　庄重性

契约文本属冷峻的书面语体，行文刻板，给人以庄重感。这种庄重感主要体现在词语的使用上。例如：

　　Term：The term of this lease <u>shall commence</u> on August 20，1997 and <u>shall terminate</u> on June 30，1998 unless <u>terminated</u> sooner as <u>herein provided</u>. <u>In the event that</u> the Tenant transfers from the unit rented under this lease to another unit the Tenant <u>shall</u> have three consecutive calendar days from the "<u>termination</u> of this lease" to move to the new unit and <u>shall</u> be billed on all additional days on a per-diem basis.

以上英文是租房协议的期限条款，其中画底线的词语都是非常正式的用语。下面是随意从几个法律文本中摘录的正式词语，其中有些可称为法律性或半法律性词语，试与日常使用的词语比较：

正式词语	日常词语
adjacent to	close to; near
aforesaid	mentioned above / before
applicable to	suitable for
arise	happen
at liberty	free
be entitled to	be given the right to
by reason of	because of
by virtue of	by means of; as a result of
cease	stop
commence / commencement	begin / beginning
deem	consider
deliver	send
dwelling	house
eligible	suitable for; qualified for
execute	deal with; carry out

implement	carry out
in respect of	with regard to; concerning
in so much as	since; because
in the event that; in the event of	if
in the vicinity of	near; around
notwithstanding	in spite of
otherwise	differently
participate in	take part in
prior to	before
provided that	if; but/except; also
pursuant to	under; by; according to
purchase	buy
said (*adj.*)	the; this; that
(the) same (*pron.*)	it; them
save (*prep.*)	except
shall	must; have a duty to
sole	only
subject to	depending on
submit	send; present
such	this; that; those; the
terminate / termination	end; ending
undertake (to)	agree to
upon receipt of	as soon as it is received
warrant (to)	promise to
without prejudice to	without doing harm to

在法律文本中还有一整套副词+介词的组合词，如 herein, hereto, herewith, hereunder, hereof, hereby, therein, thereto, thereupon, therefor, whereby 等。以 herein 为例，它表示 in this (agreement, etc.)，其他词语的意思大致可以类推。比如，therein 则表示 in it, in them, inside。这些词无休无止地穿插在句子中间，往往使初涉契约语言的学生望而生畏。实际上，这些词与其说是"句意"的要求，不如说是"文体"的要求，因此，如果以"不变"应"万变"的方法，多数时候几乎可以忽视它们的存在，这样，句子的意思反而更为清楚。

英译汉时，为使译文获得同样的庄重感，应尽量避免使用口语词语。酌情使用文言虚词及其他书面词语，往往可以起到言简意赅的效果，也可以改善长句的分、接问题。

庄重语体习用语	日常口语习用语
即（连词；副词）	也就是；马上
兹、现、今（副词）	现在
均、皆、概（副词）	都、全
本（代词）	我们，这个
如（连词）	如果
之（助词）	的（用于名词性偏正结构中）
未（副词）	没有
至（介词）	到
系（动词）	是
于（介词）	在
自（介词）	从
其（代词）	它（的）；它/他们（的）
视为（被动结构）	被认为
不得/不可（副词）	不可以
已/业已（副词）	已经
此处（代词、形容词）	这里
与否（助词，位于肯定的动词或形容词后）	是不是

总之，无论是英语，还是汉语，使用两套不同的词语写成的文本，其区别就如穿西装与穿休闲服一般，给人的感觉大不相同。本节开头的"期限条款"可用庄重的语体翻译如下，注意粗体字部分：

　　本协议**自**1997年8月20日生效**至**1998年6月30日**终止**。除本合同另有规定，**方可**提前**终止本**协议。**如**承租人从租约的单元**移至**另一单元，承租人**自**"终止本协议"**之**日起将有连续三日时间搬离，**如**超过三日，超过部分**均**按日计租。

下面是更多的一些译例：

1. On condition that your order more than 2 000 sets, we are prepared to offer

special price of US$9.10 per set, a 5% discount.

如订购2000套以上，我方准备特价报盘，每套9.10美元，**即**给5%的折扣。

2. This is to certify that the English translated copy attached hereto is in conformity with the Chinese original copy.

兹证明，英文译本与中文正本内容相符。

3. In reply to your inquiry of 25th March, we are pleased to offer you the following:

现函复贵方3月25日询价，并报盘如下：

4. This Contract shall come into force from the date of execution hereof by the Buyer and the Builder.

本合同**自**买方和建造方签约**之**日生效。

5. According to the terms agreed upon, we have drawn on you at sight against shipment through Bank of China here. We would ask you to protect the draft upon presentation.

根据双方协议条款，我们**已开具了**这批船货的即期汇票，通过**此处**中国银行转去，请见票**即**付。

文本的庄重感也体现在句型的选择上。例如，在英语的契约文本中随处可见的以where引导的条件句（与日常英语中表示地点状语的用法不同）比使用if或when引导的条件句显得更为正式。在汉译时一般采用"……的"句式，而不采用"如果……"句式，更符合我国契约文本的行文习惯。例如：

<u>Where</u> an Agreement is signed before the completion of the typescript the Publisher shall reserve the right not to publish the Work if the Publisher or its advisers thinks that it is not of the extent, character or standard which has been agreed or might reasonably be expected. In this event the Publisher shall immediately decide not to publish the Work, so notify the Author and cancel the Agreement whereupon the typescript and all rights therein shall automatically become the property of the Author, but the Publisher shall be at liberty to commission some other person to write a similar work.

作品脱稿之前签订协议**的**，作品脱稿后，若出版商自己或其顾问认为作品在篇幅、性质或水准上与原先协议不符，或超出可接受的范围，

出版商保留不予出版该作品的权利。这种情况下，出版商须立刻做出终止出版的决定，并及时知会作者和取消出版协议。作品及其所有权利自动归属作者，但出版商可以委托第三者撰写同类作品。

在我国的涉外法规的英译中，我们也常常使用这个句型。例如：

第十九条 外资企业的组织形式为有限责任公司。经批准也可以为其他责任形式。

外资企业为有限责任公司**的**，外国投资者对企业的责任以其认缴的出资额为限。外资企业为其他责任形式**的**，外国投资者对企业的责任适用中国法律、法规的规定。（《中华人民共和国外资企业法实施细则》北京：中国对外贸易出版社，1992）

Article 19 A wholly foreign-owned enterprise shall take the form of a limited liability company. It may also with approval take other forms of organization.

<u>Where</u> a wholly foreign-owned enterprise is a limited liability company, the foreign investor shall be liable to the enterprise within the limit of the capital subscribed by it.

<u>Where</u> a wholly foreign-owned enterprise takes other forms of organization, the liability of the foreign investor to the enterprise shall be determined according to the Chinese laws and regulations.

在英语的契约文本中，尤其在合同条款中，还有一个以"provided that"开头的典型句型，常位于主述条款之后，表示与主述条款相反的"例外"，通常汉译为"但"或"但是"，因此，法律界将这种条款称之为"但书"（proviso）。请看下列出版协议中的一个条款：

The Publishers shall make the following payments to the Author, namely:

(1) The sum of £500.00 (Five hundred pounds) in advance and on account of any sums which may become due to the Author under this Agreement, payable in the following manner, namely:

(a) The sum of £200.00 (Two hundred pounds) on signature of this Agreement which sum shall be repaid to the Publishers by the author in the event of the Author failing to deliver the said copies of the typescript of the Work.

(b) The sum of £ 150.00 (One hundred and fifty pounds) on the receipt and approval by the Publishers of the said copies of the typescript of the Work.

(c) The sum of £ 150.00 (One hundred and fifty pounds) on the day of publication of the Work.

(2) On the British published price of all such copies sold, excluding such copies as may by subsequent clauses of this Agreement, or as otherwise mutually agreed, be sold subject to a different Royalty:

(a) A Royalty of Nine per Cent. on all copies sold from the first printing.

(b) A Royalty of Ten per Cent. on all copies sold from the second and subsequent printings.

Provided that if at any time the corrections to a printing of the Work make it necessary in the opinion of the Publishers to substantially reset the Work for the issue of a New Edition shall commence at the original rate of Nine per Cent. of the British published price on all copies sold from the first printing rising to Ten per Cent. of the British published price on all copies sold from the second and subsequent printings, subject to the general terms and conditions of this Agreement. (285 words)

试译如下：

出版商须支付作者如下款项：

(1) 总额伍佰英镑（£500）的预付款，该款按本协议约定分期支付，即按以下方式支付：

(a) 签订本协议，即付贰佰英镑（£200）。如作者未能履约提交书稿，该款须由作者返还出版商。

(b) 出版商一经收到并认可书稿，即付壹佰伍拾英镑（£150）。

(c) 作品出版之日，即付壹佰伍拾英镑（£150）。

(2) 除本协议另有补充条款或双方另有约定版税外，所有出售的该书册，均按英国出版定价的以下比例支付版税：

(a) 第一次印刷销售的所有书册，按9%的版税率支付版税。

(b) 第二次印刷及后续印刷销售的所有书册，按10%的版税率支付版税。

但根据本协议总的条款，无论何时，若出版商认为重印该作品时如果修改过大，有必要重新制版的，则每次新版的以英国出版定价销售的所有书册按原先初版9%的版税率支付版税，相应第二次印刷及后续印刷的以英国出版定价销售的所有书册，按10%的版税率支付版税。（376字）

第六节　简明化

法律文本的负面特点，可能就是臃肿、晦涩、冗长。三者绞在一起，即便专业人士也往往退避三舍，一般人看了，更少不了有敬畏之感。要谈契约语言的"简明化"，似乎与上面讨论的"严谨性""庄重性"等章节背道而驰，然而实际上并不矛盾。一方面，我们必须了解契约语言的沿革，做到首先能看懂别人写的文字；另一方面，我们又必须明确契约语言演变的正确方向，做到在自己写作或翻译契约语言时能与时俱进，不落窠臼。

契约语言的简明化也可以从词汇和句法入手。为便于衔接，我们先讨论句法。英语契约文本中的典型句型，多数有故弄玄虚的嫌疑，而其中受到最多批评的也许就是以"provided that"引导的"但书"条款：本来可以平行陈列的几个事件，却非得绕着弯儿说出来。该句型有三个方面的危险：一是语义不清，因为它既可表示"前提"（on condition that），也可表示"例外"（except），还可表示"追加"（also）；二是该"前提"所限制的范围不确定，使读者不得不回头多读几遍；三是无故地使句子枝蔓。因此，有文体学家建议："Don't use provisos."我们试以上一节结尾的句子为例来说明这种简明化的可能。

The Publisher shall make the following payments to the Author, namely：

(1) The sum of £ 500 (Five hundred pounds) in advance, payable in the following manner, namely：

(a) The sum of £ 200 (Two hundred pounds) on signing this Agreement which sum shall be repaid to the Publisher by the Author if s/he fails to deliver the typescript of the Work.

(b) The sum of £ 150 (One hundred and fifty pounds) on the receipt and approval by the Publisher of the typescript of the Work.

(c) The sum of £ 150 (One hundred and fifty pounds) on the day of publication of the Work.

(2) All copies sold on the British published price, except by subsequent

clauses of this Agreement, or as otherwise mutually agreed upon a different Royalty, shall be subject to the general terms and conditions of this Agreement:

(a) A Royalty of Nine per Cent. (9%) on all copies sold from the first printing.

(b) A Royalty of Ten per Cent. (10%) on all copies sold from the second and subsequent printings.

(c) A Royalty of the original rate, i. e. Nine per Cent (9%) on all copies sold from each first printing of a reset New Edition and a Royalty of Ten per Cent (10%) on all copies sold from the corresponding second and subsequent printings. (215 words)

根据改写后的英文稿（也包括句型以外的改写），此条款可翻译如下：

出版商须支付作者如下款项：
(1) 总额伍佰英镑（£500）的预付款，该款按以下方式支付：
(a) 签订本协议，即付贰佰英镑（£200）。如作者未能履约提交书稿，该款须由作者返还出版商。
(b) 出版商一经收到并认可书稿，即付壹佰伍拾英镑（£150）。
(c) 作品出版之日，即付壹佰伍拾英镑（£150）。
(2) 除本协议另有补充条款或双方另有约定版税外，按英国出版定价出售的所有书册，须符合本协议总的条款：
(a) 第一次印刷销售的所有书册，按9%的版税率支付版税。
(b) 第二次印刷及后续印刷销售的所有书册，按10%的版税率支付版税。
(c) 每次重新制版的新版作品，第一次印刷销售的所有书册，按初版版税率，即按9%的版税率支付版税，相应第二次印刷及后续印刷的所有书册，按10%的版税率支付版税。(316字)

在词汇层面，"and/or"也许是使用得最滥的一个组合。最早的出发点可能是为了严谨，比如，试图把想到了的情况和没想到的情况"一网打尽"。结果，久而久之，这成了契约文书的起草人偷懒的伎俩，不管它有无必要，为了逃避责任、不出纰漏，一股脑儿都写成了"and/or"。而翻译的人也不分青红皂白，以为把它译成"和（或）"就万事大吉了。实际的情形是，可能有接近一半的时候它只表示简单的并列（and），还有接近一半的时候它只表示选择（or），极少数时间才表示并列兼选择（即 "and/or"）。因此，甚至有的文体学家说，要把这个组合从法律语言中清除出去，因为它非但没有使文字表达更严谨，反而让认真的人浪费精力去揣摩它的真正含义。请判断下面的例子：

1. In credit operations all parties concerned deal in documents and not in goods, services and/or other performances to which the documents may relate.
2. The Cardholder agrees to pay the Bank's initial and/or periodical fees for the Card. Fees will be debited to the Card Account when due and are not refundable.
3. Should the Publishers fail to fulfill or comply with any of the provisions of this Agreement within three months after written notification from the Author of such failure, or if the Work be allowed to go out of print and not be available in any edition, format, or medium, and the publishers shall fail to put in hand a reissue or a new edition within nine months of having received a written request from the Author, then and in any of these events, this Agreement shall terminate after notice in writing from the Author without prejudice to all rights of the Publishers in respect of any agreements or negotiations properly entered into by Publishers with any third party prior to the date of such termination and without prejudice to any claim which the Author may have for monies due and/or damages and/or otherwise. (143 words)

稍作停留，我们就能看出，例 1 中的 and/or 只表示选择，而例 2 中的 and/or 只表示并列，因此，它们可分别翻译如下：

1. 在信用证事务中，各有关方面处理的是单据，而不是与单据有关的货物、服务或其他行为。
2. 持卡人同意向本银行缴付信用卡的首期和定期费用。该费用按时从信用卡账户扣减，并不予退还。

例 3 的情况复杂些，其中接连使用了两个 and/or 结构。如果要"滴水不漏"地译成汉语的话，也不是不可能。比如：
3. 如出版商未能履行或遵守本协议的任何规定，经作者通知 3 个月内

第八章 契约语言的特点与翻译

仍未更正，或出版商停印作品，造成该作品的任何版本、格式或媒介脱销，而出版商收到作者书面请求后 9 个月内仍未安排重印或再版，如发生上述情况或上述情况之一，经作者书面通知，协议即终止，但在本协议终止之前出版商与任何第三方所签订的任何协议或进行的各种谈判所涉及的出版商权益不受影响，作者所享有的任何权益，包括到期稿酬及赔偿金**等任何一项或多项权益**，均不受影响。（204 字）

再仔细斟酌，后一个 and/or 并没有增添任何实际的内容，也不可能给当事人带来额外的好处，完全是一个虚文，而前一个 and/or 结构也只表示并列，无必要兼表选择。例 3 的英文还有其他看似严谨的表达，是契约语言中十足的"八股"，如果将它"瘦身"一番，一定会变得更为轻快：

3. Should the Publisher fail to comply with this Agreement within three months after a written notice from the Author of the failure, or if the Work be allowed to go out of print in any format or medium, and the publisher shall fail to put in hand a reissue or a new edition within nine months after a written request from the Author, in any of these events, this Agreement shall terminate after a written notice from the Author without prejudice to all rights of the Publisher in respect of any agreements properly entered into by the Publisher with any third party before the date of the termination and without prejudice to any claim which the Author may have for monies due **and** damages. (124 words)

　　如出版商未能履约，经作者通知 3 个月内仍未更正，或出版商停印作品，造成该作品的任何格式或媒介脱销，而出版商收到作者书面请求后 9 个月内仍未安排重印或再版，如上述任一情况发生，经作者书面通知，协议即终止，但在本协议终止之前出版商与任何第三方所签订的任何协议所涉及的出版商权益不受影响，作者所享有的任何权益，包括到期稿酬**及**赔偿金**等**也不受影响。（167 字）

需要说明的是，上面汉语译文中的"等"字也是虚文，这是汉语的行文习惯，因此，在汉译英时，也未必每一个"等"字须对应英语的"and so on"或"etc."。因此，无论是起草人还是译者，关键是确定你究竟要表达哪层意思，只要思路清楚，就可以避免或少用像"and/or"这样含混的词语。比如，我们可

以试验将第三节中英译汉的一个句子回译成英文:

4. 对托运人申报的货物数量、重量、尺码与内容,承运人有权在启运港或目的港**选择核查**,也有权在上述两个港口**重复核查**。

The carrier is entitled, at both ports of shipment and destination or at either of the two ports, to verify the quantity, weight, measurement and contents of the goods as declared by the shipper.

契约语言臃肿、冗长的主要原因就是偏爱使用繁复的短语,比如"遵守中华人民共和国法律、法规的规定",给依样画葫芦地翻译成"comply with the provisions of the laws and regulations of the People's Republic of China",实际上省去 provisions 丝毫不影响意思;"外资企业的营业执照签发日期"给翻译成"the date of issue of the business licence of foreign-capital enterprise",而不取简洁的"the date of issuing the business licence of foreign-capital enterprise";"促进和发展"给翻译成"promote and develop",而不选择更为准确的"facilitate"。这种舍简就繁的表达法大致可分为以下三大类:一是使用双联词组或三联词组(doublets and triplets),二是使用各类繁复的短语,三是使用替代简单动词的 of 结构(包括类似结构)。

臃肿的表达	简明的表达
acknowledge and confess	acknowledge
adequate and effective	effective
by and between	by
covenant and agree	agree
due and payable	due
each and every	each
final and conclusive	final
give, devise and bequeath	give
if and only if	only if
if and when	if / when
in full force and effect	in full force
indemnify and save	indemnify
null and void	void
sole and exclusive	sole / exclusive
unless and until	unless / until

第八章　契约语言的特点与翻译

臃肿的表达	简明的表达
an adequate number of	enough
at the time when	when
be able to	can
by reason of	because of
during / after the period of	during / after
during such time as	while
during the course of	during
for a period of (one year)	for
for the reason that	because
in respect of / with respect to	concerning
in the event that	if
inasmuch as	since, because
not less than /no fewer than	at least
notwithstanding the fact that	although
on a daily basis	daily
the majority of	most

臃肿的表达	简明的表达
conduct an examination of	examine
in the opinion of	think
make a decision of	decide
make an assignment of	assign
make an investigation of	investigate
promote the development of	promote / develop / facilitate
provide an illustration of	illustrate
submit an application for	apply
take into consideration	consider
undertake the representation of	represent

要使契约英语简明化，自然就要对症地在这词语结构上下功夫。请看下面的实例：

5. The monthly rental to be paid by the Tenant **for the lease of** said premises

· 173 ·

shall be in the amount of $428.00, due and payable in advance without notice of demand on the first day of each and every month during the term of this lease; except that if the tenancy commences on a day other than the first of the first month, the rent for the first month shall be pre-rated for that month and shall be due and payable on or before the beginning date of this lease. (90 words)

上述房舍每月租金为428美元，由承租人在本协议存续期间提前于每月一日支付，不再另行通知。如租期不是从一日开始，第一个月的租金提前计算，并在本协议开始执行之日（含当日）前付清。

如果有谁平时也是这样讲话，一定会让人不胜其烦。但要简化这个句子并不难，只需稍做变化，注意比较前后两种写法：

5. The monthly rent to be paid by the Tenant of the premises shall be $428.00, due in advance without notice of demand on the first day of each month under this lease; except that if the tenancy commences on a day other than the first of the first month, the rent for the first month shall be pre-rated for that month and shall be due on or before the beginning date of this lease. (74 words)

6. 第五十六条　侵犯商标专用权的赔偿数额，为侵权人在侵权期间因侵权所获得的利益，或者被侵权人在被侵权期间因被侵权所受到的损失，包括被侵权人为制止侵权行为所支付的合理开支。（《中华人民共和国商标法》，北京：法律出版社，2002）

   Article 56 The amount of compensation for infringement of the exclusive right to the use of a trademark shall be the amount of the profits that the infringer has earned as a result of the infringement during the period of the infringement, or the amount of the losses that the infringed has suffered as a result of the infringement during the period of the infringement, including any reasonable expenses the infringed has paid in its effort to put an end to the infringement. (83 words，编辑符号编者所加)

此例原文为表达"严密"，写的就是一段绕口令，也许读一遍还不能保证能弄明白是什么意思。如果不是先看汉语，而是先读英文，恐怕更会如在云里雾里。但汉语英语对照着看,你不得不承认,这是十分忠实的翻译。但如果在现译的基础上丢开原文,根据英文的行文习惯,还是有可能写得言简意赅的。试改译如下:

6. **Article 56** The compensation for infringement of the exclusive right to use a trademark shall be the amount of the profits that the infringer has earned from the infringement <u>during that period</u>, or the amount of the losses that the infringed has suffered from the infringement <u>during that period</u>, including any reasonable expenses the infringed has paid to end the infringement. (61 words)

改译压缩了1/4,意思并没有改变,实际上只是消化了一些短语,如果胆子再大一点,还可将两个 during that period 拿走(看不出会因此产生歧义)。文体学家建议,如果发现太多的 of 短语,尝试删去一半,看来是经验之谈。原译中的 of 短语在改译中已经减少了2/3,此法可谓立竿见影。

契约语言(或法律语言)简明化是西方学者首先提出来的,这是一种很务实的态度。就怎样使语言简明化,他们还提出了一些其他的建议。例如,避免使用不必要的行话(像 shall, same, such, said, 甚至有人认为 said 是法律术语中最害人的一个),避免使用多重否定结构,能用单数形式就不用复数形式(因为复数形式更容易产生歧义),能用主动语态就不用被动语态,等等,限于篇幅,本节无法一一赘述。我们的意见是,契约语言历史悠久,自有它的惯性。因此,对于正式的用词、惯用的结构和行话,适当地保留和有选择性地删除都是必要的。契约文本的起草人和译者,要像走平衡木一样,努力使自己笔下的文字正式而不陈腐,简明而不简单。

第七节 小 结

本章讨论了契约语言的六大特点及相应的翻译策略,其实,还有一大特点没有谈到,即契约语言的**专业性**。要做好契约语言的翻译,不懂法学、公文等相关的专业知识,不了解术语的既成译法是难以想象的。但法学像汪洋一片,译者的专业知识只有靠自己穷年累月地去获取,不是本章所能办到的。即使已经涉及的六大特点也只是冰山一角,只能作为入门指要。比如契约文本的格式,这里只提供了售购合同、学位证书等几种格式,但还有结婚证、离婚证、信用证、公证书、招投标书、委托书等数以百计、数以千计的不同契约文书,而各种契约文书的格式又各有面貌，这不是每一个人都能掌握或有必要掌握的。最合理的做法自然是在入门之后结合自己的工作从事实践和研究，逐步使自己成为某一局部领域的专才。

【练习题】

I. 试将下列汉语句子译成英语。

1. 改进和开发的技术，其所有权属于改进和开发的一方。
2. 合营企业的一切活动应遵守中华人民共和国法律、法令和有关条例规定。
3. 本协议之中、英两种文本均属正本，每种文本一式四份，双方各执两份。
4. 本合同签字之日 3 个月内，即不迟于 2001 年 8 月 31 日支付本合同总金额的 50% 的预付款，计 50 万美元整（大写：伍拾万美元整）。
5. 据报道，中国自 1979 年以来已对外签订技术引进合同 5600 多项，合同总额达 400 余亿美元，完成的合同数和金额分别为此前 30 年总和的 6.6 倍和 3.5 倍。
6. 根据国家统计局的一份报告，从 1953 年至 1993 年，国内生产总值累计增长 17 倍，平均年增长 7.3%。
7. 在经济方面，基本保持稳定快速增长的格局。在即将过去的 5 年中，国内生产总值提前实现比 20 世纪 80 年代翻两番的目标。
8. 按照本合同第 2 条规定的合同内容和范围，甲方应向乙方支付合同总价为 3642 美元（大写：叁仟陆佰肆拾贰美元整）。
9. 离婚时，夫妻的共同财产由双方协议处理；协议不成时，由人民法院根据财产的具体情况，照顾女方和子女权益的原则判决。
10. 中国广东 ABC 轻工集团公司（以下简称甲方）和德国 XYZ 公司（以下简称乙方）根据《中华人民共和国中外合资经营企业法》及中国的其他法规，本着平等互利的原则，通过友好协商，决定共同投资成立合资经营公司，特订立本合同。

II. 完形填空练习。

下面所选是英语合同或法规中常见的句子，填空后再将它们译成汉语，可测试对契约语言的熟悉程度。

1. This Agreement shall be __(1)__ in both English and Chinese languages, but in the __(2)__ of inconsistency or difference between the English language version and Chinese language version of the Agreement, the Chinese language version hereof shall __(3)__.

2. In witness whereof this (1) parties hereunto set their (2) and seals (3) 20th day of August 1997 and the Tenant as an individual (4) that s/he is age eighteen or (5) and that s/he has read and understands the terms of the Lease Agreement, by signing this Lease s/he (6) receipt of the Security Deposit information and "Statement of Condition". （租房契约）

3. All disputes (1) from the execution of, or in connection with the contract shall be settled through friendly consultation between both parties. In (2) no settlement can be (3) , the dispute shall be (4) for arbitration.

4. The contract shall be (1) for five years from the (2) date of the contract. The contract shall become (3) and (4) automatically (5) the expiry of the contract's (6) of validity.

5. This Agreement may be terminated by (1) Party upon three month's written notice delivered or sent by registered mail to the (2) , or may be terminated at any time, without (3) notice, upon (4) of any of its terms and (5) .

6. This set of detailed rules goes into effect as (1) the date of (2) promulgation.

7. **Important Note** We cannot accept (1) for death, damage or injury or for any (2) to perform properly any of the terms of this contract which is caused by (3) which are not our or our suppliers' fault. Accordingly, if death, damage or injury is caused by something which could not have been (4) or avoided even if we or our suppliers had taken all (5) care or by an unusual or unforeseen event (6) our or our suppliers' control which we could not have avoided, we can not be liable to you. Also, if it is your own fault or the fault of anyone else in your party, or the fault of some (7) party unconnected with us or our suppliers and is unforeseen or unavoidable, then we (8) not be responsible to you.

8. **Liability** Your travel agent shall, on the (1) of any monies, hold such monies for you until the booking is (2) at which time those monies shall be remitted promptly by your travel agent to us. All such monies received by us will be deposited as required by law. We (3) be entitled to keep each account any interest earned on (4) monies. All monies paid by you to us through your travel agent or (5) , whether in (6) of the deposit or full payment, may be disbursed by us as and when we see fit, in respect of services to be provided and/or fees payable (7) the tour program. The payment of a deposit or any other monies in respect of your tour shall be (8) to be authorization to disburse thereof as aforesaid.

III. 试根据契约英语简明化的理念及写作技巧改写下列句子，注意在改写句子时不能改变原来句子的意思。

1. Where a trademark is registered in violation of the provisions of Article 10, 11, or 12 of this law, or it is registered by deceitful or other illegitimate means, the Trademark Office shall cancel the trademark. （汉语原文：已经注册的商标，违反本法第十条、第十一条、第十二条规定的，或者是以欺骗手段或者其他不正当手段取得注册的，由商标局撤销该商标。）

2. Courts have identified a number of factors as relevant to a determination of whether the defendant's use of another's registered trademark is likely to cause a state of confusion, mistake, or deception.

3. If the spouse of a member of the armed forces on active service insists on divorce, consent must be obtained from the member concerned. （汉语原文：现役军人的配偶要求离婚，须得军人同意。）

4. It is not necessary that an investment adviser's compensation be paid directly by the person receiving investment advisory services, but only that the investment adviser receive compensation from some source for his or her services.

5. A member who has no fewer than 25 years of credited service but has not yet attained the age of 60 years and is not eligible for retirement may not voluntarily retire early without first filing a written application with the board.

6. Each member shall have the right to sell, give, or bequeath all or any part of his membership interest to any other member without restriction of any kind.

7. The Chinese Government protects, by the legislation in force, the investment of foreign parties, the profits due them and their other lawful rights and interests in equity joint ventures, pursuant to the agreements, contracts and articles of association approved by the Chinese Government. （汉语原文：中国政府依法保护外国合营者按照经中国政府批准的协议、合同、章程在合营企业的投资、应分得的利润和其他合法权益。）

8. The State shall not nationalize or requisition any equity joint venture. Under special circumstances, when public interests require, equity joint ventures may be requisitioned by following legal procedures and appropriate compensation shall be made. （汉语原文：国家对合营企业不实行国有化和征收；在特殊情况下，根据社会公共利益的需要，对合营企业可以依照法律程序实行征收，并给予相应的补偿。）

9. To assign a registered trademark, the assignor and assignee shall sign an assignment

agreement and jointly file an application with the Trademark Office. The assignee shall guarantee the quality of the goods on which the registered trademark is used. (汉语原文：转让注册商标的，转让人和受让人应当签订转让协议，并共同向商标局提出申请。受让人应当保证使用该注册商标的商品质量。)

10. The exclusive right to the use of a registered trademark shall be limited to trademarks which are registered upon approval and to goods the use of a trademark on which is approved. （汉语原文：注册商标的专用权，以核准注册的商标和核定使用的商品为限。）

11. Any income tax on income earned by Consultant within PRC pursuant to this Contract and subject to taxation according to Income Tax Law of the PRC concerning Enterprises with Foreign Investment and Foreign Enterprises and other relevant laws and regulations shall be paid by Consultant.

12. Subject to the provisions of this Ordinance it shall not be lawful for any person to use, or to cause or permit any other person to use, a motor vehicle on a road unless there is in force in relation to the user of the vehicle by that person or that other person, as the case may be, such a policy of insurance or such a security in respect of third party risks as complies with the requirements of this Ordinance. ［汉语译文：除本条例另有条文规定外，任何人在道路上使用汽车，或致使或允许任何其他人在道路上使用汽车，除非就该人或该其他人（视属何情况而定）对车辆的使用已备有一份有效的和符合本条例规定的第三者风险保险单或保证单，否则并不合法。——香港法例第272章《汽车保险（第三者风险）条例》第4（1）条。］

IV. 下面这份中英对照的合同印制在中国国际航空公司的"客票及行李票"上，英语是原文，汉语是译文。根据契约语言的特点，译文存在诸多问题，请仔细对照阅读并订正和改进译文。

NOTICE：If the passenger's journey involves an ultimate destination or stop in a country other than the country of departure the *Warsaw Convention* may be applicable and the Convention governs and in most cases limits the liability of carriers for death or personal injury and in respect of loss of or damage to baggage. See also notices headed "Advice to International Passengers on Limitation of Liability" and "Notice of Baggage Liability Limitations".

CONDITIONS OF CONTRACT

1. As used in this contract "ticket" means this passenger ticket and baggage check, of which these conditions and the notices form part, "carriage" is equivalent to "transportation", "carrier" means all air carriers that carry or undertake to carry the passenger or his baggage hereunder or perform any other service incidental to such air carriage. *WARSAW CONVENTION* means the Convention for the Unification of Certain Rules Relating to International Carriage by Air signed at Warsaw, 12th October 1929, or that Convention as amended at The Hague, 28th September 1955, whichever may be applicable.

2. Carriage hereunder is subject to the rules and limitations relating to liability established by the *Warsaw Convention* unless such carriage is not "international carriage" as defined by that Convention.

3. To the extent not in conflict with the foregoing carriage and other services performed by each carrier are subject to: (i) provisions contained in the ticket; (ii) applicable tariffs; (iii) carrier's conditions of carriage and related regulations which are made part hereof (and are available on application at the offices of carrier), except in transportation between a place in the United States or Canada and any place outside thereof to which tariffs in force in those countries apply.

4. Carrier's name may be abbreviated in the ticket, the full name and its abbreviation being set forth in carrier's tariffs, conditions of carriage, regulations or timetables; carrier's address shall be the airport of departure shown opposite the first abbreviation of carrier's name in the ticket; the agreed stopping places are those places set forth in this ticket or as shown in carrier's timetables as scheduled stopping places on the passenger's route; carriage to be performed hereunder by several successive carriers is regarded as a single operation.

5. An air carrier issuing a ticket for carriage over the lines of another air carrier does so only as its Agent.

6. Any exclusion or limitation of liability of carrier shall apply to and be for the benefit of agents, servants and representatives of carrier and any person whose aircraft is used by carrier for carriage and its agents, servants and representatives.

7. Checked baggage will be delivered to (the) bearer of the baggage check. In case of damage to baggage moving in international transportation complaint must be made in writing to carrier forthwith after discovery of damage and, at the latest, within 7 days from receipt; in case of delay, complaint must be made within 21 days from (the)

date the baggage was delivered. See tariffs or conditions of carriage regarding non-international transportation.

8. This ticket is good for carriage for one year from date of issue, except as otherwise provided in this ticket, in carrier's tariffs, conditions of carriage, or related regulations. The fare for carriage hereunder is subject to change prior to commencement of carriage. Carrier may refuse transportation if the applicable fare has not been paid.

9. Carrier undertakes to use its best efforts to carry the passenger and baggage with reasonable dispatch. Times shown in timetables or elsewhere are not guaranteed and form no part of this contract. Carrier may without notice substitute alternate carriers or aircraft, and may alter or omit stopping places shown on the ticket in case of necessity. Schedules are subject to change without notice. Carrier assumes no responsibility for making connections.

10. Passenger shall comply with Government travel requirements, present exit, entry and other required documents and arrive at airport by time fixed by carrier or, if no time is fixed, early enough to complete departure procedures.

11. No agent, servant or representative of carrier has authority to alter, modify or waive any provision of this contract.

Issued by AIR CHINA

声　明

　　如旅客航程最终目的地点或经停地点不在出发地点所在国家内,《华沙公约》可以适用于该项运输,且该公约决定并在一般情况下限制承运人对旅客伤亡以及行李遗失或损坏所负的责任。请参阅"国际旅客责任限额通告"和"行李责任限额通告"。

合同条件

1. 在本合同中所用的"客票"指客票及行李票,本条件及声明构成其一部分;"载运"相同于"运输";"承运人"指载运或约定载运旅客或其行李,或实施因此种航空运输而产生的其他服务的所有航空承运人。《华沙公约》指1929年10月12日在华沙签订的统一国际航空运输某些规则的公约或经1955年9月28日在海牙修订的该公约,何者适用即指何者。

2. 根据本合同进行的运输，应遵守《华沙公约》所制定的有关责任的规定和限制，除非此种运输不是该公约所下定义的"国际运输"。

3. 只要与上述不相矛盾，各承运人提供的运输和其他服务应遵守：①本客票中包含的规定条款；②适用的运价；③作为本条件一部分的承运人运输条件和有关规定（可向承运人办事处索取）。美国或加拿大境内一点与其境外任一点之间的运输除外，上述两国公布的有效运价适用于该项运输。

4. 承运人的名称在客票中可用简称，其全名及简称见承运人的运价表、运输条件、规章或班期时刻表；承运人的地址应为客票中与承运人名称第一个简称相对的出发地机场；经同意的经停地点是本客票中所列的那些地点，或在承运人的班期时刻表中所列在旅客航路上规定的经停地点。由数个承运人连续承担的运输，应被认为是一个单一的营运活动。

5. 一个空运企业填开另一个空运企业航线上运输的客票的做法，只能作为是该另一个空运企业的代理人。

6. 对承运人责任的任何排除或限制，应适用于并有益于承运人的代理人、雇员和代表以及承运人所用航空器进行运输的任何该航空器所有人及其代理人、雇员和代表。

7. 交运的行李应交付给行李票的持有者。遇有行李在国际运输中损坏时，应在发现损坏之后立即向承运人提出书面意见，最迟亦应在收到行李后 7 天内提出。遇有延误时，必须在行李交付之日后 21 天内提出异议。对于非国际运输的行李，请参阅运价表或运输条件。

8. 本客票自出票之日起一年内有效，除非在本客票、承运人的运价表、运输条件或有关规章中另有规定。所列的运输票价可在开始运输之前改变。如未交付适用的票价，承运人可以拒绝运输。

9. 承运人将尽最大努力以合理的快速承运旅客及行李。在班期时刻表内或其他地方所列的时间是不予保证的，也不构成本合同的一部分。承运人无须事先通知可以改换备用承运人或飞机，在必要时可以改变或取消客票上所列的经停地点。班期时刻可不事先通知而改变。承运人对航班的衔接不负责任。

10. 旅客应遵守政府对旅行的要求，出示出境、入境和其他必要的文件，并按照承运人规定的时间到达机场。如未有确定时间，则应提早至足以办完离境手续。

11. 承运人的任何代理人、雇员或代表均无权改变、修改或废止本合同中的任何规定。

中国国际航空公司

第八章　契约语言的特点与翻译

Ⅴ. 根据契约语言的特点，试将下面这份英语旅游保险合同译成适当的汉语文本。

CERTIFICATE OF INSURANCE

Cover applies to the person (s) named on this certificate of insurance and for whom a premium has been paid. Important—Please refer particularly to the Conditions (on page 30), Warranty (page 11) and the reference to the material facts at Condition 11 (page 30), as failure to comply with them could affect a claim.

This policy has been arranged by Accident & General International Ltd, 34 Lower Abbey Street, Dublin 1. Ireland.

The policy is underwritten by the Home & Overseas Insurance Company Limited, Regent Arcade House, 19 – 25 Argyll Street, London W1V 2HQ.

The £ symbol denotes pounds sterling.

WARRANTY

It is your promise to us at the time of taking out this insurance policy that:

1. You are not aware of any reason why the trip could be cancelled or curtailed or of any medical condition which could result in a claim.
2. You will obtain from your doctor a "certificate of fitness" confirming your ability to travel and endure the trip if you are undergoing medical treatment as a hospital out-patient at the date the final cost of the trip is due to be paid.
3. You have obtained written medical advice from your doctor on the advisability of taking the trip where you have received treatment as hospital in-patient or out-patient during the six months prior to the booking of the trip.
4. You are not receiving or awaiting the treatment as a hospital in-patient. If any claim arises directly or indirectly from this treatment, it will not be covered.
5. You are not traveling against medical advice or for the purposes of obtaining medical treatment or where terminal prognosis has been given.

   If you find you cannot comply with the terms of this Warranty between the date this policy is purchased and the first date of travel you must notify us.

NOTE: We must be informed of any fact which is likely to influence us in the acceptance, assessment or continuance of this insurance. Failure to do so may invalidate this insurance leaving you with no right to make a claim.

CONDITIONS

1. No payment will be made under sections 1, 2, 3, 6 or 7 without an appropriate medical certificate or other certification as required.
2. Any certificates, information, evidence and receipts required by us must be obtained at your expense (originals must be provided), if we require a medical examination you must agree to this and in the event of death we are entitled to a post mortem examination, both at our expense.
3. You should take all reasonable steps to recover any lost or stolen article.
4. If any claim is found to be fraudulent in any way this policy will be cancelled and all claim denied.
5. The original of this Insurance Certificate should be produced before any claim is paid.
6. You should not admit liability, offer or promise to make any payment without written consent from us.
7. We are entitled to take over any rights in the defense or settlement of any claim and to take proceedings in your name for your benefit against any other party.
8. We may at any time pay to you our full liability under this policy after which no further payments will be made in any respect.
9. No refund of premium is allowed unless the policy is cancelled within seven days of purchase, the travel date has not commenced and a claim has not been made.
10. The period of cover under this policy can only be extended by the issue of a continuation policy provided no claim is pending or known to be about to arise, the maximum period of cover is 24 months from the date of first issue.
11. It is a condition of this insurance that all material facts have been disclosed to us, failure to do so may invalidate this insurance leaving you with no right to make a claim.

NOTE: the Insurers must be informed of any fact which is likely to influence the Insurers in the acceptance, assessment or continuance of this insurance. Failure to do so may invalidate this insurance leaving you with no right to make a claim.

第九章　涉外广告的特点与翻译

第九章
涉外广告的特点与翻译

美国的 Coca-Cola 问世已经 100 多年了。一个多世纪中，它真正称得上名扬天下，誉满全球。Coca-Cola 之所以如此成功，有商品本身特异质量的因素，更重要的是有其广告、商标的宣传作用。自 Coca-Cola 问世以来，Coca-Cola 公司在不同的时期，针对不同的国家，坚持不懈地开展了一个又一个的广告战。"Coca-Cola"一词，朗朗上口，易写易记，适于译成不同的文字，其中"可口可乐"这一中文译名，更是有口皆碑，成为中国翻译史上的一段佳话，也为 Coca-Cola 打开中国这个人口大国的市场立下了汗马功劳。可见，要开拓国际市场，创国际名牌，搞好广告的翻译是十分重要的。

广告是种独特的文体，像广告的标题、口号，可以说常常都在玩弄"文字游戏"，这给翻译带来特殊的困难，也给传统的翻译标准提出了挑战。如何翻译广告，国内还未见系统的研究，好在翻译本无定规，这里就笔者所收集到的一些典型例子，加以分析和归类，谨供参考。

一则完整的书面广告通常由五个部分组成，即标题、正文、口号、商标、插图。本章只讨论文字部分。

第一节　广告标题、口号的句法与修辞特点

许多广告口号都是从一些著名的标题演变而来的，所以我们把标题和口号放在一起讨论。俗话说："好的开端，成功的一半。"人们看广告，首先看到的就是标题或口号。广告标题和口号的质量，往往决定了整个广告的成败。有权威断言：一则广告，标题无力，则起码浪费了 80% 的金钱。因此，许多厂商对产品广告标题和口号的译写都特别重视。

除为了专门的目的，一般的大众都是消极地接受广告。出色的广告标题和口号能一下子吸引潜在的顾客，诱导读者进一步阅读广告正文，进而采取行动（如购买其宣传的产品或服务）。因此，出色的广告标题和口号必具**独特性**、**诱导性**、**针对性**、**口语化**等特点。通俗地说，出色的广告标题和口号应该是别出心裁、朗

朗上口、余味无穷、过目不忘。

为了使广告标题和口号具备这些特点，撰稿人往往搜索枯肠、挖空心思运用各种特殊甚至离奇的句式和修辞手段。

一、巧设问句

据有关统计，在广告英语中，每30句话就有一句是疑问句。作为广告标题，疑问句显然比陈述句更能吸引人的注意。因为人们都有一种探奇心理，即越不知道的东西就越想知道。下面是一则煤气广告的两个标题：①

> Only Gas gives you
> tankful after tankful of hot water
> 3 TIMES FASTER

> WHY Gas gives you
> tankful after tankful of hot water
> 3 TIMES FASTER???

第一个标题为陈述句，首先告诉读者广告的产品，接着介绍产品所能提供的利益，一览无遗。这样，广告正文就显得多余了。第二个标题只是在第一个标题的基础上改了一个词，即将"Only"改成"Why"，也就是在原句的基础上改成了疑问句，给读者造成悬念，效果就大不一样了。

疑问句的运用多种多样，有一般疑问句、特殊疑问句，还有反意疑问句；有一问一答的，也有只问不答的（当然撰稿员心中早已有了预定的答案）。无论哪种形式，只要运用巧妙，都颇具威力。下面介绍几则成功的广告标题：

---

① 引自李中行、戚肖山、张惠：《广告英语》，湖南教育出版社1986年版，第25页。

第九章 涉外广告的特点与翻译

Would you be more careful if it was you that got pregnant?[①]

这是一则计划生育咨询中心的广告标题。插图是位目光呆滞、满面愁容、挺着个大肚子、左手撑腰、右手位于腹前呈抚摸状的男子。整幅广告极富创意，效果不同凡响，国外多种广告书刊广为引述。

Wouldn't you protest
If Shell ran a pipeline through this
beautiful countryside?

They already have!

You can be sure of Shell.[②]

这是世界著名的 Shell 石油公司做的一幅广告。广告的布局为左右两大块，左边是文字部分，分上、中、下三个位置书写，右边是一幅山清水秀、一尘不染的乡村景色（图略）。广告文字第一部分提出问题，第二部分的回答大大出人意料。但仔细一想，这个句子看似答非所问，却暗示了铺设石油管道与"秀美"乡村的关系。第三部分得出结论："Shell——信得过！"标题文字分三部分编排也是独具匠心，它引导读者一步一步地思考。

二、使用省略句，诱发联想

广告有两大类型，一类是硬卖型的（hard-sell ads），即"王婆卖瓜，自卖自夸"，一再强调自己产品的优点；另一类则是软卖型的（soft-sell ads），仅是诉诸于暗示和作用于人的情感进行间接宣传。广告中最常见的软卖型标题就是使用省略句。省略句由于给读者留下广阔的想象空间，很容易激发读者的兴趣。下面试

[①] [②] 两例均引自 Sally King, *Pocket Guide to Advertising*. Basil Blackwell (UK) and the Economist Publications, 1989, p. 93 / p. 75。

举一例：

> They Laughed When I Sat Down
> At The Piano
> But When I Started To Play!

这是美国一所音乐学校的广告①。"当我坐在钢琴旁的时候，他们开始狂笑"，但是"当我开始演奏的时候"，情况又是怎样呢？由于"laugh"的陪衬和"but"的转折，读者不禁要想：那肯定是"鸦雀无声了"。为什么在一阵"狂笑"过后会"鸦雀无声"呢？那想必演奏"精彩极了！"，以至于一个个听得目瞪口呆吧。

三、使用祈使句，发出召唤

广告的目的就在于诱导人们认同某种观点，因而广告中大量使用含有请求、号召意义的祈使句。祈使句运用得当，给人一种亲切、自信的感觉。万宝路香烟的广告标题就是一个典型的例子。

> Come to where the flavor is
> Come to Marlboro Country!

四、突出利益

从内容上来说，怎样才算是好的广告标题，三言两语很难说清，但一点可以肯定，那就是要突出广告产品将给消费者带来什么样的利益，要在有形无形中让读者感到"有利可图"。在中外广告中，这方面成功的例子不少：

---

① 引自 Sally King, *Pocket Guide to Advertising*. Basil Blackwell (UK) and the Economist Publications, 1989, p. 108。

第九章　涉外广告的特点与翻译

> HOW TO WIN FRIENDS
> AND INFLUNCE PEOPLE①

这是美国代尔·卡耐基（Dale Carnegie）给读者许下的诺言，曾风靡世界，令数以百万的人为之动心。

> I'll do a lot for love, but
> I'm not ready to die for it.②

这是一则推销避孕套的广告标题。这类广告标题最令撰稿人头痛，要么太俗太露，受到大众的批评，传播媒介也不易接受；要么过于笼统，不着边际，让人看了莫名其妙。这则广告标题的成功之处，在于抓住了人们恐惧艾滋病的心理，含蓄地表达了这一主题，真可谓"雅俗共赏"，实在难得！

五、利用反论

广告标题要引人注意，利用反论（Paradox）是绝招之一。一些标题乍看之下自相矛盾，或违反常识，或荒谬透顶，这就激发了读者探其究竟的兴趣。在推敲之后，你会茅塞顿开，觉得这些话言之有理，甚至妙不可言，让人佩服。请看大众牌汽车（Volkswagen）的一则广告标题：

> Ugly is only skin-deep.

这则标题乍看之下十分古怪，但我们马上会联想到"Beauty is only skin-deep"这么一则谚语。该谚语原指"漂亮的外表是富于欺骗性的，在漂亮的外表

---

① 引自 Sally King, *Pocket Guide to Advertising*. Basil Blackwell (UK) and the Economist Publications, 1989, p. 108。

② 引自 Dorothy Cohen, *Advertising*, U.S.A.: Scott, Foresman and Company, 1988, pp. 582-583。

之下可能有非常不相称的品质"。将"beauty"巧妙地改为"ugly",不就成了"丑陋的外表之下有十分可贵的品质"吗?自然,广告的本意不是说大众汽车"外表丑陋","偷梁换柱"的目的在于突出它的"内在美"。从广告正文中,我们可以进一步了解到,"大众"汽车之所以外表"奇特",是因为它具有许多其他汽车所不具备的功能和优点,而正是这些特殊功能和好处,要求"大众"的造型与"众"不同。一旦你真正了解了"大众",你也就不会在乎其"丑陋"的外表了,甚至你会喜欢它现在这个样子,因为它给你带来那么多的"实惠"(请参阅本章第五节该广告的正文)。

实际上,在汉语的广告语中也经常能见到这种独出心裁的例子。例如某茶店的广告语:

> 客至心常热,人走茶不凉。

六、活用成语、名句或谚语

这是许多广告撰稿人的看家法宝。成语、名句或谚语,其结构、用词和使用场合都是相对固定的,但有时广告撰稿人故意"张冠李戴"或"移花接木",借成语、名句或谚语原来的结构或含义诱发读者的联想,诙谐成趣,耐人寻味,造成特殊效果,给读者留下深刻印象。例如:

> A Mars a day keeps you work, rest and play.

这是 Mars 巧克力糖的广告,在英国的一些街头巷尾都能看到。它的成功之处在于针对儿童的特点,巧妙地套用了英语中两个家喻户晓的谚语,即"An apple a day keeps the doctor away."和"All work and no play makes Jack a dull boy.",整句口号的弦外之音就是 Mars 巧克力功效非凡,每天一块既保健又益智。这给闹吃巧克力糖的小朋友提供了正当理由。广告口号既押韵,节奏感又强,朗朗上口,更适于口边传咏,这当然能起到很好的促销作用。

> Now You Can Have Your Cake And Diet Too.

这是一则蛋糕广告。"减肥"是当今社会女性的热门话题。这则广告标题对那些既想吃零食又担心发胖的人非常有诱惑力,它也是套用了一句谚语,即"You can't eat your cake and have it.",字面意思是"吃了蛋糕就不能再拥有蛋糕,想拥有蛋糕就不能吃蛋糕",即"两者不可兼得"。如果直接套用,那就是:"Now you can not eat your cake and have diet."(你想减肥就别吃蛋糕,你若吃蛋糕就必定发胖。)但撰稿人一反常规(即利用上文中提到的"反论"),将原来的否定形式改成肯定形式,变成了"减肥蛋糕",这不让体胖的人垂涎三尺吗?

> If you are what you eat, a visit to North Carolina could make you a very interesting person, indeed.①

这是 North Carolina(北卡罗来纳)的旅游广告,画面是各种新鲜水果和蔬菜。广告表现手法非常含蓄,耐人寻味。它套用了一句英语谚语:"You are what you eat.(人者人所食。)"原指从生理学的角度说,正是人吃的食物构成了人的躯体,并影响人的健康和气质。换言之,你吃什么,你就会变成什么样的人。广告的弦外之音不难体会,即"北卡罗来纳:食物丰富,新鲜可口,到此一游,你定能吃得健康,玩得开心,何不一试?"。

七、巧用修辞

广告撰稿人,为达到广告的注意价值和记忆价值,总是力求在遣词造句上标新立异,采用各种修辞常常能获得理想的效果。

(一) 双关

> A Deal With Us Means A Good Deal To You.

---

① 引自 Dorothy Cohen, *Advertising*, U.S.A.: Scott, Foresman and Company, 1988, pp. 454–455。

这是某百货公司的广告,巧就巧在将"a good deal"的常用意义"许多/很多"和广告所要表达的特殊含义"一笔好买卖"有机地结合在一起。①

> Give a SEIKO to all, and to all a good time.

"走时准确"(keep a good time),是任何手表的基本特点,但 SEIKO 却异乎寻常,它还能令戴表的人"心情愉快"(have a good time)。

(二) 重复

> Vandermint isn't good because it's imported;
> it's imported because it's good.②

这是一则巧克力酒的广告,用词之妙,堪称一绝。两个分句,事实上只用了 7 个单词,撰稿人把这 7 个单词神奇地组合在一起(其中"it's"重复了两次,"imported""because""good"分别重复了一次),一再强调一个概念:Vandermint —— 不同凡响!

> Reliably Solid, Solidly Reliable.③

这是一则汽车广告,十分有特色,它不是简单的重复,而是通过改变词性和颠倒词序,造成特殊效果。读完之后,"Solid, Reliable; Reliable, Solid"似乎不绝于耳。

---

① 引自侯维瑞:"漫论广告英语",载《中国人民解放军外国语学院学报》1988 年第 1 期和第 2 期。

② 引自 Donald A. Daiker et al, *The Writer's Option*, New York / London: Harper & Row · Publishers, 1982, pp. 232-233。

③ 摘自 *South China Morning Post*。

（三）隐喻

> You're better off under the Umbrella.

这是旅游保险公司的广告，语言诙谐，喻义一目了然。

（四）对比

> A Business in Millions
> A Profit in Pennies

其他修辞手法还有拟人、夸张、押韵等，这里就不再赘述。以上归类，有所侧重，仅是为了叙述方便，许多广告标题，可能综合运用几种技巧。

第二节　广告标题、口号的翻译

每一则出色的广告标题或口号都是撰稿员精心创意的结果。要将这些创意转换成另一种语言谈何容易！翻译这些广告标题或口号很难定出什么条条框框，有时靠巧合，有时靠灵感。上一节已大篇幅介绍了广告标题或口号的句法和修辞特点，目的就是让学习者在翻译实践时加以模仿，在模仿的基础上发挥各自的创造性。下面介绍几种常见的翻译方法。

一、直译法

直译法就是基本保持原句的句法和修辞特点，语言形式与内容一致。能够做到这一点，那是最理想的。

> At 60 miles an hour
> the loudest noise in this new Rolls-Royce
> comes from the electric clock.

试译：

> 时速60英里
> 这款新式"劳斯莱斯"轿车里最响的噪音
> 是来自车内的电子钟。

这则广告标题是美国广告撰稿人 David Ogilvy 的成名之作①。广告质朴无华，但构思独特。译文保留原广告的风格，按陈述句直译，效果相当，就像一位天生丽质的少女，无须打扮也是漂亮的。

> They Laughed When I Sat Down at the Piano.
> But When I Started to Play！

试译：

> 当我坐到钢琴旁时，他们开始狂笑。但是当我开始演奏时！②

> Reliably Solid, Solidly Reliable

试译：

> 安如磐石，磐石之安。

---

① 引自 Sally King, *Pocket Guide to Advertising*, Basil Blackwell (UK) and the Economist Publications, 1989, p.108。

② 出处同①，p.108。凡本章编者所译的广告标题或口号均标注"试译"字样。

第九章 涉外广告的特点与翻译

You're better off under the Umbrella.①

试译：

置身保护伞下，何惧不测风云！

A Business in Millions
A Profit in Pennies
百万生意，毫厘利润。

KODAK
With You
请你随身携带柯达

这是柯达公司1910年推出的一幅广告。广告上方的文字就是"KODAK With you"。文字下方是一幅挎着女用包、手拿照相机、端庄质朴的"柯达姑娘"（KODAK Girl）的插图，柯达姑娘是人们想象的美女的化身。因此，广告标题中的KODAK一语双关。译文配上图片能保留原来的修辞特点。

一旦绿色消失
Once The Green Is Fading Away.

---

① 英语原文引自赵静：《广告英语》，外语教学与研究出版社1992年版，第34页。

天有不测风云	Up in the sky there is unforeseen storm
但是	But
如果你参加保险	If you buy insurance
那么……	Then…

上一例是林业部广告，图案是黄土龟裂、仅存北极一小块绿色的地球。下一例是中国人民保险公司推出的一幅广告。两则广告的英语译文在措辞、句式和修辞特点上与中文一致，效果甚佳。

二、意译法

意译法，即改变原文的修辞特点或基本句式的译法。由于两种语言存在着词义、结构、文化等多方面的差异，在很多情况下都不宜直译，或无法直译。尤其是一些修辞特点，如"双关"和一些玩弄文字游戏的特殊句式，如果勉强直译，不但不能忠实原文，达到预期目的，反而弄巧成拙。在这些情况下，我们采取意译。

Women Can Indeed Go Bald.

试译：

谁说女子不秃头？

某护发中心广告。如果直译，就是"女子的确可能秃头"，这就不像广告了。现改用反诘句，原来靠"Indeed"一词加强语气，译文则靠句式来引起读者的注意，译文句式变了，用词变了，但效果无不及而有过之。

A Mars a day keeps you work, rest and play.

试译：

每天一颗"火星"，让你万事称心。

> Can't Beat The Real Thing.
> 挡不住的诱惑！

这是美国可口可乐广告标语。引自《国际广告》1994 年第 3 期，译文颇传神。

> 汲取生物精华，焕发生命潜能。
> Essence of Living Beings
> Energy for Life

这是广东"太阳神"口服液广告。汉语是两个并列的祈使句，译者则用排偶的手法，凭借两个并列的名词短语和它们的前后顺序来暗示"生物精华"和"生命潜能"的关系。

> 让"上宝交通"驰名世界，让世界遍布"声佳"电器。
> Our aim:
> Make a global hit —Shengjia Auto Electric

这是一则上海户外广告。汉语采用了对偶和顶真的手法，是一个不错的广告语。如果直译成英语，不是不可能，但势必十分单调刻板。英语完全跳出了原文的句式，采取宣言式的写法，很有气势，很有新意。

三、四字结构法

这是专门针对英译汉来说的。汉语广告多用四字结构，原因很简单，因为四字结构节奏感强，朗朗上口，便于记忆。因此，用四字结构来译广告口号是很自然的。试举几例：

Taste that beats the other Colds. (Pepsi-Cola 广告)
百事可乐,冷饮之王。

Fresh up with Seven-up (Seven-up 广告)
君饮七喜,提神醒脑。

Good to the last drop. (Maxwell 咖啡广告)
滴滴香浓,意犹未尽。

Tastes too good for words (某食品广告)

试译:

其味无穷,妙不可言。

The more you write
The more you satisfy. (某自来水笔广告)

试译:

一写满意,再写难忘。

The Globe brings you the world in a single copy. (杂志广告)
一册在手,纵览全球。

FIYTA Watch, Once Possessed, Nothing More Is Expected. (手表广告)

"飞亚达"表,一旦拥有,别无所求。

国外有些厂商在中国做的汉语广告也是采用四字结构,如日本 Sony 公司在北京的一块户外广告是这样写的:

Sony 彩电,单枪三束,气贯长虹,颜色鲜明。

四、套译法

什么是套译法呢?用一句话来概括,就是借用译入语中某些惯用结构来进行翻译的一种方法(structure borrowing)。被借用的结构可以是成语、谚语、一句诗,或者本身就是广告标题或口号。总而言之,这个被借用的结构必须是人们喜闻乐见、家喻户晓的。试举例说明。

Ugly is only skin-deep.

试译:

其貌不扬。

英语原文套用了一句英语谚语,取的是话外音。我们试套用了汉语里的另一个成语,取的也是话外音。两者看似风马牛不相及,但仔细推敲,却有异曲同工之处。另外,汉语中还有其他可套用的成语,如"金玉其外,败絮其中",利用反论,可译成"败絮其外"。但考虑到词的搭配习惯、产品特点以及该成语可能给读者唤起的形象,笔者以为,"其貌不扬"可为上选。

> I'll do a lot for love, but
> I'm not ready to die for it.

试译：

> 情爱诚销魂，生命价更高！

如果把原标题直译为"我愿为爱情付出许多，但我不准备为爱情牺牲"，那就淡然无味了。我们试着套用了在中国传咏甚广的匈牙利诗人裴多菲的几句诗："生命诚可贵，爱情价更高。若为自由故，两者皆可抛。"译文取"反论"，一拍即合。也许"风流"两字比"情爱"更为贴切，但考虑到中国国情，选取"情爱"两字则更为稳妥和高雅。

> Vandermint isn't good because it's imported;
> it's imported because it's good.

试译：

> 好酒不在进口，进口必是酒好。

"Vandermint"为酒名，请参照前节分析。中国有句俗语，叫作"山不在高，有仙则名；水不在深，有龙则灵"。译文仿此结构，并在词序上作技巧处理，最大限度再现了原广告语的风貌，也可看作直译的一个例子。

> 有了南方，就有办法了。[①]
> Where there is South, there is a way.

这是南方科技咨询服务公司的广告。这个译文显然是套用了英语中最常见的一句谚语，即"Where there is a will, there is a way."。译文只换了一词，但因与

---

① 摘自《中国科技翻译》1993 年第 4 期。

该公司服务特点挂了钩，恰到好处，韵味无穷。给顾客的印象是：这家咨询公司的办法的确不少！

食在广州。

试译：

East or west, the Guangzhou cuisine is best.

在广州，茶楼酒家星罗棋布，名菜美点品种繁多，小吃摊档更是数不胜数，历史上早有"食在广州"的美誉。然而，要将这朴实无华但却寓意深刻的广告语译成相当的英语，则颇费心思。广州某大酒店把它译为"Eating in Guangzhou"，这显然是逐词死译，既不合文意，也令人没有胃口。在几本介绍广州的宣传册子里，还可以见到这样几种译文：1) Guangzhou is the place to eat. 2) If you like great cuisine, come to Guangzhou. 3) Guangzhou, the paradise for gourmands. 三种译文各有各的问题。本书的翻译是套用了英语谚语："East or west, home is best."即走南闯北，家乡最美。经替换后，不就成了"走南闯北，广州菜最美"了吗！这样翻译不仅意思正确，还人情味十足，若是出现在大酒店，效果更佳。

从本章中的许多中英文广告标题、口号可以看出，套用人们耳熟能详的成语、名句或谚语也是用母语制作广告的绝招之一，这就难怪套译法能取得较好的效果。除上面提到的许多英文的例子外，中文的例子也不难找到。例如：

山不在高，有林则贵。
（资生堂"不老林"养发精广告）
胃病患者"治"在"四方"。
（广州"四方"牌胃片广告）
中国美食在广州，广州美食在中国。
（广州"中国大酒店"广告）

日本某些大企业就深得其中的奥妙，他们常常根据目标市场的文化制作专门的广告，以赢得消费者的好感。比如日本的汽车制造行业在中国做的几则广告都大胆套用了中国家喻户晓的古谚：

> 车到山前必有路，有路必有丰田车。
> 路遥知马力，日久见丰田。
> 古有千里马，今有日产车。
> 有朋自远方来，喜乘三菱牌。

针对美国市场，日本三菱汽车公司的广告则是这样写的：

> Not all cars are created equal.

这套用了《美国独立宣言》中的第一句话：All men are created equal.（众生平等。）言外之意就是：车与车是不一样的，且看我三菱汽车。

针对英国市场，日本本田汽车公司也有一则很妙的广告：

> Home Sweet Honda.

这则标题从结构上看就已经够古怪的了，名词＋形容词＋名词，既不像个短语，又不像个句子，但撰稿员却谙熟英国文化。原来，这则广告是套用了英国妇孺皆知的一则歌谣。这则歌谣的名字就是：Home, Sweet Home. 原指英国人传统上都十分恋家。撰稿人将 Honda 套到歌谣里，Honda 不就成了"甜蜜的家"吗？妙就妙在 Honda 与 Home 有谐音之趣。

日本航空公司对欧洲大陆的一则广告标题也很独特：

> One man's sushi is another man's steak.

这则广告标题套用了英语谚语：One man's meat is another man's poison. 即

"一个人的佳肴,却是另一个人的毒药"。套用后的广告便成了:"一个人的寿司,也是另一个人的牛排。"或倒过来说:"一个人的牛排,也是另一个人的寿司。"换言之,乘坐日航航班,无论是日本人(或东方人),还是欧洲人(或西方人),都可以享受到可口的餐饮服务,不会因口味的不同而有任何的不快。

由此可见,套译法,如果运用得当,不仅能很好地传递原广告语的意义,还能很好地保存原广告语的风格,从而引起译入语读者的强烈共鸣,是翻译广告标题、口号的上选方法,值得研究和推广。

第三节 广告标题、口号翻译应注意的问题

一、广告标题或口号的翻译贵在创新,切忌步人后尘

这一点尤为重要。实际上,用原语创作广告也是如此。比如,看到人家的"'飞亚达'表,一旦拥有,别无所求",你也来一个"××××,一旦拥有,别无所求",他再来一个"××××,一旦拥有,别无所求",拾人牙慧,步人后尘,再好的东西也会令人反感。套译法是翻译广告标题、口号的一个很好的方法,但同样不能鹦鹉学舌。例如英谚"Seeing is believing."这个结构就被许多中文广告的翻译所套用,什么"Tasting is believing."(某粮油食品公司广告),"Seeing is believing."(某电视机广告),"Using is believing."(某护肤霜广告),不一而足。从套译技巧上来说,如能在被套用结构上有所变异(如本章中多次提到的"反论"),则更能吸引读者。

二、广告标题或口号的翻译应注意中英广告语的不同特点

从以上例子中不难看出,中文广告直接型、宣示型的多。比如上面提到的"食在广州",还有"桂林山水甲天下""洛阳牡丹甲天下"等等;而英文广告含蓄型、委婉型的多。比如同样是旅游广告,他们却饶有兴趣地说:"If you are what you eat, a visit to North Carolina would make you a very interesting person."(请参阅前一节)这样的例子在英语的广告里不胜枚举,也是值得我们广告撰稿人或翻译工作者学习的地方。显然,含蓄或委婉型的广告给人更多的回味。

中文广告里短语结构多(如四字结构),并列结构多(如对偶句);英语广告也用短语和对偶,但结构更富于变化,并且在很多场合更偏爱使用句子(如前面所介绍的疑问句、祈使句、省略句等)。因此,英译汉时,我们可发挥汉语优势,多采用四字结构、并列结构;但汉译英时就大可不必一律译成四平八稳的结

构。如某名牌铅笔的广告语"品质优良，书写润滑，美观大方"的译文是"Superior in quality, Smooth in Writing, Excellent in Appearance"。这种译文可谓"忠实"有余，但"味道"不足。又如浙江省的旅游广告"诗画江南，山水浙江"的英译文是"Poetic Jiangnan, Picturesque Zhejiang"；《漓江游》的广告词"百里漓江，百里画廊"的英译文是"A hundred miles Lijiang River, A hundred miles Picturesque Gallery"。我们不是反对使用这种平稳的结构（过于"平稳"就会显得"呆板"），而是强调要了解中英文广告语的这种区别，不要过度追求这种结构。自然，同样的结构，也会有效果很好的。例如2008北京奥运的口号"同一个世界，同一个梦想"的公选英译文就是"One World, One Dream"。

在英文的广告语里，使用句子的效果往往比使用短语的效果好，这一点很容易被我们忽视，因为在中文里，我们历来讲究锤炼词句，而使用句子就难免"不够简洁"。但短语和句子的韵味有时是很不一样的。请看广东利莱时装有限公司的广告语的翻译就处理得很不错：

> 利莱时装，真我个性，淑女形象
> Lilai gives you a sense of time,
> a true yourself and a pretty girl.
> 利莱时装，时代的感觉。

广告还配有身着"利莱"时装、摆着不同走姿、呈倒"品"字分布的三位妙龄女性，图文并茂。

三、广告标题或口号的翻译可采用更为灵活的方法

国内许多广告标题或口号本身质量就不高或不宜转换成外语，如需翻译，应大胆变通，甚至重写。比如某时装厂的广告口号是"天天×××，成功每一刻"，翻译人员勉为其难地把它译为"××× BRINGS YOU SUCCESS"。又如，"长城电扇，电扇长城"，其中"长城"的英语名为"the Great Wall"，如果照原文字面直译，看来是难以达到预期的效果的。另外，国内的一些涉外广告有的是以厂家名称代替标题，这不利于促销。翻译时可征得厂家的同意，增加英语标题或口号。

第四节 商标的特点与翻译

一、商标的特点

商标一般包括三个部分：商标牌号（brand name）、厂商名称和视觉标记。本节只讨论前面两个部分。

商标是企业的无形资产，它体现了企业的形象及其产品或服务的信誉。名牌商标一旦树立，可给企业带来巨额利益。在现代社会中往往出现这种情况，同一种类的商品，其质量、原料或成分相当，名牌产品可以比普通产品的售价高出几倍，甚至几十倍。因为许多消费者，与其说他们能真正分辨质量的好坏，不如说是心理因素在起作用，他们购买商品实际上是在购买品牌。

俗话说"不怕生坏相，就怕起坏名"。一个不具任何意义的商标，即使产品很好，也难以在消费者心中树立良好形象。正是基于这种认识，一些有远见的企业在给产品确定牌号时决不掉以轻心。美国一家眼镜厂以三个英文字母"OIC"作为商标，一眼看去，构图酷似一副眼镜，而读起来犹如"Oh, I see!（啊，我看见了！）"。世界胶卷之王"柯达"公司，是以照相时快门的声音来确定胶卷的牌子，而广告口号则是"请你按下快门，其余的由我们来做"。其用心之良苦，由此可见一斑。现在国内越来越多的企业也认识到好商标的重要性，有的不惜重金征集商标，也有不少外商为使其产品打入中国市场，以高薪聘请中方翻译人员反复推敲，再三筛选，确定最佳译名。

好的商标应具有哪些特点呢？事实上，给商品命名与父母给孩子取名的道理是一样的。中国的命名学有着悠久的历史，所谓"义求隽永含蓄、音讲响亮好听、形看工整简易"，所谓"别致、典雅、浑成"，这些对产品的命名都有参考价值。从广告学的角度说，商品命名须考虑以下的因素。

是否具有新意。是否给人以崭新的感觉？是否好念、好听、好写、好记、好联想？广州市商业中心有家无人不晓的百货公司——"新大新"，这个牌号真是令人耳目一新，拍案叫绝！"日新月异""新的姿态""新的面貌""新的服务"等任你联想，并且左念右念都一样。过去初来广州的人唯恐没有光顾"南方大厦"，而今日乍到广州的人则问"怎么去'新大新'？"。可见"好的名字"即是企业或商品最贴切的自我推销。

能否暗示产品的功能和利益点。这一点十分重要。有些商标，看似堂皇，却与产品特性没有挂钩，没有针对性。这很难引起消费者的购买欲。比如，"男子汉"在现代社会中倍受人们的青睐，它可象征健壮或刚强，但若用做牙膏的品牌，恐怕就不那么恰当了。目前电视上有关保健口服液的广告做得特别多，但多数牌号不尽如人意，当然也有十分出色的。如杭州的"娃哈哈"，"娃"字暗示了主要消费对象是小孩，"哈哈"两字包含四个"口"字，表示是"吃"的东西，"哈哈"一词又是对这种商品的承认和赞美。汉语中能暗示产品功能和利益点的佳例还有不少，如"鸭鸭牌"羽绒衣、"不老林"养发精、"黑而亮"鞋油、"美好挺"衬衫、"美加净"牙膏、"味全"酱油等等。

是否具有适应性。比如，是否容易转换成外国语言？在给商品命名时，可同时考虑翻译问题。这种做法省去了以后许多麻烦，值得提倡。因为有的商标中文很有新意，但要找个相当的英文译名却不易，甚至不可能。国外有些企业为了开拓中国市场，就自己取了个汉语牌号，如生产复印机的 Xerox Corporation 的中文名字叫"施乐公司"，Goodyear Tire & Rubber Co. 的中文名字叫"固特异"。日本厂商的精明让人佩服，他们许多产品的牌号一开始就使用英文，如 Canon，Sony，Casio，可见他们产品的宗旨就是面向世界的。现在，国内也有许多品牌一开始就有中英两种牌号，如广东的"乔士"衬衫的英语牌号为"Choose"。"Choose"一词用得不错，很有商品味。上海的名牌产品"美加净"牙膏，不但中文名字取得很美，它的英文名字"MAXAM"也颇具新意。它既像是个土生土长的英语单词，又不是个现成的英语单词，它是个有创意的英文商标。从形态上看，四平八稳，左念右念都一个样，也十分便于记忆。另一个可与之媲美的例子是广东的"太阳神"（Apollo）口服液，"Apollo"在希腊神话里是主管光明、青春、音乐、诗歌、医药等的神，又是青年美男子的化身。"太阳神"（Apollo）正像它的广告语"当太阳升起的时候，我们的爱天长地久"那样，充满着活力，充满着诗情画意！

能否获准注册，取得法律上的保障。所有商标均须向所在国家的商标管理机构申请注册，商标一经注册，商标注册人即享有商标专用权，受法律的保护。因此，商标要注册，首先要避免与他人已注册或已申请注册的商标相同或近似。除此以外，不能或较难获准注册的还有以下几种情况：

（1）商品通用名称或标志。
（2）国家名称、国旗、国徽、军旗等国家标志或者近似的。
（3）国际组织的名称、标志或者近似的。
（4）过分简单而缺乏识别性的标志。
（5）通用的姓氏名称。
（6）地理名称或标志。
（7）违反法律、公共道德、公共秩序或带民族歧视性的。

(8) 直接表示商品的质量、主要原料、功能、用途、重量、数量及其他特点的夸大宣传并带有欺骗性的。

美国 Coca-Cola 公司原先只以"Coca-Cola"作为该饮料的注册商标，但人们习惯上把它简称"Coke"。其他一些厂商为投公众所好，开始用"Coke"一词作为商标。Coca-Cola 公司于是向法院起诉。1920 年，美国最高法院做出裁决，认为"Coke"和"Coca-Cola"同出一源。Coca-Cola 公司胜诉以后，也以"Coke"一词作为商标注册，并写成广告口号："Coca-Cola is Coke，Coke is Coca-Cola"。从这一点看，做好商标的自我保护也是十分重要的。根据西方学者的研究，商标词可分为四大类，它们的法律保障按顺序由强到弱，这四类商标词是：

第一类：创造词或随意词（invented or arbitrary），前者如 Kodak 胶卷，后者如 Apple 电脑。

第二类：暗示性词（suggestive），如用"Ivory（象牙）"作肥皂的商标来暗示该肥皂的纯度。

第三类：描述性词（descriptive），如用"Comfort（舒适）"作鞋类的商标。

第四类：商标通用词（generic），如 Cola。

因此，好的商标一般都选用第一类或第二类词，尽可能避免使用第三类词，而不使用第四类词。除此以外，法律保护系数小的商标词还有：赞美称颂之词（laudatory names），如"perfection"（完美）、"modern"（摩登）、"super"（超级），等等；纯粹的字母组合或数字组合（IBM 等只能算是特例）。

二、商标的翻译

商标的翻译与商标的设计一样，主要也是从音、形、意三个方面考虑。音，即好读、好听；形，即易写、简单、工整；意，即隽永、典雅。从现在的商标译例来看，商标的翻译可分音译法、意译法和谐音联想法三大类。

（一）音译法

按"名从主人"的原则，根据原语发音译写。

英译汉的例子：

Ford	福特（轿车）
Lincoln	林肯（轿车）
Rolls-Royce	劳斯莱斯（轿车）
Sony	索尼（电视机）
Casio	卡西欧（电子琴）

Marlboro	万宝路（香烟）
Parker	派克（钢笔）
Nike	耐克（运动系列）
Gillette	吉列（剃须刀）
Rolex	劳力士（手表）

汉译英的例子：

神州（燃气具）	Shenzhou
春兰（空调器）	Chunlan
虹美（电视机）	Hongmei
工夫（便拖鞋）	Gong Fu
万家乐（燃气具）	Wan Jia Le
华生（电扇）	Watson
美晨（牙膏）	Mason
美加净（牙膏）	MAXAM
美的（家电）	Midea
添美食（快餐店）	Timmy's

音译看似简单，却也有许多讲究，译者在动笔之前，都有斟酌比较的过程。这其中有客观的原因，如有的商标更便于音译或只宜音译；也有主观的原因，要不然同是以姓氏命名的汽车，有的按音译，如"Lincoln"（林肯）；有的却采用谐音联想译法，如"Benz"（奔驰），并且这个商标的汉语译名还是从音译"本茨"改译过来的。这种情况也许与该姓氏的知名度有关。另外，如果是以常用姓氏或重要地理名称来命名的商标，音译时最好查查《人名译名手册》或《地名译名手册》，如不要将"Ford"轿车译成了"福德"。

从音译的例子来看，其"音"的译写并不是很严格的（也没有必要那么严格）。可见虽然不是"意"译，选词也有一定的考虑，好的音译商标总是能从某个侧面揭示该商品的特点。例如，"索尼"给人一种典雅温馨的感觉，"卡西欧"富于一种节奏感，而"万宝路"则充满豪迈劲。

音译商标也有一定技巧，其原则是力求简短，省略某些非重读音节。如将"Parker"译成"派克"而不译成"派克尔"，将"Rolls-Royce"译成"劳斯莱斯"而不译为"罗尔斯·罗迈斯"。

如系汉译英，有两种情况：一是按汉语拼音，二是谐音造词。后者值得提倡，本节所举的后5个例子都颇具创意。国内目前大多数音译商标是以汉语拼音转写的，我们觉得应尽量少用，尤其是有些汉语拼音几个音节是分开书写，连贯性差，于读于写都不方便。另外，值得注意的是，若用汉语拼音做商标，最好查查英文词典，看英语中是否有与该拼音商标完全一样的词，若有，应弄清该词词义是褒、是贬，或与该产品是否相符。这巧合不是没有可能。有学者指出，我国曾经有种"芳芳"牌的化妆系列产品被译为"Fang Fang"，不幸，英语"fang"一词却是指"蛇"等的"毒牙"。

与其他两种方法相比，音译法有一定局限，商品气息差些。比如"派克"和"劳斯莱斯"，它们本身并没有告诉消费者什么，如属新产品，人们也很难猜到它们分别是"钢笔"和"汽车"商标，这不便于商品促销。

但另一方面，由于音译商品均系随意词或创造词（arbitrary or invented names），它们与别的商标雷同的可能性小，并且作为新词，更能引起读者的注意，这是音译商标的优点。

(二) 意译法

意译法即按原语基本词义译写的一种方法。
英译汉的例子：

Orient	东方（手表）
Microsoft	微软（公司）
Volkswagen	大众（汽车）
Ivory	象牙（香皂）
Camel	骆驼（香烟）
Shell	壳（石油）
Apple	苹果（电脑）
Good Companion	良友（香烟）
Rock	滚石（唱片）
Gulf	海湾（石油公司）

汉译英的例子：

小天鹅（洗衣机）	Little Swan
太阳神（口服液）	Apollo
"葵花"牌（电扇）	Sunflower

"永久"牌（自行车）	Forever
"黑旋风"（杀虫剂）	Black Swirl Wind
"王朝"（葡萄酒）	Dynasty
"蝴蝶"牌（缝纫机）	Butterfly
"海鸥"牌（相机）	Sea-gull
"双喜"牌（香烟）	Double Happiness
"熊猫"牌（电子）	Panda

意译商标也应有一定的根据：有的按音译太长（如 Volkswagen）；有的则在取名时就有某种象征意义（比如用国宝"熊猫"暗示电子的高质量，用洁白的"小天鹅"表示洗衣机的优良性能，用"黑旋风"象征杀虫剂的威力）；有的意在创新（如用惹人喜爱的"Apple"喻电脑）；有的具有一定的纪念意义（如 Shell 石油公司的创始人原来是靠 shell 起家的）。翻译这类以"意"命名的商标时，借用"名从主人"的原则，还是还其本来面目为宜。

意译也应力求简短，比如"黑旋风"这一商标名别开生面，但"Black Swirl Wind"这个英译商标却似乎太长，不如改成"Black Wind"，或干脆就用"Swirl"，干脆利落，更显威力！国内许多英译商标多喜欢用"brand"一词，如"××"牌自行车译为"×× Brand Bicycle，而根据英文的习惯，在大多数情况下该词纯属多余。

（三）谐音联想法

所谓谐音联想法，即音译原文近似，意取音之联想。这种翻译方法既不同于音译法，又不同于意译法。音译法纯系谐音，不考虑词义问题；意译法不能脱离原文词义，但不必兼顾语音。谐音联想法则要音义兼顾，而词义又往往非原词词义，须加创造。这种方法若使用得当，可顾名思义，联想到产品的特点或性能，从而诱发消费者的购买欲。又因为这种方法吸收了音译法和意译法的长处，因此越来越受到广大翻译人员的青睐。

英译汉的例子：

Coca-Cola	可口可乐（饮料）
7 – Up	七喜（饮料）
Sprite	雪碧（饮料）
Holsten	好顺（啤酒）
Simmons	席梦思（床具）

Colgate	高露洁（牙膏）
Avon	雅芳（化妆品）
Pentium	奔腾（微处理器）
Pif Paf	必扑（杀虫剂）
Benz	奔驰（轿车）

汉译英的例子：

仙泉（酒店名）	Century
四通（电脑公司）	Stone
回力（运动鞋）	Warrior
乔士（衬衫）	Choose
北大方正（集团）	Founder
海信（集团）	Hisense
格力（家电）	GREE
海尔（空调）	Haier
雅戈尔（西服）	Youngor
联想（集团）	Legend（后因注册问题更名 Lenovo）

Coca-Cola 的汉译就是运用这一方法的杰出例子。"可口可乐"真是有"口"皆碑！到目前为止，还没有谁想出比这更好的译名。这一译名就连美国 Coca-Cola 公司也十分赞赏，1912 年有一则广告竟把"可口可乐"回译成英语，作为广告进行宣传：

> Here's
> The Road to Comfort
> Coca-Cola
> Delicious — Refreshing
> Thirst— Quenching[①]

---

① 引自 Dorothy Cohen, *Advertising*, U. S. A. : Scott, Foresman and Company, 1988, pp. 6 – 7。

在上面所举的例子中，"Pif Paf"的汉译也是出神入化，叹为观止！"Pif Paf"原为拟声，并且一语双关，即可指喷药时的声音，又可指那些蚊子、蟑螂等害虫掉下来时噼噼扑扑的声音。汉译名"必扑"也可既拟声，又双关，简直完美无缺。更妙的是，其中"必"字还可理解为"必定"，"扑"字为"扑灭"，可见这种喷雾剂是"药"到"虫"灭！

采用这一方法汉译英的例子少些，看来还须大力推广。所举10个例子，个个独具匠心。"Century"与汉语的"百年老字号"旗鼓相当；用"Stone"（石头）来命名电脑公司，实在是妙趣横生！最后3例也很特别："gree"是苏格兰方言中的一个古词，作名词用时表示"优越、善意、恩惠"等意思，作动词用可当作"agree"的变体，另外，它还可能让你联想到"green"（暗示"安全、环保"）；Haier虽是汉语拼音，但读音与英文 higher 一致，寓意"追求完美"；而"Youngor"则让你"误读"成"younger"（越发年轻），这种"篡改"的字词还有一个额外的好处，就是十分便于注册。

谐音联想法的运用要求译者既有丰富的想象力，又有遣词运字的良好基本功，还要有较强的鉴赏能力。如"7-Up"的汉译，以"喜"译"Up"，是神来之笔！"Up"有"在上、向上"的含义，由此而引申为"奋起""精神焕发"。然而，如果将它译为"七上"，则读者、饮者必是马上想到"八下"，那就是十足的败笔了！另一个有趣的例子是，德产名车 Benz（原为德国汽车工业先驱之一 Karl-Friedrich Benz 的姓，汽车牌全名为 Mercedes Benz，但人们习惯上称它为 Benz），最早的译名是音译"本茨"，后来改译为"奔驰"。现在台湾译为"宾士"（最初译为"朋驰"），香港译为"平治"。"宾士"虽显高雅，而"平治"则格调又胜一筹，但两者都没有体现轿车的特点，相比之下，显然"奔驰"更入佳境。如果是初译，说不准译为"平驰"（平稳、安全、快捷），就更上一层楼了。

三、商标翻译应注意的事项

商标翻译，无论采用哪种方法，都应注意目标市场文化。比如，国内许多厂家喜欢用动物名作商品牌号，如"白象"牌电池（"White Elephant" battery），"金鸡"牌闹钟（"Golden Cock" alarm clock），"蝙蝠"牌电扇（"Bat" electric fan），"五羊"牌自行车（"Five Rams" bicycle），应有尽有。上述以动物命名的品牌在汉语中也许意念不错，如"白象"：力大无比；"金鸡"：雄鸡报晓；"蝠"：即"福"也；而"五羊"则取自于一个美丽的传说。但这些相应的英语商标却有悖英语文化："White Elephant"指"大而无当的东西"，"Bat"与"瞎"相联系（如"as blind as a bat"），"Ram"则是"好斗的象征"。由此看来，以动物命名商品应该谨慎，归纳起来原因有二：一是可用来做商品牌号的动物不多,并且好的别人已捷足先登;二是对同一动物,不同的民族可能赋予完全不同的喻义。

要了解目标市场文化,就必须对该市场做充分的调研。一分耕耘,一分收获。美国宝洁公司在中国成功开拓市场,毫无疑问其品牌命名是重要决策之一,这也为中国企业走向世界树立了典范。请看宝洁中国公司的系列产品:Rejoice / 飘柔, Pantene / 潘婷, Head & Shoulder / 海飞丝, Pampers / 帮宝适, Whisper / 护舒宝, Tide / 汰渍, Ariel / 碧浪, Crest / 佳洁士, Zest / 激爽, Safeguard / 舒肤佳。这些渗透中国文化的知名商标就像一个个身怀绝技的小精灵,在中国这个大商场攻"城"略"地"。该公司中文译名"宝洁"本身也是适应中国文化的产物,英文原名"P & G"(Procter & Gamble)只不过是该公司的两位创始人的姓氏。

第五节 广告正文的特点与翻译

广告正文,千变万化,不拘一格。既可以是小说体、说明体、论述体,也可以是对话体、诗文体,还可以是各种体裁和语体的混合。拟稿人根据不同的广告目标和广告媒体,标新立异,灵活运用。

一则好的广告正文,必定是广告标题的延伸,即对广告标题加以详尽的说明、解释,或是对广告标题所做的承诺加以证实,或是对广告产品或服务的特点以及与同类产品竞争的优势加以阐述。就其方法来说,要么以理服人,要么以情感人。

广告正文的语言,如同广告标题和口号的语言一样,应尽可能采用各种修辞手段,以期简明、生动、有趣、出其不意、引人入胜,把消费者带到感情的高潮,从而让他们认同广告所宣传的理念,采取购买行动。下面是3则精选的英文广告实例,并附上本书作者的汉语译文,供欣赏、模仿或课堂讲评。

Ugly Is Only Skin-deep[①]

---

① 英语广告原文选自 Dorothy Cohen, *Advertising*. U.S.A.: Scott, Foresman and Company, 1988, p.197。

It may not be much to look at. But beneath that humble exterior beats an air-cooled engine. It won't boil over and ruin your piston rings. It won't freeze over and ruin your life. It's in the back of the car for better traction in snow and sand. And it will give you about 29 miles to a gallon of gas.

After a while you get to like so much about the VW, you even get to like what it looks like.

You find that there's enough legroom for almost anybody's legs. Enough headroom for almost anybody's head. With a hat on it. Snug-fitting bucket seats. Doors that close so well you can hardly close them. They're so airtight, it's better to open the window a crack first!

Those plain, unglamorous wheels are each suspended independently. So when a bump makes one wheel bounce, the bounce doesn't make the other wheel bump. It's things like that you pay the $1 585 for, when you buy a VW. The ugliness doesn't add a thing to the cost of the car.

That's the beauty of it.

笔者参考译文：

其貌不扬

　　"大众"或许不中看，但在其陋表下跳动的却是一台心脏部件：气冷式发动机。它不会因沸溢而毁坏活塞环，也不会因结冰而误了您的事。它位于车的后部，以增大雪地沙土上行驶的牵引力。约莫29英里，仅耗汽油1加仑。

　　稍待您喜爱上"大众"，您甚至对其丑貌也会情有独钟。

　　您会发现其足够的伸腿空间，再长的腿也得以舒展；绰绰有余的头部空间，再高的个子戴上帽子也可昂首挺胸；凹背单人座椅，舒适贴身；关闭得再好不过的车门是如此密不透风，您最好先把车窗留条缝。

第九章　涉外广告的特点与翻译

其朴实无华、不显魅力的车轮各自独立悬挂。当颠簸使一轮跳起时，弹跳不会波及其他车轮。只要支付1585美元，那样的尤物就归您了。其丑陋的外表丝毫不增添您购车的费用。

这就是"大众"之美！

这是"大众"牌轿车（Volkswagen）的一篇广告正文。标题已是独出心裁，正文更是别具风味。正文运用了各种修辞手段（如拟人、排偶、重复、对照），语言诙谐幽默，在娓娓谈笑之中让你领悟到"大众"牌汽车之所以"其貌不扬"，是因为它"构造特异，功能超群"，最后引出结论："大众"牌轿车——金玉其中！

How to Fly Japanese Style

One Man's Sushi Is Another Man's Steak. ①

There's just no second guessing about taste. So, to keep everyone happy, we have a simple solution.

  Two cuisines.
  One is Japanese.
  The other is Continental.

No matter which one you choose—the familiar or the adventurous—one thing remains the same: the elegant, understated service that is ours alone.

It's reflected in the smile of your JAL hostess as she offers you a steaming oshibori towel to refresh yourself. Her delicate grace as she pours your sake. The very special way she makes you feel like an honored guest at a family banquet.

---

① 英语广告原文选自 William M. O'Barr, *Culture and the Ad: Exploring Otherness in the World of Advertising*, Boulder, San Francisco, Oxford: Westview Press, 1994, p. 169。

· 215 ·

Unique service like this doesn't just happen at mealtime. From our first hello to our last sayonara, we do our best to prove there's as much difference between airlines as between airline menus.

We're the one where East meets West.

JAPAN AIR LINES

笔者参考译文：

> **何谓日本特色的飞行？**
> **寿司牛排，各有所爱。**

君之口味，非此即彼。要想皆大欢喜，妙计在这里。

  两种菜肴：
  一为日本式，
  一为欧陆式。

  无论您选择哪一种——吃惯了的，还是从未尝过的——唯一不变的是：我们独一无二、典雅、谦恭的服务。
  日航服务，无微不至。它荡漾在空姐那柔美亲切的微笑里，当她奉上一方热气腾腾的香巾，让您提神醒脑时；它表现在空姐优雅细腻的举止中，当她给您斟上一杯日本清酒时；它还渗透在空姐独一无二的处事方式中，当她待您如家宴中的上宾时。
  这样独特的服务，并不限于用餐时间。从我们见面时的第一声"哈啰"，到我们送别时的"沙扬娜拉"，自始至终，我们都竭力向您证明：不同的航空公司不但食谱迥异，其提供的服务也千差万别。

  东西合璧，尽在日航公司！

日本航空公司

第九章　涉外广告的特点与翻译

Queen Elizabeth 2[①]

The fastest way to Europe is not the necessarily the best way. Sailing on Queen Elizabeth 2 is a vacation in itself, you do not arrive in a frazzle, more tired than when you left. You arrive as you should: refreshed, with new friends and new experiences.

There are more things to see and do abroad Queen Elizabeth 2 than there are in most European towns. She's 65 000 tons, 13 stories high, and longer than three football fields. Queen Elizabeth 2 is one of the great sights of Europe.

An airplane provides a seat, Queen Elizabeth 2 provides a stateroom nicer than most hotels in Europe. Room for room, she has the largest stateroom, wardrobes, dressing rooms, and bathrooms of any ships afloat.

Queen Elizabeth 2 has a staff of over 900. This means at least one crew member for every two passengers. When you ring for your steward or stewardess, the call is answered with dispatch. Like a good English butler or maid, they are there when you want them and not there when you don't want them.

Queen Elizabeth 2 carries so many passengers, you are bound to meet a host of people you like, or love. (Is there time to fall in love on an airplane?) And if you should happen to meet someone you don't like, a game of hide-and-seek aboard Queen Elizabeth 2 can last until Southampton.

Airplanes have a baggage limit of 44 pounds. Queen Elizabeth 2 has a baggage limit of 275 pounds, you may buy a car in Europe and bring it home in our garage. It will hold 80 cars. Our hold holds countless antiques.

---

① 英语广告原文转引自李中行、戚肖山、张惠：《广告英语》，湖南教育出版社1986年版，第37－39页。标题另加。本书作者在翻译此广告时曾参考过该书的译文。

$46 a day includes your stateroom, food and entertainment. Or you can spend $193 a day. The price depends on the size and location of your stateroom or suite and the time of year you sail. $46 per day in total is $321. This is $5 more than one-way economy air fare.

Imperial Iranian Beluga Caviar in First Class. As much as you want, whenever you want. At no extra charge. In the finest New York restaurants, it can cost $12.50 a serving.

After a few days at sea, look in the mirror, you will like the person you see. So will your spouse.

They may never build another one like her.

笔者参考译文:

伊丽莎白女王2号

赴欧洲旅行,最快的旅程未必就是最佳的选择。比如,乘坐伊丽莎白女王2号漂洋过海,虽耗费时日,但度假休闲自此开始。当您到达目的地时,您会像刚出发时那样,丝毫不觉旅途劳顿。当您到达目的地时,您应该是精神焕发,有了新友,还大增了见闻。

乘坐伊丽莎白女王2号,您可观赏许多景致,还可纵情娱乐。这为大多数欧洲城镇所不及。伊丽莎白女王2号,排水量为65000吨,高达13层,长于3个足球场,本身就是欧洲胜景之一。

飞机仅为乘客提供一个座位,而伊丽莎白女王2号却为您提供一个舱房,其豪华舒适,欧洲大多数旅馆要为之逊色。就房间而论,它的舱房、衣柜、化妆室和盥洗间较任何一艘船的都大。

伊丽莎白女王2号拥有900多位工作人员,这意味着每两位乘客至少有一位船员侍候。当您按铃叫唤服务员时,他们会随叫随到,就像训练有素的英国家仆,招之即来,挥之即去。

伊丽莎白女王2号载客如云,您无疑可遇见许多有趣的人,或您所爱的人(乘坐飞机有时间谈情说爱吗?)。即使碰巧遇上个不喜欢的人,您也尽可在船上和他（她）玩玩捉迷藏的游戏，避而不见，可一直玩到船抵南安普敦。

乘飞机旅行，行李限重仅44磅，但乘伊丽莎白女王2号，行李限重则高达275磅。您可在欧洲买辆轿车，停放在我们的汽车间，与您一同返家。该汽车间可停放80辆轿车。船上的专用货舱可任君存放多少古玩珍品。

一天46美元，就可全包舱房、膳食和娱乐。船上的最高收费也只不过是每天193美元，其价格的高低取决于舱房的大小、所处的位置、家具的陈设和航行的季节。以每天46美元计算，总航程共需321美元，该费用仅比单程经济机票贵5美元。

如果乘坐头等舱，您可随时尽情享用帝国伊朗白鲸鱼子酱，不另收费。若在纽约的上等餐馆，一份这样的鱼子酱，可高达12.50美元呢！

在海上航行数日后，再照照镜子，您定会喜欢镜中人，您的爱人想必也会如此。

或许永远也不会造出另一艘可与之媲美的船了。

这是美国Cunard航运有限公司宣传伊丽莎白女王2号客轮的广告正文的一部分。全文列举了为什么要乘坐伊丽莎白女王2号而不乘坐飞机（或其他客轮）的27条理由，读后怎能不令人动心！

第六节　广告正文汉译英存在的问题

在上一节，我们引用了3则国外的广告，目的在于借鉴。下面再看看国内的广告是个怎样的情形。

例1：

××厂是广东省机械厅定点专业厂，具有20多年的历史，占地面积有32万多平方米，水陆交通方便。产品有"××"牌圆锥滚子轴承系列和"××"牌橡胶密封元件系列。企业技术力量雄厚，设备先进，质量符合国际标准。荣获省优质奖和"星火计划"奖的称号，并取得国家"工艺突破口"会诊良好的成绩和出口产品质量许可证……

原译文：

Occupying an area of 320 000m², this 20-year-old factory is a designated enterprise under Guangdong Department of Machinery. It boasts substantial technical forces and advanced equipment backed up by easy transport. Its products include "××Brand" taper-roller bearings and "××Brand" rubber sealing components, the quality of which comes up to international standards. They won provincial "Superior Quality Product", "Sparkle Plan" Prize, satisfactory results at the "Technological Breakthrough" Appraisal sponsored by the State and the quality licence for export products …

例2：

　　该厂隶属××省第四建筑公司，系全民所有制企业。年产值过千万。本厂始建于1990年，拥有年生产1500吨矿泉水的两条国内先进生产线，初期投资280万元。产品投放市场后，深受消费者的欢迎，并于1991年被评为旅游商品国际博览会金奖，1992年成为全国十大优质瓶装矿泉水之一。

原译文：

　　Our factory is a State-owned enterprise under ×× No.4 Construction Co. Its annual output exceeds 10 million yuan. The factory was founded in 1990. It now has 2 advanced 1 500T mineral water production lines. The initial investment was 2.80 million yuan. Our Mineral Water is deeply favoured by endusers. In 1991, it won a gold medal for tourist commodities in an international fair. In 1992, it became one of the ten best bottled mineral waters of China.

　　以上两则广告都是从中国进出口商品交易会会刊上摘录的，避开英译广告的语言问题不谈，中英广告的差异是一目了然的。其中最重要的差别，就是我们的宣传导向不同。许多广告似乎是在推销"厂家"（即使是推销"厂家"，国外的广告宣传的内容也大相径庭，比如我们几乎看不到人家宣传厂房的建筑面积），而不是在推销其"产品"或"服务"，而在推销某产品时，又似乎不是在宣传该产品的特点，而是一味强调该产品荣获多少"奖"项，什么省优、部优、国优，金龙奖（Golden Dragon Prize），星火计划奖（Spark Plan Prize），火炬计划项目（Torch Program），等等，而这名目繁多的奖，许多国人也未必明白它们的确切含义。近年来，这种荣获各种奖项的宣传少了些，但取而代之的则是强调通过了什么 ISO 等国际质量体系认证。

中英文广告的第二大差别，就是我国企业对待广告正文没有像对待广告标题、口号和商标那样重视。换言之，就是广告原文本身的质量就差。如例 1 中的"具有 20 多年的历史"，这并没有什么值得炫耀的；例 2 中"该厂隶属××省第四建筑公司"，也看不出与"矿泉水"有什么关系。像这样的广告原文，译者如果亦步亦趋，当然不可能有好的译文。从语言文字的角度看，我们的多数广告只是基本信息的堆积，因此，雷同的情况处处可见，再加上板着一副面孔说话，就更让人不愿多看了。国外一些成功的广告（如本章所引用的 3 则）诙谐成趣，娓娓道来，读者就像是在听故事，或可当作文学、艺术作品来把玩和欣赏。可以想见，他们制作广告就如同设计产品本身那样追求卓越。

最后，不得不提的是，许多英译中文广告错误迭出，不堪卒读。既有拼写错误，也有句法错误；既有用词错误，也有文化错误，还有"胡译""死译"造成的错误。因此，这种粗制滥造的广告不但起不到应有的作用，反而造成极大的浪费，损害企业的形象和信誉。

要解决广告正文汉译英的问题，我们认为可以采取相应的措施：一是提高广告原文的质量，模仿国外一些成功的广告，消除我国广告的一些积习；二是实行广告宣传"内外有别"的原则，针对目标市场，拟定专门的对外广告，也可以直接用英文撰写广告；三是领导授权译者或译者征得商家的同意，在翻译时，可根据广告原文酌情增删、变通，充分发挥译者的创造力；四是慎重选用译员，或请专家审稿把关。

【练习题】

Ⅰ. 关于商标的翻译，实际情形比本章所论述的三种主要方法复杂得多，应注意的事项也未能穷尽。试比较和评析下列中英品牌命名及翻译方法。

1. Welcome　　　　　　　惠康（超市名）
2. Sports　　　　　　　　舒跑（饮料）
3. Giordano　　　　　　　佐丹奴（服装）
4. McDonald's　　　　　　麦当劳（快餐店）
5. Goldlion　　　　　　　金利来（领带）
6. Mickey Mouse　　　　　米老鼠（卡通形象）
7. SEIKO　　　　　　　　精工（手表）
8. Citizen　　　　　　　　西铁城（钟表）
9. Rejoice　　　　　　　　飘柔（洗发露）
10. Bausch & Lomb　　　　博士伦（隐形眼镜）

11. Head & Shoulder　　　　　海飞丝（洗发露）
12. Clean & Clear　　　　　　可伶可俐（护肤系列）
13. 三枪（内衣）　　　　　　Three Gun
14. 大宝（化妆品）　　　　　Dabao
15. 娃哈哈（饮料）　　　　　Wahaha
16. 非常可乐（饮料）　　　　Future Cola
17. 李宁（运动系列）　　　　Li-Ning
18. 旁氏（化妆品）　　　　　Ponds
19. 美雅高（服饰）　　　　　Miyako
20. 红日（炉具）　　　　　　Red Sun
21. 华帝（燃具）　　　　　　Vantage
22. 白翎（自来水笔）　　　　White Feather
23. 白象（电池）　　　　　　White Elephant
24. 轻身减肥片（中成药名）　Slimming Pills

Ⅱ. 试讨论如何将下列中文广告译成英文，将英文广告译成中文。

说明：其中有些广告本身有过译文，或有人翻译过，但从学习和研究的角度，任何译文都不是唯一的。运用"脑风暴"法（brain-storming），效果会更好。学生人多，角度不同，常常能产生佳译。比如，在本书作者的课堂上就曾讨论过"食在广州"的翻译，有学生采用"套译法"将它翻译为：Love Food, Love Guangzhou. 这个思路非常新鲜，可以说该译文与本书提供的译文殊途同归，难分轩轾。

1. 食在广州。
2. 桂林山水甲天下。
3. 阳朔山水甲桂林。
4. 上有天堂，下有苏杭。
5. 黄山归来不看山，九寨归来不看水。
6. 五岳归来不看山，黄山归来不看岳。
7. 不识庐山真面目，只缘身在此山中。
8. 她工作，你休息。（洗衣机广告）
9. 山不在高，有林则贵。（养发精广告）
10. 要想皮肤好，早晚用"大宝"。（护肤霜广告）
11. 中国美食在广州，广州美食在中国。（广州"中国大酒店"广告）
12. Not all cars created equal. （日本三菱汽车广告）

13. You know who you are. （法国 Peugeot 汽车广告）

14. Now you can have your cake and diet too. （蛋糕广告）

15. A deal with us means a good deal to you. （百货公司广告）

16. Give a SEIKO to all, and to all a good time. （日本精工手表广告）

17. Would you be more careful if it was you that got pregnant? （计划生育宣传广告，请参阅本章该广告说明）

18. If you are what you eat, a visit to North Carolina could make you a very interesting person, indeed. （旅游广告，请参阅本章该广告说明）

19. The driver is safer when the road is dry; the road is safer when the driver is dry. （交通广告）

20. No Excuses, Guaranteed, Best for Quality, Always Available, Right Price, At Your Service. （ASDA 超市广告）

Ⅲ. 下面是一篇广告文案①，供练习或欣赏之用。用作练习时，请注意标题和口号的翻译。

THIS AD IS FULL OF LIES

LIE #1: ADVERTISING MAKES YOU BUY THINGS YOU DON'T WANT.

Advertising is often accused of inducing people to buy things against their will.

But when was the last time you returned home from the local shopping mall with a bag full of things you had absolutely no use for? The truth is, nothing short of a pointed gun can get anybody to spend money on something he or she doesn't want.

No matter how effective an ad is, you and millions of other American consumers make your own decisions. If you don't believe it, ask someone who knows firsthand about the limits of advertising. Like your local dealer.

LIE #2: ADVERTISING MAKES THINGS COST MORE.

Since advertising costs money, it is natural to assume it cost your money. But the truth is that advertising often brings prices down.

Consider the electronic calculator, for example. In the late 1960s, advertising

---

① 选自 Dorothy Cohen, *Advertising*, U.S.A.: Scott, Foresman and Company, 1988, p. 571。

· 223 ·

creates a mass market for calculators. That meant more of them needed to be produced, which brought the price of producing each calculator down. Competition spurred by advertising brought the price down still further. As a result, the same product that used to cost hundreds of dollars now costs as little as five dollars.

LIE #3. ADVERTISING HELPS BAD PRODUCTS SELL.

Some people worry that good advertising sometimes covers up for bad products.

But nothing can make you like a bad product. So, while advertising can help convince you to try something once, it can't make you buy it twice. If you don't like what you've bought, you won't buy it again. And if enough people feel the same way, the product dies on the shelf.

In other words, the only thing advertising can do for a bad product is help you find out it's a bad product. And you take it from there.

LIE #4. ADVERTISING IS A WASTE OF MONEY.

Some people wonder why we don't just put all the money on advertising directly into our national economy.

The answer is, we already do.

Advertising helps products sell, which holds down prices, which helps sale even more. It creates jobs. It informs you about all the products available and helps you compare them. And it stimulates the competition that produces new and better products at reasonable prices.

If all that doesn't convince you that advertising is important to our economy, you might as well stop reading.

Because on top of everything else, advertising has paid for a large part of the magazine you're now holding.

And that's the truth.

ADVERTISING: ANOTHER WORD FOR FREEDOM OF CHOICE

American Association of Advertising Agencies

第十章
对外传播的问题与对策

　　对外传播，过去习惯称之为对外宣传，是一个十分庞大的概念（也有人称之为"大外宣"），涉及对外交往的各个方面，内容包括旅游资料、产品推销、企事业单位和文化娱乐场所（如公司、大学、宾馆、博物馆、游乐园）等的介绍。媒介包括电视、报纸、杂志、图书、画册、城市建筑（如商店标志、户外广告）等。对外传播的问题，这里指的是上述这些材料的汉英翻译问题。

　　对外传播的材料大致属广告文体，具有两大功能，一是广而告之、传递信息的功能，二是动之以情、引导劝说的功能。因此，宣传若做得好，可提升知名度、产生经济效益或赢得良好的声誉。可是，众所周知，我国内地（即除香港、澳门和台湾外）目前的对外传播，问题相当严重，尤其是非正式出版物，几乎到了无错不成译的地步。像"当心滑到 / Be Careful to Slippery Down""公安值勤 / Be on Duty of Police"（某国际机场所见）这类令人啼笑皆非的双语公示语在旅游或其他公共场所俯拾即是。大量不合格的对外传播资料无疑有损国家形象，也会给国家在经济上带来无谓的浪费。

　　要解决好对外传播中的问题，首先必须找出产生这些问题的原因。翻译中的谬误一般表现为拼写错误、用词错误、语法错误、逻辑错误、逐字死译、文化语用错误等等。所以每当看到不堪卒读的英语译文，人们大多指责译者的英语水平或职业操守，但通过多年的观察和研究，我认识到，除此之外，翻译谬误的背后还有其他更深层次的原因。本章将就此展开讨论。

第一节　问题产生的原因

一、人们对翻译的普遍误解

　　英国著名文学评论家理查兹（I. A. Richards）曾把翻译过程描述为"极有

可能是迄今为止宇宙间最复杂的事件"①。理查兹的话也许有点夸张，但至少说明翻译的复杂性是难以估计的。但社会上人们对翻译的认识却远非如此。最近我在互联网上用 Google（谷歌）搜寻关键词"翻译公司"，再点击报价系统，结果很令人惊讶。下面是根据搜索的信息编制的一个表②：

2006 年北京、上海、广州、重庆 翻译报价列表（单位：人民币元/千字中文）

英语公司	外译中		中译外	
	普通类	技术类	普通类	技术类
A	130	–	150	–
B	150	200	170	230
C	120～148	150～180	190～220	200～230
D	110	–	130	–
E	90～120	140	160	180
F	90～120	140～180	160	180～220
G	140（2万字内） 130（2万～5万字） 120（5万字以上）	160（2万字内） 150（2万～5万字） 140（5万字以上）	160（2万字内） 150（2万～5万字） 140（5万字以上）	180（2万字内） 170（2万～5万字） 160（5万字以上）

这 7 家公司基本上是随意点击的，只是适当照顾了地区的分布。外译中，"普通类"报价往高处计算平均每千字 131 元，"技术类"报价往高处计算（B、C、E、F、G 5 家公司）平均每千字 172 元。中译外，"普通类"报价平均每千字 164 元，"技术类"报价往高处计算（B、C、E、F、G 5 家公司）平均每千字 208 元。

翻译的整体报价如此之低，一方面反映的是翻译质量得不到保证，另一方面反映的是人们对翻译的普遍误解。多数人认为，翻译算不了什么大学问。因此，只要学了点外语，借助词典人人都会做翻译。让人啼笑皆非的是，这种情况还不独在中国。我曾在德国学者 Paul Kussmaul 写的书里③读到下面这样一段话：

> Unfortunately, there are translators on the market who lack professional expertise. There are quite a number of translators with no professional training

---

① 转引自 Nida, 1964：10，编者译文。

② 这是本书修订版（2007 年）时的搜索结果。今天中国翻译市场的情况虽有些变化，但其低价竞争的基本面并没有改变。

③ 引自 Paul Kussmaul, *Training the Translator*, Amsterdam/Philadelphia：John Benjamins Publishing Company, 1995：146－147。

第十章 对外传播的问题与对策

who only have limited, and sometimes very limited, knowledge of foreign languages. There is the secretary who is supposed to know some German or French. There is the colleague who has worked abroad for some time. Translator, unfortunately, is an unprotected profession. Anyone can call himself or herself a translator.

很不幸,市场上竟然有缺乏专业技能的译者。有相当多的译者,不仅缺乏专业训练,其外语知识也很有限,有的甚至是非常非常有限。要做翻译了,就去找来某个秘书,因为听说他(她)懂点德语或法语;或去找来某个同事,因为他(她)在国外工作过一段时间。很不幸,翻译是个不受保护的职业,任何人都可自称他(她)是译者。

这番话简直就是中国翻译现状的写照。其实,作为个人译者,能力是相当有限的,哪怕是大学外语教授,也未必个个能做好翻译,或样样都能翻译。即便是有一定规模的翻译公司,也会有所长所短。可是很少人真正懂得翻译的困难和复杂性,因而给翻译足够的重视,或对翻译抱应有的敬畏。实际的情况却往往是,受委托者,尤其是某些翻译公司,既不问材料的性质,也不问自己是否有这个能力,只要有利可图,一般都是来者不拒、多多益善,其结果就可想而知了。下面是一则我收集到的翻译实例:

金茂大厦纪念卡

88层的金茂大厦位于上海浦东新区陆家嘴金融贸易区中心,高420.5米,总建筑面积29万平方米,是目前中国第一、世界第三高楼,大厦集办公楼、酒店、会展、观光、娱乐为一体,荣获新中国50年上海十大经典建筑金奖第一名。

本卡专为迎接2003年而限量发行,面值50元,可代替88层观光门票使用。

Souvenir Card —Jin Mao Tower

The 88-storey Jin Mao Tower, located in the center of the Lujiazui Finance & Trade Zone, Shanghai Pudong New Area, is 420.5 meters high with a total construction area of 290 000 square meters. The Jin Mao Tower currently ranks first in China and third in the world in height. The Tower offers a series of services for business, hotel, conference exhibition, shopping, and recreation. Jin Mao Tower won Golden Award of the Toppest Classic Buildings in Shanghai for the 50th Anniversary of the Founding of the People's Republic of China.

The souvenir cards will be issued at a limited quantity to greet the arrival of the Year 2003. Each card values RMB 50.00, can be used as an entry admission to the Observation Deck at level 88.

上海金茂大厦观光层的设计可说是商业运作十分成功的例子，但很可惜，这张观光纪念卡①的翻译没有引起项目策划者同等的重视（虽然这还算不上十分糟糕的翻译）。我们不知道这个翻译是请翻译公司，还是请自由译者，或是请某个秘书或员工做的。就这么一个小豆腐块，即使按件计算，开支常规报价数倍的费用，对该公司也是九牛一毛。很难相信，若主事者懂得翻译的真谛，在卧虎藏龙的上海会找不到合适的译者。

二、人们对原文的过度迷信

据我多年的研究和观察，对外传播的种种问题，还与人们过度迷信原文关系很大，而这迷信原文又是翻译教学观念滞后的结果。传统上，我国的翻译教学基本上是经典文学翻译的教学模式。文学翻译的核心就是要"忠实"，因为在人们的观念里，原文作者一般都是像莎士比亚、曹雪芹这样的文字巨匠，他们的作品自然也获得了神圣不可侵犯的光环。换言之，人们认为，翻译就是模仿，不仅在意义上，而且在风格上，愈接近原文愈好。可是，在非文学的应用翻译中，尤其是在对外传播的汉译英中，因作者的文字水平相差悬殊，原文的质量也就千差万别了。如果原文的文字本身质量低劣，你也不折不扣地去模仿原文，怎么能将一篇不好的原文翻译成一篇好的译文呢？这在逻辑上也说不通。殊不知，在某些语境中，绝对忠实的翻译，便成了绝对荒谬的翻译！

因此，我于2005年提出了"应用翻译"的一个基本原则，即"**应用翻译的第一道工序就是修改好原文**"②。当然，**修改原文的前提是原文不好**。如果原文没问题，自然还是按传统的"忠实"原则来翻译。请看下面一篇旅游宣传文字的翻译：

---

① 我前后收集到3张金茂大厦纪念卡，但发现只是年份和面值不同，其余均未改动。
② 刘季春：《为什么对外宣传中常有翻译谬误?》，载于《上海翻译》2005年第2期。

第十章　对外传播的问题与对策

含鄱口

横亘在五老峰和九奇峰之间有一座逶迤的山岭，下面有一个大豁口，大有汲尽鄱阳湖水之势，故称含鄱口。含鄱岭前有一座石牌坊。拾阶而上便是含鄱亭。站在这里，远望鄱阳湖，景色变化万千：湖面时而平静如镜，渔帆点点；时而碧波连天，银光闪闪；时而为云海所蔽，似湖涨半天。晨曦尤蔚为大观：红日喷薄跃出，湖天尽赤，紫霞映辉，金光万道。浓雾迷漫的早上，游客有时会突然看见自己的身影出现在云雾的屏幕上，影子的外围，环绕着两圈五色的光环，好似菩萨头上的灵光，人们称之宝光。云雾中的含鄱口，有时还能看到另一种奇景。那就是在云海的波涛从四面八方袭来时，四周云墙高垒的含鄱岭的中间，有一块纤雾不染的"云中净地"，这不仅可以使游人饱尝大自然的美景，而且是摄影爱好者拍摄神话般境界的良好时机。含鄱亭上方百米远处，有望鄱亭。在此夜赏明月，别有情趣。

Hanpo Pass

Lying between Five Old Men Peak and Nine Wonder Peak is a mountain range below which is a colossal depression known as Hanpo Pass. It is shaped as though sucking in the waters of Poyang Lake. Stone steps from a stone structure at one end of the mountain lead to Hanpo Pavilion at the top. From here one can view the entire scene, with Poyang Lake receding into the distance. Smooth as a mirror and dotted with white-sailed fishing boats at times, its blue waters ripple silver against the skyline, but in storms they leap and roll in giant waves. In the morning sun the lake shimmers crimson and merges with the sky, or veiled in heavy mist it appears as a mass of clouds surrounded by a rainbow-coloured double ring, or "divine light", as people often call it. Through the mists here one may even glimpse fleeting clouds arising from every side, whirling within the confines of Hanpo Pass, then magically leaving the place clear of not so much as a wisp of cloud. Visitors feast their eyes on such scenes; shutter bugs feel they are in heaven. A hundred meters above Hanpo Pavilion is Overlooking Poyang Lake Pavilion, another magical site, especially in moonlight.

这篇翻译摘自（汉英对照）画册《庐山》（外文出版社1983年版，译者不详）。再重读一遍原文，你会发现，作者颇得章法，一两句话，似不经意，却一下把你带到一个奇妙的所在，跟随他的描写，缓缓展现在眼前的竟是一幅万千气象的画卷。从细节处理上看，译者秉承的基本是"信、达、雅"的翻译理念。我很佩服译者的英文功力。你看：无论是遣词用字，还是布局谋篇，还有中文旅游文字里许多独具特色的表达，译者竟能在另一种文字里游刃有余、曲尽其妙！

可是，对外传播中大多数中文原文都不尽人意。上文提到，修改原文的前提是原文不好。但判断原文的好坏不是件容易的事情，需要一定的理论修养。经多年的研究，**我发现，原文不好可分两种情况：第一种情况就是文字质量差**。比如用词累赘、衔接欠妥、逻辑混乱等。有些文字初看尚可，但直到落笔翻译时才发现它的毛病。这也不难理解，因为要将一种文字转换成另一种文字，译者考虑得最仔细。① 请看下面两个例子：

例1：
　　上海××饭店主楼高25层，是一家集客房、餐饮、商场、娱乐、旅游为一体的大型综合性涉外饭店。
　　With its main building 25 floors high, ×× Hotel is a large comprehensive star-rated hotel receiving both domestic and foreign guests, supplying them with lodging, catering, shopping, recreational and traveling services.

这是摘自某酒店宣传册子的句子。看中文原文，似乎感觉不到有什么不妥。但看英文翻译，你就会发现，原来句首的状语与后面的主句并不形成因果关系。

例2：
　　对内新闻报道在写作上往往习惯于逻辑思维演绎法，先从立意、命题再到论理、论据，即一般是首先明确提出一个主题或道理，然后再用事实材料或议论去破题，总是从观点和结论出发去讲道理，似乎记者在报道中如果不点明主题或提出明确概念和意图，读者就难以理解，报道就上不了纲，就缺乏思想性，结果是宣传思想显露。（145字）

---

① 若把自己的作品翻译成另一种文字，也很容易发现原文的瑕疵，这就是为什么几乎没有哪个作者译者（author-translator）翻译时不偏离原文的，并且作者译者比非作者译者更不忠实于原文，这种现象不独见于非文学翻译，也许更多见于文学翻译。

我做过一个实验，要求学生将某本书里的两段话（这是其中的第一段）翻译成英文。作业交上来后我并没有批改。在下一次上课时，我问学生翻译时遇到的主要问题是什么，学生告诉我说："感觉原文怪怪的，且有不少重复"。尽管如此，因为我事先没有说明做题的目的和要求，学生几乎都是按原文译出，不敢删减，结果译文累赘不堪。其中"逻辑思维演绎法"的翻译特有意思，受原文的影响最为明显，比如不少学生的译文是"the deductive method of logical thinking"（还有不合"逻辑思维"的演绎法吗？）。下课前，我要求学生做第二次翻译，即要求学生先修改好原文，在不改变原作者意图的情况下，将原文大致压缩1/3，然后按修改后的原文再翻译一次交上来。结果学生第二次交上来的翻译，普遍比第一次交上来的提高了许多。比如在讲评作业时，我将上面这段文字修改如下：

> 对内新闻报道在写作上往往习惯于演绎法，即先从立意、命题开始，再到论理、论据。换言之，他们总是从观点或结论出发。似乎记者在报道中不点明主题，读者就难以理解，报道就缺乏思想性。结果，宣传的意图暴露无遗。（99字）

想想看，即便是同一个译者，翻译修改后的这段话是不是可以翻译得清楚、明了得多呢？

原文不好的第二种情况，就是不合目的语文化与行文习惯。这种情况往往和第一种情况混在一起，因此更为隐蔽和复杂。下面是几则典型的例子，读者不妨先自己分析一下，看看将这样的原文忠实地译成英语会有什么问题。

例3：
宝墨园四时青翠，鸟语花香。景点有聚有散，步移景换，美不胜收。诸如艺林览胜、瑞霭琼林、千年罗汉、荔岛凝丹、群芳竞秀、柳剪春风、榕荫古渡、桂苑浮香，令人陶醉；青春长驻的玫瑰香园，洗涤尘襟的荷花胜境，绿云碧水的逍遥三岛，惠风和畅的紫竹幽居，令人赏心悦目，俱为避暑胜地。（旅游宣传册）

例4：
张家界国家森林公园，有三千多座奇峰异石，似人似物，神形兼备，或粗犷，或细密，或奇绝，或诡秘；浑朴中略带狂狷，威猛中又带妖媚，危岩绝壁，雍容大气。（"旅游在中国"丛书《张家界》画册，

中国旅游出版社1999年版，第20页）

例5：
　　"采菊东篱下，悠然见南山。"奇秀甲天下的庐山，曾凝聚了多少诗人的向往和留恋！那篇篇锦绣，字字珠玑，是如临仙境时吐露的内心独白。山石奇峻，千姿百态，白雾茫茫，云蒸霞蔚，身在其中，不由得问一句："陶令不知何处去，桃花源里可耕田？"（中英文双语版《长江史话》，中国大百科全书出版社2008年版，第60页）

例6：
　　城市面貌日新月异，昔日落后的边陲小镇，已发展为初具规模的园林式、花园式现代化国际性城市；社会主义精神文明建设成就显著，人民生活水平稳步提高。深圳先后荣获"国家卫生城市""国家园林城市""国家环境模范城市"和"全国双拥模范城市""全国科教兴市先进城市""中国优秀旅游城市""国家花园城市"等称号。（《今日南粤》，第78页，非正式出版物，无年份）

例7：
　　业务范围包括：开展国内外旅游业务，招徕、接待国内外游客，办理组织中国公民出境旅游业务，代订全国各地机票、火车票和酒店订房服务。本社一贯以"真诚待客，信誉第一"为宗旨，将一如既往地做到最好，让旅游者满意，同行放心。（某旅行社宣传册）

例8：
　　上海国际会议中心位于东方明珠塔西南方，沿浦东滨江大道与外滩隔江相望。上海国际会议中心占地4.5万平方米，其中绿地广场3万平方米，建筑面积11万平方米。整个项目由以下几个部分组成：现代化的会议场馆，有4400平方米的多功能厅（宴会可容纳3000人，会议可容纳4000人，可兼作展厅），2500平方米的展厅，800人会议厅一个，200人会议厅两个，100人、50人等各种规格的会场近20个；豪华的宾馆客房，有总统套房、商务套房、标准间共259套；高级的餐饮设施，有中西餐厅、咖啡厅等；舒适的休闲场所，有夜总会、歌舞厅、KTV包房、室内高尔夫、健身房、游泳池、保龄球、桌球、桑拿、商场等；1500平方米的地下停车场，设计车位达600余辆。（宣传册）

下面是这6个例子原来的英语译文（包括拼写、标点在内的各类错误依原稿），我们来看看不修改原文直接翻译，译文会是个什么样子：

例3：

　　Baomo Garden has perennial green, singing birds and blossoming flowers. The scenic spots are distributed reasonably. Wherever you go, you will get quite a different view. One can hardly take all the beautiful scenery in. Such scenic spots as "Wonderful Art Circle", "Green Forest Amidst Auspicious Haze", "Litchis Forest on Litchis Island", "Blossoming Flowers", "Weeping Willows in Spring Breeze", "Ancient Ferry under Shade of Banyan" and "Osmanthus Yard with Light Fragrance" are worth appreciating. The ever blossoming Rose Garden, the refreshing Lotus Pool, the tranquil free island and the breezing Baomo Garden please both the eyes and the minds and they are ideal places for summer resort.

也许有译者会认为，这是一篇不错的原文（如果这样认为，那就更糟糕了！）。你看：那一大串四字结构的描写，念起来如潺潺流水、铿锵有力。但一旦下笔翻译，你就会发现，这些四字结构的结构，实际上并不一致：有偏正结构，有并列结构（有的并列结构中还含偏正结构），有主谓结构，有动宾结构，等等，再加上中式思维的景点名和描写混杂在一起，有谁能用英文保留原来的结构达到相同的效果呢？我曾将这篇材料给研究生做练习，很多学生的译文甚至更为忠实于原文，结果却越发不伦不类、佶屈聱牙——真是费力不讨好啊！

例4：

　　The Park possesses more than three thousand grotesque peaks and rare stones. They appear to be at once human figures and animals, tangible or intangible. They display a strong tinge of either uninhibitation, or delicacy, or uniqueness, or surreptitious.

与原文对照，译者去掉了后一个分句，但可以看出译者仍在极力模仿原文的措辞和结构。译者去掉后一个分句，我想一定是译不下去了。

例5：

　　"From the eastern hedge, I pluck chrysanthemum flowers, and idly look towards the southern mountains." How much poets' yearn and nostalgia the spectacular Lushan inspires! Those wonderful poems were the interior monologues of the poets who felt as if they were in the fairyland. There are grotesque rocks of various shapes, and the view from Lushan Mountain is misty and cloud-enshrouded. Seeing all these, one may ask, "Where has Tao Qian gone? Is it true that he could till fields of Peach Blossom soils?"

英美读者读了上面这段英文，一定会觉得自己身处云里雾里，摸不着头脑。早有外国友人批评这种英语翻译："（他们）想当然地认为，（我们外国）读者对中国历史和文化也（像他们自己那样）了如指掌。"

例6：

The city has changed its appearances with each passing day, and the past frontier small town has grown into a landscape and garden-like, modernized and international city with a definite size. The level of the socialist cultural life has been remarkably raised and the people's living standard improved steadily. Shenzhen has successively been awarded the titles of "State Hygienic City", "State Garden City", "Environment Model City" and "National Double Support City" (Support the army and give preferential treatment to the families of the armymen and martyrs, and support the government and cherish the people), "National Advanced City of Science and Technology Promotion", "China Excellent Tourist City", "International Garden City" and so forth.

这段话涉及中国国内的政治生活，结果给原原本本地翻译成了英文。中文文字质量也差，具有中国特色的各种难以言喻的奖项，不加选择地堆砌在一起，即使本国人读中文也会不胜其烦吧。

例7：

Its business scope: to deal with overseas and domestic tour business, to attract and receive tourists from all over the world, to organize outbound tours for Chinese citizens, to book on behalf of customers air or railway tickets and reserve guestrooms from all over the country. China Travel Service (××City), continuously sticking to the aim of "Treat Customers Honestly and Take Reputation First", will do its best as always to satisfy tourists and let the units of the same trade rest assured.

这是个内稿外用的极端例子：错误连篇，无的放矢，充斥无效信息。我国目前的旅行社分两大类，一是国际社，一是国内社。如果是前者，它的业务范围自然是包括接待国内外游客；如果是后者，也就没有必要翻译成英文了。汉语原文的最后一句话"让……同行放心"竟然也搬进了英文，一定让外国人大惑不解。

例8：

　　　　Along the riverside boulevard and overlooking the Bund, Shanghai International Convention Center is located southwest to the Oriental Pearl Tower. The total area of 45 000 square meters, include the Center space of 110 000 square meters and Garden of 30 000 square meters. The Center has the following facilities: The Grand Ballroom of 4 400 square meters (seating capacity of 3 000 people for banquets or 4 000 seats for conference), Exhibition Hall of 2 500 square meters; one Conference room for 800 people, two meeting rooms for 200 people and 20 modern meeting rooms seating capacity from 100 to 50 people. Hotel has 259 luxurious rooms with Presidential Suite and 2 Executive floors, 4 restaurants—3 Chinese and 1 western; 3 bars; recreation facilities and night club, Gym, Health club, Swimming pool, Bowling alley, Billiard, Boutiques, and Low basement parking lot for 600 vehicles.

上海国际会议中心是上海地标性建筑之一。这是笔者在2001年收集到的一份宣传资料，当时那里刚开过APEC领导人峰会，可见该场所的重要性。但这份汉英对照的翻译资料却与这富丽堂皇的建筑形成极大的反差，真是是应了一句俗话："不看不知道，一看吓一跳！"从原文的角度看，主要问题又是什么呢？读者也许已经注意到了，那就是这堆似繁星般的数字了。中国人特别喜欢用数据来做宣传。的确，数据特别能说明问题，一两个数据，有时胜过千言万语。可是也别忘了，数据多了滥了，一般人都要头皮发麻，敬而远之。

由此可见，原文不好，翻译策略又不对，译文就不可能有好的效果，要是再加上译者的责任心和文字水平不够，译文就会大有问题。

第二节 解决问题的对策

一、普及翻译教育

早在20世纪90年代伊始，段连城就撰文：《呼吁：译界同仁都来关心对外宣传》（《中国翻译》1990年第5期）。10年后，爱泼斯坦、林戊荪、沈苏儒联名发表《呼吁重视对外宣传中的外语工作》（《中国翻译》2000年第6期）。在互联网上用"Google"或"百度"搜索关键词"劣质翻译"，我们会发现翻译界和读书界的有识之士一直都在关注我国的翻译质量问题。其他代表性的文章还有：季羡林、叶水夫、冯亦代、杨宪益等12位知名学者联合署名的《关于恪守译德，提高翻译质量的倡议和呼吁》（《光明日报》，2002年6月13日），刘鉴强的《劣质翻译充斥学术著作》（《中华读书报》，2003年1月15日），冯世则的《翻译：三关失守》（《文汇报》，2003年2月28日第11版），张妍妍、周润健的《翻译出版业：浮华背后的忧思》（《人民日报》，2005年5月23日第11版），以及李景端的几篇文章，如《把脉劣质翻译图书"症状"》（《中华读书报》，2005年12月28日）。

上述文章虽然多数不是直接讨论对外传播的，但学界普遍认为，劣质翻译的一个重要原因，就是译者的职业道德出了问题。因此，大家都寄希望于通过批评教育来改变这种局面。但过去20多年，几乎没有任何成效。无怪乎有人不无感慨地说："呼吁来，呼吁去，甚至是大声疾呼，情况不但没有好转，反而恶化了。"可见，道德问题仅靠呼吁和批评很难起到作用。因此，我现在有了新的思考，觉得要改变我国翻译市场劣质翻译充斥的现状，长效的途径，可能首先要想办法普遍提高人们对翻译的认识：要让全社会看好翻译（唯如此，翻译公司才不会以低价竞争），要让读者或客户有能力识别和抵制劣质翻译产品，最后达到让译者敬畏翻译。我想，这样的重任必须落实在普及翻译教育上。比如在综合性大学（不仅仅在外语院系）将翻译课开设为公共必修课（要知道，从事各类翻译的人或各类翻译的委托人，未必是英语或翻译专业毕业的）。普及翻译知识，传播翻译理念（而不是简单的、说教性质的伦理教育），经过一两代人的努力，可望消除人们对翻译的普遍误解。当然，要做到这一点，还有赖于国家的教育主管部门。

二、培养多元翻译观

谈到翻译，人们几乎总是要问：翻译的标准是什么？在我国，大家耳熟能详的就是严复提出的"信、达、雅"三字标准，后来人们又把它诠释为"忠实、通顺"。简言之，这就是翻译的"忠实"观。"忠实"观一直盛行到20世纪90年代中，虽然人们早已朦胧地意识到"忠实"观无法解释一些特殊的翻译现象。在西方，自泰特勒于1790年提出翻译"三原则"，到奈达于1964年提出"动态对等"，基本的翻译观实际上也没有跳出"忠实"的樊篱。直到20世纪70年代西方出现"翻译研究"学派和"功能"学派（参见第三章"操控论"和"目的论"），"忠实"观的一统天下才真正被打破。我国是在20世纪90年代末才开始引进西方这些理论的。也正是在他们研究的基础上，我提出了"应用翻译的第一道工序就是修改好原文"的原则。

实际上，"忠实"取向的翻译本身并没有错，错在我们把"忠实"当作唯一的翻译原则。今天大多数经典文学的翻译仍是按"忠实"的原则来翻译的，但我们必须明白，即使是经典文学的翻译，也不等于"不增、不减、不改"，因为翻译是件非常复杂的事情，有时还会涉及文本外因素的影响。非文学的应用翻译则更是如此。试想：假如我们的学生长期习惯于传统的翻译批评或名译赏析那样的课程，而从来没有哪个老师告诉过他们，做应用翻译时可以修改原文，有时甚至可以重写原文，毕业之后面对这类资料，他们怎能不重蹈覆辙呢！

按照功能翻译理论，评价翻译的标准，依据的已不再是原文，而是每一次翻译任务的性质和目的。有的看它产生的效果和影响，比如对外传播，你说得天花乱坠、空话连篇，不但没有效果，反而令人生厌；有的看客户的满意度，比如广告翻译，看它是否带来了预期的经济收益，可能与"忠实"没有多大关系，像将"Coca-Cola"翻译成"可口可乐"；有的看译文使用者对照译文能否按其指示完成某项工作，比如操作手册，花的时间愈少，出错率愈低，说明翻译得愈好。以译文与原文的关系来说，翻译有种种不同的方法，有尽量保存原文面貌和细节的全译，但应用翻译更多的是需要改变原文特征（比如长度、视角、专门程度、文化特色等）的译写。"译写"只是一个总称，它包括摘译（按各部分比例压缩，述其大意）、编译（重新编排或添加原文没有的内容）、改写（译者按自己的意图重新构思）等等。所有这些，都不是按照一个统一的"忠实"原则就能济事的。

三、增强跨文化意识

仔细分析对外传播的问题，我们可以归结到一点，即译者的跨文化意识薄弱，具体表现在翻译时内外不分。什么是"内外不分"呢？简单说来，就是在我们的对外传播中，存在大量"内稿外用"的情况。原本是说给国人听的，结果却在不知不觉中原封不动地给翻译成了外文。殊不知此时的对象已悄然发生了变化，他们具有完全不同的历史、地理和政治背景，因此也具有很不一样的思维方式、兴趣爱好和心理诉求。比如有本汉英对照《黄山》的画册，其概览中这样写道："泰岳之雄伟，华山之峻峭，衡山之烟云，庐山之飞瀑，雁荡之巧石，峨眉之清凉，黄山莫不兼而有之。"译者也如此这般照译不误。但请问那些没有去过泰山、华山、衡山、庐山、雁荡山和峨眉山的外国人如何能理解"黄山"的"兼而有之"呢？可是这种空洞的描写是我们旅游语篇里的一种惯有写法。在新闻语篇里，有很多像"坚定信心、聚精会神、攻坚克难、开拓前进"等豪言壮语，还有像"迎来新契机、构建新格局、再上新台阶、展现新气象、取得新突破"等政治行话，如果译者也不知变通、依样画葫芦把它们搬到英文里去，岂不对牛弹琴、平添笑料？

因此，在对外传播中增强跨文化意识十分重要。增强跨文化意识，首先要了解中西文化的差异，不仅在表达的内容方面，而且在表达的方式方面。先说内容方面，比如中国人旅游，期盼的是增长见闻，以补"读书"之短（所谓"破万卷书，行万里路"），所以在介绍景点时念念不忘灌输人文历史；西方人旅游，则醉心于享受休闲，以缓解工作之压力，所以在介绍景点时始终看好康乐设施和自然风光。又比如，中国大学的宣传册子，几乎都热衷于罗列多少硕博点、多少实验室或研究中心、多少科研项目、多少论文和著作，满满当当，数字成堆。但西方名校的宣传册子，突出的往往则是该大学的学术传统和办学特色，偶尔也会提及有什么世界级的人物曾在该大学学习或工作过。此外，他们还会特别介绍该大学所在的城市以及生活和娱乐设施。再比如，在介绍宾馆方面，我发现西方人首先会强调宾馆的优越地理位置：如果是在郊区，一定会告诉你交通便利，还可能告诉你附近就有海滩；如果是在市区，就少不了要告诉你"闹"中有"静"。但我看过北京有个宾馆的介绍很奇葩，它竟然是这样开头："××宾馆是隶属于国务院机关事务管理局，以接待党和国家领导人，承接国务院召开的小型会议和为外宾提供公寓服务的园林式涉外宾馆"，而英文也是照译不误。我们还习惯于夸耀宾馆建筑的高度（如果是世界或亚洲之最，或许有这个必要）。有趣的是，他们却似乎谈"高"色变，哪怕是只有三五层高的宾馆，似乎都急于要说明有电梯，有的甚至还告诉你有几个电梯。在描绘宾馆的房间时，我们热衷于宣传豪华的内部装饰，如果是五星级，还可能会告诉你是否有总统套房；他们则喜欢突出怡人的外部环境，比如是否有阳台或台地（terrace），是否有正面或侧面的"湖景""海景"或"山景"（front or side lake view or sea view or mountain view），是全景还是半景（full or side view），如果是在市中心，则可能告诉你窗户面对的是怎样的街景（如公园、广场、教堂）。因此，在对外传播中，如果不了解这种种差别，我们的宣传就会无的放矢：人家想知道的，我们压根儿没说；人家不想知道的，我们却说了一大箩筐。

再说表达方式问题。一个民族的表达方式，因行之久远，往往习焉不察。比如在旅游语篇中我们常常读到的"美文"：叠床架屋的辞藻，蜂拥而至的排比，像上文中提及的《宝墨园》和《黄山》的介绍。翻译这样的"美文"，即使译者的语言

第十章 对外传播的问题与对策

功力了得,倘若愚忠原文,也很难讨好;要是译者的语言能力不济,译文便要惨不忍睹了。新闻界前辈段连城先生写过一篇题为《讨"美文"檄文》的文章①,历数了"美文"之于对外宣传的"四大"危害:① 因词害义,使外国人感到吹嘘;②爱用典故,外国人不能理解;③诗词楹联,外国人很难欣赏;④ 缺少信息,外国人不愿看。相对于我们抽象夸张的描写,他们更偏爱具体而微的低调陈述,觉得"展出了一万余种郁金香"和"掌声持续了十多分钟",远比"美不胜收"和"掌声雷动"更具感染力。又比如,在新闻报道中,我们习惯于议论、动辄作价值判断,最典型的莫过于几大报的社论:什么是正确的,什么是错误的,要坚持什么,要反对什么,旗帜鲜明、毫不含糊。但西方人最讨厌别人代己思考、强加于人的做法。他们的记者更精于用事实说话,让读者自己得出结论。此外,还有一些更为隐蔽的情况,比如在新闻报道中,中国人习惯于按时间顺序来写,但西方记者则一般采用倒金字塔的写法,开门见山,把最重要的事情先说出来。在新闻编译中,如果不遵循这一原则,读者就不接受。因此,在对外传播中,如果不注意这种种差别,人家不但不会接受我们的观点,反而可能产生抵触情绪,与我们的初衷背道而驰。

针对对外传播中存在的大量"内外不分"或"内稿外用"的情况,**我们必须遵循的一个基本原则,就是"内外有别"和"国际视野"**②,"内外有别"与"国际视野"合起来,就是对外传播中的跨文化意识。本书第九章中提到,日本的某些大企业深得对外传播的精髓,他们不仅注意做到"内外有别",还尽可能做到"外外有别"。比如日本三菱汽车公司为中国市场写的广告口号是"有朋自远方来,喜乘三菱牌",但为美国市场写的广告口号则是"Not all cars created equal"(参见第九章解说)。日本企业的许多国际知名品牌,比如Sony, Canon, Panasonic, Olympus,等等,从一开始就采用罗马化的英文名,这是对"国际视野"的最好诠释。中国自改革开放到今天,似乎大家也都知道对外宣传的意义,因为大多数的宣传资料都是汉英对照的,但在做这些翻译的人中,很少人具有跨

---

① 刊于新华社对外部主办的《对外宣传参考》1988年第10期,转引自翟树耀:《对外宣传报道与英语写作》,厦门大学出版社2001年版。

② "内外有别"的原则,是中国共产党新闻传播工作的经验总结,在历史上发挥过重要的作用。但有学者认为,在全球化背景下,随着信息科学,尤其是网络技术的发展,新媒体时代已经来临,对外传播的生态也已经发生了根本的变化。因此,他们认为"内外有别"的原则已经过时,提出了"内外一体"的主张。但我认为,内外之间的差别始终都是存在的,将来也会存在,只是程度会有变化。尤其涉及翻译问题,只要"内稿外用"的情况不改变,"内外有别"原则的重要性也不会改变。实际的情况是,在大多数时候,我们低估甚至没有意识到内外之间的差别。为了避免某些误解,我认为,同时采用具备"国际视野"的说法也很好。

文化意识。我曾做过调研,收集了国内数百家星级宾馆的宣传册子,结果发现,如果除去港澳台的,90%以上的翻译都做得不好,有的是做得非常糟糕。语言错误暂且不说,其基本做法就是将中文宣传文字原封不动译成了英文。而仅有的几家宣传做得地道的宾馆(如广州的白天鹅宾馆、香格里拉酒店各地分店),几乎无例外地遵循了"内外有别"的原则,比如有的是委托翻译人员或外籍人士根据委托人的意图直接用英文书写,有的是做成双语对照,但各自分别行文,可对应,也可不对应,效果都非常好。请看下面两则实例,供学习和参考。

例1:

香格里拉

In Hangzhou where else but the Shangri-la

杭州香格里拉酒店

Shangri-la hotel, Hangzhou, China

Paradise on Earth

The scenic grandeur of China is elegantly captured in the mystical city of Hangzhou. Enveloped between the majestic Zhijiang River and the famous West Lake, Hangzhou's picturesque landscapes make it an ideal retreat for secluded tranquility.

Tucked away in this renowned city, in the serene, romantic surroundings of the emerald West Lake is the Shangri-la Hangzhou. Where else to experience the spectacular attractions and time-honored service of this "Paradise on Earth"?

The Elegance of the East and the Comfort of the West

In keeping with the surroundings, the 387 spacious and high-ceilinged guestrooms and suites offer unrivalled comfort and luxury.

Each room is beautifully decorated and provides all the modern amenities. All suites also offer a magical view of the lake.

The lovely furnishings are also a splendid complement to the gracious, caring service that is so much a part of the Shangri-la tradition.

The Joy of Leisure

A visit is not complete unless you experience boating on the lake. Step out of the hotel and you are immediately beckoned by the spellbinding sight of the radiant West Lake. Rent a boat and while away the hours as the gentle, alluring waters cradle you. Then, there are the hotel gardens that are a blend of walkways flanked by lush foliage, trees and flowering shrubs. Explore this enchanting scenery either by bicycle or on foot.

A World of Fine Dining

This fine Shangri-la Hotel's culinary creations will gratify the most discriminating diner. The elegant Shang Palace in the West Building will delight you with excellent Chinese cooking including one of China's greatest cuisines, Cantonese dishes. The restaurant's palatial interior offers comfort plus customary Chinese service with all its charm and grace.

At Café Peony, connoisseurs of food and wine can select from an international menu which offers everything from European and American to Asian specialities.

A Sure Hand for any Gathering

For the business-oriented client, the Shangri-La Hangzhou has extensive convention and banquet facilities available in the hotel's specially designed convention center that caters to private banquets as well as long, high-powered meetings, up to national and international levels. Most impressive is the fixed seat auditorium, accommodating 500 persons.

There is also a ballroom with a capacity for up to 450 persons and 7 smaller function rooms of various sizes. Whether it is for big or small business, this superb convention center has the facilities to meet your business needs.

例2：

香港华美酒店
The Wharney Hotel Hong Kong

Recreation
What a better way to dissolve the stresses of the day than enjoying the facilities of our gymnasium, swimming pool, Jacuzzi, sauna & steam bath.

娱乐活动
可享用健身中心各种设施：露天泳池、按摩池、桑拿及蒸汽浴室，舒缓身心，减压健体。

Lobby Lounge
The Lobby Lounge offers a perfect venue to meet friends and business associates in a refined and intimate atmosphere.

大堂酒廊
大堂酒廊午间气氛宁谧写意；晚间在舒适雅座闲聚，灯影摇曳，琴韵飘扬，身畔玻璃长窗让您透视繁华璀璨的湾仔夜色。

因长期受翻译"忠实"观的影响，多数人在评价一篇汉英对照的资料时，总是习惯于看一句译文，再看一句原文比对着看。其实，外国人并不知道，也没有必要知道汉语里写了些什么。因此，真正重要的是，译文能够**独立成篇**，即译文不依赖于原文也是一篇表意完整的地道英文。至于与原文有点出入，甚至有较大的出入，只要能促进任务的整体目标，就是一篇正当、合法的翻译。相反，若英文写得不好，内容或形式又不合目标读者的口味，或超出了目标读者的理解能力，从而影响和损害了任务的整体目标，即使在字面上看似与原文分毫不差，仍是一篇不合格的翻译。可以说，在对外传播中，改写原文是常态。或者可以说，真正翻译做得好的译者，都是具有强烈跨文化意识的译者，他们能够发现原文中的问题，并在翻译时做必要的改写，有时是做大刀阔斧的改写。比如在我们的对外传播的资料中，有一种**信息过量**的倾向，高明的译者都善于采用"**化繁为简**"的翻译策略。沈苏儒举的一个例子很能说明问题[①]。请看：

---

① 沈苏儒：《对外传播·翻译研究文集》，外文出版社2009年版，第44-48页。

第十章 对外传播的问题与对策

例3：

　　这尊已有1200多年历史、高达70多米的石刻大佛位于四川省乐山市东面三江汇合处，是我国最大的露天佛像。光是它的头部就有14.7米，宽10米。头上有螺形发髻1021个。头顶正中的螺髻可以放下一张圆桌，容纳10个人聚餐。它的耳长7米，耳内可以并排站立两人。它的脚背宽8.5米，上面站立100个人，并不显得过分拥挤。它整个地给人以"山是一尊佛，佛是一座山"的感觉，远在5公里之外，人们就能看到它那高大的身影。

沈苏儒指出，这里一口气给出了10个不同意义的数字，但并不能达到预期的效果，因为"贪多嚼不烂"，数字"贵在精不在多"。如果对原文加以简化，只保留两三个数字，反而能给读者深刻印象。因此，他建议作如下改写：

　　这尊位于四川省乐山市东面的我国最大石刻佛像有30层楼房高，远在5公里外即可望见。光是它的一只脚的脚背上就可以站立100个人。

作为译者，如果不具有很强的跨文化意识，则随时可能犯内外不分的错误。这样说并非耸人听闻，因为这种错误防不胜防、屡见不鲜。以下是收集到的一些典型例子：

1. 这里四季春常在，请到天涯海角来！（海南三亚"天涯海角"景区介绍）
   You are welcome to Tianyahaijiao, enjoy a spring climate all the year round here.

译者可能根本没有多想就照字面翻译了，原本是向游客说明当地的气候好。殊不知，每个国家的春天都是不一样的。如果是英国，春天算是个讨厌的季节：寒气未去，春雨连绵，万象萧森。英国和欧洲人特别爱去阳光充足的地方旅游，这点不可不知。

2. 天子山云雾为中外旅游者所赞叹。（《张家界》，中国旅游出版社1999年版，第58页）
   Both Chinese and foreign sightseers would gasp with admiration at cloud

and mist over the Emperor Mountain.

在许多宣传或推广文字里，经常能见到"中外"（或"国内外""海内外"）这样的表述。实际上这个表述强调的是"外"，而不是"内"，表示能得到外国人的认可，原本是民族自卑心理的折射，显然是说给中国人自己听的，但我们似乎已经觉察不到这一点了，结果这个"中外"或"国内外"便自动转换成英文了。请看人家是如何描写类似的场景，似乎没有谁会去强调游客的"国籍"。

a. It is impossible not to fall in love with Paris, city of light, of life and of culture.

b. This legendary island with its magical, dramatic landscapes has captured visitors forever.

c. Few areas of Europe can rival the charm and character of Bavaria, from its extravagant castles and medieval towns to the famed "Romantic Road".

d. No visitor to Jerusalem can fail to be affected by the unique atmosphere of this teeming, multifunctional city, sacred to Jew, Christians and Moslems alike.

3. 人们根据瀑布的声和形，予它诗一样的名字，诸如九龙瀑、人字瀑、百丈瀑、鸣弦泉、三叠泉、铁线泉、钵盂泉等等。（《黄山》，中国旅游出版社1999年版，第84页）

Poetic names are given to these waterfalls according to their sounds and shapes, such as Nine-Dragon Waterfall, 人-shaped Waterfall, Hundred-Zhang Waterfall, Singing String Spring, Three-Section Waterfall, Iron-Line Spring, Alms Bowl Spring.

且不说中文里这些"诗一样"美的瀑布和泉水名不可能翻译成同样音美、形美和意美的另一种文字；对于不通中文的英美读者，他们怎样念"人-shaped"？又怎能懂"Hundred-Zhang"呢？

4. 相传春秋时代有一位智勇双全的大臣范蠡，他帮助越王打败了吴国，成功之后，隐居在太湖之滨，保全了自己的生命。（《中国通手册——名胜古迹》，上海古籍出版社2002年版，第53页）

It is told that there was an intelligent and brave official, Fanli. He helped the King of Yue to defeat Wu. But after the conquest, he dwelled nears Taihu in seclusion and gave up the reward. His wisdom saved his own life and avoided being murdered by the king of Yue.

这是一段很离奇的英语,这里的"reward"指什么?上下文中没有任何交代。"dwelled in seclusion"与"saved his own life"有什么关系?为什么在"helped the King of Yue to defeat Wu"之后,又会"avoided being murdered by the King of Yue"?遇上个较真的外国读者,一定要大伤脑筋!中国人能看懂汉语原文,是因为他能够填补其间缺省的文化,比如他至少必须知道"伴君如伴虎"这个说法。

5. 中国是文明古国,中国人的始祖是人首蛇身的女娲和伏羲,他们交尾以后,就有了我们这些数以万计黄皮肤的"龙的传人"(蛇是龙的前身)。事实上,我们更喜欢自称是"炎黄子孙",因为华夏文明始于炎黄,正是炎黄时代,造出了第一把梳子。(《梳子史话》连环画第一集,第4-5页。产品宣传册,非正式出版物)
China is an old country with resplendent civilization. The originators of Chinese are Nv-Wa and Fu-Xi who were human-headed and snake-bodied. After the copulation of Nv-Wa and Fu-Xi, millions and millions of our yellow skinned "descendants of dragon" (snake was the old image of dragon) had been produced. Actually we'd better to call ourselves "offsprings of Emperors Yan and Huang" because the civilization of China began from the period of Emperors Yan and Huang. Just in this period, the first hair comb was invented.

《梳子史话》娓娓道来,对象原是中国人,所以文中使用了第一人称。但在翻译成英语时,站在第三者的立场来谈论中国人,译者却忘了要相应地将第一人称转换成第三人称,并做其他相应的调整。

6. 外国合营者作为投资的技术和设备,必须确实是适合我国需要的先进技术和设备。如果有意以落后的技术和设备进行欺骗,造成损失的,应赔偿损失。(中英对照《中华人民共和国中外合资经营企业法》,法律出版社1988年版)
The technology and the equipment that serve as a foreign joint venturer's investment must be advanced technology and equipment that actually suit our country's needs. If the foreign joint venturer causes losses by deception through the intentional use of backward technology and

equipment, it shall pay compensation for the losses.

这个翻译无意中造成了重大问题，因为对于不同国籍的人，"our country"代表的是不同的国家啊。因此，在对外传播中，注意不要开口闭口总说"我国"，要养成习惯多说"中国"，因为当你对外说"我国"的时候，你的立足点就不那么具有国籍视野了。

第三节　小　结

要做好翻译，基本条件是必须具备良好的双语能力，这是共识。但良好的双语能力并不一定能保证做好翻译，因为要做好翻译，还关系到译者的翻译理念和职业道德。除此之外，在对外传播中，译者还必须具备很强的跨文化意识。

双语能力的提高需要个人有意识的努力，这是一个缓慢的过程。译者的职业道德与社会整体氛围有密切联系。经验告诉我们，靠单纯的批评和说教很难见效，最终还有赖翻译教育的普及。译者的翻译理念主要来自课堂，这方面已经有了很大的改进，比如在有条件的翻译和外语院系，除了开设传统的文学翻译课程外，一般都会开设应用翻译或非文学翻译课程，使学生接触到西方功能翻译理论。

译者的跨文化意识，是我们传统翻译教学比较忽视的一块，虽然学生可能学习过跨文化交际之类的课程，但如果不与翻译结合起来讲，学生在翻译时就很难用上这些知识，结果理论与实践脱节。本章中提到的"内外有别"的原则其实并不是什么新概念，在我国新闻传媒界很早就已经是通则了，但将新闻传播的理论与翻译研究结合起来，并将这些成果写进翻译教材则是晚近的事情。实际上，早在1977年，英国作家、英中了解协会副会长费里克斯·格林，在北京的一次讲习班上，就曾批评我国的对外宣传"整体上是失败的"。他还建议，中国每一个从事对外宣传的工作者，都应该在自己的写字台上立一块标语牌，上面写着："**外国人不是中国人**"。[①]他的话给我的启发很大，时至今日，犹在耳边。他指出了中国对外传播中的最大问题就是"把外国人当中国人"。时隔数十年，我国的对外传播虽然取得了不小的进步和改观，但要在根本上改变传统思维，前面的路仍漫长而艰巨。

---

① 见刘洪潮：《怎样做对外宣传报道》，中国传媒大学出版社2005年版。

本章主要阐释了对外传播的宏观策略,但要真正做好对外传播,写出地道的英文,还需加强对各种文体的微观研究,即**对平行文本**的研究和学习,包括内容、措辞、句式、格式、思维习惯甚至呈现的方式。平行文本在应用翻译中是个重要的概念。如果我们要对外介绍一所大学,首先要去读英语国家的大学简介,了解他们的写法;如果要对外介绍一个景点,自然也首先要去读英文旅游宣传册,熟悉这种英语的特点。我们常可见到这么一种情况:一篇英文介绍文字,仔细阅读后也并未发现语法或拼写错误,也未发现跨文化方面的明显错误,但一看就知道是中国人写的英文。原因是什么?除了内容外,我想,主要原因就是译者闭门造车,未能使用英文同类资料中的惯用句式和高频词汇。比如在旅游英语中,我们喜欢使用 best, great, perfect, beautiful, marvelous, splendid, picturesque 等词语,但这还远远不够,英美人还经常使用 fine (finest, finely), glorious, fabulous, gorgeous, majestic, superb, spectacular, landscaped, amazing, stunning, awe-inspiring, impeccable, enchanting, fascinating, exclusive, unrivalled, overwhelming, most refined, 等等。**要知道,某些夸张的说法,正确的搭配比词义的精确更为重要。**

对于一个国家,搞好对外传播十分重要。我们常说"要让世界了解中国",但要想让世界了解中国,不仅需要热情,还需要正确的理论指导。我们希望有更多的有识之士来关心、研究和推进中国的对外传播事业。

附录1:翻译项目实例[①]

"千年古楼遗址"与"千年古道遗址"

这里要介绍的是作者于2003年承担的一项翻译任务的实际过程。具体任务是翻译广州市北京路"**千年古楼遗址**"和"**千年古道遗址**"的说明文字。委托方为广州市越秀区商业局。联系人是作者的一个毕业多年的学生。两篇材料极短,总计不过500多字,且有部分重叠。起初,我并不十分愿意接受这项委托,一是因为内容不熟悉,字数又少;二是以为只不过是一般的宣传册子,工作繁忙,无暇顾及。但联系人告诉我,他们规划在广州市商业中心北京路立两块大石碑,将中英对照的

---

① 承蒙委托单位同意,将相关材料写入书稿,在此表示感谢。

文字刻在上面。我立刻感到此次翻译任务的意义，便欣然答应了。

事情的进展很不顺利。如前文所言，多年的翻译实践与教学，坚定了我的一个信念，即"应用翻译的第一道工序就是修改好原文"，使它适合于对外宣传。但联系人告知，文稿不得修改，任何修改都得经市主管部门批准。而我认为，若指出了问题的所在，你们总不能不考虑吧？这样，往返的沟通和交涉就费去大量时间。以下是委托翻译材料的原始文稿，读者不妨审校一遍，看能否发现什么不妥。

"古楼"原始中文稿：

千年古楼遗址

2002年夏，在北京路步行街发现古城遗迹。经广州市文物考古研究所发掘、考证，该处为清、明、宋三个历史时期层层叠压的门楼遗址。其遗存有清代的基础垫土层与木桩的柱孔，明代的门楼西门洞铺石路面和抱鼓石等，宋代的门楼西门洞砖铺路面和石门槛等。宋代的三次建造，门楼基址逐次扩大，南北跨度依次为9米、12米和22米。该处距地表深约1.8米处已见山冈的生土，表明这里曾是山冈地段。

据《番禺县志》载：今北京路唐时有清海楼，南汉时在此叠石建双阙，宋代改为双门城楼，元代毁，明洪武七年（1374年）重建。清代重修，称"拱北楼"。民国八年（1919年）拆城开马路，拱北楼遂平。

广州市文物管理委员会
广州市越秀区人民政府
二〇〇二年十二月

"古道"原始中文稿：

千年古道遗址

2002年夏，在北京路步行街发现古道遗迹。经广州市文物考古研究所发掘、考证，古道始于唐代，至民国年间。街道路面层层叠压11层：第11层砂石路距今地表约3米，与第10、9两层铺砖路属唐代；第8、7两层铺砖路为五代南汉国年间；第6、5、4三层属宋代；第3层属南宋至元；第2层石板路属明代。往下有汉唐时期的淤积泥，到

4.5米深处发现有南越国时期遗迹，往下为淤泥层，直至7.9米深见灰红色生土，表明这里曾是河涌地段。

据史志载，今北京路自隋唐以来一直是广州城的中轴线。

广州市文物管理委员会
广州市越秀区人民政府
二〇〇二年十二月

"古楼"修订中文稿：

千年古楼遗址

2002年夏，在北京路步行街发现古楼遗迹。经广州市文物考古研究所发掘、考证，该处为宋、明、清三个历史时期层层叠压的门楼遗址。其遗存有清代的基础垫土层与木桩的柱孔、明代的门楼西门洞铺石路面和抱鼓石等、宋代的门楼西门洞砖铺路面和石门槛等。宋代门楼历三次建造，南北跨度逐次扩大，依次为9米、12米和22米。该处距地表深约1.8米处已见山冈的生土，表明这里曾是山冈地段。

据《番禺县志》载：今北京路唐时有清海楼，南汉时在此叠石建双阙。宋代改为双门城楼。元代毁。明洪武七年（1374年）重建。清代重修，称"拱北楼"。民国八年（1919年）拆城开路，拱北楼遂平。

广州市文物管理委员会
广州市越秀区人民政府
二〇〇二年十二月

"古道"修订中文稿：

千年古道遗址

2002年夏，在北京路步行街发现古道遗迹。经广州市文物考古研究所发掘、考证，古道始于唐代，至民国年间。街道路面层层叠压11层：第11层砂石路距今地表约3米，与第10、9两层铺砖路属唐代；第8、7两层铺砖路为五代南汉国年间；第6、5、4三层属宋代；第3层属宋元期间；第2层石板路属明代，最顶层属民国年间。往下为汉唐时期的淤泥层，到 4.5 米深处发现有南越国时期遗迹，往下为淤泥层，直至 7.9 米深处，见灰红色生土，表明这里曾是河涌地段。

据史志载，今北京路是唐至民国年间广州城的中轴线。

广州市文物管理委员会
广州市越秀区人民政府
二〇〇二年十二月

以上有四处重要的修改。有什么依据呢？下面依次说明。第一，将"古城"改为"古楼"，是为了与第二篇的"古道"一致，并且更为具体化；第二，将"清、明、宋"改为"宋、明、清"，是因为叙述历史事件，习惯多由"远"至"近"；第三，增加"最顶层属民国年间"，是觉得没有理由只少说"一层"；第四，将"隋唐"改为"唐至民国年间"，是因为"隋"在前文中没有任何交代，若照实翻译，外国游客会不知所以。修改后，正好能前后照应。不同的人，视角不一样，看法和修改都有可能不同。但若您是委托方，我是否已经说服了您呢？

字数不多，可翻译起来不简单！若您是译者，再回过头来看看，会遇到什么困难呢？我当时的经历，可以说是举步维艰，尤其在相关知识方面。我历来对考古没有多大兴趣，因此，花了整整两天时间泡在图书馆翻阅广州的地方志和百科全书。比如，要了解"古楼"具体指的是什么？为什么谈论广州的事情，依据的却是《番禺县志》？"清海楼"和"拱北楼"有何寓意？"叠石"怎样理解？"抱鼓石"与"双阙"有无现成的英语译名？最后，为了避免弄错年代，还把相关朝代的起讫年份列了一张总表。

两天下来，有些问题解决了。比如，了解到古时在北京路的东西两侧曾有两座小山，东侧（即广州市第十三中学现址）的叫番山，西侧（即广州百货大厦现址）的叫禺山，故广州叫番禺，不同于现在的番禺区。还了解到"拱北楼"中的"拱北"原来是古时臣民对帝王"以德治国"的赞誉，所谓"拱北楼"，即"德政楼"矣！（现在北京路东侧隔街就有一条平行的"德政路"。）但仍有一些问题，则遍寻不获。不得已，只好四处讨教。比如"古楼"和"叠石"的翻译，是咨询了考古所的专家。而几乎让我绝望的则是"清海楼"。假如不能攻克这个难题，就意味着"清海楼"和"拱北楼"都只能用没有意义的拼音来表示了，因为两者必须统一处理。后来是在内人的提醒下请教了训诂学专家谢栋元教授。他告诉我"清海楼"取意于"河清海晏"，换言之，"清海楼"即"太平楼"之谓。当时，我真不知道有多高兴！"抱鼓石"也是在他的指引下特意到古籍书店花了200元买了一本《中国美术大辞典》解决的。一般汉英词典没有该词条,但美术词典的解释很清楚——抱鼓石:"古时置于牌坊门柱侧或栏杆尽端的鼓形石雕件。……原起结构加固作用,后逐步演变为纯粹装饰物。""双阙"的译法,则是在购买美术词典时意外购得我国著名建筑家梁思成英文原著,其子梁从诫汉译的汉英双语版《图像中国建筑史》后确定的。可以想见,只有解决了以上知识方面的问题,才谈得上真正着手翻译。

再说翻译技巧吧。首先,标题的处理是一个难题。"千年"该如何翻译呢?是"a thousand years"吗?是"a millennium"吗?都不对。因为它不完全是一个确数。那么是否可译成"over a thousand years"呢?也不好。因为在欧洲和其他一些文明古国,超过"千年"并至今保存完好或屹立不倒的建筑(如城堡、教堂、宫殿)和古迹并不少见,因而起不到"震撼"的效果。最后采用的是客观的描述译法。因两块石碑相隔只有200米左右,格式与措辞都得保持一致。在选词方面,还有两个词是个挑战。一个是"生土",一个是"叠石"。前者,在一般汉英词典里很容易查到,它们都把它译为"immature soil",但显然与上下文不合,不得已,只好把它译为"fresh soil"。后者则无法在词典里找着,需要自创译文。最后根据考古专家对中文的解释及与外籍教师的讨论,勉为其难地译成"layered stone",作修饰语用。事后,我甚至在怀疑:对于一篇只供一般游客观赏的说明文字(而不是考古文献或学术著作),是不是有必要翻译得那么准确和详尽呢?在句子结构的安排上,第二篇的二三句之间的衔接有相当的困难,我也忘记了当时换了多少个句型,但结果还是比较满意,读者在阅读下面的译文之前,也可不妨试试。

"古楼"修订中文稿英译初稿:

The Site of a City Gate Dating Back to the Seventh Century

In the summer of 2002, the remains of an ancient city gate were discovered under the pedestrianized area of Beijing Road. Based on the excavation by Guangzhou Research Institute of Cultural Relics and Archaeology, Beijing Road has proven to be the successive sites of a city gate in the respective Song, Ming, and Qing Dynasties (960 – 1911 A. D.), each on top of the previous. What can be seen today are the foundation soil layer and some wood pile holes left over from the Qing Dynasty, the flagged floor and drum-shaped supporting stones at the western entrance of the Ming gate, and the brick floor and the stone threshold at the western entrance of the Song gate, etc. During the Song Dynasty, the city gate underwent reconstruction three times, the north-south span being extended from 9 meters, 12 meters, and 22 meters. From about 1.8 meters below the surface emerges fresh soil, which reveals that the site was first set on a low hill.

According to *The History of Panyu County* (an ancient name for Guangzhou), as early as in the Tang Dynasty (618 – 907 A.D.), there stood a city gate named Qinghai Lou (Times of Peace Gate) on the site of the present Beijing Road. During the Southern Han period (917 – 971 A.D.), a pair of layered stone gate piers was constructed. The paired gate piers were replaced in the Song Dynasty by a pair of city gates, which were destroyed in the Yuan Dynasty (1279 – 1368 A.D.) and reconstructed in the 7th year under the reign of Emperor Zhu Yuanzhang of the Ming Dynasty (1374 A.D.). In the Qing Dynasty the paired city gates were renovated and came to be known as Gongbei Lou (Rule of Virtue Gate). However, they were demolished in the 8th year of the Republic of China (1919 A.D.) for the sake of building a road.

The Cultural Relics Management Committee of Guangzhou
The People's Government of Yuexiu District of Guangzhou
December, 2002

"古道"修订中文稿英译初稿:

The Site of a City Street Dating Back to the Seventh Century

In the summer of 2002, the remains of an ancient street were discovered under the pedestrianized area of Beijing Road. Based on the excavation by Guangzhou Research Institute of Cultural Relics and Archaeology, the origin of the street has been dated back to the Tang Dynasty (618 – 907 A.D.). Between then and the period of the Republic of China (1912 – 1949 A.D.), 10 additional layers were added: the 11th layer is around 3 meters below the present surface and it, as well as the 10th and 9th brick layers, belongs to the Tang Dynasty; the 8th and 7th brick layers belong to the Southern Han period of Five Dynasties (907 – 960 A. D.); the 6th, 5th and 4th layers belong to the Song Dynasty (960 – 1279 A. D.); the 3rd layer belongs to the Song Dynasty and the Yuan Dynasty (960 – 1368 A. D.); the 2nd flagged layer belongs to the Ming Dynasty (1368 – 1644 A. D.), and the final layer to the Republic of China period. Beneath the street is a thick layer of silt formed during the Han and the Tang Dynasties. At a depth of 4.5 meters, the remains of the Southern Yue Kingdom (203 – 111 B. C.) were found. Further downwards is again a thick layer of silt. From 7.9 meters below the surface lies gray-red fresh soil, which reveals that the site used to be a riverbed.

According to historical records, the **site** of the present Beijing Road was the axis of Guangzhou **City** from the Tang Dynasty to the Republic of China period.

The Cultural Relics Management Committee of Guangzhou
The People's Government of Yuexiu District of Guangzhou
December, 2002

翻译的初稿出来了,但心情仍不得轻松,准确地说,是忐忑不安。这是做汉译英时常有的情形。在选词、语法、衔接、逻辑等方面做了几次修改,然后又带着疑问约请英国朋友讨论了几回,最后才定稿。读者可不急于往下看,先对上面的英译稿认真审校一遍,看看从你的角度能发现什么问题。

"古楼"修订中文稿英译定稿:

The Site of a City Gate Dating Back to the Seventh Century

In the summer of 2002, the remains of an ancient city gate were discovered under the pedestrianized area of **this road**. Based on the excavation by Guangzhou Research Institute of Cultural Relics & Archaeology, Beijing Road has proven to be the successive **site of city gates** in the respective Song, Ming, and Qing dynasties (960 – 1911 A. D.), each **site** on top of the previous. What can be seen today are the foundation soil layer and some wood pile holes left over from the Qing **dynasty**, the flagged floor and **a block of drum-shaped supporting stone** at the western entrance of the Ming gate, and the brick floor and the stone threshold at the western entrance of the Song gate, etc. During the Song dynasty, the city gate underwent reconstruction three times, the north-south span being extended from 9 meters to 12 meters, and finally to 22 meters. From about 1.8 meters below the surface lies virgin soil, which reveals that the site was first set on a low hill.

According to *The History of Panyu County* (an ancient name for Guangzhou), as early as in the Tang dynasty (618 – 907 A.D.), there stood a city gate named Qinghai Lou (Times of Peace Gate) on the site of the present Beijing Road. During the Southern Han period (917 – 971 A.D.), a pair of layered stone gate piers were constructed. The paired gate piers were replaced in the Song dynasty by paired city gates, which were destroyed in the Yuan dynasty (1279 – 1368 A.D.) and reconstructed in the 7th year under the reign of Emperor Zhu Yuanzhang of the Ming dynasty (1374 A.D.). In the Qing dynasty the paired city gates were renovated and came to be known as Gongbei Lou (Rule of Virtue Gate). However, they were regretfully demolished in the 8th year of the Republic of China (1919 A.D.) for the sake of building a road.

The Cultural Relics Management Committee of Guangzhou
The People's Government of Yuexiu District of Guangzhou
December, 2002

"古道"修订中文稿英译定稿:

The Site of a City Street Dating Back to the Seventh Century

In the summer of 2002, the remains of an ancient street were discovered under the pedestrianized area of this road. Based on the excavation by Guangzhou Research Institute of Cultural Relics & Archaeology, the origin of the street has been dated back to the Tang dynasty (618 – 907 A.D.). Between then and the period of the Republic of China (1912 – 1949 A.D.), 10 additional layers were added: the bottom grit layer (the 11th layer) is around 3 meters below the present surface and it, as well as the 10th and 9th

brick layers, belongs to the Tang dynasty; the 8th and 7th brick layers belong to the Southern Han period of Five Dynasties (907 – 960 A. D.); the 6th, 5th and 4th layers belong to the Song dynasty (960 – 1279 A. D.); the 3rd layer belongs to the Song dynasty and the Yuan dynasty (960 – 1368 A. D.); the 2nd flagged layer belongs to the Ming dynasty (1368 – 1644 A. D.), and the final layer to the Republic of China period. **Immediately beneath** the street is a thick layer of silt formed during the Han and the Tang dynasties. At a depth of 4.5 meters, the remains of the Southern Yue **kingdom** (ca 203 – 111 B. C.) were found. Further downwards is again a thick layer of silt. From 7.9 meters below the surface lies gray-red **virgin soil**, which reveals that the site **was once** a riverbed.

According to historical records, the **location** of the present Beijing Road was **Guangzhou's hub** from the Tang dynasty to the Republic of China period.

The Cultural Relics Management Committee of Guangzhou
The People's Government of Yuexiu District of Guangzhou
December, 2002

为什么要做这些修改呢？先说英国朋友的意见。她帮我将"fresh soil"改为"virgin soil"，似乎毫不费力。原来所谓"生土"，即所谓"处女地"啊！这是说母语人的语感，但我们常常会感到很无助。另外两个意见则是事先没有想到的。一处是第二篇的"the 11th layer"，她告诉我，他们习惯上是由下往上数，因此"the 11th layer"可能会理解为"the top layer"。另一处是"中轴线"的译法。她认为"axis"有言外之意。我在E-mail中告诉她，"中轴线"是中国传统建筑中的一个重要概念，不好随便换词。但她回复时仍坚持说：But I think the connotation is important. "Axis" is now strongly associated with George Bush's dreadful "axis of evil" speech so perhaps change it to avoid the connotation! Another negative connotation is to the Second World War, when Germany and its allies were known as the "axis powers". （翻译这两篇文字的时候，正值美国攻打伊拉克期间。）最后我只好将"axis"换成"hub"，毕竟英语是给外国人看的！此外，"hub"在英语的旅游资料中也是一个常见的词。

我自己也做了一些重要的修改。比如，将"Guangzhou Research Institute of Cultural Relics and Archaeology"中的"and"改成"&"，理由是在单位名称中，

连接并列成分时，使用符号比使用词语更为常见；将"抱鼓石"的复数形式改为单数形式，是因为有一天我专门到现场去了一趟，发现只有一块"抱鼓石"。另外，在南越国的起讫年份前加了一个"ca"，是表示大约，因为不同的文献记载的时间略有出入。最后，我将以大写字母开头的"Dynasty"全部改成了小写字母开头的"dynasty"。这个词的大小写很令人困惑，因为即使在外国人的著作里也常常不一致。就这个问题我也请教了英国朋友，她的回答是小写的"dynasty"，我不知道她依据的是什么，不过为了把事情弄清楚，我查阅了Collins 系列和 Longman 系列词典，它们举的例子是：the Kennedy dynasty, the Habsburg dynasty, during the Ming dynasty in China（Longman），也就是说，无一例外都是小写的"dynasty"。其他一些修改，读者大致能揣摩出译者的用意，在此不赘。

到此，委托的翻译算是完成了（虽然事后还发现一些不妥的地方，比如，第一篇英文稿的第二句话的结构 "Based on…, Beijing Road has proven to be…" 就不太合逻辑）。但万万没有想到的是，联系人第二天又拿着翻译的稿子回来了。他告诉我：英文太长，石碑太小，刻不下！他还带来了中文原稿，单位领导在上面删除了一些句子。他们希望我能按新的原文重新组织英文。我一看，原来的翻译几乎等于报废，因为句子之间不可能再连起来！万般无奈，我只好叫他们另请人翻译。但在请示领导后，联系人又回来了，说还是要请我翻译，原文由我删减。而实际上，删减原文并不可能完全由我做主，比如说，"广州市文物考古研究所"该不该删除啊，这牵涉到很复杂的关系。长话短说，最后我们达成了一个折中的意见，即汉语文稿基本不变，英文文稿由我决定取舍。

实际碑刻"古楼"中文稿：

千年古楼遗址

2002年夏，在北京路步行街发现古楼遗迹。经广州市文物考古研究所发掘、考证，该处为宋、明、清三个历史时期层层叠压的门楼遗址。其遗存有宋代的门楼西门洞砖铺路面和石门槛，明代的门楼西门洞铺石路面和抱鼓石等，清代的基础垫土层与木桩的柱孔等。宋代门楼历经三次建造，南北跨度逐次扩大，依次为9米、12米、22米。该处距地表深约1.8米处已见山冈的生土，表明这里曾是山冈地段。

据《番禺县志》载：今北京路唐时有清海楼，南汉时在此叠石建双阙。宋代改为双门城楼，元代毁，明洪武七年（1374年）重建。清代重修,称"拱北楼"。民国八年(1919年)拆城开路,拱北楼遂平。

广州市文物管理委员会
广州市越秀区人民政府
二〇〇二年十二月

实际碑刻"古楼"英译稿:

The Site of a City Gate Dating Back to the Seventh Century

In the summer of 2002, the site of the respective city gates of the Song, the Ming and the Qing dynasties (960 – 1911 A. D.) was discovered under the pedestrianized area of this road, each site on top of the previous.

According to *The History of Panyu County* (an ancient name for Guangzhou), as early as in the Tang dynasty (618 – 907 A. D.), there stood a city gate named Qinghai Lou (Times of Peace Gate) on the site of this road. During the Southern Han period (917 – 971 A. D.), a pair of layered stone gate piers were constructed. The piers were replaced in the Song dynasty by paired city gates, which were destroyed in the Yuan dynasty (1279 – 1368 A. D.) and reconstructed in the 7th year under the reign of Emperor Zhu Yuanzhang of the Ming dynasty (1374 A. D.). In the Qing dynasty the paired city gates were renovated and came to be known as Gongbei Lou (Rule of Virtue Gate). However, they were regretfully demolished in the 8th year of the Republic of China (1919) for the sake of building a road.

The Cultural Relics Management Committee of Guangzhou
The People's Government of Yuexiu District of Guangzhou
December, 2002

实际"古楼"英译依据稿:

千年古楼遗址

2002年夏,在北京路步行街发现宋、明、清三个历史时期层层叠压的门楼遗址。据《番禺县志》载：今北京路唐时有清海楼，南汉时在此叠石建双阙。宋代改为双门城楼。元代毁。明洪武七年重建。清代重修，称"拱北楼"。民国八年拆城修马路，拱北楼遂平。

广州市文物管理委员会
广州市越秀区人民政府
二〇〇二年十二月

实际"古道"碑刻中文稿：

千年古道遗址

2002年夏，在北京路步行街发现古道遗迹。经广州市文物考古研究所发掘、考证，古道始于唐代，至民国年间，层层叠压，共11层。第11层砂石路距今地表约3米，与第10、9两层铺砖路属唐代，第8、7两层铺砖路为五代南汉国年间，第6、5、4三层属宋代，第3层属宋元期间，第2层石板路属明代。第11层下有汉唐时期的淤积泥，到4.5米深处发现有南越国时期遗迹，往下为淤泥层，直至7.9米深见灰红色生土，表明这里曾是河涌地段。

据史志载，今北京路是唐至民国年间广州城的中轴线。

广州市文物管理委员会
广州市越秀区人民政府
二〇〇二年十二月

实际"古道"碑刻英译稿：

The Site of a City Street Dating Back to the Seventh Century

In the summer of 2002, the remains of an ancient street were discovered under the pedestrianized area of this road. Field and textual research has dated the origin of the street back to the Tang dynasty (618 – 907 A. D.). Between then and the period of the Republic of China (1912 – 1949 A. D.), 10 additional layers were added. The bottom grit layer is around 3 meters below the present surface. At a depth of 4.5 meters, the remains of the Southern Yue kingdom (ca 203 –111B. C.) were found. From 7.9 meters below the surface lies gray-red virgin soil, which reveals that the site was once a riverbed.

According to historical records, the location of the present Beijing Road was Guangzhou's hub from the Tang dynasty to the Republic of China period.

The Cultural Relics Management Committee of Guangzhou
The People's Government of Yuexiu District of Guangzhou
December, 2002

实际"古道"英译依据稿:

千年古道遗址

2002 年夏,在北京路步行街发现古道遗迹。据发掘考证,古道始于唐代,直至民国时期,街道路面层层叠压 11 层。最底层砂石路距今地表约 3 米。到 4.5 米深处发现有南越国时期遗迹,至 7.9 米深处,见灰红色生土,表明这里曾是河涌地段。

据史志载,今北京路是唐至民国期间广州城的中轴线。

广州市文物管理委员会
广州市越秀区人民政府
二〇〇二年十二月

最后,我向委托方递交了两份中英文对照稿,一份是简化的,供碑刻使用;一份是完备的,供印刷品使用。实际上,以上翻译的过程还是简化了的,只是为了更有条理,方便读者。总共 500 多字,前后花了令人难以置信的近 20 天时间。但至此,我的心还没有完全放下来,我最担心的,是文稿在碑刻时会出现差错,因为这太常见了。比如,一个定冠词在移行时给分成了上下两半。因此,我再三叮嘱联系人,要他亲自监工。当联系人电话告诉我碑刻已经完成时,我很快就赶去现场,急切地看了一遍,又看一遍。当我确定没有差错时,才真正松了一口气!我原来希望这个碑刻的翻译能成为一个样板,但碑刻完成后,更多的是忐忑不安。我要感谢委托方的联系人,也是我过去的学生,我也要对他说声"抱歉"。他处于一个十分尴尬的位置:一方是自己的领导,一方是自己的老师。如果没有他高超的协调能力,这次任务是无法完成的。

本次翻译任务的经验与教训:

(1) 不能轻易接受中译外的任务,尤其是不熟悉的领域,对自己的所长所短要有认识。一个人的能力是很有限的,而翻译所涉及的知识是无限的。我的建议是:学习翻译的学生或在职人员,在打好语言基本功的前提下,可结合自己所学专业或工作性质,专攻相关领域的翻译,使自己成为某一领域的翻译行家。

(2) 要养成与委托方订立"翻译指令"(translation brief,或可翻译为"翻译述要")的习惯(参阅第三章)。要善于替委托方提供专业意见。本次任务中,委托方按理是不可随意变更翻译要求,但译者也有部分责任。比如,有经验的译者可能就会主动询问石碑的大小。

(3) 要较好地完成一项翻译委托,译者还要不断提高人际沟通的能力,要有耐心。译者不但要做翻译,还要做翻译理念的宣传员。译者要有责任心,为维护和提高翻译行业的声誉尽心尽力。

附录2:应用翻译示例

《北京老街》前言

下面这篇古色古香的"前言",是摘自陈永祥等的《北京老街》(中英对照彩绘本)①。这本铅笔淡彩画集,精美绝伦,从一个侧面栩栩如生地再现了老北京的风貌。更难能可贵的是,所配的英文翻译也功力非凡,文字与画面相映生辉。仔细对照阅读,我们会发现,译者化繁为简,取舍有度,其方法与当今西方倡导的功能主义翻译理念不谋而合,因此可作应用翻译的一个参考。

前　言

这本铅笔淡彩画集的"源头",是1950年代初期,我在北京人民艺术剧院任舞台设计期间,为了当时创作的需要,在街头巷尾体验生活、收集素材的一些记忆。光阴荏苒,时过境迁,心里对于往昔生活的怀念却是越来越强烈。为了保留一些逝去岁月的痕迹,为了再现记忆中的故都面貌,

---

① 浩力:《北京老街》,陈永祥绘,索毕成、史宝辉译,社会科学文献出版社2006年版。承蒙陈老慨允,在此向几位作者和译者致谢。为方便读者对照阅读,排版有所调整。

第十章 对外传播的问题与对策

我在10多年的时间里陆陆续续地画出了100余幅铅笔淡彩画。我当然不敢奢望，以这么一点儿零星的图片来表现老北京的全貌，这确实差得太远了。我只是希望对自己有个交代。或许，这也算是对历史的一个交代。

This collection of light-color pencil drawings has its origin dating back to the 1950s, when I was a set designer at Beijing People's Art Theater and did much research in collecting scenes of the city for the stage design. The memories have grown stronger as time passes by. In order to reproduce the scenery of the old city, I have drawn over a hundred color sketches. I cannot expect to give a whole picture of Old Beijing in these limited drawings, but I feel this is something I can contribute to the history of Beijing.

老北京城的建筑多为砖木结构，无论城垣、店铺门面、牌楼和四合院民居，均体现着中国建筑的传统风格，营造出恬静、安详的生活氛围。在当时的街道上，车辆稀少。除了公共交通工具有轨电车外，汽车很少见到，随处可见的只是自行车和人力三轮车。然而这样简单的交通工具，并未让北京市民感到出行如何不便。

The constructions in Old Beijing were mostly structure of wood and brick, exhibiting a style of traditional Chinese architecture and a life of tranquility and peacefulness. There was little traffic apart from the public buses and trams, though bicycles and rickshaws could be seen everywhere. Such simple means of transport, however, did not put the citizens into any inconvenience.

值得一提的，是老城老街难以言表的味道。例如，老北京店铺特有的中国龙形象，虬龙木雕挑头，雕刻精美，造型生动；其他如雕工细致的挂檐板，油漆彩绘的木梁柱，变化多端的木质窗棂，屋顶上格式各异的朝天栏杆，古色古香的匾额，等等，虽经雨打风吹，早已破旧不堪，但是浸透在里面的浓浓的北京味儿丝毫不减。那些耸立在街头巷尾的各式木结构的牌楼，以其五光十色、重重叠叠、镂空架起的斗拱而夺人眼目。这些历尽沧桑、形迹斑驳的艺术瑰宝，含蓄地诉说着当年的辉煌。

What is worth mentioning is the unique taste of the streets, as seen in the vivid carvings of Chinese dragon figures on the facades of the shops, the painted beams, the variety of window frames, and so on. Despite the fact that they have been worn with years of wind and rain, condensed in them is the taste of Old Beijngers in the bygone times. The wooden archways standing in the streets appeal to the eyes of everyone. These artistic treasures seem to be telling people about their magnificent past.

星罗棋布在北京各个区域的古建筑群,其布局也是颇讲章法的。记得在1951年,我曾聆听建筑大师梁思成先生所做的关于老北京城市规划的报告,很值得一提。其一是,北京城在世界都市规划中,有一条举世闻名、独一无二的南北方向的"中轴线"。它最南段的起点是永定门,向北依次经正阳门(即前门)、中华门、天安门、故宫端门、午门、前三殿(即太和殿、中和殿、保和殿)、后三殿、神武门、北山门、景山万春亭、寿皇殿、地安门、鼓楼,直至最北端的钟楼为终点。这条"中轴线"全长7.5公里,由明朝至今已历经数百年。所有皇家宫殿、坛庙、街署等古建筑群均依附着这条"中轴线",紧密相连在一起,以此昭示皇权至尊和一统全局的观念。

The old buildings distributed in the various areas of Beijing follow regular patterns. I remember that in 1951 I attended a lecture given by Liang Sicheng, the renowned architect, on the planning of reconstructing Beijing, who said that for one thing, Beijing had a unique axis from the south up to the north, starting from Youngdingmen (the Gate of Lasting Peace), the southern terminal, there was successively Zhengyangmen (the Gate of Direct Sunshine, also known as Qianmen, the Front Gate), Zhonghuamen (the Gate of China), Tian'anmen (the Gate of Heavenly Peace), Duanmen (the Southern Gate of the Forbidden City), Wumen (the Meridian Gate), the Outer Court (the Halls of Supreme Harmony, Central Harmony and Preserving Harmony), the Inner Court, Shenwumen (the Gate of Spiritual Valor), Beishanmen (the Northern Gate of the Forbidden City), Wanchunting (the Pavilion of Springs on the Prospect Hill), Shouhuangdian (the Palace for Worshipping Ancestors), Di'anmen (the Gate of Earthly Peace), Gulou (the Drum Tower), and Zhonglou (the Bell Tower) at the very north. This central axis was built in the Ming dynasty (1368–1644) and extended for seven and a half kilometers. All the imperial palaces, altars, temples, and government offices clustered along the axis, making obvious the supreme authority and national unity.

其二是,建筑群体的布局均为东西或南北对称排列。比如,天坛在南,地坛在北;日坛在东,月坛在西;太庙(今日的劳动人民文化宫)在东;社稷坛(今日的中山公园)在西。又如,城垣布局也是对称的,内城东为东直门,西为西直门;东南为崇文门,西南为宣武门。紫禁城的安排更是对称的,东门为东华门,内为文华殿;西门为西华们,内为武英殿;城垣四角更有对称修建、遥相呼应的四座角楼。市井商贸中心地区的建筑群,布局亦复如是。比如东城有东四牌楼、东单牌楼,西城有西四牌楼、西单牌楼。

The pattern of the buildings was purely symmetrical. For example, the Temple of Heaven was in the south, with the Temple of Earth in the north, the Temple of Sun in the east and the Temple of Moon in the west. The Altar of Ancestors and Gods was in the east (now the Working People's Cultural Palace) and the Altar of Earth and Harvests was in the west (now the Zhongshan Park). The arrangement of the city walls, the halls in the Forbidden City and the Corner Towers of the city walls were also symmetrical. So were the trading centers.

其三是,老北京的城墙,无论是外城、内城还是紫禁城,尽管其地基起伏不定,内外城墙高低有别,但各自的城脊却奇迹般地坐落在同一水平线上,无一例外。这在世界测量史和建筑史上都是一个奇迹。

The third point was that although the old city walls were of various heights, the spine of the walls was miraculously on the same horizontal level, without exception. A miracle in the international history of surveying and architecture!

这本画集划分为中轴地区、东侧地区、西侧地区三个部分,每个部分都按照从南向北和从东到西的顺序排列,这样可以比较清楚地展示老北京城区的格局。

This collection of drawings consists of three parts: the Central Axis Area, the Eastern Area and the Western Area. Each of those parts in the book is distributed from South to North and also from East to West to show the old city of Beijing in a clear order.

由于年代久远，记忆难免有模糊不清之处。这本画集的部分图画和文字内容，参考了人民中国出版社出版的《旧京大观》、外文出版社出版的《京城胡同留真》、北京美术摄影出版社出版的《北京的胡同》等文献，谨在此向热心研究北京历史卓有贡献的专家——江涛、韦木、刘日祥、金维娜、曾牛耕、柴亦倩、刘富扬、李维维、赵衍、张先得、马洁、熊英、王琼、沈延太、王长清、丁幼华、张承志、许延增诸先生，表示衷心的感谢和敬意。

In drawing and writing this book, I have consulted several major works on Old Beijing, including *Perspectives of Old Beijing*, *Photo Album of Hutong in Beijing*, and *Hutong in Beijing*. I'd like to express my gratitude and appreciation to the following people, who have made outstanding contributions to research in the history of Beijing: Jiang Tao, Weimu, Liu Rixiang, Jin Weina, Zeng Niugeng, Chai Yiqian, Liu Fuyang, Li Weiwei, Zhao Yan, Zhang Xiande, Ma Jie, Xiong Ying, Wang Qiong, Shen Yantai, Wang Changqing, Ding Youhua, Zhang Chengzhi, and Xu Yanzeng.

同时，向策划本书出版的王好立先生，英文翻译索必成、史宝辉先生，以及社会科学文献出版社祝得彬、孙元明诸公致以谢意。最后，还要向多年来默默无闻、与我相扶相伴的夫人王桂玲女士说一声：谢谢。

I would also like to thank Mr. Wang Haoli, who arranged the publication of this book, Mr. Suo Bicheng and Mr. Shi Baohui, who translated the text into English, and Mr. Zhu Debin and Mr. Sun Yuanming of the Social Science Academic Press. Last but not least, I must say "Thank You" to Wang Guiling, my wife, for her love and care throughout all these years.

陈永祥

2005 年 9 月 10 日

第十章　对外传播的问题与对策

【练习题】

Ⅰ．完形填空练习。下面所选段落都是地道的英文，可测试对旅游资料文体在遣词造句方面的熟悉程度。

White Swan Hotel（Guangzhou）

___1___ on the historic Shamian Island, ___2___ the Pearl River, where the earliest Western traders settled, the Hotel is ___3___ enough to provide a respite from the ___4___ of the city, yet close enough to offer ___5___ access to shopping and tourist attractions.

Holland

___1___ it's not windmills you think of when you think of Holland, it's flowers. The country has established itself as Europe's premier flower-growing nation, and show off its most valuable assets with pride. There is ___2___ better to experience this than Keukenhof（地名）, which boasts a ___3___ display of more than 6 000 000 tulips and other varieties, ___4___ over 65 acres of lovingly-tended gardens.

France

Just 20 or so miles across the Channel lies another world. France, the largest country in Western Europe, has a wonderful ___1___ of scenery and culture. the famous North Coast ports, including lively, bustling Calais; the majestic chateaux of the Loire Valley; the ___2___ vineyards of Burgundy and Bordeaux; elegant cities ___3___ Toulouse and Lyon; the glamorous Riviera; the quaint, Spanish-style towns of the Pyrenees; the ___4___ goes on and on. ___5___ in history, yet always looking forward, France is a fascinating ___6___ of ancient and modern. You can marvel at the ___7___ magnificence of a thirteenth century cathedral or enjoy "state of the art" shopping in vast malls to ___8___ any in America. In the glorious, ___9___ countryside, you're as ___10___ to come across a horse and cart wending its way to market, as to see a sleek, super-modern TGV train ___11___ between cities. As for the people, at first they may seem a little "stand-offish", but try just a few words of French and you'll be sure to receive a warm welcome ___12___ you go.

The Romance of Paris

No other place __1__ the imagination __2__ like Paris. This beautiful city __3__ oozes charm—from the splendid, tree-lined Champs-Elysées to the tiny, winding alleyways of Montmartre, where you can be __4__ by one of the many street artists as a souvenir of your visit. An organized city tour by __5__ is the easiest way to see all the major sights, __6__ Notre Dame, the Eiffel Tower, the Arc de Triomphe and Sacre Coeur. But don't forget—Paris is just __7__ for walking, whether you want to __8__ around the famous-name fashion houses or visit some of the many __9__ art galleries and museums. As for Paris by night, there's plenty of entertainment on __10__—from cinema to cabaret. Or why not take to the water for a romantic dinner cruise on one of the brightly-lit "bateaux mouches" which __11__ up and down the Seine?

Israel

The multi-cultural melting pot of Israel holds a unique __1__ for many of the world's peoples—Christian, Jew and Muslim __2__. This relatively small country is a __3__ in historic terms, the very __4__ of religion and the "Promised Land" of the Bible. It is also, of course, the place where you'll find perhaps the most famous historical __5__ in the world, Bethlehem, the birthplace of Jesus. At the same time, its historical __6__ is matched by natural beauty, with a fifth of the country covered by some 300 national parks. It is also a land of stark __7__, its landscape varying from the lush, __8__ hills of the north to the parched desert country of the south.

Ⅱ. 校改练习。

下面是从一本英国作者编写的翻译教材①的附录里摘选的一篇中英对照文字（已删除一段关联不大的文字，段落重新编号）。英语为原文，汉语为译文。原文是幻灯片的说明文字，每一张幻灯片（原书未附图片）配一段文字。译者可能是中国留学生或访问学者。译文中存在许多错误，请认真校对译文，看看能否找出并订正这些错误，尤其是跨文化交际和知识方面的错误。请反复校改译文后，再对照书后提供的参考译文。

---

① 引自 Mona Baker, *In Other Words: A Coursebook on Translation*, London: Routledge, 1992, Appendix 3。

China's Panda Reserves

1. An adult panda munches bamboo. This attractive black and white mammal has widespread human appeal and has become a symbol for conservation efforts both within China and internationally as the symbol of the World Wide Fund for Nature (WWF).

2. Today there may be no more than 1 000 giant pandas left in the wild, restricted to a few mountain strongholds in the Chinese provinces of Sichuan, Shaanxi and Gansu.

3. For most people their only chance of seeing a giant panda is in a zoo. These young pandas in Beijing Zoo are great crowd pullers.

4. The panda is something of a zoological mystery. Its closest relative is the smaller red panda with whom it shares its range. The red panda's striking appearance indicates the close relationship between pandas and the racoon family.

5. There is also strong evidence, however, that giant pandas are related to the bears. This Asiatic black bear shares the panda's range in China.

6. The panda's mountain home is wet and lush. Today pandas are only found at high altitude, wandering the broadleaf forests and subalpine woodlands.

7. Only occasionally are they found in the lower mixed broadleaf forests for these are the areas most accessible to and disturbed by Man.

8. The panda's mountain home is rich in plant life and gave us many of the trees, shrubs and herbs most prized in European gardens. Species like this mountain rhododendron were collected by 19th century botanists and shipped back to Europe for horticultural collections.

9. The adult pandas at the centre sleep in cages and are fed a well-balanced and nutritious diet; many have been nursed back to health from the brink of starvation. They also have access to a large outdoor compound where they can roam among natural vegetation in semi-wild conditions.

10. Many of the species growing wild here are familiar to us as plants cultivated in European gardens-species like this exotic lily.

11. The Chinese people have already made substantial efforts to protect the giant panda, which is considered to be a national treasure. Nevertheless we are at a critical

time for this species. Without immediate and effective protection and management of the giant panda and its remaining habitat this will become an increasingly rare sight—a loss both for China and the whole world.

中国的熊猫保护区

1. 一只成年大熊猫在咀嚼竹子。这一吸引人的黑白哺乳动物为人们所广泛地喜爱。作为世界自然基金会（WWF）的标记，熊猫已经成为中国和国际性自然保护努力的象征。

2. 今天，仍处于野生状态的大熊猫可能只有1000只，仅限于中国的四川、陕西和甘肃省内的一些山区。

3. 对大多数人来说，能看见大熊猫的唯一机会便是在动物园里。北京动物园里的这些幼熊猫吸引着大量的观众。

4. 熊猫可以被称为动物学里的一个谜。其最近的亲属是与其分享活动领域的更小的红熊猫。红熊猫引人注目的外貌表明了熊猫和浣熊科之间的紧密联系。

5. 但是，也有较强的证据表明大熊猫与熊有亲属关系。这一亚洲黑熊分享熊猫在中国境内的活动区域。

6. 熊猫的山区栖息地是潮湿、茂盛的。今天，只有在高海拔地区才有熊猫漫游于阔叶森林和亚高山的林地之中。

7. 偶尔也见于较低地区的混合阔叶森林之中，因为这些地区是人类最容易进入、干扰最多的地方。

8. 熊猫的山区定居地有着丰富的植物种类，有着欧洲园林所珍视的许多树木、灌木和草木植物的种类。像这一山杜鹃花等种类为19世纪的植物学家所采集，然后运回欧洲作为园艺收藏品。

9. 该中心的成年熊猫睡于笼子里，供应的食物匀称、营养丰富；许多熊猫已从饿死的边缘被护理恢复了健康。它们还享有一个大型的户外院子，可以漫游于半野生状态的自然植物中。

10. 这里野生的许多种类我们很熟悉，是欧洲园林内种植的种类——像这一奇异的百合花等种类。

11. 中国人民已经做了许多工作来保护被视为国宝的大熊猫。但是，我们正处在熊猫生死存亡的关键时刻。如果没有对大熊猫及其仅剩的栖息地进行及时的、有效的保护和管理，这样的景象就将会越来越难看到——这对中国和整个世界都将是个损失。

第十章　对外传播的问题与对策

Ⅲ. 下面是在北京八达岭实录的一篇汉英对照的景点介绍。请根据原文提供的信息修改译文，或重新制作一篇译文。

万里长城·八达岭

长城是中国古代最宏伟的建筑和最伟大的军事防御体系，是世界上的奇迹，中国的骄傲。

春秋战国时期（公元前770—221），诸侯割据，为了防御临近诸侯的侵扰，在各自的领地边境上，筑起了防卫的城墙。公元前三世纪，秦始皇统一中国，将北方的各段城墙连接起来，筑成了万里长城。以后许多朝代因军事防御的需要，都对长城进行过不同规模的修筑和改建。但由于历史原因，长城都有过不同程度的损坏，现在保存较好的只有明代长城了。

明长城东起鸭绿江边，西至嘉峪关，绵延万余里。跨越我国北部的辽宁、河北、天津、北京、山西、内蒙古、陕西、宁夏、甘肃等省、市、自治区。

八达岭是万里长城居庸关的前哨。墙高7米有余，顶部宽约5米，在城墙的转角和要冲处，筑有城台和敌楼，是万里长城的精华部分。新中国成立后，人民政府曾不断对八达岭这段长城加以维修，使它保持了原来的雄伟面貌。1961年，八达岭被国务院列为全国重点文物保护单位。1988年，八达岭作为万里长城的杰出代表，接受了联合国教科文组织颁发的世界人类文化遗产证书。八达岭是驰名中外的旅游胜地，是世界人类文化遗产的一部分。

BRIEF INTRODUCTION OF THE GREAT WALL (BADALING)

The Great Wall is one of the greatest wonders in the world, also it is the most magnificent architecture and the greatest military defences in ancient China.

Construction of the Great Wall first began during the Spring and Autumn period and warring states period (770 – 221 B. C.) At that time, walls were built by some warring states to protect their territories. In the 221 B. C., Qin Shihuang, who was the first emperor in Qin unified China, he linked up the separated walls and had them exceeded into ten thousand-li wall. From then on, the Great Wall was rebuilt with great efforts in some dynasties. But most of them were damaged in varying degrees because of the historical reasons. At present, only the Ming wall is best preserved.

The Ming wall stretched from east Yalu River to the west Jayuguan Pass. Covering a total length of more than 6 000 kilometers. It traverses 5 provinces, 2 autonomous regions and 2 municipalities in the north part of China. They are Liaoning, Hebei, Tianjin, Beijing, Shanxi, Inner Mongolia, Shaanxi, Ningxia and Gansu.

Badaling is the advanced point of the Jiayuguan Pass. The Great Wall is more than 7 meters high and 5 meters wide. Many fortresses and beacon towers constructed at the strategic point along the Great Wall. The Great Wall was designated major historical relics under states protection in 1961.

The Chinese government has paid great attention to Badaling section of the Great Wall since the P. R. C. is founded. Badaling Great wall is essential one of the Great Wall. In 1988, it received the world's mankind culture heritage certification applied by the United Nations Educational Scientific and Culture Organization. And now, she is preserved as a historical monument and has become one of the most popular tourist spots in the world.

第十一章
涉外文书常用词语的翻译

在涉外文书中，有些词语的使用频率很高，因此了解其特点和含义，研究其翻译方法，对提高翻译的效率和译文的质量都有积极的意义。

第一节 be interested in

"be interested in"这一短语在日常英语中表示的是"对某事感兴趣"，但在外贸函电中，该短语被广泛应用，并逐渐获得了一种新的含义。在不同的上下文中，很难用"对……感兴趣"这种一刀切的译法，否则，译文常常可能文理不通。请看下面的例子：

1. We would be interested in receiving your inquiries for all types of Electric Goods.
   译文：我们对收到你们对各种电器用品的询函**感兴趣**。
2. Should you be interested in supplying, we would be more than pleased to enter into business activities with you.
   译文：如果你们对供货**感兴趣**，我们很愿意与你们建立业务关系。
3. We are interested in your "Sea Gull" brand woman's wrist watches and shall be glad if you should make us an offer for 1 000 pieces with details.
   译文：我们对你们的"海鸥"牌女装手表**感兴趣**，如果你们能给我们1000只这种表的详细报盘，不胜高兴。

以上3句译文，前两句摘自学生的练习，第3句摘自公开出版的书籍，可见都是"对号入座"。这些译文说通也通，说不通也不通。说通，是说读后能基本明白其意思；说不通，是说译文表达不贴切，且不合汉语行文习惯。试分别改译如下：

1. 欢迎贵公司来函询购各款电器产品。
2. 如贵公司有意供货，我们十分乐意与你们建立业务关系。
3. 我们欲购你厂"海鸥"牌女装手表，请报1000只详盘。

从以上3个句子可以看出，"be interested in"不仅仅表示对某事的一种"兴趣"，而且还明确地表示做某事的"意向"。当然，我们并不是说不能将"be interested in"译成"对……感兴趣"，只是提醒读者，翻译时应根据不同的上下文，灵活措辞。

第二节 （be） subject to

"（be）subject to"的翻译可谓五花八门，不易掌握。也许最可靠的办法还是从它的释义开始。subject 用作形容词，根据 *Oxford Dictionary Thesaurus & Wordpower Guide*（2001）的解释，它有3个意思：① likely or prone to be affected by (something bad)（可能或易于遭受坏事的影响）；② dependent or conditional upon（"依赖于"或"以……为条件"）；③ under the control or authority of（"受制于"或"在……的管辖之下"）。第一个义项常见于外贸英语中，但也用于日常英语，最后两个义项尤其多见于契约和公文语言中。请看下面的例子：

1. The treaty is subject to ratification.
   本条约**待批准后生效**。（或：本条约未经批准无效。）
2. This contract is binding subject to the fulfillment of the following conditions.
   本合同**须满足下列条件**方始生效。
3. This credit is subject to the Uniform Custom and Practice for Commercial Documentary Credit.
   本信用证**以**"跟单信用证统一惯例"**为准**。
4. Our prices are subject to fluctuation of the market.
   我方价格得**随市价波动而调整**。
5. This kind of glassware is subject to breakage during transit.
   这种玻璃器皿在运输途中**易受破损**。
6. Foreign citizens in China are subject to Chinese laws.
   中国境内的外国公民**必须遵守**中国法律。（或许也可译成：中国境内

第十一章 涉外文书常用词语的翻译

的外国公民**适用**中国法律。)

7. You'll be transferred to the permanent staff <u>subject to</u> your satisfactory completion of the probationary period.

   只要圆满完成试用期,即可转为正式员工。

8. The contracted goods could be delivered at any time <u>subject to</u> the availability of shipping space.

   合同所订货物**如**有舱位可随时装运。

9. The property is sold and will be conveyed <u>subject to</u> the following conditions.

   该财产**须按**下列条款出售和转让。

10. The purchaser shall have the full power, <u>subject to</u> the provisions hereinafter contained, at any time during the contract to issue instructions to the contractor so as to alter, amend, omit, or add to any of the project services.

    购买方享有充分权利在合同有效期间的任何时候向承包方发出指令,以对任何工程服务项目进行修改、补充、删减或增加,**但在行使该权利的同时**,购买方**必须遵守**本章下述条款。

11. **第十六条** 公民为完成法人或者非法人单位工作任务所创作的作品是职务作品,**除**本条第二款的规定**以外**,著作权由作者享有,但法人或者非法人单位有权在其业务范围内优先使用。有下列情形之一的职务作品,作者享有署名权,著作权的其他权利由法人或者非法人单位享有,法人或者非法人单位可以给予作者奖励:

    (一) ……

    (二) 法律、行政法规规定或者合同约定著作权由法人或者非法人单位享有的职务作品。

    Article 16 A work created by a citizen in the fulfillment of tasks assigned to him by a legal entity or entity without legal personality shall be deemed as a work created in the course of employment. The copyright in such a work shall be enjoyed by the author, <u>subject to</u> the provisions of the second paragraph of this Article, provided that the legal entity or entity without legal personality shall have a priority right to exploit the work within the scope of its professional activities. In the following cases the author of a work created in the course of employment shall enjoy the right of authorship while the legal entity or entity without legal personality shall enjoy other rights included in the copyright and may reward the author:

(一) (omitted)

(二) Works created in the course of employment where the copyright is, in accordance with laws, administrative regulations or contracts, enjoyed by the legal entity or entity without legal personality.

此例选自《中华人民共和国著作权法》第十六条（《中华人民共和国对外经济法规汇编》1991年卷，中国对外经济贸易出版社，1992）。为了更清楚地了解"subject to"的用法，所以引用了完整的上下文（这里不讨论其他部分）。本条文中"除……以外"被翻译为"subject to"。但要注意的是，如果将它回译成中文，也有可能是"在与本条第二款的规定不抵触的情况下"，换言之，在这类上下文中，"除……以外"未必是"subject to"的最好或唯一译法。

从上面的译文看，似乎没有什么规律可循，但只要从该短语的核心意义出发，仔细琢磨句子间各成分的关系，再根据汉语行文习惯重新组织句子，就有可能写出准确、通顺的译文。

第三节　responsible for/responsibility 与 liable for/liability

上面这组词，都可译成"对……负责"，或"责任"，但如果是汉译英的话，就可能造成混乱了。事实上，这两个词（组）是有区别的，它们意思相近，但侧重点不同。根据 *Collins Business English Dictionary* 的释义，"responsible"有两个基本含义：一是"in charge of"（对……负责，即享有权威，享有安排和督促有关事宜进行的职责）。比如：You will be responsible for the conduct of the new sales campaign.（这次促销由你负责。）二是"capable of being blamed"（可能引咎受罚或遭到谴责）。比如：If anything goes wrong, you will be held responsible.（事情如有差错，将由你负责。）而"liable"则是指"being legally responsible for loss, damage, debts, etc."（对……丢失、损坏、债务等承担法律上的责任）。由此看来，"responsible"一词适用的范围更广，并侧重"道义"上的责任；而"liable"则强调与"loss, damage, debts"等有关的"法律"责任，换言之，事情如有差错，当事人须负赔偿或刑事责任。试看下面一些例子：

1. Party A shall be responsible for the completeness, correctness and legibility

of the product design drawings and manufacturing Technical Documentation sent to Party B.

甲方**对**提供给乙方的产品设计图纸和制造技术资料的**完整性、正确性、清晰性负责**。

2. She is responsible for making sure orders are processed on time.

她**负责**安排生产，以确保如期完成订单。

3. The pilot of the plane is responsible for the passengers' safety.

飞机驾驶员**对乘客安全负有责任**。

4. The carrier shall not be liable for loss or damage arising or resulting from defects not discoverable though the carrier has exercised due diligence as aforesaid.

承运人**对**前款规定已经谨慎处理后仍不能发现的由货物本身缺陷所造成的**货物灭失或损坏免除责任**。

5. The Company shall be liable for total or partial loss of the insured goods caused in the course of transit by natural calamities — heavy weather, lighting, floating ice, seaquake, earthquake, flood, etc. or by accidents—grounding, stranding, sinking, collision or derailment of the carrying conveyance, fire, explosion and falling of entire package or packages of the insured goods into sea during loading or discharge, etc.

本公司**负责赔偿**被保险货物在运输途中由于遭受暴风、雷电、流冰、海啸、地震、洪水等自然灾害或由于运输工具搁浅、触礁、沉没、碰撞、出轨、失火和爆炸以及在装卸过程中整件货物落海等意外事故而造成的**全部或部分损失**。

6. The seller shall not be liable for any claims unless they are made promptly after receipt of the goods and due opportunity has been given for investigation by the seller's own representatives.

除非买方收到货物即刻提出索赔，并给予卖方的代表有调查的相当机会，否则卖方**对于索赔不予负责**。

7. In all circumstances, the carrier shall be discharged from all liabilities in respect of loss or damage unless suit is brought within one year after delivery of the goods or the date when the goods should have been delivered.

关于货物**灭失或损坏**赔偿的要求，应自交货之日或应交货之日起一年内提出，否则在任何情况下承运人**免除一切责任**。

8. My partner and I are jointly and severally liable for any debts.
我和我的合伙人均负有个别及连带**承担偿付一切债务的责任**。

9. Parents and guardians may avoid liability for their children's crimes if they can satisfy the court that they have done everything they can to prevent it.
孩子的父母或监护人，只要能向法庭证明他们已采取一切必要措施防止其孩子或被监护人犯罪，可免除**承担**其孩子或被监护人犯罪的**法律责任**。

"responsible for/responsibility"与"liable for/liability"各自的适用范围有时也是很难区别的。比如有时在负有道义责任的同时，也可能须负赔偿、刑事等法律责任。为使译文严谨。我们可以看到，在翻译法律性文件时，常常同时使用两个词。例如：

10. 银行**对于**天灾、暴动、骚乱、叛乱、战争或本身无法控制的其他原因，或任何的罢工或关厂而中断营业所引起的后果，**概不负责**。
Banks assumes no liability or responsibility for consequences arising out of the interruption of their business by Acts of God, riots, civil commotions, insurrections, wars or any other causes beyond their control, or by any strikes or lockouts.

第四节　abide by/comply with；according to/ in line with /in accordance with

以上两组词在契约语言中广为使用，也特别容易混淆。"abide by"和"comply with"都可译为"遵守"，但前者的主语一般是人（其他动词还有"obey""observe"），后者的主语为事或物。试比较如下：

1. 合营公司**全体员工**都应**遵守**项目所在国的法律和法令，尊重当地的风俗和习惯。
All the personnel of the Joint Venture Company shall abide by the laws and decrees in the project-host country and respect the local customs and traditions.

2. 双方的**一切活动**都应**遵守**项目所在国的法律、法令和有关条例规定

第十一章 涉外文书常用词语的翻译

All the activities of both parties shall comply with the provisions of laws, decrees and pertinent regulations in the project-host country.

在表示"根据（依照）合同、规定、贸易惯例"等时，第二组词一般可以通用，但"according to"较口语化，"in line with"和"in accordance with"为书面语体，并且后者最为正式。例如：

3. 合作企业须**按照**国家有关规定聘任中国注册会计师进行查账验证。
   The Joint Venture shall, in line with related provisions of Chinese laws, commission accountants registered in China to audit and check their financial accounts.

4. **根据**《中华人民共和国外资企业法》第23条规定，制定本实施细则。
   The Detailed Rules are formulated in accordance with the provisions of Article 23 of *Law of the People's Republic of China on Foreign Capital Enterprises*.

另外，"according to"还可作为"根据某人的意见""根据……报告"解，此时不能与"in accordance with"或"in line with"通用。例如：

5. **根据市场调查**，明年上半年石油化工产品的价格可望回升。
   According to a market research, the prices for petrochemicals during the first half of next year are expected to pick up.

第五节　against

"against"是个多义词，在外贸英语中广为使用，翻译时需根据上下文仔细选择词义。

表示"防止……"

1. We will not effect the payment of the withheld goods value unless you ensure against the recurrence of the damage to packing of the coming goods.

· 277 ·

只有你方**保证**今后**不再**发生包装破损的现象，我们才会支付拒付的货款。

2. We wish to ensure the following consignment <u>against</u> all risks for the sum of U.S. $3 600.

  我们要为下列货物按3600美元保额**投保**综合险。

表示"根据／凭……"；"以……为条件"

3. The Bank of China, London can open an L/C in RMB for you <u>against</u> our sales confirmation.

  伦敦中国银行，可**凭**我方销售确认书开立人民币信用证。

4. We hereby issue in your favour this documentary credit which is available by payment <u>against</u> presentation of the following documents.

  现开立以你方为受益人的跟单信用证，**凭**下列单证议付。

5. documents <u>against</u> payment（D/P）

  付款交单

6. documents <u>against</u> acceptance（D/A）

  承兑交单

第5、6两例均是国际贸易的常用术语。"付款交单"系指边付款边交提单及货运单据的一种结算方式。进口商在国外所订货物运抵口岸时，经银行通知，于汇票到期日或到期以前，将票面金额付清，银行将提单及其他单据（包括发票、保险单、磅码单等）交给进口商凭以提货。"承兑交单"系指先交提单及货运单据后付款的一种结算方式。进口商在国外所订货物运抵口岸时，将未到期汇票承兑后，即可先向银行取得提单及其他单据（包括发票、保险单、磅码单等），凭以提货，银行于到期日再行收款。

表示"违反……"

7. It is <u>against</u> the contractual stipulations that you failed to establish the covering L/C 30 days before the time of shipment.

  贵方未在交货期前30天开立有关的信用证，这是**违反**合同规定的。

表示"对……不利，反对"

第十一章　涉外文书常用词语的翻译

8. In case you should fail to effect delivery in April, we will have to lodge a claim <u>against you for the loss</u> and reserve the right to cancel the contract.

如果你们4月份尚不能交货，我们只好**向你们提出索赔**，并保留取消合同的权利。

　　表示"与……比较/对比"

9. <u>Against</u> the invoice weight the consignment was found short of 1 350kg.

　　与发票重量**相比**，货物短重1350公斤。

第六节　offer，quote/quotation，bid

"offer"、"quote/quotation"和"bid"在外贸业务中有它们各自的含义和用法，须加以区别。

"offer"译为"报盘"或"发盘"，是外贸业务中的一个环节，通常是指卖方向对方提出贸易成交条件，如货名、数量、规格、价格、船期、效期。

"offer"既可作名词，也可作动词。作名词时，又可分为实盘/确盘（firm offer）和虚盘（non-firm offer）。实盘须附有效期，如firm for 5 days。虚盘须附有条件，如subject to our final confirmation（以我方最后确认为准）；subject to our prior sale（货未售出为有效）。一切报盘如果规定了效期而未附加任何条件，即使无"firm"字样，也默认为实盘。

除实盘和虚盘外，外贸业务中还有搭配报盘，即"combined offer"（或称联盘，即指两种以上的商品）和买方的还盘，即"counter-offer"。

"offer"经常与下列动词搭配，以表示报盘的各个方面：

　　to make / forward an offer　　发盘
　　to accept an offer　　接收报盘
　　to decline an offer　　谢绝报盘
　　to entertain an offer　　考虑是否接受报盘
　　to extend an offer　　延长报盘
　　to renew an offer　　恢复报盘
　　to withdraw an offer　　撤回报盘

请看下面的句子:

1. Please make us an offer C. I. F London for 20 metric tons peanut.
   请报 20 公吨花生伦敦到岸价**实盘**。

2. This is a combined offer, which must be accepted in its entirety.
   此系**搭配报盘**,必须一起接受。

3. We renew our offer for reply here Wednesday our time.
   兹**恢复报盘**,以我方时间星期三复到为有效。

"quote"用作动词,其后可接两个宾语。作"报价"解时,其直接宾语只能是"price"或是与"price"相关的价格术语,如"FOB""C&F""CIF"等,或两者同时出现。例如:

4. Please quote (us) your lowest price CIF London for walnut.
   请**报**我方胡桃最低伦敦**到岸价**。

"quotation"为"quote"的名词形式。它与"offer"(报盘)不同,主要是指"提出价格",一般可译为"报价""行市""行情""时价"等。例如:

5. Please send us your lowest quotation CIF London for walnut.
   请**报**我方胡桃最低伦敦**到岸价**。

6. These quotations are said to be nominal.
   这些价格据说是有**行**无**市**。

7. These are the latest quotations from the Stock Exchange.
   这些是证券交易所的最近**行情**。

"bid"译作"递盘/递价",与"offer"相对,系指买方的主动出价。买方还价时说"counter-bid"或"counter-offer"。"bid"既可用作名词,也可用作动词。作动词时,其句型与"quote"相似。另外,"bid"系不规则动词,其过去时和过去分词均为"bid",词形不变。例如:

8. We will try to get a bid from the buyers.
   我们要设法从**买主**那里获得一个**递盘**。

9. As your prices were too high, we made a counter-bid at RMB ￥4 000 per ton.

第十一章 涉外文书常用词语的翻译

由于你方价格太高，现**还价**每吨人民币 4000 元。

10. Last week we <u>bid</u> RMB ￥4 000 per ton for Green Tea. Now we can do a little better.

上周我方绿茶**递价**每吨人民币 4000 元，现在我方可以**递价**稍高些。

第七节 if, in case 及其他

英语中由"if"和"in case"引导的表示将来的从句，在许多场合下都可能译成汉语的"如果……"（或"如……""若……"），英译汉一般不成问题。但是，在汉译英时，如果将"if"和"in case"当作等值之词，却可能产生语气上的毛病。例如：

1. 如果本合同自签字之日起 6 个月仍不能生效，本合同对双方任何一方均不具约束力。

    _____ the contract cannot come into force within six months after the date of signing the contract, the contract shall be binding neither to Party A nor to Party B.

2. 如果贵方有意购买我出口目录中任何一项商品的话，请与我各有关分公司接洽。

    _____ you have interest in any of the items listed in our export catalogue, you are welcome to get in touch with our competent branches.

以上两个英译文都留出空格，哪处该用"if"，哪处该用"in case"呢？同是一个"如果"，但在特定的上下文中，其语气却可能截然相反。比如，例 1 中的"如果"，指的是说话者不愿看到的结果；例 2 中的"如果"，则是指说话者希望发生的情况。在英语中，"if"常用来表示可能性大的假设，而"in case"则一般来表示可能性小的假设。据此，在例 1 中理应选"in case"，在例 2 中选"if"。如果选择相反，例 1 就可能暗示合同签订之初双方均无信心，而例 2 就不可理解了。有哪家公司希望自己的产品无人问津呢？

在汉译英时，还应注意"if"与"provided"的区别。如果从句的内容是一种纯粹的假设，通常用"if"表示；如果从句属一种先决条件，那就用"provided"表示（或用"on condition that"表示）。一般说来，能用"provided"的场合，也可用"if"；但可用"if"的从句却未必能换用"provided"，如上文例

· 281 ·

2就不能换成"provided"。又如：

3. 如果你方接受我们提出的数量，我们就接受你方的报价。
We will accept your price <u>provided / if</u> you take the quantity we offer.

此外，能用"in case"的场合，也可换用"should"，或根据上下文的词句结构，改用"in case"的异体形式。例如：

4. 如果卖方在规定的日期前未收到信用证，本确认书即告无效。
<u>Should / In case</u> the L/C fail（s）to reach the Seller before the stipulated expiry date, this sales confirmation shall be considered null and void.

5. 如果发生索赔，双方应友好协商解决。
<u>In case of</u> claims, the Parties involved should seek a settlement through amicable negotiations.

6. 如果本合同提前终止，本合同之附件也随之终止。
<u>In the event of</u> premature termination of this Contract, the Contract Appendices shall likewise terminate.

第八节　shall 及其他

在英语的法律文献中，"shall"几乎被认为是法律行业标志性词语之一，法律文献起草人动辄使用"shall"，以显示其专业水准。然而，实际的情况是，有相当多的法律文献起草人并不十分了解该词的准确用法，只是为"专业性"而"专业性"，在法庭上阅读法律文献的人每次遇到"shall"，也只把它作当然之物，不去究其所以。并且这种做法在法律界或在法学院一再被强化，逐渐成了一种痼习。因此也可以说，"shall"这个词是法律文献中使用最滥的词语之一。难怪有法律文体学家建议："Delete every shall"（Garner, 2001: 105）。

既然是痼习，就不可能一说要去掉就能马上去掉的，因此，现在仍有必要了解它的一些基本用法。"shall"的主语为第三人称（与日常英语不同），它不是表示"将来"，而是表示法律意义上的命令、义务、职责、权利或许诺等，在英语中相当于"must"（或"have a duty to""be required to"），但很少用"must"，即不如此则须承担违反法律的后果。无独有偶，在中文法律文献中，属强制性范畴、使用频率相当的词语就是"应"，其含义相当于"须"，但多数情况下使用

第十一章 涉外文书常用词语的翻译

"应"替代"须"。由此，在英汉互译时就产生问题了。

英译汉时，"shall"按理说该译成"应"，但在汉语中，"应"既可理解为"必须"（即"shall"的正解），又可理解为"应当"（即一般义务或道义上的义务）。此外，英语中的"should"又该怎么翻译呢？有人提议，将"shall"译成"应"，而把"should"译成"应当"，以示区别。但在汉语词典里，"应"与"应当"恐怕并无这样的区别，因此，如此翻译也就没有根据了。我们认为积极的办法不如将"should"译成"应当"或"应该"，而把"shall"尽可能地译成"须"，坚持下去，也许可以慢慢改掉中文法律文字中混用"应"与"须"的陋习。例如：

1. The payment of the aforesaid expenses shall be effected against presentation of original vouchers after being checked.
上述有关费用均**须**凭核实的原始单据支付。

如果将此句中的"shall"译为"应"，那就可能给钻空子了，即最好凭原始单据支付，但若实在没有，也只好作罢，换言之，仍有商量的余地，这就与句子原来的意思不符。

汉译英时，如上所述，最根本的方法恐怕还是要在动笔之前认真辨义，看"应"是属于法律范畴，还是非法律范畴。如属前者，则译作"shall"，如属后者，则译作"should"。例如：

2. 合营公司**应**按贷款协议的规定偿还到期**应**偿还的贷款本金。
The Joint Venture Company shall repay the principal on loans that fall due and should be paid in accordance with the provisions of the loan agreement.

英文法律文字中"shall"的滥用自然也导致了法律文献汉译英时"shall"的滥用。例如：

3 (a) 商标注册人享有商标专用权，受法律保护。（《中华人民共和国商标法》，法律出版社 2002 年版）
The owner of a registered trademark shall enjoy the exclusive right to the use of the trademark, which shall be protected by law.

· 283 ·

原文只是陈述一个事实，而译文却变成了一道命令，似乎连商标注册人本人也无选择的权利。上句可稍作修改，译为：

3（b） The owner of a registered trademark **has** the exclusive right to the use of the trademark, which **is** protected by law.

另一方面，中文法律文献，根据行文习惯，有时"应"字并不出现。这种情况在英译时往往容易错用"will"替代"shall"。例如：

4. 合作企业的清算事宜，依照国家有关法律、行政法规及合作企业合同、章程的规定办理。
The liquidation of the Joint Ventures **shall**（不用"will"）be handled in accordance with related State laws and administrative regulations and rules as well as the ventures' contract and the articles of the association.

与"须"相对，由"shall"构成的否定句，在中译时一般可使用"不得"。例如：

5. The Chairman and Vice-chairman of the Standing Committee **shall** serve **no** more than two consecutive terms. ①
委员长、副委员长连续任职**不得**超过两届。

值得注意的是，当以"neither""nothing""no"等否定词语开头的英文句子，后面的"shall"并不具有"have a duty to"的意义，因此，为了避免混乱，最好用"may"或"be allowed to"替换"shall"。例如：

6（a） **Neither** party **shall** assign this Agreement, directly or indirectly, without the prior written consent of the other party（Garner, 2001: 105）.
任何一方未经另一方事先书面同意，无论是直接还是间接，均**不得**转让本协议。

---

① 见 *The Basic Law of the Hong Kong Special Administrative Region of the People's Republic of China*，转引自李克兴、张新红：《法律文本与法律翻译》，中国对外翻译出版公司 2006 年版，第 173 页。

上面这个英文句子最好改写成:

6（b） **Neither** party **may**（或"**is allowed to**"） assign this Agreement, directly or indirectly, without the prior written consent of the other party.

这样的句子并不少见,又如:

7. **No** departments of the Central People's Government and no province, autonomous region, or municipality directly under the Central Government **may** interfere in the affairs which the Hong Kong Special Administrative Region administers on its own in accordance with this law.①
中央人民政府所属各部门、各省、自治区、直辖市均不得干预香港特别行政区根据本法自行管理的事务。

8. **Neither** of the Parties hereto **may** at any time during the continuance of the Agreement deal with any of the shares of the Joint Venture Company owned by it whether by sale, pledge, gift or otherwise in any manner inconsistent with the carrying out of its obligations hereunder.
本协议任何一方均不得在本协议存续期间采用出售、抵押、赠送或其他与履行本协议规定不一致的方式处理其拥有的合营公司的任何股份。

总之,"shall"在英语的法律文献中是一个意义十分晦涩的词,给汉译英也带来不小的麻烦。如果表示强制意义,有法律专家建议统统使用"must"来替换"shall"。但显然这需要一个过渡时期,而多数法律文献的起草人更容易接受少用"shall"的折中做法。比如不用"shall be entitled to""shall have the right to",而直接使用"be entitled to""have the right to",或改用"be allowed to""may"等。

---

① 见 *The Basic Law of the Hong Kong Special Administrative Region of the People's Republic of China*,转引自李克兴、张新红:《法律文本与法律翻译》,中国对外翻译出版公司2006年版,第175页。

【练习题】

I. 试将下列英语句子译成汉语，注意画线词语的译法。

1. Promotion is automatic subject to passing internal examinations.

2. All rates are subject to 15% service charge. All rates are subject to change without prior notice.（宾馆）

3. You will receive 2% commission subject to (your) selling more than 5 000 articles a year.

4. We accept this order subject to your agreement that delivery of the goods is to be made in May.

5. Our terms are cash within three months of date of delivering, or subject to 5 percent discount if paid within one month.

6. The export trade is subject to risks：ships may sink, consignments may be damaged in transit, exchange rates may alter, buyers may default, or governments may suddenly impose an embargo.

7. We propose to pay any Bill of Exchange at 30 d/s, documents against acceptance.

8. We have packed goods in such a way as to ensure them against any possible damage during transit.

9. We have sent you under separate cover a complete list of books published here. Please check the names of the books in which you are interested in and return the list to us.

10. Any income tax on income earned by Consultant within PRC pursuant to this Contract and subject to taxation according to *Income Tax Law of the PRC concerning Enterprises with Foreign Investment and Foreign Enterprises* and other relevant laws and regulations shall be paid by Consultant.

II. 试将下列汉语句子译成英语，注意选用本章所学词语。

1. 我们对这些费用概不负责。
2. 她亲自接管了这项工程。
3. 夫妻应平等承担抚育孩子的责任。
4. 全部损失由我们一方负担是不公平的，因为责任是双方的。
5. 我们认为买主不会出更高的价。
6. 凡适合妇女从事劳动的单位，不得拒绝招收女工。
7. 卖方须在规定的装货时间，至少14天前用电报方式将装船条件告知买方。

买方或其他代理人须将装货船只预计到达装货港口的时间告知卖方。
8. 合营企业的有关外汇事宜，应遵照中华人民共和国外汇管理条例办理。
9. 如果因人力不可抗拒的事故延续 60 天以上，买方有权撤销合同。
10. 如果你方报价很低，足以吸引此地买主，我们就能成功地推销你方产品。
11. 董事会会议每年至少召开一次，由董事长召集并主持。董事长如因特殊情况不能履行职责，由董事长指定副董事长或其他董事召集并主持。如 1/3 董事提议，可召开临时董事会会议。

第十二章
企业名称的翻译

每一个企业,要进行对外业务和对外宣传,首先应该有个对外的名称。因此,如何翻译企业名称,是涉外工作人员常常要遇到的问题。本章拟就英语企业名称的汉译和中国企业名称的英译进行讨论。

第一节 英语企业名称的汉译

英语的企业名称,可分为两个部分,如"Hewlett-Packard Company",可分为第一部分的"Hewlett-Packard"和第二部分的"Company"。在英语中,企业名称的第二部分较为简单,尽管有十多个词可供选择,但绝大多数要么是"Company"(缩略形式为"Co."),要么是"Corporation"(缩略形式为"Corp.")。无论是哪一个词,一律可汉译为"公司"。有时在两个词之后加上"Ltd."或"Inc."。前者是"Limited"的缩写,后者是"Incorporated"的缩写,均译为"(股份)有限公司"。"Ltd."在英国、欧洲大陆和日本用得多一些,美国则多用"Inc."。也有不少公司,把"Co."或"Corp."省去,直接使用"Ltd."或"Inc."。企业名称的第一部分较为复杂。一般原则,实义词译义,人名、地名及创造词译音,或采用"谐音联想"的方法(详见第九章)。如上文的"Hewlett-Packard Company",原是两位企业创建人的姓名构成的公司名,大陆曾长期使用音译名"休利特-帕卡德公司",但近年来已逐渐被谐音联想名"惠普公司"所取代。有些企业,其生产或经营的性质,从名称本身就能一目了然,因此,汉译时一般不成问题。例如,"American Motors Corporation"就可直译为"美国汽车制造公司"。但还有相当多的企业,其名称并不说明什么,如果按音直译,效果往往不佳。例如上面提到的"Hewlett-Packard Company",不管译成"休利特-帕卡德公司",还是译成"惠普公司",它们都不能告诉读者这是一家什么样的公司。就像商品名称一样,译名最好能暗示该商品的特点。企业名称的译名,也应成为自身的广告。要达到这样的目的,一般有两种途径:一是在译音方面做文章。例如,"Otis Co., U.S.A"被译成"美国奥梯斯公司",其中"梯"字有可能让人联想到这是一家"电梯"公司;二是采用添词的办法,这种办法更为普遍和简单易行。例如,"E. R. Squibb Co., U. S. A"被译为"美国施贵宝**制药**公司","Gillette Co., U. S. A"被译为"美国吉列**刀片**总公司","Bell Telephone Co., Belgium"被译为"比利时贝尔电话**设备制造**公司","Hewlett – Packard Co., U. S. A"也可改译为"美国惠普**电子**公司"。

由两个人名构成的企业名称,翻译时往往容易发生问题。例如,"Brown and Root Inc., U. S. A.",有的书把它译成"美国布朗·路特公司",这就译错了。因为原文显然是两个人名,但译文却有可能被误会为一个人名。正确的译法应该将中间的小圆点"·"改成连字符"–",即"美国布朗–路特公司"。应注意的是,连字符的宽度只有一个汉字的一半,目前的出版物中常有错误。另外,少数由几个人名构成的企业名称,中间并没有用"and"字样,也没有"–"或"&"符号,翻译前应尤其小心,分辨清楚。

英语企业名称中常可见到"&"这个符号。"&"有时用来连接两个人名,如"Smith & Johnson Co.",可译做"史密斯–约翰逊公司"。以"人名 + & + Co."命名的公司,"&"一般略去不译。例如,"James Hill & Co."可译做"詹姆士·希尔公司";如果是"T. Holden & Son"则可译做"T. 荷登父子公司"。由"&"连接两个实义词构成的企业名称,"&"有时译成"和",有时不译,这主要取决于译文是否产生歧义和读起来是否自然顺口。例如,"Minnesota Mining & Manufacturing Company"被译成"明尼苏达采矿和制造公司",而"AT & T"被译成"美国电话电报公司","Sanyo Clock & Watch Corp., Ltd., Japan"被译成"日本三洋钟表有限公司"。

我们还经常看到一些企业的缩写名称。这些缩写名称在国际贸易界长期使用,以至于它们原来的全名反而鲜为人知。这种特殊的企业缩写,常可免译。例如上面提到的"Minnesota Mining & Manufacturing Company",可免译简写为"3M"公司;又如"International Business Machines Corporation"(美国国际商用机器公司),可免译缩写成"IBM"公司。

第二节 汉语企业名称的英译

目前,中国企业的名称,大都也以"公司"命名。为讨论方便,我们也可将企业的名称分成两大部分。例如:

· 289 ·

1. 天津　丽明　化妆品‖工业公司
　　A　　B　　C　　　D
　Tianjing Liming Cosmetics Industry Company
2. 香港　美丽华　酒店‖有限公司
　　A　　B　　C　　　D
　Hotel Miramar Co., Ltd., Hongkong
3. 中国　东方　科学仪器‖进出口公司
　　A　　B　　C　　　D
　China Oriental Scientific Instruments Imp. & Exp. Corporation

以上3个公司的名称，基本上反映了中国企业名称的构成方式。如上所示，A，B，C为第一大部分，D为第二大部分。一般说来，B和D为中国企业名称不可缺少的组成部分。在第一大部分里，A为企业注册地址（这是中国企业名称的一大特点），B为企业专名，C为企业生产对象或经营范围。第二大部分则表明企业的性质。

我们先讨论第一大部分的翻译问题。A属地名，按地名翻译的原则处理，即除少数特例外（如国名China；特别地名Hong Kong，Macao），一律采用汉语拼音；B可译音，也可译义。译音者如例1，将"丽明"按汉语拼音译成"Liming"，又如例2，将"美丽华"按英语拼写方式译为"Miramar"；译义者如例3，将"东方"译成"Oriental"。C属通名，且为实义词，须译义。C常有两个并列成分，翻译时一般用符号"&"连接起来，例如，"中国科学器材公司"译为"China Scientific Instruments & Materials Corporation"。但应注意的是，不宜在一个公司名称里使用两个"&"符号，例如，"中国工艺品进出口公司"译为"China National Arts and Crafts Import & Export Corporation"，在前一个并列结构里，我们用"and"替换了"&"。

中国企业名称的翻译，当属第二大部分中有关"公司"的译法最为复杂，下面我们分别讨论。

一、"公司"的译法

根据英语企业的名称，"Company"和"Corporation"是大多数翻译人员翻译"公司"时的首选之词。但究竟在什么情况下该选用哪个词，就存在很大分歧。要解决这个问题，我们认为可以从如下两个方面入手：

第一，从词典释义入手。试比较下面词典的解释：

第十二章　企业名称的翻译

Longman Dictionary of Contemporary English：
* **Company**：a group of people combined together for business or trade
* **Corporation**：a large business organization

Collin's Cobuild English Language Dictionary：
* **Company**：a business organization that exists in order to make money by selling goods or services
* **Corporation**：a large business or company, or a group of companies that are all controlled and run together as a single organization

根据以上两本词典的解释，我们可以明确三点：一是在规模上，Corporation ≥ Company；二是在语域方面，Corporation ≤ Company，因为后者不仅指工商企业，还包括或侧重服务性行业；三是在释义方面，两本词典均有交叉循环现象，这也许正是人们在实际使用这两个词时造成混乱的根源。下面我们来分析几个实例：

1. 北京家务服务公司
   Beijing Housework Service Company
2. 东北建筑工程咨询公司
   Northeast Construction Project Consulting Company
3. 中国兴华工程咨询公司
   China Xinghua Engineering Consulting Corporation
4. 中国造币公司
   China Mint Company
5. 北京特种工艺公司
   Beijing Special Arts and Handicrafts Company
6. 深圳特种工艺公司
   Shenzhen Special Arts and Crafts Corporation
7. 首都钢铁公司
   Capital Iron and Steel Company

以上公司的译名摘自新华社对外新闻编辑部编《中国组织机构英译名手册》（新华出版社，1986）。从汉语角度看，例1至例3均属服务性行业，例4的规模则不可能太大，因此，选用"Company"一词是比较得体的；例5和例6的规模可大可小，企业性质可"工"可"商"，选用"Company"一词则比较保险；例

7是典型的大型企业，译文不如改为"Corporation"。顺便提一下，我国其他几大钢铁公司（如武钢、鞍钢、包钢）的英译名虽然都使用"Company"一词，但香港一些报刊在提到这些企业时常改用"Corporation"，看来这是不无道理的。

第二，从用词习惯入手。通过对国外许多企业名称的分析，关于"公司"的选词，我们不难找到与词典释义相悖的例子。比如说，某些小企业的名称使用的是"Corporation"，而某些大企业的名称却使用的是"Company"（有规则就有例外，这也是正常的）。因此，"公司"的翻译显然不能仅凭其规模大小而采取一刀切的做法。在英语中，"Company"和"Corporation"的运用有时似乎并没有什么道理可言，只是与用词习惯有关。

首先，"Company"和"Corporation"的使用可能有国别之分。比如在英国，公司法被称为"Company Law"，而在美国，公司法则被称为"Corporation Law"。因此，英国的大多数企业选用"Company"来命名，相反，美国的大多数企业则选用"Corporation"来命名。日本的企业大多偏爱"Company"一词，因此，我们在翻译中日合资企业时可以大胆地使用"Company"。例如，"福建日立电视机有限公司"被译为"Fujian Hitachi TV Sets Co., Ltd."，"上海三菱电梯有限公司"被译为"Shanghai Mitsubishi Elevator Co., Ltd."，"佳能大连办公设备有限公司"被译为"Canon Dalian Office Equipment Co., Ltd."。与此相反，中国的大多数企业则偏爱"Corporation"一词。比如，对外贸易经济合作部的几十个总公司，绝大多数都采用"Corporation"，并且许多地方大企业也喜欢选用"Corporation"来命名。

其次，特定的行业也可能会有自己用词的习惯，久而久之便成了行规。比如"保险公司"，似乎与国别关系不大，规模大小也不是问题，多数称作"Insurance Company"。其他与行业有关，习惯上多用"Company"来命名的企业还有一些。比如，"公共汽车公司"译为"Bus Company"（但"公共汽车制造公司"则通常译为"Bus Corporation"），"航运公司"译为"Shipping Company"（但"船舶工业公司"则通常译为"Shipbuilding Corporation"），"电气公司"译为"Electric Company"，"石油公司"译为"Oil / Petroleum Company"，"出版公司"译为"Publishing Company"。

"公司"一词的英译，除选词外，也涉及翻译技巧。例如，利用"增词法"常可避免译文歧义："中国汽车公司"译为"China Automotive Industry Corporation"，"上海直升飞机公司"译为"Shanghai Helicopter Service Company"。

二、"总公司"的译法

不少中国企业都喜欢在其名称中加上个"总"字，以示规模的庞大。在汉译英中,"总"字的处理可归纳为如下几种情况。

(一) 将"总"字译成"general"

多数人一看到"总"字,往往首先就联想到英语的"general"一词,即基本上把它们看成是可以互译的等值之词。但在英语的企业名称中实际使用"general"一词的并不多。尽管如此,由于我们一时难以改变这种非"general"不显其"大"的思维习惯,这种以"general"来译"总"字的做法已逐渐被大家接受。例如,"北京建筑材料集团总公司"被译为"Beijing Construction Material Group General Corp.","抚顺石油工业总公司"被译为"Fushun General Petroleum Industry Corp."。另外,以"general factory"来译"总厂"的情况也很普遍。例如,"上海上菱电冰箱总厂"被译为"Shanghai Shangling Refrigerator General Factory","大庆石油化工总厂"被译为"Daqing Petrochemical Industry General Factory"。值得指出的是,目前"general"一词的使用很混乱,其位置有前有后(如上例所示),造成修饰关系不清,这就很容易与美国的"General Motors Corporation"和"General Electric Company"中的"general"一词相混淆了。在这两家美国企业中,"general"并不表示"总"的意思,而是表示"一般用途"的意思。它们长期以来分别被译为"美国通用汽车制造公司"和"美国通用电气公司"。中国也有类似性质的企业,其中"通用"一词理应同样处理。例如,"上海通用机械(集团)公司"被译为"Shanghai General Machinery (Group) Corp."。据此,我们认为,为避免歧义,如果是表示"总"的意思,最好将"general"与"Company"或"Corporation"紧放在一起,中间不宜被其他修饰成分隔开。

(二) 将"总"字译成"national"

我国对外贸易经济合作部直属的几十家企业,凡名称中有"总公司"字样的,其英译名几乎都使用了"national"一词。看来,用"national"来表示该行业的最上层机构"总部"是非常恰当的,并且这种统一的译法值得提倡。"national"一词的位置绝大部分放在 China 之后。例如,"中国化工进出口总公司"被译为"China National Chemicals Import & Export Corporation"。但也有个别特殊的情况。例如,"中国华润总公司"被译为"China Resources National Corporation"。显然,这种说文解字式的公司译名中间是不宜被隔开的。

(三) 将"总"字省译

"总公司"是相对于"分公司"而言的,因此,如果用不同的词来表示分公司，总公司的"总"字自然也就可以免译了。这正是大多数英语大型企业名称的命名方法。例如，"Sullair Corporation, Subsidiary of Sunstrand Corporation"，我们从中就可知道，"Sunstrand Corporation"是总公司，"Sullair Corporation"是分公司。也正因为如此，在中国企业名称汉译英中，这种省译"总"字的做法越来越普遍，下面的译例可见一斑。

1. 中国对外贸易仓储总公司
   China Foreign Trade Storage Corporation
2. 中国国际图书总公司
   China International Book Trading Corporation
3. 北京对外贸易总公司
   Beijing Foreign Trade Corporation
4. 中国石油化工总公司
   China Petrochemical Corporation
5. 上海轴承总公司
   Shanghai Bearing Corporation

三、"分公司"的译法

在英语中，分公司常用"Subsidiary"来表示。在汉译英时，我们也偶尔照此办理，或改用"Branch"一词。由于中国企业素有使用注册地址命名的习惯，因此，对于我国各级全民所有制企业，用地方名称来区别其总公司是最简捷和最普遍的做法。但是，在处理"分公司"和"总公司"之间的关系时，各部分的布局是颇费心思的。有些译文虽然说不上谁对谁错，但从翻译的角度看，其中却有好坏优劣之分。试比较下面几组实例：

1. ⎧ 中国粮油食品进出口总公司
      China National Cereals, Oils and Foodstuffs Import & Export Corporation
   ⎨
   ⎩ 陕西省粮油食品进出口公司
      Shaanxi Cereal, Oils and Foodstuffs Import & Export Corporation

第十二章 企业名称的翻译

2. ⎰ 中国机械进出口总公司
   ⎱ China National Machinery Import & Export Corp.
   ⎰ 陕西省机械进出口公司
   ⎱ China Shaanxi Machinery Import & Export Corp.

比较以上两组分公司的译文，我们觉得第二组好得多。与其"总公司"的译文相比，该"分公司"的译文只是用"Shaanxi"替换了"National"，但它们之间的隶属关系却一目了然。

3. ⎰ 中国出口商品基地建设总公司
   ⎱ China National Export Bases Development Corp.
   ⎰ 中国出口商品基地建设湖南公司
   ⎱ China National Export Bases Development Hunan Corp.

比较第2、3两组，其分公司的译法只是地方名称的位置不同，目前两种译法都很普遍。如果要统一，可按第二组统一。此外，公司的中文名称也应规范化，比如将"陕西省机械进出口公司"改成"中国机械进出口总公司陕西省分公司"，将"中国出口商品基地建设湖南公司"改成"中国出口商品基地建设总公司湖南分公司"。

4. ⎰ 中国华润总公司
   ⎢ China Resources National Corporation
   ⎢ 华润贸发进出口公司
   ⎨ China Resources Trade & Development Co., Ltd.
   ⎢ 华润（悉尼）有限公司
   ⎢ Sino-Resources (Australia) Co., Ltd.
   ⎢ 安徽华润有限公司
   ⎱ CRC, Anhui Branch

在这一组中，第二例用"Trade & Development"来替换"National"，说明它是中国华润总公司属下主管"贸易与发展"的分公司，译法类似第二组。在措

· 295 ·

辞上，将"Corporation"改成"Co., Ltd"，比其他译法技高一筹。根据英语词典的释义，"Corporation"是可以由"Company"组成的，这类似于"University"可以由"Colleges""Faculties""Schools"或"Institutes"组成。第三例将分公司地名放入括号内，这是一种十分简约的处理方法。又如，南京四通计算机公司：Stone Computer（Nanjing）Co., Ltd,；"中国银行（深圳分行）"：Bank of China（Shenzhen Branch），"巴黎国家银行（香港）"：National Bank of Paris（Hong Kong）。第四例是个特例，可供参考，缩写词的位置可前可后。又如，中化辽宁进出口公司：SINOCHEM，Liaoning Import & Export Corp.；中国海洋石油总公司渤海石油公司：Bohai Petroleum Corporation，CNOOC（CNOOC 即 China National Offshore Oil Corporation）。

5.
中国轻工业品进出口总公司
China National Light Industrial Products Import & Export Corporation

广东东莞轻工业品进出口公司
Dongguan Light Industrial Products Import & Export Corporation of Guangdong

中国轻工业品进出口总公司广东省分公司东莞支公司
China National Light Industrial Products Import & Export Corporation, Guangdong Branch, Dongguan Office

比较这一组中地名的不同布局。第二例显然是为了避免将两个地名重叠在一起，因为地名一般都是汉语拼音，如果几个拼音词叠在一起，往往十分别扭，这一点在翻译企业名称时应尤其注意。第三例译文，小单位放在大单位后面，似乎有悖英语的习惯，但用的时间长了，慢慢也被大家接受了。这种译法特别适用于放在广告、产品目录或信笺上方。

四、其他各类"公司"和"厂"的译法

公司的名称可谓五花八门，现在最时髦的有"实业公司""开发公司"和"集团公司"等。根据汉语词典的解释，"实业"系指"工商"企业，因此，许多实业公司被译为"Industry and Commercial Corp. / Co."。为方便起见，不少实业公司被简译为"Industry Corp. / Co."。所谓"开发公司"，其含义并不清楚，有学者指出：有哪家公司不锐意开发呢？据此，在许多公司名称中，"开发"一

词似乎可以免译。如果非译不可，则按现在流行的做法，将"开发公司"译成"Development Corporation/Company"。"集团公司"，现在一般译做"Group Corporation / Company"，有时也译做"Holdings Corporation / Company"。这两个词很难说有什么区别。"Group"和"Holdings"常被放在括号内。例如，"华润（集团）有限公司"被译为 China Resources (Holdings) Co., Ltd.。

在翻译各类公司的时候，还应注意一词多译、多词同译或交叉互译的现象。例如，"实业"还有译成"Enterprises"，或译成"Industry"。但另一方面，"Enterprises"和"Industry"又分别与汉语的"企业（公司）"和"工业（公司）"相对应。除"开发公司"外，根据现有的众多实例，"发展公司"和"建设公司"也有译成"Development Corp / Co."的。

还有许多企业是以"厂"命名的。在英语中，表示"厂"可用"factory""mill""plant""works"等词。大多数"厂"可用"factory"来译。大型冶金和机械工业企业则使用"plant"或"works"，这两个词没有多少区别，前者的使用频率高一些。主要生产设备是大型旋转装置的厂，可译为"mill"。例如，"轧钢厂"可译为"Steel Rolling Mill"，"造纸厂"可译为"Paper Mill"，"纺织厂"可译为"Textile Mill"，"水泥厂"可译为"Cement Mill"。除此之外，还有一些厂名需要用专词来表示。例如，"造船厂"可译为"Shipyard"，"酒厂"可译为"Distillery"，"啤酒厂"可译为"Beer Brewery"，"精炼厂"可译为"Refinery"。"总厂"用"General Factory"来译，"第三卷烟厂"可译做"No. 3 Cigarette Factory"。"分厂"则用"Division"或"Branch"来表示。例如，"第二分厂"可译为"No. 2 Branch"。

第三节 小 结

综上所述，企业名称的翻译是个错综复杂的问题，以上讨论只能起一个抛砖引玉的作用。目前的实际情况是，理论研究远远落后于实践，大家都是各自凭经验翻译，因此，企业名称的译名非常混乱。这种情况对企业的自我宣传非常不利，亟待国家有关部门加以规范。总而言之，我们在翻译企业名称时，一方面应尊重词典的释义，小心选词，另一方面又不能忽视用词和翻译的现状，局限于某些条条框框；我们既要参照国外的情况，又要根据国情及中国企业名称的特点，灵活变通，形成一套具有中国特色的译法。另外，认真研究和比较现有企业名称的译名，分析其利弊，是提高企业名称翻译质量的一条有效途径。

主要参考文献

[1] Allen, Bryan. *The Business Letter* [M]. London: Evans Brothers Limited, 1978.

[2] Baker, Mona. *In Other Words: A Course on Translation* [M]. / 换言之: 翻译教程 [M]. 北京: 外语教学与研究出版社, 2000.

[3] Baker, Mona. *Routledge Encyclopedia of Translation Studies* [M]. / 翻译研究百科全书 [M]. 上海: 上海外语教育出版社, 2004.

[4] Cohen, D. *Advertising* [M]. U.S.A.: Scott, Foresman and Company, 1988.

[5] Daiker, Donald A; Kerek, Andrew; Morenberg, Max. *The Writer's Options* [M]. New York / London: Harper & Row · Publishers, 1982.

[6] Garner, Bryan A. *Legal Writing in Plain English* [M]. Chicago: The University of Chicago Press, 2001.

[7] Garner, Bryan A. *The Elements of Legal Style* [M]. Oxford University Press, Inc. 2002.

[8] Hermans, Theo. (ed.) *The Manipulation of Literature: Studies in Literary Translation* [M]. London / Sydney: Croom Helm, 1985.

[9] Isaacson, Walter. *Steve Jobs* [M], London: Little, Brown Book Group, 2011.

[10] Jakobson, Roman (1959). "On Linguistic Aspects of Translation", in Lawrence Venuti (ed.). *The Translation Studies Reader* [M]. London and New York: Routledge, 2000.

[11] Kalb, Marvin & Bernard Kalb. *Kissinger* [M]. Boston-Toronto: Little, Brown and Company, 1974.

[12] King, S. *Pocket Guide to Advertising* [M]. Basil Blackwell (UK) and the Economist Publications, 1989.

[13] Kussmaul, Paul. *Training the Translator* [M]. Amsterdam: John Benjamins B. V., 1995: 147.

[14] McMordie, Seidl. *English Idioms and How to Use Them* (Reprinted) [M]. Oxford University Press, 1978.

[15] Murphy, J M. (ed.) *Branding—A Key Marketing Tool* [M]. London: the Macmillan Press, 1987.

[16] Nauheim, Ferd. *Letter Perfect* [M]. U.S.A.: Van Nostrand Reinhold, 1982.

[17] Nida, E A. *Toward a Science of Translating* [M]. Leiden, Netherlands: E. J. Brill, 1964.

[18] Nida, E A & Taber, C R. *The Theory and Practice of Translation* [M]. Leiden, Netherlands: E J Brill, 1969.

[19] Nida, E A & Jan de Waard. *From One Language to Another* [M]. Nashville, Tennessee: Thomas Nelson, Inc., Publishers, 1986.

[20] Nord, Christiane. *Translating as a Purposeful Activity* [M]. Manchester: St. Jerome Publishing, 1997.

[21] O'Barr, William M. *Culture and the Ad: Exploring Otherness in the World of Advertising* [M]. Boulder, San Francisco, Oxford: Westview Press, 1994.

[22] Pinkham, Joan. *The Translator's Guide to Chinglish* [M]./中式英语之鉴[M]. 北京: 外语教学与研究出版社, 2000.

[23] Pousma, Richard H. *An Eventful Year in the Orient* [M]. Grand Rapids, Michigan: WM. B. Eerdmans Publishing Co., 1927.

[24] Shuttleworth, Mark & Cowie, Moire, *Dictionary of Translation Studie* [M]./翻译学词典 [M]. 上海: 上海外语教育出版社, 2004.

[25] Steiner, George. *After Babel: Aspects of Language and Translation* [M]. Oxford: Oxford University Press, 1992.

[26] T K Ann. *Cracking the Chinese Puzzles* [M]. Vol. 1, Hong Kong: Stockflows Co., Ltd. 1982: 142.

[27] Trace, Jacqueline. *Style and Strategy of the Business Letter* [M]. New Jersey: Prentice-Hall, Inc., 1985.

[28] Tytler, A F. *Essay on the Principles of Translation* [M]. London, 1970.

[29] Venuti, Lawrence (ed.). *The Translation Studies Reader* [M]. London / New York: Routledge, 2000.

[30] 艾萨克森. 贾伯斯传 [M]. 廖月娟, 姜雪影, 谢凯蒂, 译. 台北: 天下远见出版股份有限公司, 2011.

[31] 艾萨克森. 史蒂夫·乔布斯传 [M]. 管延圻, 等译. 北京: 中信出版社, 2011.

[32] 陈浩然. 外贸英语翻译 [M]. 北京: 中国对外经济贸易出版社, 1987.

[33] 陈文伯. 教你如何掌握汉译英技巧 [M]. 北京: 世界知识出版社, 1999.

[34] 陈永祥, 浩力, 索毕成, 史宝辉. 北京老街 (中英对照彩绘本) [M]. 北京: 社会科学文献出版社, 2006.

[35] 陈忠诚. 《中外合资企业法》两种英译文评讲 [J]. 法制论丛, 1992 (4).

[36] 程镇球. 翻译问题探索 [M]. 北京: 商务印书馆, 1980.

[37] 崔刚. 广告英语 [M]. 北京：北京理工大学出版社，1993.
[38] 邓炎昌，刘润清. 语言与文化 [M]. 北京：外语教学与研究出版社，1989.
[39] 狄更斯. 大卫·考坡菲 [M]. 张谷若，译. 上海：上海译文出版社，2003.
[40] 段连城. 对外传播学初探 [M]. 北京：中国建设出版社，1988.
[41] 高尔斯华绥. 苹果树 [M]. 董衡巽，译. 北京：中国和平出版社，2005.
[42] 高尔斯华绥. 苹果树 [M]. 屠枫，译. 北京：人民文学出版社，2006.
[43] 赫胥黎. 天演论 [M]. 严复，译. 郑州：中州古籍出版社，1998.
[44] 胡文仲. 现代实用英语例解 [M]. 上海：上海外语教育出版社，1987.
[45] 黄学范. 翻译新语 [M]. 台北：东大图书股份有限公司，1989.
[46] 黄自来. 英汉语法对比 [M]. 台北：文鹤出版有限公司，1987.
[47] 卡尔布·马文，卡尔布·伯纳德. 基辛格（上、下）[M]. 齐沛合，译. 北京：生活·读书·新知三联书店，1975.
[48] 黎松峭，鲍学谦. 中外成功广告900例 [M]. 南宁：广西民族出版社，1993.
[49] 李克兴，张新红. 法律文本与法律翻译 [M]. 北京：中国对外翻译出版公司，2006.
[50] 李文成，吴雨初. 世界自然与文化遗产——黄山 [M]. 凌原，译. 中国旅游出版社，1999.
[51] 李中行，戚肖山，张惠. 广告英语 [M]. 长沙：湖南教育出版社，1986.
[52] 林煌天，陈彦田，袁锦翔. 中国翻译词典 [M]. 武汉：湖北教育出版社，1997.
[53] 林克难，籍明文. 英语天下行——旅美生活自助宝典 [M]. 天津：南开大学出版社，2001.
[54] 刘洪潮. 怎样做对外宣传报道 [M]. 北京：中国传媒大学出版社，2005.
[55] 刘季春. 扬起创造的风帆——许渊冲学术思想研究 [J]. 山东外语教学，2003（1）.
[56] 刘季春. 为什么对外宣传中常有翻译谬误？[J]. 上海翻译，2005（2）.
[57] 刘季春. 基础笔译 [M]. 北京：外语教学与研究出版社，2015.
[58] 刘宓庆. 文体与翻译 [M]. 北京：中国对外翻译出版公司，1985.
[59] 刘靖之. 翻译工作者手册 [M]. 香港：商务印书馆，1991.
[60] 刘勰. 文心雕龙注释 [M]. 周振甫，注. 北京：人民文学出版社，1981.
[61] 陆文慧. 法律翻译——从实践出发 [M]. 北京：法律出版社，2003.
[62] 鲁迅. 且介亭杂文二集 [M]. 北京：人民文学出版社，1973.
[63] 吕俊. 论翻译研究的本体回归——对翻译研究"文化转向"的反思 [J]. 外国语. 2004（4）.

[64] 吕和发，单丽平. 汉英公示语词典 [M]. 北京：商务印书馆，2004.

[65] 吕叔湘. 吕叔湘译文三种 [M]. 北京：外语教学与研究出版社，1992.

[66] 罗新璋. 翻译论集 [M]. 北京：商务印书馆，1984.

[67] 钱歌川. 翻译的技巧 [M]. 北京：商务印书馆，1981.

[68] 乔海清. 翻译新论 [M]. 北京：北京语言学院出版社，1993.

[69] 诺德. 译有所为：功能翻译理论阐释 [M]. 张美芳，王克非，译. 北京：外语教学与研究出版社，2005.

[70] 萨克雷. 名利场 [M]. 杨必，译. 北京：人民文学出版社，1994.

[71] 商友敬. 中国通手册——名胜古迹 [M]. 汪磊，译. 上海：上海古籍出版社，2002.

[72] 思果. 翻译研究 [M]. 台北：大地出版社，1972.

[73] 思果.《名利场》选评 [M]. 北京：中国对外翻译出版公司，2004.

[74] 宋毅英. 国际贸易实用合同 [M]. 香港：星海图书公司，1984.

[75] 沈苏儒. 对外传播·翻译研究文集 [M]. 北京：外文出版社，2009.

[76] 苏福忠. 译事余墨 [M]. 北京：生活·读书·新知三联书店，2006.

[77] 孙德权. 白象非象——浅谈商品牌名的英译问题和其他 [J]. 现代外语，1988（1）.

[78] 田贵君等撰文. 张家界 [M]. 吴中平，译. 北京：中国旅游出版社，1999.

[79] 王宏志. 重释"信达雅"：二十世纪中国翻译研究 [M]. 上海：东方出版中心，1999.

[80] 王萍. 外贸应用文大全 [M]. 北京：现代出版社，1991.

[81] 王佐良. 美国短篇小说选 [M]. 北京：中国青年出版社，1980.

[82] 翁显良. 意态由来画不成？[M]. 北京：中国对外翻译出版公司，1983.

[83] 吴景荣，丁往道，钱青. 当代英文散文选读 [M]. 北京：商务印书馆，1980.

[84] 萧伯纳. 卖花女 [M]. 杨宪益，译. 北京：中国对外翻译出版公司，2002.

[85] 许国烈. 中英文学名著译文比录 [M]. 西安：陕西人民出版社，1985.

[86] 许渊冲. 翻译的艺术 [M]. 北京：中国对外翻译出版公司，1984.

[87] 许渊冲. 追忆逝水年华 [M]. 北京：生活·读书·新知三联书店，1996.

[88] 许渊冲. 文学翻译谈 [M]. 台北：书林出版有限公司，1998.

[89] 杨全红. 汉英词语翻译探微 [M]. 上海：世纪出版集团/汉语大辞典出版社，2003.

[90] 杨全红. 走近翻译大家 [M]. 长春：吉林人民出版社，2004.

[91] 杨全红. 也谈汉英公示语的翻译 [J]. 中国翻译，2005（6）.

[92] 杨晓荣. 翻译理论研究的调整期 [J]. 中国翻译，1996（6）.

[93] 余光中. 余光中选集第四卷（语文及翻译论集）［M］. 合肥：安徽教育出版社，1999.

[94] 袁锦翔. 名家翻译研究与赏析［M］. 武汉：湖北教育出版社，1990.

[95] 翟树耀. 对外宣传报道与英语写作［M］. 厦门：厦门大学出版社，2001.

[96] 张达聪. 翻译之原理与技巧［M］. 台北：国家书店有限公司，1983.

[97] 张经浩，陈可培. 名家　名论　名译［M］. 上海：复旦大学出版社，2005.

[98] 张梅岗，等. 实用翻译教程（上）［M］. 武汉：湖北科技出版社，1993.

[99] 张南峰. 中西译学批评［M］. 北京：清华大学出版社，2004.

[100] 张培基. 习语汉译英研究（修订本）［M］. 北京：商务印书馆，1979.

[101] 张培基，喻云根，李宗杰，彭谟禹. 英汉翻译教程［M］. 上海：上海外语教育出版社，1980.

[102] 张信雄. 实用商业英语［M］. 台北：暖流出版社，1987.

[103] 张玉玫. 中英对译技巧［M］. 台北：学习出版公司，1987.

[104] 赵一鹤. 对中外合资企业法英译文的体会［J］. 编译参考，1979（8）.

[105] 支懋彤. 外贸英语常用词手册［M］. 天津：天津科学技术出版社，1987.

[106] 周兆祥. 译评：理论与实践［M］.//黎翠珍. 翻译评赏［M］. 商务印书馆（香港）有限公司，1996.

[107] 诸葛霖. 外贸实用英语手册［M］. 北京：商务印书馆，1981.

[108] 庄绎传. 英汉翻译教程［M］. 北京：外语教学与研究出版社，1999.

[109] 北京语言学院/北京对外贸易学院. *Business Chinese* 500［M］. 北京：外文出版社，1982.

[110]［111] 庐山（汉英对照画册）［M］. 北京：外文出版社，1983.

[111]［112] 新华社对外新闻编辑部. 中国组织机构英译名手册［M］. 北京：新华出版社，1986.

[112] 中国翻译工作者协会《翻译通讯》编辑部. 翻译研究论文集（1894-1948）. 翻译研究论文集（1949-1983）［M］. 北京：外语教学与研究出版社，1984.

[113] 中华人民共和国对外经济贸易部条法司. 中华人民共和国对外经济法规汇编（1991年卷）［M］. 北京：中国对外经济贸易出版社，1992.

[114] 中华人民共和国婚姻法［M］. 北京：法律出版社，1986.

[115] 中华人民共和国外资企业法，中华人民共和国中外合作经营企业法，中华人民共和国中外合资经营企业法［M］. 北京：法律出版社，2002.

[116] 中华人民共和国著作权法［M］. 北京：法律出版社，2002.

附录一

英语常用公示语例解

英语中的"sign"一词，汉语的"对应词语"则多种多样，比如标志语、标识语、揭示语、公示语。"揭示语"的用法稍微老些，目前中国多数学者采用"公示语"一词，为了术语的标准化，本书也采用"公示语"的说法。公示语一般制成标牌，材料可以是木质、金属、塑料或纸片（有时也直接书写在物件或墙壁等显眼的地方），除文字外，常常伴有图案。公示语主要具备"指引"和"警示"两大功能。

受书写空间的限制，公示语的最大特点就是用词简约，最少的只用一个词。为了简约，有时可以省略冠词、物主代词、被动语态中的系动词 to be，有时也忽略单复数。例如，Beware of Dog; Caution: Do Not Cross in Front of Bus; Please Register Smart Cards Here; No Pets Allowed, Switch off Mobile Phone。公示语常常全部使用大写字母，可以不用标点，寥寥几个词语往往也会分数行排列，公示语的完整意义有时还依赖于图案。例如，Stop Request（电铃按钮图案旁：停车请按铃）。Temporarily Out of Service When Lit（指示灯图案旁：灯亮时暂停服务）。Stop / For Your Safety（分上下两行排列，中间插图：禁止攀越）。

仔细阅读英语的公示语，我们还会发现一些词法和句法上的特点。例如，大量使用名词性短语（主要是表示"指引"的公示语，常伴有箭头图案），大量使用祈使句（尤其是否定的祈使句，主要是表示"警示"的公示语），大量使用被动语态（通常比主动语态更为婉转）。有些词语的使用频率相当高。例如，表示请求的 please；表示限制的 only；表示禁止的 allow（否定的被动句中），forbid, prohibit；表示惩罚的 to be prosecuted, to be fined；表示警示的 watch / mind, notice, caution, warning, danger（应注意其语气强弱的变化）；表示程度的 strictly, absolutely；表示强制的 must。我们还会注意到个别平时比较不习惯使用的词汇，比如（on the）premises（包括建筑在内的经营场址）。

随着我国改革开放的深入，各大城市国际化程度的提高，汉英双语的公示语随处可见，但英语之滥也是触目惊心。目前翻译界一些学者和机构正在致力于改善这一情况。我们认为，公示语的汉译英，可以从宏观和微观两个层面逐步完善。在宏观上，一方面，政府要加强引导和管理；另一方面，也有必要认识到，双语公示语不是越多越好。这样说，避短是一个考虑，但更实际的是，有些汉语公示语，也许根本就没有必要配上英语。在微观上，自然要重视对英语公示语本身的研究。

根据英语公示语的特点，汉语公示语的英译大致可以采用两大策略：一是**借用法**，二是**仿拟法**。借用法是最为自然的方法，因为在英汉两种语言中，存在大量的使用场所相同、意义和功能完全一致的公示语，最为成功的借用要数"小心地滑"：Caution / Wet Floor（在笔者的记忆中，似乎还没有见到这个标牌上的英语写错了的）。采用仿拟法，是因为也存在大量的情形不尽一致的场合。国情和生活方式不一样，需求自然也不一样，并且英语公示语本身也在不断变化。从以上的综述可以看出，英语公示语，作为一种特殊但成熟的语体，已经形成了自身的语言规范，即使英语中没有现例照搬，我们同样能译写出适合中国语境的地道的英语公示语，比如学会了英语的 Staff Only，就可以根据新的语境写出 Passengers Only（车站）、Members Only（俱乐部）、Adult Only（书店成人专柜）、Ticket-Holders Only（剧院）、Teachers Only（学校教师阅览室），等等，而不需要问在英语的实际语境中是否存在这样的公示语。

在实地考察和收集英语公示语的过程中，我们还注意到，表达同一主题的英语公示语，其写法也是多种多样。这里的情况比较复杂：有标牌书写空间大小的考虑，有语体和场合正式与否的区别，有规范（如交通标志）和灵活的界限，有国别和偏爱的关系（如美国英语和英国英语），有行文统一的要求（比如同一场所的公示语），有观念认识的差异（最为典型的例子就是 W. C. 的用法，过去有人认为这是一个不雅的词汇，但近年来，不断有在国外考察过的学者指出，这是一个误会。笔者也曾去过欧洲多个国家，证实该用法最为普遍。从传播学的角度看，该用法的流行自有其道理：简明、省力、醒目）。另外，各种写法还有好坏正误的可能，就如我们用母语写公示语或其他标语一样，撰稿人的学识、认真的程度都不可能一样，结果自然就不一样了。因此，在借用和仿拟的过程中，要仔细鉴别，学会因地制宜，做到去芜存菁。

目前，汉语公示语的英译，除不堪入目的拼写和基本语法错误外，最常见的毛病就是脱离语境（包括忽视标牌图案）逐字翻译，结果画蛇添足、不伦不类。改善这类公示语的有效方法，就是采用**核心词法**，这也是英语公示语的特点之一。例如，本书第十章提到的国内某国际机场的双语公示语："公安值勤/ Be on duty of police"（当然这条公示语的英语写法在语法上也不通），如果没有见过英语的公示语，直接使用其核心词语 POLICE，大概不会有什么问题。还有许许多多这样的例子，请看：参观由此去 / This Way to Visit（图案为箭头）；环保垃

圾筒 / Environment-Protection Trash Box；禁止乱扔污物 / DON'T THROW SOMETHING DIRTY ON THE FLOOR（T160次广州东至青岛列车）；注意安全 / Take Good Care of Yourself。如果采用核心词法，上述汉语公示语可分别改译为："This Way"；"Recyclable"；"No Littering"；"Danger!"。

最后再补充一点：传统上，公示语因其指引和警示的功能，常常给人居高临下、盛气凌人的感觉，但今日世界，英语公示语的写法已悄然地发生了变化：诙谐幽默的公示语、温馨提示式的公示语越来越受到人们的青睐。笔者在英国进修期间常常看到这样一条公示语：Merchandise in this store is protected by an electronic tagging system. If the alarm sounds, please return to the cash desk to have the stock control tag removed. 国内媒体曾报道不少超市保安与顾客发生冲突和误会的事件，我在想，如果我们也挂上这样的公示语，对双方都是一个很好的提醒，类似不愉快的事情就可以减少或避免。可喜的是，比如我们的某些建筑工地，已经开始出现一些更为人性化的标语，例如，"施工给您带来许多不便，感谢您的理解和支持"。笔者相信，人的行为是会受语言的影响。因此，建立一个和谐社会可以从提倡美的语言开始。

以下的英语公示语主要有三个来源（只保留本书初版的个别条目）：一是笔者在英国进修期间实地收集的；二是朋友帮笔者在英国收集的①；三是通过国外相关网站搜索的。所收集的英语公示语，其数量不是很多，种类也远非齐全，但经过筛选，从用词和句法特点来看，仍有相当的代表性，可供读者参考。②

一、使用核心词语（可以是动词、过去分词、形容词或名词）

1. Pull
2. Push
3. Ring
4. Stop!

---

① 肖武东老师为作者提供他在英国进修期间拍摄的部分照片，在此表示感谢。
② 几点说明：1）大多数英语公示语的意思都一目了然，因此，除少数有可能造成问题的，一般不配汉语译文。2）英语公示语的书写可以全部采用大写，但考虑到国内读者的阅读习惯，本书采用大小写混排的做法。一般说来，英语的公示语，短语形式的，多用大写；句子形式的，除句子首字母大写外，其余小写；句子或短语字符数少的习惯用大写，字符数多的，除句子首字母外，习惯用小写。实际制作标牌时可斟酌处理。3）分类既按结构，也按功能，主要是从借用和仿拟的实际出发，个别条目的重复是有意保留的。4）因每类的条目不多，排列主要按结构或意义的相近，适当照顾排版的美观，与一般词典按音序排列的做法不同。5）由单句构成的公示语，除感叹号和冒号外，一般不使用标点。

5. Danger!
6. Dip 陡坡
7. Emergency
8. Toxic
9. Recyclable
10. Closed 打烊
11. Vacant 无人（厕所）
12. Engaged 有人（厕所）
13. Occupied 有人（厕所）

二、使用名词和名词性短语

14. Exit
15. Entry
16. Entrance
17. Telephone
18. Inquiries
19. Information
20. Tollgate 收费站
21. Donation 捐款箱
22. Reception 接待处
23. Car Wash
24. Bike Route
25. First Aid 急救
26. One Way Traffic
27. Currency Exchange
28. Dead End 此路不通
29. Taxi Stand / Taxi Zone
30. Baggage Claim 行李提取处
31. Bicycle Shed 自行车停放处
32. Complaints Box 意见箱
33. Comments & Suggestions 意见箱
34. Level Access（残疾人通道）
35. Mail Drop / Pigeonholes 信箱
36. Bus Loading Zone 公交车上落点

37. Car Park（英国）；Parking Lot（美国）

38. Box Office（戏院、影院、歌舞厅等的）售票处

39. Booking Office 售票处（英国）；Ticket Office（美国）

40. Stop Request 需要停车请按铃（公交车上电铃按钮旁）

三、使用祈使句

41. Please Pay Here 收银台

42. Please ring for attention

43. Please wait here for service

44. Please queue this way 请排队（箭头图案）

45. Visitors please sign here 来宾请签到

46. Please call again! 欢迎再次光临!（超市出口处）

47. Please do not park bicycles against the glass windows or doors

48. Fasten seat belts

49. Push for Emergency

50. Reduce speed now

51. Ring bell for service

52. Wear eye protection

53. Wear face field / mask

54. Wear foot protection

55. Wear hand protection

56. Wear hearing protection

57. Post No Bills 禁止张贴

58. Keep off the Grass / Lawn

59. Keep your distance（保持车距）

60. For Police, Fire, Medical Assistance, Dial 911（美国）

61. Give Way! 当心来车!（交叉路口）（英国）；Yield（美国）

62. Do not disturb

63. Do not break seals

64. Do not touch exhibits

65. Do not block this area

66. Do not use elevator in case of fire

67. Do not distract the operator while the train is moving
68. Do not speak to the driver while bus in motion

69. No Cycling
70. No Fishing
71. No Littering
72. No Parking
73. No Eating, Drinking, or Smoking

74. No Dogs
75. No Entry
76. No Cameras
77. No Pedestrians
78. No Motor Vehicles
79. No Pedestrian Access
80. No Entry by This Door
81. No Unauthorized Access
82. No Naked Flames（严禁明火）
83. No Admittance except on Business
84. No Access for Unauthorized Persons
85. No U-Turns 禁止掉头（交通标志）
86. No Vehicle Excess（车辆禁止入内）
87. No Unauthorized Vehicles beyond This Point
88. Strictly No Admittance
89. Absolutely No Bikes or Skateboards on Sidewalks

四、must 和被动语态的使用

90. Ear protection must be worn
91. Eye protection must be worn
92. Foot protection must be worn
93. Hair protection must be worn
94. Protective clothing must be worn
95. Seat belts must be worn
96. Safety helmets must be worn in this area

97. This area must be kept clear at all times
98. Security: ID must be displayed at all times
99. This is a secure area. Identification must be displayed at all times
100. These seats must be vacated for seniors and disabled persons 请为长者和残疾人士让座

101. This door must remain closed at all times
102. This college is closed to visitors / tourists
103. All visitors must report to reception 来访请登记
104. Unauthorized entry to this area is strictly forbidden
105. Library users who cause a disturbance will be asked to leave
106. Notice: No persons under 18 years of age will be served on these premises
107. Guests must be over the age of 21 with appropriate identification to enter the service

108. All reserved（包场）
109. Detour / Road Closed！请绕行
110. No pets allowed
111. No children allowed
112. Bicycles strictly forbidden
113. Pedestrians prohibited
114. Swimming prohibited in this area
115. Pedestrian area: All vehicles prohibited
116. Beer and alcoholic beverages prohibited
117. Caution: Foot protection required
118. Handicapped parking, permit required

五、其他结构

119. Admission Free
120. Open to Visitors
121. Closed to the Public
122. Falling Objects 当心落物
123. Lost and Found 失物招领
124. Risk of Falling 当心滑倒

125. Fragile / Handle with Care

126. Private Property / Keep Out

127. Slow / Children at Play（交通标志）

128. Push button / Wait for walk signal（斑马线处）

129. Stop / For your safety 禁止攀越（交通护栏）

130. Exact Fare / Ready Please 自备零钞，恕不找赎（公共汽车）

131. Out of Order 暂停使用（电铃、热水器、水龙头等因故障、损坏需要维修时）

132. In an emergency, use hammer to break window / Penalty for improper use（公共汽车）

六、相近主题表达法

133. Please call again! 欢迎再次光临！（超市出口处）

134. Thank you for your custom 谢谢惠顾（超市出口处）

135. Automatic Door / Keep Moving

136. This door is not in use / Please use other door

137. Stand Clear / Inward Opening Door（车门向内开，请勿靠近）

138. Lockers 存包处

139. Guest Lockers

140. Free Coin Return Lockers 硬币退还存包处

141. Position Closed 暂停服务

142. Out of Service 暂停服务

143. Temporarily Out of Service When Lit 灯亮时暂停服务

144. No Food or Drinks to Be Brought in Shop

145. No Outside Food or Beverage Please 拒绝外带食品和酒水

146. Entry

147. Entrance

148. Enter Here

149. Exit

150. Fire Exit
151. Fire Escape
152. Emergency Exit

153. Shop to Let
154. For Hire （出租车）空车
155. To Let 出租（房屋、店铺等）
156. For Rent 出租（房屋、店铺等）
157. For Lease 出租（交通工具、房屋、土地等）

158. Road Closed
159. Workers Ahead
160. Road Work Ahead
161. Road Construction Ahead
162. Construction Site / Keep Out
163. Caution: Construction Work Ahead

164. W. C.
165. Toilets
166. Restrooms
167. Disabled Toilet
168. Gents / Ladies
169. Public Toilets
170. Public Restrooms 公共厕所（美国）
171. Public Conveniences 公共厕所（英国）

172. Trash 垃圾箱（美国）
173. Litter / Thank You 垃圾箱（分两行排列）
174. Recyclable
175. Recycle Here
176. Recycle plastic bottles here
177. Recycle your drinks cans here
178. Material for Recycling
179. General Waste

180. Paper Waste Only
181. Hazardous Waste
182. Place rubbish in bins.
183. Do not drop litter. Use the bins provided.

184. Toxic
185. Explosive
186. Radioactive
187. Toxic Material
188. Explosive Material
189. Flammable Material
190. Radioactive Material

191. Smoke Free
192. No Smoking
193. Smoking Area
194. No Smoking Area
195. Non-smoking Area
196. Thank you for not smoking
197. This is a smoke free station
198. No Smoking beyond This Point
199. Welcome to our smoke free facility
200. This is a non-smoking facility（本大楼内禁止吸烟）
201. You are now entering a non-smoking zone. Thank you for your assistance.

202. Half Price
203. Sale Price
204. Extra Value
205. Special Buy
206. Terrific Value
207. Christmas Sales
208. Clearance Price
209. Unbearable Offers
210. Best Value in Town

211. Buy One, Get One Free

212. No Parking
213. Reserved Parking
214. Short Term Parking
215. Customer Parking Only
216. Emergency Parking Only
217. Handicapped Parking Only
218. Parking: Permit Holders Only
219. Valet Parking Only 清洗停车
220. Have you paid and displayed?
221. Pay at meter / Display ticket
222. Car Park: For Use of Patrons Only 顾客专用（酒吧等场所）

223. Admission by Ticket Only
224. Adult Only 成人专柜（书店）
225. Authorized Personnel Only
226. Authorized Vehicles Only
227. Members Only （俱乐部）
228. Passengers Only 送客止步
229. Wheelchair Entrance Only
230. Wholesale Customers Only
231. Cash and Checks Only / Thank You
232. Staff Only 职工专用；顾客止步；闲人免入
233. Self-Serve: Debit and Credit Cards Only. No Cash Accepted
234. Warehouse: Authorized Persons Only 仓库重地，闲人免入

235. Tow-Away Zone 严禁停车，违者拖车
236. Cars parked in unassigned spaces may be towed
237. No Dumping. / Violators will be prosecuted
238. Unauthorized vehicles will be towed away at owner's expense
239. Strictly No Camping / Trespassers will be evicted & prosecuted
240. Reserved parking by permit only / Violators will be fined $25.00
241. Notice / Vehicles and contents are left here entirely at owners' risk

242. Warning / Vehicles parked here without authorization will be wheel clamped. Release fee £ 50

243. Dogs must be carried
244. Dogs must be kept on leads
245. Dogs must be on leash at all times
246. Dogs are not allowed, except on a leash
247. Dogs must be leashed. Owners must clean up after dogs
248. Please be a responsible dog owner. Clean up after your dog.
249. No person shall be allowed to walk dogs in this park
250. The walking of dogs is not allowed in this park 公园内严禁遛狗

251. Fire Door / Keep Shut
252. Fire Exit / Keep Clear
253. Flammable / Keep Fire Away
254. Flammable / No Smoking
255. In case of fire / Do not use lift. / Use stairs.
256. In case of fire / Use stairway for exit / Do not use elevators
257. No Parking or Standing / Fire Lane 消防通道，禁止停站
258. Petroleum Spirit (Vapor) / Highly Flammable / No Naked Lights

259. Caution /Wet Floor
260. Caution / Slippery Floor
261. Caution / Slippery Surface
262. Caution / Uneven Surface
263. Caution / Slippery When Wet
264. Caution / Floor May Be Slippery
265. Caution / Watch your steps. Floor may be slippery at times

266. Caution: Wet Paint!
267. Caution: Keep Clear 注意：保持畅通
268. Caution /Maintenance in progress
269. Caution / Construction work in progress
270. Caution / Beware of snow sliding from roof

271. Caution / Do Not Stop in Doorway. Automatic Sliding Door

272. Caution：Speed Ramps
273. Caution：Two Steps Ahead
274. Caution：Slow Ramps Ahead

275. Mind the step
276. Mind your head
277. Watch your head 当心碰头
278. Watch your steps 留神脚下
279. Watch for pedestrians 当心行人

280. Beware of Dog
281. Beware of Pickpockets
282. Beware of Shark
283. Warning! Security Dog 注意：内有警犬！
284. Security：Do not leave bags / property unattended. 安全提示：请照看好随身携带物品。

285. Warning / CCTV Cameras 闭路摄像
286. Warning / CCTV in Operation 闭路监控
287. Warning / These premises are under CCTV surveillance
288. Notice / Closed Circuit Television operates at this station
289. Notice / Concealed CCTV cameras operate on these premises.
290. Warning! Video security cameras are in use. With constant on-screen monitoring and tape recording, you have already been observed and filmed.

291. Danger! Do Not Enter
292. Danger! Demolition in Progress
293. Danger! High Voltage / Keep Out
294. Danger! Construction Area / Keep Out
295. Danger! Explosives / No Trespassing
296. Danger! High Speed Trains / Do Not Enter

七、温馨告示

297. Thank you for not smoking

298. Thank you for using the ashtry

299. Welcome to our smoke free facility.

300. Have you paid and displayed?（停车场）

301. Thank you for keeping your voices down.

302. Enjoy your national forest. Please don't litter.

303. Save our time. / Save your time. / Please shut the door.

304. You are now entering a non-smoking zone. Thank you for your assistance.

305. Please leave this place as you would wish to find it. （厨房、餐厅等处）

306. Is this what your kitchen look like at home? Let's keep the kitchen clean please.

307. If it breaks we consider it sold to you. Look with your eyes. Please do not touch.

308. Parents and guardians are advised to warn children of the dangers of entering this area.

309. Reminder / Please remember to remove your card from the ATM machine / Thank you.

310. These seats are particularly appreciated by the elderly and infirm. （公共汽车靠中门下车处）

311. In consideration of fellow guests, we ask that noise levels in corridors be kept to a minimum.

312. Look around the kitchen and find out where the items on this table come from and how they get here.

313. LLRS Mobile Phones Policy

    If it's silent, you're fine. If it's not, you're fined!
    Stay safe—Switch it off.

314. National Museums Liverpool

    Apologize for any inconvenience caused during the alterations to this area.

315. Sorry about the mess

    We are making this a more pleasant place for you to shop and for us to work. （商店装修）

316. <u>Security Barrier</u>

If alarm sounds while passing through the barrier, please return to counter and speak to counter staff. The barrier is monitored by CCTV 24 hour recording in operation.

317. <u>Attention</u>: Our merchandise has a hidden security device. Upon purchase it will be deactivated.

318. If the alarm sounds, please contact a member of staff for assistance. （商店出口处）

319. Merchandise in this store is protected by an electronic tagging system. If the alarm sounds, please return to the cash desk to have the stock control tag removed. （商店出口处）

英语公示语实例：

附录一　英语常用公示语例解

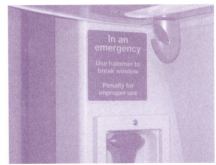

附录二

补充练习材料

本附录选取了几个主要应用文体的八篇英语材料,作为英译汉的补充练习。这些英语材料也可看作汉译英的范本。

一、贸易往来信函

以下是两封贸易往来信函①,第一封是客户的抱怨信,第二封是厂家的回函。试将两封信函翻译成汉语,特别注意两封信函在措辞上的不同语气。

信函 1:

Gentlemen:

More than three weeks ago I saw your ad in the *PDQ Trade Journal*. I wrote to you, in response to the ad enclosing my check for $142.78, a copy of the ad, and a covering letter, ordering one gross of your Model 0021, to be shipped to me Express collect.

I have not received the merchandise. You haven't even had the courtesy to acknowledge my order. If you are not prepared to ship the ordered merchandise, immediately return my check.

Sincerely,

O. P. Hattery

---

① 选自 Ferd Nauheim, *Letter Perfect*, U.S.A.: Van Nostrand Reinhold, 1982, pp. 203–208。

信函 2:

Dear Mr. Hattery,

One gross of Model 0021 left here by Air Express this morning, twenty minutes after your letter arrived. By this time, you've had my telegram advising you of the shipment.

My warmest thanks, Mr. Hattery, for writing and bringing this inexcusable delay to the surface. You've been very patient.

The moment your shipment was out of here and the telegram sent, I started an investigation. Until you've had some more experience with us, you'll find it hard to believe, I'm sure, but this is far from our normal method of handling orders.

The rule here is that an order is acknowledged the day it arrives and, if humanly possible, the goods are shipped that same day. The longest we normally take to make a shipment is 48 hours, unless we have no inventory of the item requested. That's why your well justified complaint constituted a serious mystery here.

I didn't have to look far. The first place checked was the accounting department. Your order and check went there first to be entered on the books and to permit them to search the files to see if you were a new customer or not. They found that you had placed one previous order nearly three years ago. And that's where it happened. When the old folder was returned to the file your new order went in the file too. That's where it was found this morning.

No heads rolled. Nobody was fired. The folks working in that department are good. They handle thousands of details each week and they make amazingly few errors. But they are human and mistakes will happen. We had a little meeting and showed them what had occurred in your case. It put everyone that much more on their toes to safeguard against a similar slip in the future.

So, we owe you more than a deeply sincere apology, Mr. Hattery. We owe you a vote of genuine appreciation. The incident will make us even more efficient in the future.

I do hope that the delay didn't cause you any serious inconvenience. Please accept our warmest thanks for your business. I look forward to hearing from you again so that we'll be able to demonstrate the far more normal courtesy and speed with which your orders will be handled. Although your letter specified that the merchandise should be sent express collect we have prepaid the shipment, to demonstrate our desire to make amends.

Sincerely,

二、契约文本

文本 1：旅游保险

INSURANCE ①

It is our policy to ensure that all our customers are comprehensively covered by insurance when buying our holidays. We have therefore negotiated good value premiums which give above average insurance benefits.

You will automatically be insured with us unless you indicate otherwise on the Booking Form, and give us details of your insurance which should give at least equal cover. Customers choosing to take an alternative scheme must ensure that they can contact their own insurance company in an emergency. The Magic of Italy（旅游公司名）cannot be held responsible for any inability to make immediate payment of emergency expenses in the resort for customers not covered by our insurance.

OUR INSURANCE

We have arranged a special holiday insurance scheme for any persons living in and traveling from the UK through Aon, Cork Bays and Fisher Ltd. （保险公司名），a division of Aon Risk Services (UK) Ltd., which is underwritten by Certain Underwriters at Lloyds. The full terms, conditions and exclusions are incorporated in the Master Certificate which alone constitutes the contract of insurance between the Insured

---

① 选自国外旅游宣传册，非正式出版物。

Person and the Insurers in the event of a dispute regarding the terms and conditions of the insurance the terms and conditions of the Master Certificate shall prevail. The policy is governed by English law. On this page are brief details only. Individual policies will not be issued, although a more detailed summary will be sent to you with your confirmation invoice, and you may inspect the Master Certificate at our offices.

POLICIES

You will receive an insurance document with details of the cover and this, together with the premium shown on your confirmation invoice, will be evidence of your having effected the insurance cover. Both documents are needed in the event of a claim. Always take your insurance document with you on holiday.

EMERGENCY ASSISTANCE

The 24-hour Emergency Assistance Service of Medicall Ltd is available in the event of an emergency overseas relating to medical problems for which the costs would be recoverable under the Medical Expenses and Personal Accident sections of the policy.

DELAYED DEPARTURE BENEFITS

Regrettably there are times when, for reasons beyond our control, flights are delayed. The policy of this company in the event of a delay in departure from your UK airport, for reasons other than those which are the responsibility of the airline, is to arrange for our customers to be provided, whenever practical, with the following welfare arrangements: 2 ~ 4 hours delay—light refreshment; over 4 hours delay—main meal. In addition, our Travel Insurance gives improved financial compensation should the commencement of your holiday or return journey be delayed as a result of failure or disruption of transport services: A benefit of £ 25 after 12 hours delay will apply. (See Cover for details.)

PRE-EXISTING HEALTH CONDITIONS

If any person to be insured has received in-patient treatment in the last 12 months or are taking prescribed medication, on receipt of your certificate the Insured Person must contact the Medical Underwriting Helpline. You must make the call personally and will need to quote your certificate number. The telephone will be answered by trained staff who will ask questions in order to assess whether cover can be granted for your health condition. All calls are treated in the strictest confidence and other than your name and address, trip details and medical condition (s) most answers will be YES or NO so that personal information is not overheard. Should we require an additional premium and you accept our offer, this should be paid to the Medical Helpline either by Credit card or cheque. Full confirmation will be sent to your address after your call. If your call is within 7 days of your trip departure and an additional premium is required, only payment by credit/debit card can be accepted. You can obtain a refund of the basic premium within the 14 days cooling – off period if you do not find the terms acceptable, providing the trip has not commenced or a claim been made.

CLAIMS

If you wish to attempt a claim, telephone or write to: Van Ameyde & Wallis. 34 The Mall, Bromley, Kent. BR I ITS. TEL. 0181 466 6034 requesting a Claims Form relevant to the section you wish to claim under. Complete and return the form to Van Ameyde & Wallis together with your confirmation invoice and any other documentary evidence you have in support of your claim. In all correspondence please quote your certificate number as shown on the insurance document issued to you.

WARRANTY

The insured person warranties that at the time of effecting this insurance:
a) No circumstances are known that are likely to lead to cancellation or curtailment of the holiday (e. g. the known health condition of a close relative).
b) The insured person has disclosed all material facts concerning this insurance to the Insurers.
c) No travel will be undertaken against a medical practitioner's advice.

PREMIUMS (NON-REFUNDABLE)

Up to 4 nights	£ 25.00
Up to 9 nights	£ 30.00
Up to 16 nights	£ 36.00
Up to 22 nights	£ 45.00
Up to 31 nights	£ 48.00
Each additional week or part week	£ 10.00 (Maximum period 3 months)

Premium inclusive of insurance Premium tax. For persons aged 71 years or over, the premium is increased by 50% (e.g. up to 9 nights increases from £ 30 to £ 45). Children under 16 on departure date—HALF PRICE. Infant under 2 on departure date accompanied by insured adult—FREE.

COVER

The cover provided is as follows:

Section 1—Personal Accident

(a) Death	£ 15,000
(b) Loss of one or more limbs and/or sight in one or both eyes	£ 15,000
(c) Permanent Total Disablement from following any occupation	£ 15,000

Section 2—Medical & Additional Expenses Up to £ 5,000

This section includes emergency assistance services

Section 3—Hospital Benefit **£ 20 per day up to £ 600**

Section 4—Baggage, Personal Effects

Any one article pair or set up to £ 250

Cameras and Jewellery limited in all up to £ 250 Up to £ 1,500.

This section includes emergency purchases if baggage delayed for more than 12 hours Up to £ 100

Section 5—Personal Money (£ 300 Cash limit) Up to £ 500

Section 6—Personal Liability Up to £ 1,000

Section 7—Travel Delay (Exceeding 12 hours) **Up to Holiday Cost**

Either

£ 25 for the first full 12 hours, £ 15 for each complete 12 hours thereafter

up to £ 100 or

should you decide to cancel after 12 hours, up to the holiday cost

Section 8—Loss of Deposit or Cancellation Up to holiday cost

Section 9—Curtailment Up to holiday cost

Section 10—Missed Departure Up to £ 500

Section 11—Legal Expenses Up to £ 25,000

Policy excess: Sections 1, 3, 6, 7a, 10 & 11—Nil; Sections 2, 4, 5, 7b, 8 & 9—£ 35 each and every loss (Loss of deposit £ 5, delayed baggage—Nil)

文本 2：聘用合同

Employment Agreement

THIS AGREEMENT is made this 16th of January 2006 by and between:

a) Beijing Relay International School ("BRIS"), hereinafter referred to as "Employer" and
b) Barrie Jones hereinafter referred to as "Employee".

NOW, THEREFORE, in fulfillment of the obligations of this Agreement, the Employer agrees to employ this Employee, and the Employee agrees to work for the Employer in accordance with the following stipulations and benefits:

1. The Employee shall be employed for the purpose of **School Assistant,** but may be assigned to other or additional duties within the training and capabilities of the Employee. The Employee signing the contract should not be bound by any other employment contract.
2. The Employee's employment shall begin as of January 22, 2006 and shall continue for the remainder of the 2005/2006 school year, as set forth in the official School Calendar, attached as Exhibit A.
3. The Employee shall be compensated on an hourly basis at the rate of US＄8.00 per hour. The number of hours per week and the day(s) of the week have been agreed upon by the Employer and the Employee and a memorandum setting forth the agreed upon schedule is hereby incorporated into this Agreement as Exhibit B. The Employer will deduct from all payments made to the Employee, any applicable Chinese taxes and any other deduction required by the Chinese Law. The Employee is responsible for all home country tax return preparation and payments.
4. If at the request of the Director, the Employee is required to work hours in excess of those set forth in Exhibit B, the Employee shall be paid at the hourly rate as set out in (3) above.
5. The Employee is entitled to sick leave at the rate one (1) day for each month of service or ten (10) working days per year of contractual service. Sick days are to be taken for legitimate illness and not used as vacation or personal leave. The Employer reserves the right to require a signed medical certificate stating the nature

and seriousness of the illness. Sick leave not taken by the end of the contracted period may be reimbursed but may not be accrued for the purpose of adding them to the next contract period. The sick leave reimbursement will be determined by the following formula: Allowed days less used days, multiplied by the employee's daily rate.

6. The Employee may elect to treat up to three (3) days of sick leave as personal leave per school year. Personal days not taken by the end of the contract period may be reimbursed. Days of absence for illness beyond the number of days earned shall result in a deduction of an amount equal to 100% of the employee's daily rate. Absences other than sick leave and personal leave will be taken as unpaid leave of absence and will be deducted from the employee's daily rate. The daily rate of pay will be calculated by the following formula: hours worked per day multiplied by the hourly rate.

7. The Employee is required to abide by the Policy and Regulations ("Regulations") established by the Board of Directors and in force as of the date of execution of this Agreement. Execution of the Agreement acknowledges that the Employee has been given access to these Regulations and that the Employer agrees to provide Employee with continued access to all Regulations.

8. This Agreement may be terminated by either party in writing with ninety days' notice, or by the Board of Directors according to the procedures set forth in Board Policy. Furthermore, if the Board of Directors determines that the level of enrollment no longer justifies the employment of the Employee, this Agreement may be terminated without notice.

9. Disputes between the Employer and the Employee arising out of this Agreement shall be decided by majority vote of the Board of Directors.

This Agreement has been executed and signed at Beijing Relay International School, Beijing, the People's Republic of China, this 16th day of January 2006.

By the Employer represented by   By the Employee
(Signature)   (Signature)
Director of BRIS   Barrie Jones

Date:

三、广告文案①

文案1：

HEALTH INSURANCE

One of the best ways to insure good health is to eat a well-balanced diet that includes nutritious foods like Campbell's Soup.

That's not just our opinion. The fact is university researchers found that soup plays a significant part in a nutritionally healthy diet.

That Campbell's Tomato Soup up there, for instance, is an important source of vitamin C. While Campell's Vegetable Beef contains more than 1/3 of the day's allowance of vitamin A in just a single serving.

And not only are most Campbell's Soups a rich source of nutrition, they're also light on your stomach, and easy to digest.

So when you're picking out a good health insurance policy, remember to pick up a few cans of your favorite Campbell's Soups.

If you have any questions, talk to one of the best insurance agents around.

**Campell's
Soup Is Good Food**

---

① 选自 Dorothy Cohen, *Advertising*. U. S. A. : Scott, Foresman and Company, 1988, p. 179。

文案 2:

You can count on Sears to replace it free if it fails to satisfy you ever

"If any Craftsman® hand tool ever fails to give complete satisfaction, return it to the nearest Sears store in the U. S. and Sears will replace it free." This full unlimited warranty tells you a lot about Craftsman tools—and about Sears.

How can Sears offer such a sweeping warranty? Because Sears goes to such lengths to make sure you'll get complete satisfaction from any Craftsman hand tool you buy.

When you buy a Sears product, you should be able to count on Sears for good design, good workmanship, good materials, and good value.

So Sears digs into the details. If you were to visit the factory that makes the Craftsman pliers in our picture, you might run into a Sears engineer working to streamline production methods. Or a Sears tool buyer discussing possible improvements — perhaps a slight change to make the handle more comfortable.

At the Sears laboratory, you would see some of the tests that over ten thousand products go through every year. Tests of children's swing seats for strength, of bedding for flame resistance, of washing machines for performance.

After Sears approves a product and offers it for sale, Sears responsibility carries on. If what you've bought requires installation, Sears will make sure it's done right. And when it comes to service, Sears runs one of the world's largest service organizations, with Sears-trained repairmen buzzing around all fifty states in over 16 000 service trucks.

It all adds up to a sense of responsibility to you that starts with the development of the product and stays alive and active after the product enters your home. From sewing machines to jeans to towels to tools, for products you can count on, you can count on Sears.

四、旅游文本 ①

文本1：

Austria

With its wealth of history, breathtaking scenery and friendly people, it's no surprise that Austria has become one of the world's most popular touring destinations. Whether you choose to step back in time to the days of the Habsburg Empire or follow the nature trail through acres of open, rolling countryside, you'll return home with lots of lasting memories of this charming country.

Imperial cities

Austria's three great cities are packed with pleasures for the visiting tourist. In Vienna, home of the world-famous Boy's Choir and Spanish Riding School, you can sit in a coffee-house, enjoy a decadent slice of Linzertorte and drink in centuries of history, preserved in the wonderful architectural gems which surround you. Salzburg, birthplace of Mozart, is an unrivalled place of pilgrimage for music and art lovers, as well as being one of the most picturesque cities in Europe, its skyline of medieval spires, domes and turrets set against a stunning mountain backdrop. And then there's Innsbruck, the ancient capital of the Tyrol, where you can wander the maze of narrow, medieval streets, and browse through the little shops which sell all kinds of souvenirs—from exquisitely painted ornaments to crystals carved out of the Alps.

Mountain scenery

It may be best known as a winter wonderland, but from early June, when the spring flowers carpet the landscape, the Austrian Tyrol becomes the classic picture-postcard

---

① 选自国外旅游宣传册，非正式出版物。

destination. Quaint villages with traditional chalets and rustic inns nestle in deep green valleys, surrounded by towering, snow-clad peaks. Lakes, streams and cascading waterfalls glisten in the sunshine. And as you ramble through the glorious scenery, you can feel the exhilarating effects of the crisp, clean mountain air. "Gemutlichkeit" is the Austrian word for the unique atmosphere of old-world charm and congeniality which characterizes this welcoming corner of the world, and there's no better place to experience it than a traditional Tyrolean evening, as you enjoy a glass or two of beer and sing along to the local "oompah" band. With its colourful, gabled buildings and cobbled streets, the 14th century town of Kitzbuehel is the very essence of Tyrolean charm. It's also a paradise for walkers, with 180 kilometres of marked trails ideal for anything from a gentle stroll to an adventurous hike.

Hearty eating

All that fresh air is sure to give you an appetite. But don't worry, there's plenty of hearty local dishes to oblige, including Germknodel (a yeast dumpling filled with plum jam), Kasespatzle (baked pasta dumplings with a cheese topping), and Kaiserschmarrn (sweet pancakes served with preserved fruit). And of course, there's Austria's world famous pastry dessert, strudel. As for drinks, the local beers and wines are generally good and inexpensive.

文案2：

Italy

What sums up Italy? Scenic splendour? Cultural treasures? Mouth-watering cuisine? In fact, it's all these and more. Because besides its well-known artistic and architectural wonders, this fascinating country has a myriad of other pleasures to offer, whether you're enjoying the peace and beauty of the Lakes, exploring the history of Rome, or touring the picturesque, white-washed towns and villages of the Bay of Naples. Throughout the many vastly different regions which stretch from top to toe of Italy's instantly-recognisable boot-shaped land mass, centuries-old traditions-open-air markets, bread and cheese-making, time-honoured recipes—live on, sitting comfortably alongside the fast-moving developments of modern society, which have made the country a world-leader in fashion and design.

Historic cities

No other country in the world has more famous sights than Italy, and a large proportion of these can be found in the three great cultural centres—Rome, Florence and Venice. Rome's mighty Colosseum, fascinating Roman remains, glorious churches and elegant squares; the Tuscan capital, Florence, with its awe-inspiring Duomo and the 14th century Ponte Vecchio which spans the broad Arno River; the gorgeous city of Venice, divided by 177 canals and blessed with superb buildings such as the Doge's Palace and St Mark's Cathedral; the list of unmissable attractions is almost endless.

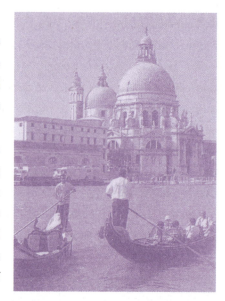

Lakes and mountains

With its sparkling waters backed by stunning mountain scenery, the Lakes region of Northern Italy has been a popular holiday playground since Roman times, drawing visitors like a magnet year after year with its irresistible blend of beauty, elegant "Belle Epoque" hotels and temperate climate. Then, of course, there's the excellent local food and drink, including lake trout, fresh or sun-dried, and the light, red Bardolino wine from the eastern shores of Lake Garda.

The rivieras

Italy's coastline is also full of infinite variety. The Venetian Riviera, its most popular resort the lively Lido di Jesolo, has broad expanses of sand, gently sloping into balmy waters, perfect for swimming and snorkeling. The dramatic Neapolitan Riviera has towering cliffs with pretty fishing villages cascading down the hillside to bays of sparkling blue water. And nestling at the "toe of the boot" is the ravishing, sun-kissed island of Sicily with its spectacular scenery and miles of soft, golden sand.

A food lover's paradise

It's impossible to talk about Italy without talking about food. Forget the pre-packed pasta and pizzas which proliferate outside the country. Italy's cuisine today still offers a kaleidoscope of authentic regional dishes, created from fresh local produce and lovingly prepared to age-old recipes. What's more, the country is one of the world's largest wine producers, with many excellent lesser-known varieties to choose from in addition to the ever-popular favourites like Chianti and Frascati.

附录三

各章练习参考答案

第一章

第二节

a) dry goods　　　　　　纺织品
b) wet goods　　　　　　酒类商品
c) dry state　　　　　　禁酒的州（美国）
d) wet state　　　　　　非禁酒州（美国）
e) dry law　　　　　　　禁酒法令（美国）
f) white goods　　　　　白漆家用电器
g) white wine　　　　　　白葡萄酒
h) dry white wine　　　　干白葡萄酒
i) toilet water　　　　　花露水
j) to close the switch　　开电闸

第二章

I.

1. 在这儿等我，别走开。
2. 车未停稳，请勿开门。
3. 现在的收音机没有不是立体声的了。
4. 地球在太空运行的同时也在自转。
5. 我们正要入睡，门铃就响了起来。
6. 新的价格从明年1月1日起开始实行，那时以前，下列旧价格依然有效。
7. 乔布斯认为，所谓简约设计，就是想办法使产品设计得简单易用。
8. 前人种树，后人乘凉。我想，大多数有创造力的人，都不会忘记感谢前人的努力。

9. 记得亨利·福特说过:"要是我最初问顾客需要什么,他们一定会告诉我:'一匹跑得更快的马!'。"实际上,在你还没有将产品摆在顾客面前之前,他们并不知道真正需要什么。因此,我从来不依赖市场调查。我们的任务就是要读懂还没有落在纸上的东西。

10. 人们热衷于提出各种新的历史研究方法,与其说是因为学科外的学者不承认历史这个学科,还不如说是因为学科内历史学家之间的相互诋毁。

11. 惯用法才是唯一的取舍标准。假如有两个短语,一个是平易自然,但不合语法,另一个是语法正确,但隐晦生硬,我是宁要前者而不要后者的。

12. 我写的东西,很少是觉得无法改进的,更多的情况是心有余而力不足,结果只好罢了。

13. 那是一部很有价值的著作,我想即使文笔很好的人也能从中学到很多东西。

14. 有些作家思路不清,却往往认为自己的思想并不像乍一看那样肤浅,而是有更深刻的含义。

15. 别忘了,耶路撒冷也是个现代、繁华的城市,流光溢彩的商店、灯红酒绿的餐厅,使你忍不住停下观光的脚步。

Ⅱ.

1. 原文中"all...not..."是个部分否定结构,此外,"this Corporation"为"本公司/我公司"的意思。拟改译:来函所询商品**不全是**我公司经营的。

2. 原文属"多枝共干"结构。拟改译:这些文件详细载明了所调查事件中的姓名、日期、地点和全部经过。

3. 原译中"正本两份"有歧义,即不清楚是"同一合同的正本",还是"不同合同的正本"。拟改译:今寄上标题合同正本一式两份,请会签后寄回一份,以便存档。

4. 原文"as specified in Appendix 8"不是修饰谓语动词,而是修饰"the working and living conditions"。拟改译:……要求承包方对发现有错误的工程服务迅速返工而不增加购买方的费用。但是,购买方须按附件8向返工人员提供规定的工作和生活条件。

5. 原译中"应该包括"与"不限于"同义重复,漏译"storm";此外,原译词序不当。拟改译:任何双方无法控制的事件或情况 —— 不仅限于火灾、风灾、水灾、地震、爆炸、战争、叛乱、暴动、传染病及检疫——均应视为不可抗力事件。

Ⅲ.

Treasure Island

By Robert Louis Stevenson

Chapter XV　The Man of the Island

From the side of the hill, which was here steep and stony, a spout of gravel was dislodged, and fell rattling and bounding through the trees. My eyes turned instinctively in that direction, and I saw a figure leap with great rapidity behind the trunk of a pine. What it was, whether bear or man or monkey, I could in nowise tell. It seemed dark and shaggy, more I knew not. But the terror of this new apparition brought me to a stand.

第四章

Ⅰ.

1. The bank refused further credit to the company.
2. We will contact you as soon as fresh supplies are available.
3. Please find enclosed the copies of the shipping documents.
4. We trust you will honor our draft on presentation.
5. Please change L/C to read "Negotiable in Guangzhou".
6. If one side fails to honor the contract, the other side is entitled to cancel it.
7. Unfortunately, we cannot accept your offer, your prices are prohibitive.
8. In order to conclude the transaction, we think you should reduce your price by at least 5%.
9. Our terms of payment are by a confirmed, irrevocable L/C available by draft at sight.
10. Enclosed are our Purchase Confirmation No. 4567 in duplicate. Please sign and return one copy for our file at your earliest convenience.

Ⅱ.

1. 这期间，窗户的一块玻璃一直不停地发出格格的响声。这时并没有风吹过。这个长江低谷地带大概是世界上最不可能发生地震的地方了，可是我还是很想知道明天的报纸是否报道有别的地方发生了地震。

附录三 各章练习参考答案

2. 德国改革宗教会的乔治·斯奈德牧师大人夫妇远在中国腹地。有电报要他们撤离，但鉴于他们所在地没有发生骚乱，他们回电说还是留在那里。后来又给他们发过一封电报，比第一封电报更紧急，却没有收到回音。论私交，我们很关心斯奈德一家，因为去年夏天他们与我们是"威尔森总统号"上的同船旅客，且两家在一起相处得很好。

3. 在去码头的路上，我们就已经感受到了一点局势紧张的气氛——只见横冲直撞的士兵和四处奔波的苦力，大有山雨欲来风满楼之势。

4. 不久，我们听到增援的汽车在街道上疾驰，因此我们考虑是否有必要逃到军舰上去。

5. 有一本语法书，既大又重，但印刷精美，作者是位来自荷兰格罗宁根的波斯玛先生，我怀疑这位先生是不是我的哪个远房表亲。

6. 到这儿的头天早晨，我们就被步枪和机关枪的枪声吵醒了。我知道长江上游好几百公里远的地方正在打仗，因此担心是不是有支部队已经神不知鬼不觉地来到了下游在攻打南京了。还好，我后来得知，那只不过是打靶练习，让我们虚惊了一场。

7. 我听说在南京赌博是违法的，尽管我见到过大量的证据，证明这规定是一纸空文。但庆祝新年期间通常是"法外开恩"，因此赌博可以不受约束地进行。这情景让我们想起主耶稣在耶路撒冷的圣殿，用鞭子将商人赶出去的传说，我们真搞不懂为什么异教徒的僧侣不用鞭子将寺院里这些亵渎神灵的人赶出去呢？

8. （一路上）我们看到好几窝猪。一般是一头母猪带着三到七头小猪，在稀疏的草地上啃食，旁边有个小男孩看着。这些猪的背脊虽不能说像剃刀片，但猪的腰身无疑是瘦骨嶙峋，猪没猪样。我不禁突发奇想，要是把这些黑毛牲畜，在我们爱荷华州农场主那丰美的草场放养一个月，它们该何等欢喜！

9. 在（南京城墙上的）多个地点，我们发现了一些奇怪的大石板，石板厚约 15 厘米，宽约 30 厘米，高约 1.2 米。这些石板相对而立，每块石板上开有两个直径为 10 厘米左右的孔洞。石板牢牢插入城墙的地面。我们很好奇，这些石板在远古时作何用途。我们猜想，也许当年石板的孔洞里安装了木头，用来固定将人或物拉到城墙上来的绳索。

10. 我们大家都心神不宁，寝食难安，戚戚然不知道未来一两个月等待我们的是什么。据我看，疾风暴雨就在前头。

第五章

1. 丧失了道德，便丧失了一切。
2. 水冷却到一定程度便成了冰。
3. 凶手是谁，一点线索也没有。
4. 冰的密度比水的小，因此，冰浮于水。
5. 电源线接错了，就会损坏发动机。
6. 录用的女服务员，须试用3~6个月。
7. 那人黑衣、黑鞋、黑胡须，满脸愁容。
8. 他显然具备了钓鱼者最重要的品质，那就是以钓为乐，钓少钓多一个样。（倜西、董乐山译，反面着笔）。本例也可从正面着笔来翻译：不用说，他具备了钓鱼者最重要的品质，那就是以钓为乐，钓多钓少都不在乎。
9. 物质热胀冷缩是个普遍的物理现象。
10. 使用燃料的损失率依其方式不同而异，直接使用，损失率最低，为10%~20%，用于发电再加送电，损失率最高，达65%~70%。（王季良 译）
11. 如谈判未能解决，争执之事可提交仲裁。
12. 你方索赔歉难接受，因为装船时箱子都完好无损。
13. 我们越来越离不开三种基本的运输方式，即海、陆、空运输。
14. 从他那儿我懂得一名能干的政治家的标志在很大程度上是善于审时度势。他在适当的时机说适当的话。（齐沛合 译）[1]

    本书改译：

    从他身上，我懂得了怎样才是一个杰出的政治家，其基本标志就是能审时度势，知道什么时候说什么话。
15. 我之所以当教师，也不是我自认为能够回答学生的问题，或我觉得有满腹的学问，非与别人分享不可。有时我真的很吃惊，我课上讲的，学生竟然作了笔记！

第七章

I.

1. We shall appreciate it if you would inform us of your trade terms and conditions.

---

[1] 马文·卡尔布等：《基辛格》（上、下），齐沛合译，生活·读书·新知三联书店1975年版，第51页。

附录三　各章练习参考答案

2. We highly appreciate your effort in pushing the sale of our slippers.
3. We shall appreciate it if you will forward the following to the above address at your earliest convenience.
4. We are pleased to advise you that the captioned goods were shipped yesterday per S. S. "Peace".
5. Enclosed please find our Sales Contract No. HN38 in duplicate.
6. Shippers are requested to note particularly the exceptions and conditions of the Bill of Lading with reference to the validity of the insurance upon their goods.
7. We have the pleasure of sending you by separate post our latest catalog of manufactures with their price-list. We hope the prices and quality will be satisfactory.
8. We appreciate your proposal of acting as our agent. However, as we are not yet thoroughly acquainted, we think it is better to discuss the matter sometime later when some practical transactions have been done.
9. We acknowledge with thanks the receipt of your facsimile letter dated August 31, 2005. We appreciate your interest and sincerity in cooperation with us. We will do what we can to bring about the arrival of cooperation between us at an earlier date.
10. Enclosed is our Proforma Invoice No. 5368 in duplicate covering 500 Forever Bicycles for shipment during October 1993. We wish to state that the Proforma Invoice is valid till September 1, 1993.

II.
1. 感谢贵方12月22日来函，但遗憾的是，我们目前暂不能提供苦杏仁。
2. 如蒙告知贵行客户中可靠的进口商号及地址，并附其资信报告，我们将不胜感激。
3. 3月2日来函及所附贵厂产品价目单均收悉。
4. 兹通知，我方4265号化肥订单舱位订妥，由"和平"号装运，该轮预计5月15日抵达。
5. 该货起订量为1000码，根据订单大小，我们可提供高达25%的折扣。
6. 随函附寄最新目录和价目单。请注意，我方货物系自己生产，且不通过任何中间商直接出口，故价格比其他竞争者均优惠。
7. 兹寄上本公司订单，请立即发运100包"美利奴"羊毛。
8. 万一发生索赔，必须于货到目的地后30天内提出，过期不予受理。
9. 6月5日函、样品和价目单均收到，谢谢。我们业已选妥，并随附368号订单。

10. 请寄橡胶鞋目录一份，并注明付款条件及最大折扣。

Ⅲ.
奥伯曼女士：
　　您好！
　　谢谢您在圣诞来临之际又给我们发来了订单。遗憾的是，您所要的座钟是乔·斯托公司经营的。然而我们也有同类的，且颇具特色（夜光指示，可旋底座）的41型座钟，其单价只略增1.50美元。请查阅随函所附我公司函购商品目录第131页。
　　我们已特意为您留了100只这种今年极为畅销的座钟，全部包装整齐，随时待发。如您决定订购，请于本周五前打受话方付款电话回复为盼。
　　此致
敬礼！

第八章

I.

1. The improved and developed technology shall be owned by the party who has improved and developed the technology. 或：
   The ownership of any improved and developed technology shall belong to the party who has improved and developed the technology.
2. All the activities of a joint venture shall be governed by the laws, decrees and pertinent rules and regulations of the People's Republic of China.
3. The Chinese and English texts of this contract are each prepared with four originals. Each Party shall keep two copies of each text.
4. Fifty per cent (50%) of the total amount as advance payment, viz. 500 000 U.S.D. only (SAY FIVE HUNDRED THOUSAND U.S. DOLLARS ONLY), shall be paid within three (3) months, after signing this contract, i.e. not later than August 31, 2001.
5. Over 5 600 technological import contracts involving a total value of over US$40 billion have reportedly been signed by China since 1979, 6.6 and 3.5 times the respective figures of the previous 30 years.
6. According to a report compiled by the State Statistics Bureau, from 1953 to 1993, the gross domestic product (GDP) of the country multiplied 18 times at an annual rate of 7.3%.

7. In the area of economy, it has kept a steady and rapid growth. In the last five years, its gross domestic product (GDP) quadrupled that of the 1980s in advance of the scheduled time.

8. The total contract price to be paid by Party A to Party B in accordance with the content and scope stipulated in Article 2 to the Contract shall be 3 642 U. S. Dollars (SAY: THREE THOUSAND SIX HUNDRED AND FORTY TWO U. S. DOLLARS ONLY).

9. In case of divorce, the disposal of the joint property of husband and wife is subject to agreement between the two parties. In cases where agreement can not be reached, the people's court should make a judgment after considering the actual state of the family and the rights and interests of the wife and the child or children.

10. In accordance with *The Law of the People's Republic of China on Chinese Foreign Equity Joint Ventures* and other laws and regulations of China, and on the basis of equality, mutual benefit and friendly negotiations, Guangdong ABC Light Industry Group Corp. of the People's Republic of China (hereinafter referred to as Party A) and XYZ Corp. of Germany (hereinafter referred to as Party B) agree to jointly establish an Equity Joint Venture and hereby sign this Contract.

Ⅱ.

1. (1) executed
   (2) event
   (3) prevail

2. (1) said
   (2) hands
   (3) this
   (4) certifies
   (5) over
   (6) acknowledge

3. (1) arising
   (2) case
   (3) reached
   (4) submitted

4. (1) valid
   (2) effective
   (3) null
   (4) void
   (5) upon
   (6) term

5. (1) either
   (2) other
   (3) such
   (4) breach
   (5) conditions

6. (1) of
   (2) its

7. (1) liability
   (2) failure
   (3) circumstances
   (4) predicted
   (5) due
   (6) beyond
   (7) third
   (8) shall

8. (1) receipt
   (2) confirmed

(3) will   (5) otherwise   (7) under
(4) such   (6) respect   (8) deemed

V.

保险凭证

本保险适用于本保险凭证所指定付讫保费的被保险人。

重要事项：请仔细阅读"条款"（第 30 页）、"保证声明"（第 11 页）和"条款"第 11 项（第 30 页）有关"重要事实"的约定，若未能遵守以上规定，将影响索赔。

本保单由**意外及一般保险国际有限公司**制订（地址：34 Lower Abbey Street, Dublin 1, Ireland）。

本保单由**国内及海外保险有限公司**签署承保（地址：Regent Arcade House, 19—25 Argyll Street, London W1V 2HQ）。

本保单中符号£ 表示英镑。

保证声明

被保险人领取本保单时必须保证：

1. 被保险人对旅行的可能取消或缩短，及可能导致索赔的健康状况事先并不知情。
2. 若被保险人在旅费付讫当日是仍在接受治疗的门诊病人，被保险人须提供医生开具的"健康证明"，证明被保险人适宜旅行，并能坚持旅程。
3. 若被保险人在预订旅行的前 6 个月曾作为住院或门诊病人接受过治疗，被保险人须从医生处获得适于外出旅行的书面医嘱。
4. 被保险人不能为正在接受或等待治疗的住院病人，由这种治疗直接或间接导致的索赔，不在本保单的保险范围之内。
5. 被保险人不得违反医嘱，或以获得治疗为目的，或在自知身患绝症的情况下参加旅行。

若被保险人不能遵守本保证书所列条款，被保险人须在购买本保单之日与旅行首日间通知保险人。

备注：保险人必须被告知任何可能影响保险人受理、评估或延续本保险的事实，否则，本保险即告失效，被保险人也不再享有索赔权。

条款

1. 第 1、2、3、6 或第 7 部分所涉及的情况，若无法提供相关的医学证明或其他所需证明，概不赔偿。
2. 保险人要求提供的所有证明、资料、证据或收据（必须提供正本）的费用由被保险人承担。若保险人要求被保险人体检，被保险人不得拒绝。若不幸发生被保险人死亡，保险人有权对其进行尸体解剖，两项费用均由保险人承担。
3. 若发生物品丢失或被盗，被保险人应采取一切必要的措施挽回损失。
4. 若发现任何欺诈性索赔，本保单即告作废，保险人将拒绝任何索赔。
5. 任何索赔应在出示本保险凭证原件后赔付。
6. 被保险人在未得到保险人书面同意的情况下，不得向任何第三方承认过失，不得提供或承诺赔偿。
7. 保险人有权接管被保险人，以驳回或解决任何第三方提出的索赔，为了您的利益，保险人还有权以被保险人的名义，向任何第三方提起诉讼。
8. 保险人可根据本保单在任何时候给被保险人一次性赔付，之后不再作任何赔付。
9. 除非保单在购买后的 7 日内被取消，且旅行尚未开始，索赔尚未提出，否则保费不予退还。
10. 本保单的保险期限，只有在无尚未解决的索赔或已知即将发生的索赔的情况下，签发续保单之后才可延长，但保险最长期限为自首次签发保单起的 24 个月。
11. 本保险规定，被保险人不得隐瞒任何重要事实，否则，本保险即告失效，被保险人也不再享有索赔权。

备注：保险人必须被告知任何可能影响保险人受理、评估或延续本保险的事实，否则，本保险即告失效，被保险人也不再享有索赔权。

第十章

Ⅰ.

White Swan Hotel（Guangzhou）

1. Situated / Located   2. overlooking   3. secluded   4. bustle
5. easy

Holland

1. If   2. nowhere   3. spectacular   4. Stretching

France

1. diversity   2. rolling   3. like   4. list   5. Steeped   6. mix   7. serene   8. rival   9. unspoiled   10. likely   11. speeding / shuttling   12. Wherever

The Romance of Paris

1. captures   2. quite   3. simply   4. sketched   5. coach   6. including   7. perfect   8. window-shop   9. well-stocked   10. offer   11. slide

Israel

1. fascination   2. alike   3. giant   4. cradle   5. site   6. significance   7. contrast   8. forested

Ⅱ. 校改练习参考译文（请特别注意粗体字部分）。

中国的熊猫保护区

1. **成年大熊猫以竹子为食**。这一吸引人的黑白相间的哺乳动物广为人们喜爱。熊猫作为世界自然基金会（WWF）的**徽标**，象征了中国和国际社会为保护自然所做出的努力。

2. 今天，野生大熊猫**也许不足**1000只，仅分布在中国的四川、陕西和甘肃这些省的部分深山老林。

3. 对大多数人而言，只有去动物园才有机会看见大熊猫。比如，北京动物园里的这些幼仔大熊猫就吸引着众多游客。

4. 熊猫的**种属问题**可以说是动物学界的一个谜。它的近亲是其活动区域内体形较小的红熊猫。红熊猫**同样**引人注目的外貌特征，表明熊猫与浣熊科之间存在近亲关系。

5. 但是，也有力证表明，大熊猫与熊也有亲缘关系。比如，在中国境内，这种亚洲黑熊与大熊猫活动于同一区域。

6. 熊猫栖息于潮湿、葱翠的山区。今天，熊猫只出没于高海拔的阔叶森林和亚高山的林地之中。

7. 熊猫**只偶尔**见于较低海拔的混合阔叶森林之中，因为那里是人类可轻易闯入、干扰最多的地方。

8. 熊猫的山区栖息地植物种类繁多，其中有许多欧洲园林所珍视的**乔木**、**灌木和草本植物**。像这种**高山杜鹃**，就为19世纪的植物学家所采集并运回欧洲作为园艺收藏。

9. 该中心的成年大熊猫给安置在熊猫舍里，喂养营养均衡的食物；许多熊猫在精心护理下已从饿死的边缘恢复了健康。它们还可以进入到一个广阔的户外围场，在半野生的自然植被中自由活动。

10. 这里许多的野生植物品种**都是**欧洲园林所常见的——像这种（奇异的）百合花就是一种。

11. **中国人**已经做了大量的工作来保护**被**他们视为国宝的大熊猫。但是，人类仍处在**拯救这一物种的关键时刻**。如果再不对大熊猫及其仅剩的栖息地进行及时、有效的保护和管理，这样的景象就将会越来越难看到——这对中国和整个世界都将是个损失。

第十一章

I.

1. 只要通过内部考核，员工可自动升迁。
2. 所有房价均另加15%的服务费。房价如有调整，恕不另行通知。
3. 如果每年销售5000多件，你方可获2%的佣金。
4. 我方接受这笔订货，但你方必须接受5月份船期。
5. 我公司的条件是，自交货之日起，3个月内必须支付现金。如1个月内付款，可打5%折扣。
6. 出口贸易随时可能遭受风险，例如船舶可能沉没，货物可能在运输中受损，外汇兑换率可能变动，买主可能违约，或政府可能突然宣布禁运。
7. 我们建议以见票30天付款的汇票承兑交单。
8. 货物已妥善包装，保证在运输途中不致受损。
9. 我们已另寄此间出版社的图书全套目录，请你们在标明所感兴趣的书籍之后退回。
10. 顾问按本合同在中国境内赚取的所得，按《中华人民共和国外商投资企业和外国企业所得税法》以及其他有关法律法规须纳税的，应由顾问缴

纳所得税（麦兆龙　译）①

II.

1. We shall not be liable for any of the charges.
2. She herself took over the responsibilities for the project.
3. Husband and wife should be equally responsible for bringing up their children.
4. It would not be fair if the loss is totally thrown on us as the liability rests with both parties.
5. We don't think buyers will bid a higher price.
6. No unit suitable for women to work in may reject any female applicants for employment.
7. The Seller shall telex to the Buyer advising the loading conditions at least 14 days before the fixed loading time. The Buyer or his agent shall advise the Seller of the vessel's estimated time of arrival at the port of loading.
8. An equity joint venture shall handle its foreign exchange transactions in accordance with the regulations on foreign exchange control of the People's Republic of China.
9. If the force majeure incident lasts over 60 days, the Buyer is entitled to cancel the contract.
10. Provided your quotation is low enough to attract the buyers here, we can push the sale of your products successfully.
11. Meetings of the Board of Directors shall be convened at least once a year and be chaired by the Chairman. Should the Chairman be unable to chair the meetings, one of the deputy chairmen or any director designated by the Chairman shall call and chair the meetings. If one third of the directors of the Board so propose, the Board may call an interim meeting.

---

① 引自陆文慧：《法律翻译：从实践出发》，法律出版社2004年版，第272页。